The North Road

'Haunted and haunting: Cowen tracks the London–Edinburgh highway
in a mesmerising exploration of time, place, memory and identity.
A dazzlingly inventive work of literature.'
Robert Macfarlane

'In combining deep history, travel, memoir, fiction and so much more
besides, Rob Cowen has created something stunning and utterly unique.
The North Road sits in a genre of one. He's a wandering wizard, a magician
whose brilliance lies not in trickery, but in real talent and a wild, untamed
imagination that's capable of transcending time.'
Benjamin Myers

'*The North Road* is stunning, weaving an intricate tapestry
of tarmac, humanity and time, as rich as the dark earth on
which his many threads lie. It will stay with me.'
Raynor Winn

'When I began this book, I wondered if it would be for me. I didn't think
I was interested in roads. But *The North Road* is a wonderful, epic braiding
of history, geography and personal memoir. It made me think deeply about
who we are, and where we came from; our country in this moment in time,
and how we can learn from our past. I couldn't put it down.'
James Rebanks

'A dazzling, dogged, layered account of one road's passage through place,
time and an ordinary family's history, *The North Road* truly is a trip.'
Melissa Harrison

'Epic, magisterial, hard-won, properly-wrought – much like the Great
North Road itself. Truly, a tour de force . . . you may read another
book in 2025, you will not read a better one.'
John Lewis-Stempel

'Masterful. One of the best books I've read in a long time.'
John Mitchinson

'This book will have you tripping on England. Rob Cowen
has made the great portrait of the A1, "the main road" par excellence.
His text is a glimmering cocktail of memory and diachronic history,
a plait of three enchanted cords – the ancient highway itself,
the life of the land, and Cowen's personal story.'
Damian Le Bas

'A deep and richly satisfying, mind-bending exploration of space, place and
memory. I loved the many, many colourful layers of *The North Road*.'
Clover Stroud

'A masterful weaving of time and place. *The North Road* offers a rare,
strong blend of national and personal – sweeping, sensitive and enduring.'
Tristan Gooley

'A road, like a story, is never just that. Both have roots, tributaries,
ancestors and consequences. From first step to surprise destination,
The North Road is as layered and braided as the route it follows,
and as brutal, beautiful and unique as a life. With his singular
blend of research, personal exploration and intensely visceral
storytelling, Rob Cowen is truly in a class of his own.'
Amy-Jane Beer

'Rob Cowen brings a highway to living sentient life, from nowhere to
everywhere in this elegant, moving mind-map of a storied road.'
Philip Hoare

'Rob Cowen is an enchanter, and he has conjured up a classic with this
extraordinary, multi-layered knockout of a book. *The North Road* asks
all the big questions – identity, history, memory, belonging – and
offers riffs and responses that are both personal and universal,
never glib, always beguiling.'
Dr Sharon Blackie

'Rob Cowen's account of a journey on foot fragments – startlingly –
into history, fiction, philosophical enquiry and fearless memoir.
A beautifully woven and mesmerising book.'
Tom Bullough

'Rob Cowen weighs up the mighty A1 from the hard-packed
solum beneath its pitch to the aerial maps by which so many
steer its course. *The North Road* is by turns brilliant, questing and
poignant. Equal parts ardent asphalt anthem and song to belonging,
Cowen's new book is a north/south tour de force.'
Dan Richards

'I loved the combination of memoir, history, family story, the vivid fictional interludes. All the familiar places referenced along Rob Cowen's journey made *The North Road* feel universal; many will get a similar resonance from it as I did. Rob has given the A1 an entirely new sense of life.'
Luke Turner

'An extraordinary, beautifully realised road trip. Here, a road is a tributaried river, created and recreated by ourselves, our ghosts, doubles and echoes, and told as the story of us in the connections and coincidences a road engenders. This poetic, poignant and lyrically political book throws up more mysteries than it answers, as the best literature does, and leaves us wanting more.'
Nicola Chester

'This thought-provoking and beautiful exploration of that most humanised of spaces, the road, shows how our lives are always intimately bound to those of others within the social landscape. Through sharing and celebrating this common journey, Cowen manages to demonstrate the wonder of what it is to be alive. This is a book that will have your heart ringing like a bell.'
Matt Gaw

'Through Cowen's engrossing, original narrative, this Roman road proves to be anything but straightforward. In revealing buried pasts, glancing the uncanny, and exhuming the strata of both personal and national identity, Cowen explores the question of our final destination: What will remain? Reading this is a revelation.'
Jade Angeles Fitton

'*The North Road* utterly took my breath away. This genre-bending book is both lyrical and gritty, blending fiction and non-fiction. It signifies literal and metaphorical journeys: of personal evolution, the movement through time, freedom and escape, the unpredictability of life, breaking societal constraints, and connecting people, places, and ideas. Deeply researched and exquisitely poetic.'
Kathryn Aalto

'Full of unexpected diversions and detours – just like the great road itself – Rob Cowen's *The North Road* takes us on a fascinating, multi-layered journey through history, place, and personal story. Brilliantly researched, beautifully written, profound, and utterly unique.'
Brigit Strawbridge Howard

ROB COWEN

The North Road

HUTCHINSON
HEINEMANN

1 3 5 7 9 10 8 6 4 2

Hutchinson Heinemann
Penguin Random House
One Embassy Gardens
8 Viaduct Gardens
Nine Elms
London SW11 7BW

Hutchinson Heinemann is part of the Penguin Random House group of companies
whose addresses can be found at global.penguinrandomhouse.com.

www.penguin.co.uk

A CIP catalogue record for this book is available from the British Library.

ISBN 9781529152432

Typeset in 10.5/14pt Sabon LT Std by Jouve (UK), Milton Keynes
Printed and bound in Great Britain by Clays Ltd, Elcograf S.p.A.

The authorised representative in the EEA is Penguin Random House Ireland,
Morrison Chambers, 32 Nassau Street, Dublin D02 YH68

www.greenpenguin.co.uk

Penguin Random House is committed to a
sustainable future for our business, our readers
and our planet. This book is made from Forest
Stewardship Council® certified paper.

For Mum, Dad and all who've travelled with me.
And for Rosie, Tom and Bea: my road ahead.

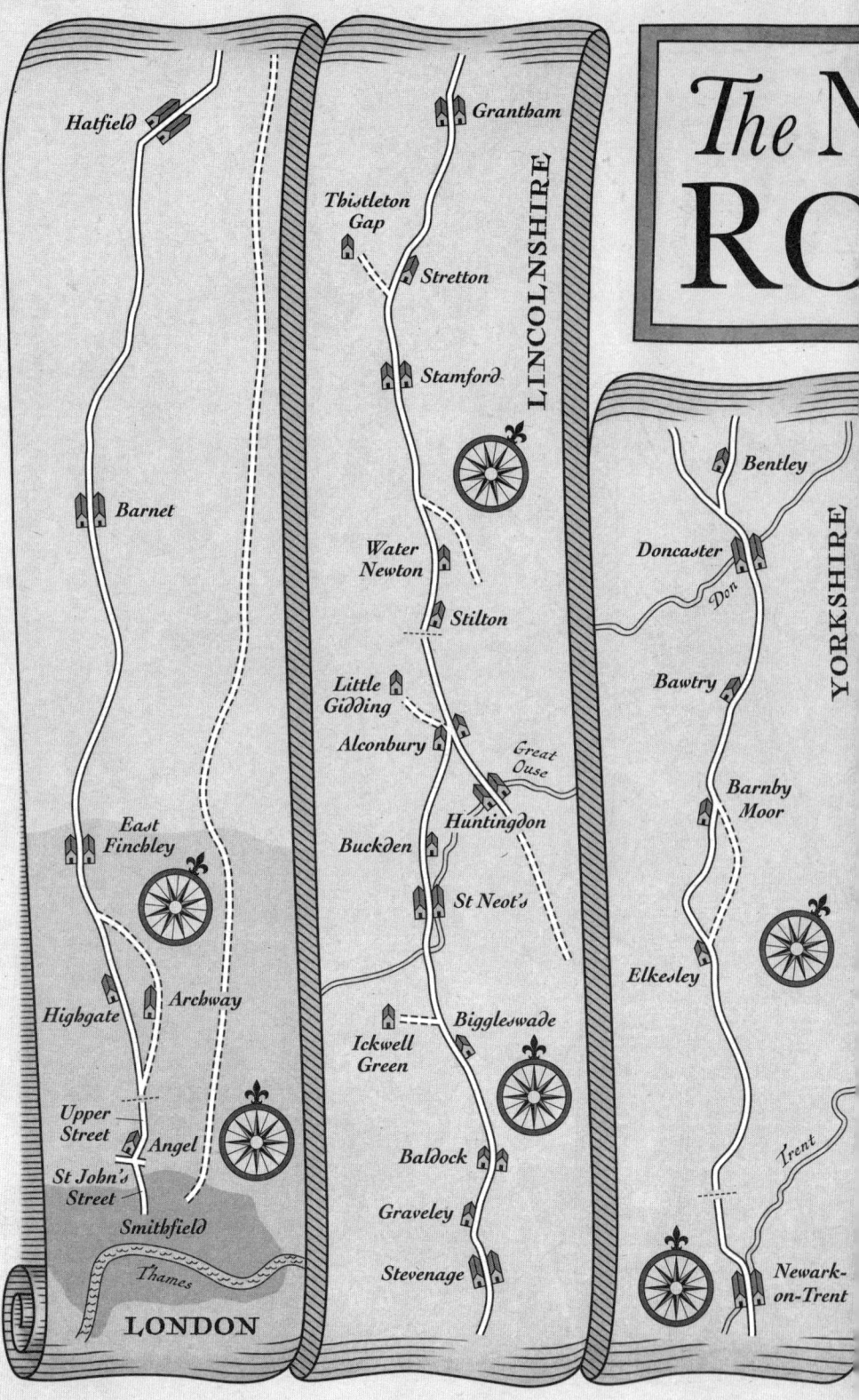

The N
RO

LONDON

Thames

Smithfield

St John's
Street

Upper
Street

Angel

Highgate

Archway

East
Finchley

Barnet

Hatfield

LINCOLNSHIRE

Grantham

Thistleton
Gap

Stretton

Stamford

Water
Newton

Stilton

Little
Gidding

Alconbury

Great
Ouse

Huntingdon

Buckden

St Neot's

Biggleswade

Ickwell
Green

Baldock

Graveley

Stevenage

YORKSHIRE

Bentley

Doncaster

Don

Bawtry

Barnby
Moor

Elkesley

Trent

Newark-
on-Trent

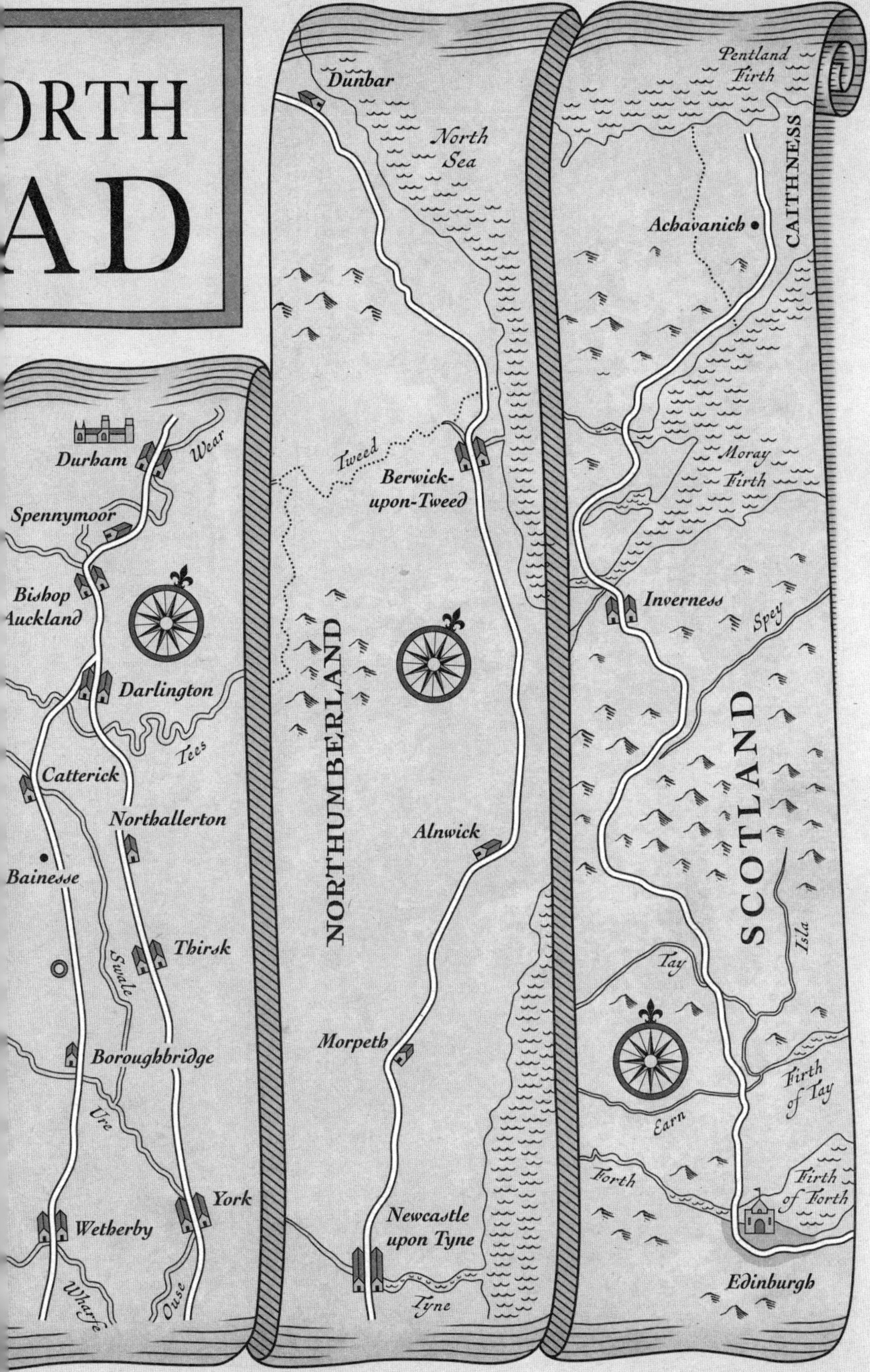

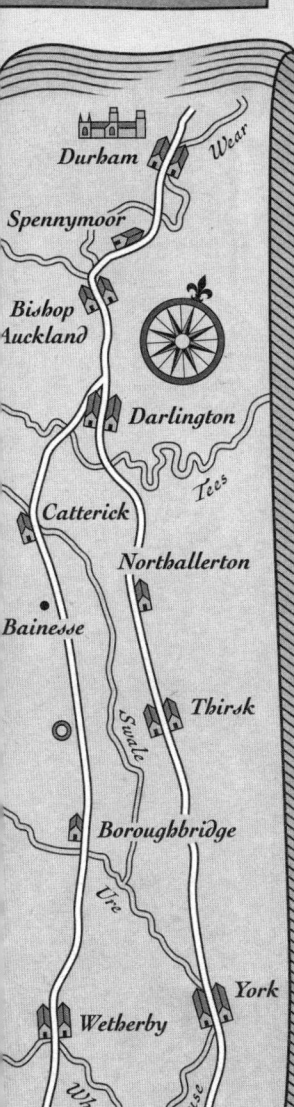

ORTH
AD

Dunbar

North
Sea

Pentland
Firth

Achavanich •

CAITHNESS

Durham

Wear

Spennymoor

Tweed

Berwick-
upon-Tweed

Moray
Firth

Bishop
Auckland

Inverness

Spey

Darlington

Tees

Catterick

Northallerton

• Bainesse

NORTHUMBERLAND

SCOTLAND

Isla

Thirsk

Swale

Alnwick

Tay

Boroughbridge

Ure

Morpeth

Earn

Firth
of Tay

Forth

Firth
of Forth

Wetherby

York

Newcastle
upon Tyne

Wharfe

Ouse

Tyne

Edinburgh

Contents

I. *Ghost Road*

II. *Open Road*

III. *Road Home*

I

Ghost Road

I love roads:
The goddesses that dwell
Far along invisible
Are my favourite gods.
Roads go on
While we forget, and are
Forgotten like a star
That shoots and is gone.

Edward Thomas

Every life is in many days, day after day.
We walk through ourselves, meeting robbers, ghosts,
giants, old men, young men, wives, widows,
brothers-in-love, but always meeting ourselves.

James Joyce

Surfacing

(Catterick)

I

There were ten of us that morning kneeling by the road, searching for the dead. Ten of us in neon jackets and hard hats, digging out those womb-like hollows in the dirt, bringing into the light that which had long lain buried. And what light it was. Bright and sharp. Northern England on the cusp of May. It had been a bitter spring of late snows but at last the land seemed to be yielding again. You could sense it in every scrape of the soil: the earth stirred and stirring, the ground giving up its ghosts.

I was being careful. Careful not to appear too inexperienced; careful to hold the trowel exactly as I'd been shown, dragging the earth towards me in short, quick strokes. This was new territory for me and it felt a little like one of those anxiety dreams where you suddenly find yourself at the controls of a plane with no idea how to fly or being ushered into a surgical theatre, dressed in scrubs and gloves, expected to operate on a waiting body. Except the body here was a large sweep of roadside field, freshly scalped by a mechanical excavator. Gone the topsoil, the skin of the land; gone the thick flush of spring grass; gone the young crops and the hedges. What remained was the hard-packed substrate a metre or so down – that which is known in archaeological circles as the *horizon*. What this horizon was exposing was what had lain undisturbed for God knows how long. But with the sun spilling over the soil, severed roots and stones it shone wetly, in the way of a new wound. The way an estuary does when the tide is out.

I scraped and I stared. This was the operation – scraping and staring at the earth. Actually, less *at* the earth. More *into* the earth, because that's the first thing you need to learn. To train yourself to look in a different way, to shift focus and see beyond the surface of things.

Digging is an exercise in awareness as much as moving matter. It requires you to be alive to the smallest changes in colour, texture or material, to recognise and read the irregularities and uneven edges. Each sweep of the trowel is like a summoning spell and, in between, you're scouring for the tiniest indications of the magic working. Sifting and sorting, you're scanning constantly for any suggestion of human hand or human remains, waiting for the moment when brain and eye align and things transform before you. Pebble into potshard. Soil and stone into spoil and bone.

The man overseeing me was called Jan. He was from Eastern Europe and had come to Yorkshire for the job, part of a community of archaeologists and diggers that move from site to site. 'Following the work', as he put it, and this was good work. A major road scheme. It was Jan who'd met me at the edge of the horizon and given me the once-over, clocking my hesitation, my notebook and the cheap trowel I was carrying. In a world where a well-worn edge earned through years of use is a badge of honour, a plastic-handled builder's trowel found at the back of a shed turns out to be a giveaway. To his credit, he had taken me under his wing, giving me a crash course in wielding the blade, before walking me over to the patch of ground he was working on. He'd explained that pressure and balance were key. 'Not firm. Not soft.' It was about scraping and clearing away the surveyed soil with a shovel and bucket as you went along. Then, once we'd reached the grave cut – a depression of darker soil edged with stones – he'd shown me what he meant. There was a rhythm to it, which I picked up quickly, although I suspect you could overthink such things. As I carefully tried to follow instructions, Jan leaned over me and hacked at a piece of dirt with something pulled from his top pocket. It took me a second or two to realise it was a dessert spoon.

The light, the earth stirred and stirring, Jan and his spoon, and me – scraping, staring, trying not to look too conspicuous. That's what I remember of that first surreal hour or so on-site. How, with my eyes down in concentration, everything seemed to fall away. How the world narrowed to the horizon beneath and all sound was drowned in the hypnotic, sea-on-shingle roar of the road. How thoughts that had swirled around my head for months escaped me, and others slipped in unexpectedly. How it was hard not to lose track of time and how, after a while, I must have done because when I sat up to wipe the sweat from my face, the day's brightness seemed to have intensified, the scrape had deepened and it no longer seemed so strange to be there. Another digger – a woman with shock-pink hair – stretched her back. She caught my gaze, then gestured at the ground. I knew what she was asking: *Have you found anything yet?* I shook my head. She flashed the thumbs-up. *You will*, she was saying. *You will.*

Ten of us kneeling by the road, searching for the dead. When I'd woken that morning and assumed the same position on the bedroom floor to change my daughter's nappy, this wasn't how I'd imagined the day unfolding. But sometimes these things happen. New horizons emerge and beckon. You chance upon a door and a crack of light and before you know what you're doing, you're pushing through to the other side.

*

It was my dad's idea to join the dig. I'd been feeling out of sorts for a while, ever since finishing writing a book and closing the cover on three years of life. Riding out the bump and crash that followed had been tough-going. The intensity of those final frenzied weeks compounded by the sheer exhilaration and exhaustion of becoming a father again. Only a few days after handing the manuscript in, our little girl, Beatrice, *Bea*, arrived like a flaming torch into that freezing January, a force of nature from the second she lit up the birthing ward with a wild cry. I've always been suspicious of claims about such things, but I swear she was born with her personality fully formed. Who she was, who she would be – there from the off. Her radiance, her defiance, her raging, irrepressible independence. Carrying her home wrapped in blankets to meet her brother, Thomas, had been like bringing in glowing coals. Our house immediately felt different. But, like a fire, you couldn't take your eyes off her for long. Perhaps understandably, she wanted to be held all the time and was resolute that she would only sleep in her mother's arms. My wife, Rosie, bore the brunt of it, but within a month we were both dead on our feet. There were things to be done at every turn: piles of washing and dirty dishes, nappies to change, and always someone to be bathed, fed, held, helped or coaxed out of a crying fit. With two children now, there was no escape for either of us any more. As any parent knows, newborns and toddlers exist entirely in the present and it quickly became clear that we would need to do the same. For a while, at least. Time slipped and snagged. A minute might catch on a moment and stretch into an hour; a day could vanish in what seemed seconds. Our universe shrank to the immediate and the essential, which made focusing on anything beyond the walls and windows of the house impossible. This presented a problem, though. The book was done and we needed money.

I searched out jobs and took writing commissions but I found that for the first time in my life the words weren't coming. Weeks passed sitting in the library staring at my laptop screen, chasing half-thoughts down dead ends, going all kinds of nowhere at once. Forcing myself to finish a page felt like learning to write again. It was less a block, more that the tank was empty. In rational moments I could convince myself it was temporary; that such phases are just part and parcel of finishing any long slog of work, but in truth it made me feel edgy and anxious, then guilty and frustrated that time was passing and I was neither helping at home nor seemingly able to bring any money in. This dragged on, all through the end of that bitter winter, into the frigid spring. Sleepwalking through days, then wide awake in the wee hours, worrying, trying to get Bea to settle for long enough to give Rosie the unbroken rest she so desperately needed. An hour or two. Three at the most. Some nights, with all ideas and internet-researched tips exhausted, I'd give up on sleep, carry Bea to the window, hug her close for warmth and wait for morning – the frozen world through the glass dulled and distant in the dark, like I was remembering it from a dream.

The road came out of nowhere. One afternoon in early April, Dad had called in on his way past from somewhere further north. While Rosie and Bea slept, we drank coffee and talked things over, helping Tom push toy cars around his favourite play mat, printed with a cartoon map of lush green fields, woods and wide, empty roads. Dad had been due earlier, but he'd been caught in traffic. Highways

England was working on or, in the wording of such things, 'improving and upgrading' twelve miles of the A1 not far from our home. The scheme involved transforming a long stretch of dual carriageway into motorway-grade six-lane, renaming it the A1(M) – part of a gradual modernising that had been happening up and down this old highway for years. The delay hadn't bothered Dad, though. If anything, he was excited to have been caught up in it all. As a member of YAHS – the Yorkshire Archaeological and Historical Society – he was privy to news filtering out from the archaeologists working ahead of, and alongside, the bulldozers – the teams tasked with surveying, recording and rescuing everything that would otherwise be buried under layers of tarmac. What they were unearthing was astonishing: flint hoards and post-holes from Mesolithic shelters; Neolithic pottery and hand axes; Iron Age settlements; thousands of Roman, Saxon and Anglian finds. In one old roadside house ear-marked to be knocked down, they had uncovered the ghost walls of a forgotten eighteenth-century coaching inn, itself built upon the bones of a medieval farmhouse.

I knew the road, of course. This was the A1 after all. *Alpha One.* Britain's primary road – a 400-mile arterial link running between London and Edinburgh like a backbone through the country. I knew too that the cipher 'A1' was only one of this highway's many incarnations, bestowed on what was previously the Great North Road during a nationwide road-numbering scheme in the years after the First World War. It is a rebrand that has never fully taken. Even a century on, the name 'Great North Road' frequently follows any mention of its successor, like a clarification. As though the speaker is divulging a truer identity: *the A1 . . . the Great North Road.* For various reasons, it's also the road I've travelled more than any other. I've never lived further than fifteen miles away from it. For six years my home was a tiny flat along one of its early stretches in London. Still, I'd be lying if I said I'd ever given it too much thought. Whenever encountering it, I found its muddle of identities and variants confusing. For all the romance of its old name, the promise of return it held for a northerner relocated to the capital, it still appeared like any modern highway: noisy, poisonous, devoid of life. Off-limits unless you were in a vehicle, whereupon it blurred into an amnesia-inducing non-place. Somewhere to be endured, transcended, en route to anywhere else.

Listening to Dad, though, it was hard not to think again. To think differently. Hard not to be a little curious and intrigued. Here was his idea: Why didn't I try to get on-site? Perhaps I could write about the excavations for a newspaper? Make some money? Either way, it would do me good, he suggested, to be proactive; to shake the listlessness and feel a new season on the skin. He had a contact if I was interested. Someone who could put me in touch with someone.

That evening, as I packed away Tom's toy cars and rolled up his play mat's cartoon vision of countryside, I mulled over what Dad had said, wondering about the hidden worlds beneath, between, beyond our own. I thought about how much we miss and how partially sighted we become, caught in the chaos of our own little universes. *You could go*, I thought. *Follow the road awhile. See where it leads.* Besides, it would only mean a day away from home. Not too long to abandon Rosie and the kids.

*

I was awake before the alarm on the day of the dig, moving on autopilot, changing Bea beside our bed. As she fed in Rosie's arms, I showered and pulled on my clothes. It was too early, I knew that, but it had been made clear to me that turning up promptly was essential, that 'time was of the essence'. And – the irony – there was always the traffic to consider. Downstairs, I made sandwiches, filled a flask with coffee and picked up a rucksack that was stuffed with a jumper, notebook and the builder's trowel. Packing that had been an afterthought. My fingers had chanced upon it as I'd been rummaging for kindling the night before. I'd joked with Rosie that it might help me look the part, but given the delicate and sacred nature of the work, I didn't really think I'd get to use it. I was there to observe and make notes and it had taken two weeks of ringing around just to get to that point. Last on the trail of numbers had been Steve Sherlock, the archaeological clerk of works and a case of nominative determinism if ever there was one. The previous day I'd dialled his phone and pitched the idea of a newspaper story about what they were finding. I expected more to-and-fro, more red tape, but he'd surprised me: 'Why don't you come in tomorrow? I'd be happy to show you around.'

Taking the main road out of town, I drove north through high-hedged lanes, blossom-set, furred with leaves. It had been a while since I'd been out at this hour and, despite the chill, I wound the windows down and took things slow. Even so, after thirty minutes I was over halfway to where I needed to be and still an hour early. I pulled up in a gateway and burned my tongue on too-hot coffee while watching the mist lift off the land. The horizon haze of yellow-grey faded into shining white; a pheasant bobbed through baby wheat. To the east I could already make out the A1. It sounded like a far-off river in spate. Driving towards it, I merged into a thick flow of northbound traffic. About ten miles on, by a junction marked 'Leeming Bar', a cluster of signs on the hard shoulder: WORKS ACCESS and SITE OFFICE ONLY. A slip road up to a shallow rise of ground parallel to the highway. The top steamrollered flat to house a huddle of large, low, interconnected buildings. Dull-grey, functional, surrounded by lights, antennae and air-conditioning units, the whole set-up looked like a lunar colony.

Seven-thirty sharp. The sky wide open. 'A great day for digging,' Steve said, shaking my hand by the car. I liked him straight away. He was, in every sense, down to earth. Trim, bearded, a weatherworn face; a wry disarming humour warmed by a soft Teesside accent. But it was immediately clear he had a lot on his plate. Steve was responsible for all the archaeological teams working on the road, from the spot where we were standing to Barton, twelve miles north. He also had the unenviable task of being the middle-man – a go-between for the archaeologists and Highways England, breaking any news about discoveries and making the case for what might need further investigation. All this while trying to keep to the pre-agreed construction timetables.

Grabbing my things, I hurried after him towards a reception building, weaving through lines of parked cars. In a battered Volkswagen lay a half-dressed man in workwear, pack of cigarettes on his belly, can of Relentless in his hand, asleep. Steve explained that some of the road's construction crew commuted from as far away as Scotland, only heading home at the end of a long series of shifts. 'In the meantime, they live in their cars,' he said, adding, over his shoulder: 'Then again, don't we all?'

Waiting inside on a sofa for the compulsory briefings while Steve shot off to take a call, I was feeling daunted, somewhat at sea. Then things happened, quickly. A safety officer showed me into a strip-lit office with desks and a screen. There were videos to watch, waivers to sign, multiple-choice tests to confirm I understood the risks of being on a road that carried upwards of 70,000 vehicles a day. *Pay attention*, a leaflet warned. *Read slowly. These words could save your life.* Its list of values was like some initiation: *We safely deliver. We collaboratively achieve ... We are responsible and we care ... We are ambitious and we improve.* I ticked the forms. Afterwards, I was directed to a changing room and issued with kit: a hi-vis jacket with PLEASE KEEP ME SAFE in reflective letters on the reverse; trousers, gloves, steel-toed boots, a white hard hat. Down another corridor, I sat in another office and waited for Steve again. Covering the wall opposite were aerial photographs and maps of the road scheme. It was difficult to make sense of. I could see the A1 and the thicker, shadow lines of the new A1(M) poised to supersede it. I knew the town displayed – Catterick – well enough and the blue bend of the River Swale, but I couldn't really tell what else I was seeing, or how it fitted together. Technical drawings showed calculations and precise positions; geophysics surveys revealed under-earth furrowed from centuries of tilling. Elsewhere computer-generated bridges, roundabouts and carriageways were superimposed on satellite shots and topographical renderings. Even I could recognise all the ambition in it, though. The intent to elevate the road from the gravity and press of its histories towards a state of pure, unimpeded flow.

Steve arrived carrying car keys. Change of plan. He had something pressing to attend to. Best thing would be to drop me off at an excavation site for a few hours, then pick me up later to show me around. 'It'll give you a great idea of what's going on,' he said, walking over to the wall. 'Here.' He was tapping one of the maps. '*Bainesse.* May as well throw you in at the deep end. Come on, I'll explain as we go.'

*

To avoid disturbing what was already known to be in the ground, Highways England had decided to deviate a small section of the new A1(M) motorway away from the course of the A1, before merging them again higher up the road. The area surrounding Catterick – what had once been the Roman fort and town of Cataractonium – had had its pockets turned out many times through history: nighthawkers, strike-it-lucky farmhands, treasure-hunting gentry, but most extensively in the 1950s during earlier A1 bypass works when the age of the motor car was hitting full throttle. Then the imperative had been to move the A1 away from the old, overburdened coaching route of the Great North Road, which intentionally cut through the hearts of villages and towns, and relocate it out to the edges. In this instance, to relieve Catterick's traffic-clogged high street. However, in doing so, the road builders had created an echo, returning this leg of the main north–south thoroughfare through Britain to its ancient antecedent and alignment, laying it over the course of the original Roman road.

Unsurprisingly, the bulldozers were soon striking archaeological features, including a long-forgotten Roman roadside settlement at Bainesse, an area named after a nearby farm. In the following decades further investigations revealed post-holes and footings from houses, streets, workshops and enclosures. Up too came emotive detritus and broken pieces of the day-to-day: pots, combs, coins, bones, bits of cavalry harness, children's toys, spearheads, hammers, keys and lucky charms. A treasure trove for the archaeologist; a minefield for the road builder. So, it was understandable that this time around, Highways England had taken the decision to leave this area well alone. The plan was to bypass the ground around Bainesse completely, swinging the new northbound and southbound carriageways for the A1(M) west of the line of the A1 by 200 metres through what they believed to be virgin fields. Except, of course, there are no virgin fields in England. Despite surveys coming back clear, and the new northbound section being constructed without hitch, no sooner had the digger buckets broken the sod for the southbound lanes than they began to harvest human bones. The suspicion was an unknown Roman cemetery, possibly hundreds of skeletons in a graveyard that had been abandoned, infilled and tilled over for what – 1,600 years? More? Long enough, though, for the site to have ended up six feet under itself. But here it was again, offering up its dead for resurrection. You can imagine the frustrations. The diggers stuttering to a stop. The climbing down from the cabs. The head-shaking and the muttering. Steve's calls back to the office. The road put on pause as its histories repeated themselves, playing merry hell with those pre-agreed construction timetables.

*

To reach Bainesse we'd climbed into one of a fleet of Highways England pickup trucks parked outside the offices, shunting north along trenches of cones overhung with yellow 50 mph speed cameras. Through the truck's tinted windows, the scarp of the Hambleton Hills, foothills to the North York Moors, brooded on the eastern horizon like a grounded thunderhead, stark and dark against the sky. To the west lay the pleated greens and ale-tinted streams of the Yorkshire Dales. The A1 cut between the two, threading through the wide flatland of rolling fields known as the Vale of Mowbray. Crops and hedges as far as you can see. Clumps of high, wild trees on gentle rises, telegraph poles, pylons. Close to the road, an old, derelict farm had broken windows and graffitied walls. There were suggestions of burial mounds, tumuli, in the ragged copses. It possessed the aura of long-worked, long-lived-in land.

As he drove, Steve explained that this low-lying plain, contained on either side by higher ground, had been an obvious place of passage for many thousands of years. Of pathway, trackway, highway, railway. Linking the Vale of York below with the lowlands of the Tees above, the Vale of Mowbray formed part of a natural land corridor that runs longitudinally through northern England and into Scotland. As you might well imagine, given this setting, it is a place that runs deep with human history.

At the point of the Roman invasion of Britain in AD 43, the Vale of Mowbray was the heartland of the Brigantes. This was the powerful northern tribe whose territory stretched from the Irish Sea to the North Sea, encompassing much of what is now Yorkshire, Lancashire and Northumberland. More likely a loose confederacy of smaller tribes united under a single identity, at first the Brigantes accepted the invaders as the governing force, meaning they were left relatively free. Less than thirty years later, disorder in the house. Betrayals, uprisings, then a full-scale anti-Rome revolt. When legionaries marched north in AD 71, they came with one purpose: annexation. The shorthand for killing, laying waste, suppressing and possessing Brigantian territory at all costs. After establishing an earth and timber fortress at a river confluence in York, Roman accounts tell us that the legionaries pushed through the Vale of Mowbray with devastating force, subduing the sacred Brigantian territory. Along the way, they fortified strategic points, like the river crossing at Catterick, as each was taken and then held. A road was extended from the fortress at York to link and supply these new outposts, overlaying in places trackways that had already run through this vale for millennia, shadowing the advancing column of marching soldiers like a trail of blood.

Eventually this road would stretch from York to the Antonine Wall, near Edinburgh – the briefly held northern extent of the Roman Empire. More famously, it was the route to Hadrian's Wall, a more enduring frontier stretching seventy-three miles between the Tyne and the Solway Firth for close to 300 years. As far as this ancient road's name goes, any records that might have shed some light are lost. Today it is referred to as Dere Street, a title from later history when the Vale of Mowbray was part of the Anglo-Saxon kingdom of Deira. What is certain is that it was thrumming from the get-go. A loaded vein for trade, communications, military, dotted with service settlements.

'If the cemetery at Bainesse tells us anything,' said Steve, gesturing as he drove, 'it's that there is a lot of archaeology lying undiscovered all around here. Towns like Catterick have been developed, and therefore quite well excavated over the years. They've found Roman bath-houses, workshops. But people don't normally dig holes in fields or along a hard shoulder for no reason. It's expensive and it's time-consuming. So, things that are buried here tend to stay buried, until a scheme like this comes along.'

Therein lay the paradox: on one hand the road building was destructive to the archaeology beneath. No sooner was it discovered than it had to be rescued or concreted over. On the other, the A1(M) project was the only reason anything was being found at all. Steve and his team were toeing a line: saving and preserving the past while

ensuring it didn't interfere with the plans of the present. But with Highways England bankrolling every penny, you got the sense that the future was the overriding imperative. The road won't wait too long for anything, even its own dead.

Steve continued: 'As I said, time is of the essence. Something like the cemetery discovery is a challenge because archaeologists and diggers are in such short supply in Britain. Even with volunteer excavators and bringing in teams from Europe, we still don't have enough people. Now that's something we could do with you reporting on . . .'

Taking the hint, I rummaged for my notebook in the rucksack, scattering its contents across my lap in the process. I'd forgotten about the builder's trowel until it fell, tangled up in my jumper, on to the seat between us. Steve passed it back to me.

'That's right,' he said. 'You mentioned doing some digging before.'

This was half-true. When we'd talked on the phone, he'd asked whether I had any experience on excavations. I'd answered that I had pitched in a few years earlier when sent by a newspaper to cover a British Army-run dig on Salisbury Plain. What I hadn't disclosed was that I'd only really emptied wheelbarrows and made sugary tea.

Then he said: 'Why don't you have a go while you're here?'

'Would that be OK?'

'Don't see why not. We're always glad of an extra pair of willing hands. I'll introduce you to Jan. He can show you the ropes. He'll keep an eye on you.'

A little further along the A1, at the road sign for Catterick, Steve indicated and turned off the highway. Flicking on the pickup's amber roof lights, we bounced along a works track, south, beside the half-built carriageways, pulling up at two yellow shipping containers that had been repurposed into a field office and a canteen. Beyond lay a large square of interlocking metal fencing, the kind that corrals an audience at a festival. Enclosed within was the open horizon, that bare earth, pockmarked with exposed graves. Fumbling for the handle as Steve killed the engine, I opened the door a little. The reek of fresh greenery under sun. The cold, damp-dirt waft of tombs.

'You ready?' Steve asked. I nodded and we pushed out, into the light.

*

I scraped and I stared and, at first, I didn't see a skull. What I saw was the edge of a pebble. I filled the shovel, turned, emptied it, leaned in again, only now Jan was studying it more closely. Something in the irregularity of shape. Not a bump, as such. More a ridge. Something about the way the mud clung. 'Wait,' he said. Then he went off to fetch some kit, returning with what looked like a stack of white ice-cream tubs. But while he was gone, I did something you're probably not supposed to do. I took off a glove, reached down and ran my finger along that ridge. A little jolt. The sudden realisation that our summoning spell had worked: *soil and stone into spoil and bone.*

Jan was soon confirming suspicions. Another body burial. One of nearly 300 graves and cremations that would eventually be unearthed at Bainesse. Then, without fuss or fanfare, he lay on his side, propped on an elbow, and began dessert-spooning the surrounding fill away, thinning the membrane of that thin place even further. I'm not sure what I thought would happen next. More action, I suppose. More drama, like in the films. Tents. Forensics. We forget that people become, if not numbed, then conditioned to getting on with even extraordinary work. That what might seem profound to one person is, to another, just one more job on a day's long to-do list.

As he worked, Jan scooped various samples of spoil into the ice-cream tubs, marking them for closer inspection. Early analysis from other graves had yielded microscopic revelations, traces of sweet-scented bedstraw and bog bean buried with the bodies. Such discoveries can be doorways into wider environmental information as well as revealing details, such as the month of burial. They explain too why 'preservation in situ' is the favoured archaeological methodology of today. The intent is to leave sites undisturbed unless they're at real risk of being damaged or destroyed, and even then – where possible – to preserve artefacts in the place they're found. The belief is that context will play a more important role in years to come; that our descendants will grimace at stripping and removal of sites in the way we do at heavy-handed eighteenth-century excavators. Technology will render locations increasingly significant, infused with decodable data. The implication being that we ghost the soil in deeper ways than we yet comprehend. That the earth is striated with our stories.

The ridge revealed itself to be part of the temporal bones of a human skull, lying sideways in the earth. That rise you can feel running back from your cheekbone towards your ear. Around it, surfaced the unmistakable curve of a cranium coated in fine clay, like brown vernix. Working quickly, Jan began to pick and brush what had been the bones of a face into being: an edge of an eye socket, a grinning jaw, unhinged, slack, as though the skull had been screaming for all its worth into the soil.

Around us, people appeared and disappeared. They'd be there one minute, in silhouette, gone the next, back into the ground. Occasionally, other diggers ambled over from their graves to have a 'nosy'. The woman with the pink hair was halfway through digging her own body out of the ground. That was the way she described it, with all the oddness of that phrasing. Notes were taken, measurements, photographs. Time was of the essence, yes, but there was also a strict process to be observed. For all the mind-blowing implication of the work, archaeology is really concerned with the details. It's about accurate data sets that can stand up to and inform scrutiny and research for decades to come. So, I kept myself out of the way, crouching at the edge of the grave scrape, leaving Jan to swiftly, skilfully, coax the past back into present.

Once a halo of space had been cleared, it was possible to see how the skull had shifted in the grave over the centuries, slipping back on itself a little, like it was glancing over its shoulder. It gave the uncanny appearance of turning away, as if straining to escape the light falling over it for the first time in two millennia. Together with that silent, mid-scream mouth, it made me think for a moment of the way a teenager rolls their head back into a pillow in protest when the bedroom curtains are flung open. *Funny*, I told myself. But I wasn't fooling anyone. There was nothing funny about it. On the contrary, in fact: it was becoming more unnerving and unsettling by the minute.

Thud-thud. Thunder behind and beneath. Felt as much as heard. Louder even than the traffic. At the edge of the site, two pile-drivers had been fired into life and were set on shoring up a half-constructed

overbridge that would straddle the new motorway. Great pendulum-looking things with wasp heads, they struck in succession, slamming rods into the ground. *Thud-thud*, in twos, reverberating in the earth, like a heartbeat. Then a high whine as they reset – that first lungful of air after diving too deep.

The head was one end of the grave. Now for the other. Jan shifted position and began to expose the area around the legs, working down towards where he guessed the feet would be. *The feet.* After a while he was confident of the position of the skeleton: the leg bones straight and parallel. The body, he determined, had been placed flat on its back, arms by its side. The way you lie on a bed when testing a mattress.

'See now,' he said, brushing a tibia. 'I guess a male. See how long they are?'

See indeed. I reminded myself that was the point of the exercise: to let the eyes adjust and see beyond the surface of things; to *see now* because who knows when you might get to see in such a way again? But for one so unused to death, seeing was also disbelieving. A too-severe shift in perspective. Here, the black mirror. Here, the skull under the skin of land. I understood then why they put fences around sites like these. Not only to keep out, but to keep in. To protect us oblivious passing by in our cars from catching sight of what we all know, but what we spend our days trying to forget. I knew too that I was getting out of my depth, but I couldn't tear myself away. That's the thing. Once you start to *see* like this, you can't easily stop.

Thud-thud. The heartbeat in the ground. The earth stirred, and stirring.

What happened next felt like being lifted by a wave. A swelling unsteadiness brought on by all the strangeness of that morning. Blame it on looking down for too long or a thin skin from too many nights with too little sleep, but I was struggling to hold on to anything familiar, struggling to process the enormity of what was in front of me. It wasn't just proximity of the emerging skeleton, but what it represented. The simultaneous flashing back and forward. The mind isn't accustomed to reality destabilising in real-time, to streams of time spilling into one another and scenes, aeons apart, coexisting in the same frame. Yet this was the sensation kneeling there between the future echoes of overbridges and those Roman bones. The world altered; all usual borders and barriers gone. There was the noise and frenzy of the present, the pile-drivers and the cars flowing by, wind-screens exploding with sun, the drone of tyres on tarmac, that sour, throat-catch stink of warm diesel, yet there was the sense of another dimension too. No less present; no less tangible: a body being placed in a plain of sky and pasture, where the flashes tracering past weren't sun on glass but stray sparks from pine fires borne on a breeze. Where the drone wasn't road noise but prayer to unknown gods in a foreign tongue. Where the oil in the air was the incense of ritual offerings. Where we weren't diggers at all, but mourners, laying flowers in a grave, reaching in to turn the face of a friend towards the distant moors and rising sun.

A few seconds, that's all. That sensation rose and passed like a shiver. Time slipped back into its usual rhythms. The machinery cut out as abruptly as it had begun. The echoes faded. Before long one of the other diggers was petitioning for lunch: 'Hey! It's nearly two!' Another yelled 'I need *cake*' in mock desperation. Everyone laughed, then drifted from their graves towards the shipping containers.

Jan was standing too, pocketing the dessert spoon, sealing up the ice-cream boxes. 'Time to go,' he said, shielding his eyes from the sky-glare. I followed the direction of his gaze and saw a Highways England pickup parked at the field's edge. In the driver's seat was Steve. Window down. Shades on. A phone clamped to his ear.

'You see what you need,' Jan said.

Only after he repeated it did I realise it was a question.

'Oh, yes. I did. Thank you.'

A shrug. 'Good.' A grin. 'Maybe take a photo too, if you want.'

And that was that. We shook hands and he was off in search of sandwiches. I stayed for a while, my shadow shrouding the skeleton, trying to take pictures on my phone. But there are things a camera can't capture, things that nevertheless fix in the memory and fix for good. Doors you push through that can't be closed again. That was the feeling as I stood there – the sense of something that couldn't be framed in a shot: something to do with the open horizon and the open grave, something in that confluence of the old road and the new, and of times intersecting. What I can tell you is this: when I turned and walked away, that feeling followed me.

*

In the afternoon Steve drove us from place to place on a tour of the other excavation sites. We were back on the A1, back amid the familiarity and the mundanity of traffic, humming along its smooth tarmac past Eddie Stobart lorries and service stations boarded with fast-food adverts and petrol prices. All of it felt different now. Oddly augmented. Under-shadowed. Wherever we went, it only seemed to sharpen this awareness of the rift below the asphalt. The aggregate beneath the aggregate.

Up where the A1 crosses the River Swale, at the site of the Roman fort of Cataractonium, a crew was upgrading the road bridge. New metal beams spanned the river on concrete pillars surrounded by scaffold. As Steve chatted with the team, I watched the water muscling past, peat-stained, creased with undercurrents. Then Steve waved me over. A flank of the southern bank had been stripped away and a section of the Roman fort wall was now visible as a seam of solid stone in the strata.

It's believed the etymology of Catterick is bound up with the Swale, with the Latin *cataracta* translating as 'waterfall' or 'lively river'. No one knows for sure, though, because it's a word that also means 'portcullis', as in obstruction, like the cataracts of the eye. It's possible too it derives from a Brythonic word meaning 'battle ramparts' and that the Romans simply co-opted it when they grabbed the land. They certainly had form in such assimilation. Words, cultural practices, even deities were lifted from areas they annexed and made their own. Gods of place, *genius loci*, adopted and appeased by those working the outlying borders of empire as they found themselves in alien locations. One stone altar, uncovered in a previous dig at Catterick, was dedicated to Veteris, a British god worshipped in the north and said to have been especially popular with legionaries stationed around Hadrian's Wall.

'There was another interesting altar discovered here a while back,' Steve said, as we climbed into the pickup and buckled ourselves in.

'It's the only one, I think, ever been found to have been inscribed to the god who devised pathways and roads.'

'Wait. The god of roads?'

'I know,' Steve said, chuckling. 'Right here by the A1. God of roads itself.'

*

Driving up and down the highway, we stopped to visit teams that had called-in that morning with questions or discoveries. In one field office, archaeologists were analysing a tray of pot fragments. Pinned on the walls around them were hand-drawn identification guides and sketches of finds. Lists of Samian-ware stamps revealed not only the names of individual makers – Sacrillus, Masclinus – but also the location of the Gaulish kiln sites where the bowls and plates had been fired. There were colour-pencil renditions of a motto beaker, an alehouse drinking cup emblazoned with a slogan, LIFE IS GOOD, as well as depictions of bits of Nene Valley ware. This type of British-made pottery was transported up the road from mass-production facilities located at Durobrivae, a once-large Roman town 150 miles to the south that, today, lies buried under fields slap-bang next to the A1 at Water Newton.

At another location we opened the doors to a shipping container to find shelved units filled with bubble-wrapped objects ready to be moved off-site to museum storage. Steve peeled open oil lamps, an altar, a statue pitted and worn with age, masonry. In a corner was a hefty stone block. Thought to have been part of a doorway or arch, it had been chiselled in such a way as to leave a good-luck sign: a large phallus standing proud as schoolboy graffiti. As we walked outside again, the sudden whine and clunk of a lorry passing on the highway made me turn. Along its side, finger-drawn into a layer of dirt, someone had carefully traced the same shape.

Time was soon pressing; thin, sharp light starting to thicken as the sun arced westward. But there was one last place to go. We took a byway with enough of a gradient to provide a viewpoint across the Vale of Mowbray, pulling up at a fence that slumped into the grass to reveal a panorama of the plateau beyond. A fitting elevation to appreciate the road. It lay there looking at once like a complete thing and a multiplicity unravelled, like when a cable gets twisted too many times and frays open, and you glimpse the wires within. You could see, in the distance, where it formed a single highway and where it split into constituent parts: where a ribbon of old coach road threaded off into Catterick, where the arrow-straight 1950s bypass continued along the course of its Roman ancestor and where the new loop of half-constructed motorway was manifesting in the fields. With the windows down and the engine off, you could hear it too. A distant inhaling and exhaling of passing cars, like breathing.

I asked Steve questions, clarified points and tried to remember things I'd meant to bring up. In between scribbling notes, I bit at my nails absentmindedly, forgetting about the dark, half-smile of dirt embedded under each cuticle, realising too late that the grit between my teeth and tongue was grave soil. Then we were off again, back down to the highway, back to that shining line leading everywhere.

II

In the weeks after the dig, I couldn't stop thinking about the road.
Our home was no less chaotic, the rollercoaster of parenthood no less
precipitous, ecstatic, wearying; sleep was still, for the most part, a virtual concept only enjoyed by others. But I'd followed the road awhile,
seen where it led, and something about it wouldn't leave me alone.
That double vision of the opened highway and the body in the earth
lingered, like some vital words I'd forgotten to say. It would have been
easy to dismiss the feeling as imagination running wild, but, in honesty, it felt like the opposite – like a sharpening of the senses. A glimpse
through a rent in the fabric at something real.

I scratched at that feeling it left in me as you do a mosquito bite.
May went about its business. Storms blew through and the air
warmed. The world threw wide its windows. Squares of light slipped
across the library walls as I searched its corners for any reference to
the A1 or the Great North Road I could find. At home, I scoured the
internet, buying and piling up out-of-print books on my desk. Books
from the 1800s and the turn of the century; books from the 1950s
and the 1970s. Books by Frank Morley, Norman Webster and C. G.
Harper, all of which bore the weight and mystery of that title: *The
Great North Road*. Obscure books on the old mail routes and the
coaching age, on early maps and Roman roads. Books by the likes of
Ivan Margary and Jessie Mothersole. Novels by Dickens and Walter
Scott, such as *The Heart of Midlothian* in which his heroine, Jeanie
Deans, tramps the road from Edinburgh to London in the 1770s. I
turned up sixteenth-century diary entries and essays in parish news-
letters; archived reports on highway accidents and magazine stories
mockingly measuring the A1 against the so-called 'epic' drives of the

world, framing the road as a barometer of British decline. Reading, researching and replaying the events of that day in my head, I often found myself wandering, and wondering: *What else did the road have to show? What else was out there waiting to be revealed?*

One night, after we'd wrestled the kids into bed and the dishes were washed and stacked to dry, I sat up late in front of my laptop, located our terrace on Google Maps and then scrolled off towards the A1 again, retracing my steps via its assemblage of satellite images. Zoomed in, the pixelated shots of summer fields, houses and highway resembled a Hockney photo collage. There were no signs of the construction works; the photos must have dated from an August a year or two before, but as I clicked the cursor and dragged north towards where I estimated Bainesse must be, something odd occurred. The grey line of the current road was clear; its coloured-dot cars and lorries frozen mid-flow, casting shadows. Yet, on either side, the satellites had captured a perspective impossible to see on the ground. In the crops edging the road, underlayers: the watermark patterns of what appeared to be paths, tracks and structures traced in the barley and wheat. Doughnut-shaped enclosures, circles, and shaky, parallel lines. Weirdest, though, was what else was visible. The new A1(M), with its roundabouts and slip roads, was already mapped out as an overlayer, ribboning through the fields in thick, opaque-white lines. As I clicked and scrolled, this virtual road moved with me, fading, reappearing. I tried flicking on to 'Street View', curious to see what future vision it might transport me to, but in the hard descent to the tarmac it vanished, depositing me in the slow lane on the current A1, crawling along behind a white van. When I zoomed out again, it was back. A glitch, but one that seemed to confirm what I already knew: that I'd been viewing this highway all wrong. There, on the screen, the road was disclosing a truer nature again. A convergence of what was, what is and what will be; a muddy river of history far deeper than it is wide. A timeline running through the land.

*

Imagine, for a moment, a topographical map of Great Britain. Place a finger on London, then draw a line north to Edinburgh avoiding major hills and mountains and you'll be tracing a road. An old road and the country's longest. A remarkable road with its roots in time out of mind; one that, in places, traces tracks laid down as far back as the Mesolithic. A road that, today, connects two nations and links eighteen counties, including the largest and smallest in England. A road bookended by frenzied capitals, that stitches together sprawling cities and suburbs, satellite developments and rural backwaters. A road that cuts along coastlines and through fields and flatlands, between once-grand towns and deserted villages, over lost graveyards and under new supermarket car parks. While not, perhaps, Britain's oldest, this haunted and haunting assemblage of prehistoric desire path, ancient trackway, Roman road, pilgrim route, turnpike, coach road, A-road and motorway has surely been its most influential and important. A driving force, facilitator and fulcrum in the long story of these shores – and at times, by extension, the world – for the last 2,000 years and counting.

Now imagine closing in on that map, stepping into it. Imagine its earliest origins around you. See meandering tracks weaving through post-tundra woodlands. See them widening and deepening. See their significance increasing as our species, conversely, shifts to sedentism. See societies forming; agriculture, farming, the creation of myth and ritual. See settlement and segmentation. See stockpiles and surpluses. See new lines being drawn over old in the name of trade and exchange. See the swift arrival of their twins: possession and war. See tracks being forcibly conjoined, straightened, widened, heightened into a long power line laid out in stone. See it carrying emperors and the enslaved, connecting forts and fledgling cities. See it named, numbered and known across the seas. See it scarred and etched with the countless footprints of the unremembered as centuries wash over it. See it regreening, flooding, overgrowing. See it surfacing and echoing again with foot and hoof and wheel. See it spreading the word of God, kings and revolutionaries burning with their righteous ideals. See it bringing battle, plague, death. See it delivering untold freedoms and subjugations. See the mass movement of people, driven by desperation and by desire. See it pumping lifeblood throughout this land, becoming the major artery of a nation again, blueprinting future patterns of flow and commerce, spinning the wheels of mass production and industry. See it empowering and arming an empire once more, enabling the export of unchecked human ambition and the want of things beyond limits across oceans and into new worlds. See all of this, and you will never look at this highway the same way again.

See now. Jan had instructed me beside the road. Well, between those bones and the pages of the books on my desk, I was starting to see. Further, deeper. Starting to see this constantly seen and yet unseen thing. I was starting to comprehend its significance and scale for what they are. Here: a seam of collective memory still whirring away, still recording, still assembling the evidence. Zoom in or zoom out, the conclusion is the same. The road was never just another everywhere-and-nowhere-land, an anonymous tarmac conveyor belt in the grim, grey web of infrastructure necessary for our survival. Here was an entity in its own right. *A1: Alpha One.* God of roads, indeed. Somewhere to be endured, but enduring. Something to be transcended, but maybe transcendent too.

There were warnings of getting too close. Not just in the old coach-road books with their tales of highwaymen and cut-throats, or in the wealth of evidence of the road's dangerous pollution levels and crash death tallies, but stranger risks. In one newspaper story from 1997, I found the road described as '400 miles of death'. In the same feature, a lorry driver named Joe Doyle had been interviewed about his thirty-year obsession with the A1. He explained that many haulage drivers chose the older north road even on journeys when the newer M1 provided a quicker, more direct route. Truckers felt 'tied' to it in ways they couldn't enunciate. He confessed also that there were rituals reserved for this highway alone. Sequences of headlamp flashes, stopping places that only the initiated knew about. 'The A1 is more than just a road,' he admitted at the end. 'It's a disease. A disease you can't get out of your blood.'

*

Somewhere along the line, amid all this discovery, I found I was writing again. As summer set out its stall and June arrived teeming with energy and expectation, the tank began replenishing itself. What had been blank screens started to fill with pages of typed-up notes. Dead ends resolved into open highways; impressions into sentences. It was the road's doing, perhaps. Dad had called it back in April – *try something to shake the listlessness and clear the steam from the glass*. He'd been right. This sort of intense concentration can create a kind of invested distraction where the mind becomes both focused and freed at once. It's like finding a thread in your clothes: the more you pull, the more it unravels, and the more it tangles up the attention. Tugging at the thread of the road brought a thaw to my fingers. While I wasn't remembering that I couldn't write, something clicked into place, and suddenly I was. Nothing polished, mind. Little more than notes and ramblings at first, but enough to feel the rhythm of writing again, to recall the rush when words seem to flow and fit together to give a sense of things. To *make* sense of things. The knock-on effect was that working hours at my laptop in the library became productive once more. Writing commissions that had stalled for weeks were completed. Deadlines met. New projects and possibilities appeared on the horizon. On my walks back home, my thinking felt clearer than it had for a long time.

What didn't shift, however, was the unease and the anxiousness – that lingering sense of being out of sorts that had dogged me for months. If anything, it increased in its intensity after that day on the road. I kept telling myself I must be coming down with something; that exhaustion was finally stamping its foot. But when I did rest, it didn't help. No virus materialised. Life continued to gather momentum. I researched, read, worked and wrote. The sun shone. Things even started to turn a corner at home. Bea was sleeping longer. Some nights she could make four hours or more in her cot. One evening she let me put her down on my own, a breakthrough Rosie and I immediately marked with a bottle of wine, then immediately regretted when she woke a couple of hours later. Not quite out of the woods, then, but still better. Easier. Our own little universe beginning to expand, merge and meld with the outside once again. We made plans. We took long moor walks in summer's warmth, carrying the children in slings, letting them crawl and toddle in the heather. We tidied the house, played, cuddled, laughed, pushed toy cars around the play mat. We let the kids air-dry after baths in our backyard with its wild dog rose in flower, and the street's swifts arrowing the sky. LIFE IS GOOD, our alehouse beaker might have read. Yet that feeling still stalked me like a shadow at my shoulder, waiting for the smallest unguarded moment when it might brush my neck and send a shock-shiver of something like sorrow and despair rippling through me. I tried my best to ignore it, to cover it whenever the feeling surfaced. I didn't breathe a word to anyone, especially Rosie, partly because it frightened and confused me and partly because it was ridiculous. *All that I love and need, all that gives my life meaning, is here, around me.* Of this I was certain. To turn while making tea and catch sight of the kids in Rosie's arms, fed, safe, giggling and healthy, was as much as my heart could ever hope for. What exactly did I have to be sad or anxious about?

As the weeks passed and nothing changed, I began to suspect this creeping dis-ease might be the road's doing too; that there was something in what had happened that day and the days that had followed, something about what had been seen and couldn't now be unseen. I started to wonder if the act of unearthing the road was unearthing something in me. Two things happened then – two moments that gave me pause. The first was a phone call. A friend asking what I'd been up to. We'd soon moved on to the subject of the highway and the dig, and I'd run through the details: Jan and his spoon, Steve and his histories, that moment I'd reached forward and touched the skull. The silence at the other end was long enough that I thought the connection had dropped. Then my friend asked: '*Why*, though? Why the hell were you doing that?' I mumbled some words, changed the subject. But his question stuck because I realised how odd it sounded, and that I didn't really have a proper answer to give. Later, awake in the night, this pulled at my heart. It hurt, and I wasn't sure why.

Another day I came back from work early. Commission finished. Rucksack clinking with shopping to cook for dinner. My world framed in the living-room window as I snuck up to take a look. Bea in a knitted white cardigan rolling around a jungle gym; her brother in a too-big firefighter helmet with a length of cut-off garden hose, putting out imaginary blazes. Rosie clocked me. Pointed. 'Who's that?' she asked. '*Daddy!*' Tom squeaked. 'Home! Daddy's home . . .' Yet in the time it took for him to toddle to the door, the feeling was there again: a surge of sadness and despair. I lifted him and he wrapped his arms around me, pressing his face into mine. A little, clumsy, lovely kiss, his eyelashes brushing my cheek. His sweet breath on my skin. 'Daddy's home,' he repeated, as he held on to me. 'Daddy's home.' And in that moment, it was me that was holding on. Holding on to that moment and to my son, trying not to cry because, for the first time, the feeling had found a voice and it was whispering in my ear, questions irrational as they were cruel: *What will happen when all of this falls apart? What will happen to them? To you? What will the children remember when all this is gone?*

III

What do we see when we look at a road? We see us, of course. The road is a human lifeline, laid out. There is no more enduring symbol or overused metaphor for our existence, in existence. We're all *on the road*, we're told. Birth marks the beginning, death the end, and it's a road in between. It's affirmed in religions and philosophies, embedded in stories, songs, poems and prose. Caught in our time along this timeline, we travel from point of departure to final destination encountering hard road and smooth-going. We experience days when the miles slip by, and others when every possible pothole, speed bump or patch of oil is felt. The start and the destination may be set, but there's autonomy along the way – forks, junctions, side roads and sharp turns to consider and take. There are roads to follow and not to follow too.

Robert Frost famously wrote: 'Two roads diverged in a wood, and I / I took the one less traveled by, / And that has made all the difference.' Playful words (how could he have known when he never took the other?), but ones that would – albeit unintentionally – push his friend Edward Thomas towards testing his mettle on the Western Front, and Thomas's journey's end in 1917. Such is the reality of travelling life's road: decisions and collisions to make and to live with. There are roads within roads too. We might take the road to freedom, recovery, sobriety, happiness, independence, understanding, redemption, success or ruin. But what we're told is non-negotiable is that our road only runs in a single direction. Entropy points to the arrow of time being a one-way street. Time flows on, within us and without us. We know this well. We're accustomed to the steady progression of days, seasons and years, to birth and growth leading one day to death and decay. We know that a cup of coffee on our desk will cool in time.

And we know we can't undo a broken thing or even the memories of it breaking because the altering of time's arrow is impossible. This instils in us a fixed notion of past and future, and the space they meet: the ever-becoming present. A continual *now* that we all exist in. *Now*, as I write this. *Now*, as you read it. To be alive is to be a laser point moving between the road travelled, and the road yet to come. The temptation – the classical conditioning – is to believe both are inaccessible. One is always behind us; one ahead. They are places we can only visit in memory and imagination. Except, I wonder now, as I circle back and think of that northern highway again, whether it's not more complicated than this.

*

Five months have passed since that morning. Five months since I knelt by the north road, scraped at that horizon and saw beneath and beyond what is normally seen. Among the traces and relics of time, I felt for a moment a sense of streams of time intersecting, converging, spilling into one another; of scenes, aeons apart, coexisting in the same frame. It occurs to me that this is part of what's stayed with me since – the awareness that perhaps past and future, far from being inaccessible, are inescapable. That although we might think of them as locked away and out of reach, they are, in fact, contained within this present, working on and through us, shaping our experience of lived time and creating this eternal *now*. That road, that multiplicity known variously as the A1, A1(M), the North Road, the Great North Road, Dere Street, Ermine Street, seemed to confirm as much, whether down on my knees beside it, my hands filthy with grave soil, or scrolling through satellite images taken from space. Those underlayers and overlayers. Those drifts of time. The very word 'street' speaks of strata. Both share a common origin; both are rare English survivors from the Roman Latin *via strata*, meaning 'a paved road of overlaid material'. There you are: roads, layered by definition. What if we are the same? We can't detach past and future from our present because we are all just jumbles of memories and anticipations. That is how our brains work. Time is not a single thing. It is all these layers altogether, all of the time. How does William Faulkner put it? 'The past is never dead. It is not even past.' Well, to that we might add some paraphrased William Gibson: 'And the future's already here.'

This is what I'm thinking as I sit with Google Maps open and my screen centred on Bainesse. It's nearly October now. Summer gone. The children asleep in the room next door. Rosie downstairs reading. In a few hours' time, it will be my thirty-ninth birthday. If you consider that neither of my grandfathers made it beyond the age of seventy-six, then I might well be crossing over to the other side of the hill about now. If fortune favours me and I'm lucky, I may be spared the same measure again. This is the middle of the road and, just like at Bainesse, it feels as though I'm caught between an old highway and an unbuilt one tonight. A place where past and future conjoin and crowd the present. A fitting place to stop shrinking from the shadow at my shoulder, and to try and face it.

*

Why, though? Why the hell were you doing that? That question. I knew in the moment of replying that the reason wasn't as simple as 'I wanted to write a piece for a newspaper' or 'I needed to try and shake a spell of writer's block and earn some money'. Those motives were real enough, but they weren't the whole story. That innocuous question made me smoulder because it reached in and grasped at thoughts and feelings I've struggled with my entire adult life. Old hurts, doubts and fears. The traces and relics of the past that I've always dug in and covered over whenever I felt them getting too close to daylight, but which I know are there just beneath the surface.

The question caught me off-guard. But ask me again, now, *Why the hell were you doing that?* and I might give another answer. A fuller answer. I might look you in the eye and tell you that when I was sixteen, I watched my home and family break into pieces. That everything I now recognise as the bedrock to a young life disintegrated around me. I might tell you that the tensions and struggles of dealing with the fallout of my parents' divorce and the sudden and complete change in circumstances and relationships it brought left me untethered and hollowed, raging with, and running on, a dangerous kind of adrenalin. I might tell you it felt like falling through a trapdoor into darkness and that over the years of denied emotional pain that followed, I found I couldn't settle down to anything, or with anyone, for very long. How I learned, self-destructively, to leave situations before they could leave me and how this made it hard to commit to things and live the kind of life that everyone else seemed to slip so easily into. The kind of life that makes sense on the surface. A life of sensible choices and financial security, of regular work and guaranteed income, of savings, pension plans, paid holidays and career ladders that would mean *of course* you wouldn't be thirty-eight years old and trying to scratch out a living as a writer, worried about paying the mortgage each month and putting food on the table. Or out there on your knees along an A-road, searching for the dead on an April morning, doing the kind of thing that would lead anyone to reasonably ask: *Why the hell were you doing that?* I might tell you that although I know the darkness and difficult days were a long time ago and that divorce and the disarray that follows it is such a normal experience for so many today that it has always felt oversensitive to be burdened with it, I've come to realise these last few months that the stories of everything that has happened to me are as much part of this here and now as the fact of me sitting here tapping out these words on a keyboard.

Nobody warned me that when you have children, as well as bringing the future firmly into the present, you may begin to relive your childhood through them. You wake up one day to find the road ahead is also, unexpectedly, a backtrack down the highway of memory. I've started to see myself in my son and my daughter all the time. Not just as I am, necessarily, but as I was. It's uncanny. Likewise, it doesn't take my mum chiding me with 'you're just like your father' at times for me to notice the many ways that I've grown to mirror him. Her too, actually. Each of us is repeating and retracing patterns. But what strikes me strongly now is that all this time Rosie and I have been building our home, our eyes and energies have been fixed on the future element of the present – on the worries, pressures and excitements that tomorrow brings to any parent. All this time I've been overlooking that other part of this present's picture. The truth is that 'home' is still a difficult place for me. A restless place. For all the joy and happiness I can recall, my memories are layered; underlaid with the negative too – with shock, sadness, the sense of an ending. I wonder if that's what's been at the root of this lingering feeling of edginess and anxiety all along. In building a home and raising a family, I've been digging up the shallow-buried fear that everything I love might break into pieces again.

*

When you're young, life's road feels like an endless highway. For a long time, it's easy to find ways to escape the things that are handed down – those tensions, traumas and unresolved conflicts we internalise and carry with us. The struggle to stay ahead of these forces can be damaging and debilitating, but it can prove productive too. Oppositions held in the heart can be an engine room for creativity, compelling us to think differently, and to try to comprehend and make sense of this beautiful, terrifying world, and our place within it. To write, even. To go on writing. Yet whatever it is we do with our days, we all, at times, find ourselves lost in the flat spin of the now, caught in the chaos of our own little universes. We become a blur making time. We rise each morning and we push on. Like those Highways England planners with their technical drawings and surveys, we do our best to escape the gravity of our histories in pursuit of a state of pure, unimpeded flow. We whisper *please keep me safe* and we pray for a smooth journey, busying ourselves with constructing our future in the present. But what I'm left with from that day on the road is that we can't avoid forever what we know to be there, because in the blink of an eye what we believed were virgin fields turn out to be graveyards. Ghosts rise. Suddenly there's a shadow at your shoulder and a voice in your ear, and you're holding on to your son fighting back tears for something that hasn't happened to him, that may never happen, and yet, at the same time, you'll never forget.

Ironic, really, for such a self-obsessed species, but sometimes the hardest thing to do is to look at ourselves. The older we get, though, the more we're aware that the long road north isn't endless. Opportunities to get things right are limited. Just as the road reveals the layers that make up this present, it discloses the evidence that the end of the road grows closer each morning. There's nothing like uncovering a skull in the earth to remind you of the folly of trying to hold on to things that never hold still. 'Death,' Saul Bellow ventured, 'is the dark backing that a mirror needs if we are to see anything.' It shows us the stakes. It stills the spin for a while, giving us moments of awakening. And it puts me here, now, still writing in these wee hours when I should be asleep. Here, halfway through a life, on a planet halfway through its existence, wondering how I might begin to untangle, understand and come to terms with the past and the road that has led me to this point. How I might learn to give myself to the present, to live *in* the present, and *be* present, with everything that entails. Because I do want to get things right. I don't want to feel listless and anxious or afraid of building a life and a home and filling them with love. The present is no place for shadows, for all we don't resolve, all we bury or bypass, we end up handing down. To move on, perhaps we must get on our knees and search through our bones and broken pieces, through all that has long lain buried, and bring it into the light.

The Ties That Bind

(Doncaster)

They must have dressed for the occasion. Put on best frocks and jackets, polished shoes, fixed hair and plucked flowers for buttonholes. Unlikely, then, that it was a working day. Maybe it was a Sunday and this a post-service picture. Except the flashes of 1920s fashion seem at odds with the formalities of church. A little too much leg. Silks and satins. More party gear; out-for-the-evening wear. There are relations dotted around the rows, but strangers too. People uncredited on the list of names that came with the image. Perhaps it was a staff shot. Workers and other halves heading off for a day at the races. Whatever the occasion, this is how we'd all like to be remembered: young, carefree, en route to somewhere exciting. Given how long it must have taken to marshal everyone, one thing irks: the alignment. The photograph is not quite level, nor the group square in front of the drab, double-fronted building. It was taken from on the road, though; snapped during a gap in traffic. But truth be told, composure-wise, they could have done with shuffling left a step or two.

There are faces I know. My grandfather, Bartley, whom I never met and who died before I was born, yet whom I recognise from my father's photographs of him around the house when I was growing up. He is a young man in this world. A cute, lopsided smile under a mop of black hair, standing far-right on the second row. His younger brother, Walter, on the step at the back, looks every inch the cheeky chappie, washed, brushed, forced into a too-big jacket, no doubt after arriving late from playing out somewhere. That same irreverent smile beams from his portrait in uniform on the cover of his war diaries, sitting on a shelf behind me. A stoicism that belies the horrors within.

Bartley and Walter's older sister, Ellen, is among the group of girls in white dresses laughing on the left. Strong, dark-eyed, with a bob-cut. Like Walter, I remember her from when she was in her eighties. It speaks of how young she remained in spirit and style that I can pick her out from an image taken sixty years before. Then there's the man in the middle. Heart of things. Centre frame. Pride of place. Suit and tie. A thin grin beneath a pair of dark, flint-hard, stare-you-out eyes. He is my great-grandfather, John William Cowen. Or 'Bill', as he preferred. Although I've heard about him countless times, I've never before seen his face. Not until a link to this photograph and fifty others dropped into my inbox, emailed by one of my dad's cousins. He'd found them while clearing out his loft. Each is fascinating in its own way, but this one, with its unexpected file name, has knocked me sideways:

The Cowen Family. 16 French Gate. The Great North Road. Doncaster.

*

The stories of my father's family and its origins have always been incomplete, half-remembered. Even our name isn't quite right, apparently. Cowen is an anglicised bastardisation of the Gaelic Ó *Cadhain*. A name rewritten on each English census, every ten years, as the accent faded: *Coyne, Coin, Cowyn*. Like my dad, all the relatives from his side of the family were Londoners, or so I'd assumed. They lived through the Blitz, fought the war in foreign climes or grew up playing in the willowherb-bursting rubble of the post-war 1950s, riding out rationing into the Land of Plenty through the technicolour curtain of the 1960s. Those still alive when I was young had, by that point, mostly dispersed into the Home Counties. My dad left London early too, moving to Yorkshire in 1964 to attend university, the first in the family to ever do so. There he met my mother and, after a few years living back down on the edge of Epping Forest, they relocated north permanently, setting up the home that my brother and I were born into. Dispersed as Dad's wider family became, whenever they met their bond was instantaneous; their collective remembering a cathartic experience. To watch them interact was to watch people fall into hardwired patterns and pecking orders. They seemed to understand each other in ways I didn't know that you could back then. How to play and tease one another. What to say to spark a flame. How to calm the fire. They were masters of needling, joking, pacifying, mollifying. So, whenever one of them, a good many glasses of something down, would tell how they'd lived in each other's houses in the warren-like Victorian terraces of North London, it wasn't hard to believe.

In the mid-1980s, by the time I was old enough to remember the gatherings of this diaspora, the family was an eclectic bunch: a semi-professional actor and road-safety campaigner; a budding TV chef. The first foreign manager of an English football club, Danny Bergara – a lovely, funny Uruguayan who'd played in the World Cups of the 1950s – was married to my dad's cousin and coaching at Sheffield United. Bill Cowen remained the spectre at the feast, though. Gone, but there. Still the beating heart of things; still drawing focus. Bill died in 1967. His wife, May, pictured two to his left in the photograph, holding my great-aunt Peg, a year later. But even in absentia, it was the stories of Bill that stuck in the mind on the late-night drives home to Yorkshire. It was the fragments of his life I tried to stitch into sense as I drifted off in the back seat.

This much I came to learn: Bill was your classic patriarch. All hard living and hard work, descended from an Irish immigrant, named Thomas, who'd fled famine and starvation in Knock, County Mayo, in the mid-nineteenth century and wound up in the slate mines of Derbyshire. Hence the old family tradition once recalled to me of Guinness at Christmas and Irish songs around a piano. Bill was a coal boy himself, born either 1889 or 1890 and raised in the slum-streets and pit terraces of Old Radford in Nottingham, an area of grime and grind that would later provide the claustrophobic doom-dark backdrop to Alan Sillitoe's *Saturday Night and Sunday Morning*. By eleven years old, Bill was working in a mine, most likely Radford Colliery, picking and sorting coal. Not long after, he was down in the tunnels working as a 'hewer' just like his father and uncle before him. There was danger money in the daily risks of collapse, rockfall, explosion and flooding, but hewing was as hard as physical work gets. It meant long shifts in near-darkness kneeling or hunched on a stool, smashing at the coal face with a pick, stripped to the waist, sweating in the heat and the airless air. Dust in the lungs and eyes. A greasy blackness that soap only chased around the skin in a tin bath before the fire.

In his early teens Bill decided to hit the road. Together with his brother and his uncle, he headed north to the boomtown of the South Yorkshire coalfields: Doncaster. For a decade, he ripped coal. He met and married May, a miner's daughter, and slowly climbed the long ladder out of the dark. About this time, another photograph shows him playing centre forward for Doncaster Rovers at the weekends.

Bill escaped the mines as soon as it was possible, saving enough to turn his work ethic to opportunities above ground – fish and chip shops, B&Bs. Many of the photographs in the cache date from this time, including the one of them lined up on the Great North Road. In others, Bill must have had a bob or two. There are studio portraits of him in plus fours; the boy-done-good look in holiday snaps at Blackpool: cloth cap, suit jacket, shorts, cigarette. May and the children grinning on deckchairs, or ankle-deep in the sea. But the story goes that these good times turned bad quickly. When the boom of the 1920s tipped into the Great Depression of the 1930s the family lost everything. At some point, for some reason, Bill packed everyone into a van and, with the extended family in tow, he drove down the Great

North Road to London. Doncaster was not to be mentioned again. The decades spent there seemingly vanishing from family memory. A chapter ripped out that no one wanted, or was willing, to reread or shed light upon.

London must have been a gamble and hard-going. Hacking out a new life from nothing. These are the times the relatives talked about freely and happily. Bill tramping streets with a barrow filled with ice and fresh fish from Billingsgate. A lease on a tiny shop in Chalk Farm that led to another. Then another. Even with the interruption of war and the Blitz, Bill and May grew a mini-empire, opening up other fish shops in Kentish Town and beside the arches of the railway bridge at Gospel Oak, installing at the tills and the frying counters those in the family who weren't fighting overseas. In later life, my great-aunt would recall, clear as day, the 3 a.m. trips to the market for the cod and haddock. The boys sat around the kitchen table as Bill fired up the engine on the van. The fortifying drinks. 'It was strong tea in the teacups and Irish whiskey in the saucers.'

The gamble paid off. Success saw Bill and May relax into a good retirement. Bill, by then chairman of the local branch of the National Federation of Fish Fryers, handed over the running of the shops to his kids and bought a pretty terraced cottage on Squire's Mount in Hampstead. It was idyllic village life. Genteel, flower-filled. Quietude on the edge of the Vale of Health. Light and air. There are photographs from this time too. A few tinted with watercolours: Bill and May, aged, happy and rotund outside the house, or raising a toast at a wedding anniversary. Bill with pipe in mouth tending hydrangeas, a fox terrier at his feet. The two of them strolling in Montreux beside Lake Geneva after the war. A place, I was told, they flew to by seaplane.

It was around this time that Bill and May struck up a friendship with the actor Richard Burton and his first wife, Sybil. Burton's brother, Ifor Jenkins, lived next door on Squire's Mount. A few years later, Burton would buy the place opposite. The Burtons and the Jenkinses adored the pair of them. Bill was an ex-miner who'd got out of the pit, but he could recall only too well the exhausted eyes and soot-blackened face in the mirror. That underworld existence. In him, Richard would have recognised the pitmen of the villages he grew up

amongst. He would have seen something of his father and, perhaps, of himself too. That paradox of seeking to escape the confines of the mining towns while, simultaneously, idolising them in his memory, measuring everything short against the community and the people left behind. Together Bill, Ifor and Richard shared a common language and experiences few others in smart Hampstead or the theatres of the West End could possibly relate to. I was told when I first moved to London that Bill and Richard would often be fished out of the same Hampstead pubs I would trek friends up to – the Wells Tavern, the Hollybush, the Flask. There Bill might be found holding court, centre frame, flanked by Burton and, once or twice, a baby-faced Peter O'Toole and Richard Harris. I was told that while my great-grandmother May was kind and loving, she was strong and fearlessly forthright too. When Burton first brought Elizabeth Taylor to their house, my great-grandmother shooed her out, chastising Richard for what he was putting Sybil and his daughters through. No lasting hard feelings, though. Burton and Taylor continued to visit Bill and May whenever in London. Another cousin of my father remembers how, sometime in the 1960s, he dropped in on 'Grandpa Bill' after school one day to find the world's most famous couple sitting in the kitchen having tea. In 1967, when Bill was dying in the New End Hospital in Hampstead, Burton and Taylor made a trip to see him. What was relayed to me was the way Richard sat with Bill alone; the way they talked in whispers there together, head-to-head. Hearing of this moment when I was young, there always seemed something of the confessional about it. I used to wonder what stories passed between them. I used to wish that I could have listened in.

It is the same now. Now, with this photograph in full screen and all the questions it raises. These questions and these silent faces smiling back at me. Bill's thin, knowing, half-grin. I hover the cursor over the file name. It pops up once more:

The Cowen Family. 16 French Gate. The Great North Road. Doncaster.

*

These have become oddly appropriate days to be thinking of identity, of origins, of the past, the future, the now. Of Britishness, of *Englishness*; of what these terms represent and mean in 2016. We've been living under strange skies. Storms battering our shores with apocalyptic intensity. Strikes. Rising inequality. Inflammatory debates on poverty, austerity, immigration, on whose flag old colonies should be living under. Out on the streets, hand-painted placards decry the exploitation of the Earth and its people; they call out the madness of end-game capitalism on a dying planet. And the backdrop to all of it? A promise of a reassessment of our role and place in Europe. A binding referendum on the UK's membership of the EU is now not long away and, though billed as a vote on economic independence and the technicalities of governance, it has, unsurprisingly, opened a Pandora's box of ideologies, historical arguments and extreme opinions. Nations, like people, are governed by narratives. Countries are composites of the stories we tell and Britain has long been an island of complex and competing truths. Layered, you might say. Written and overwritten with contrasting experiences and contradicting facts and fictions. Over these last few months, as winter has come and gone,

I've watched with a dose of déjà vu this country awakening to its shallow-buried bones and broken pieces – to its tensions, fears and anxieties. With spring stirring the earth again, we're all here, it seems. A nation paused and poised, and busy asking itself: *Who are we? Where have we come from? Where we are going?*

Before the link to my family's photographs even arrived in my inbox this bothered me. It had me looking again at the smouldering fold of old highway. Something about its indifference, its invisibility yet importance; the way its spine-like length connects body-Britain, its evolution for purpose not photo-opportunity; something in how it neither craves our gaze nor cares for it – all lend the road a kind of raw, disinterested authenticity that's in sharp contrast to the fussed-over and consciously created monuments we like to imagine explore and explain our country's histories. It's often said that the distance we've travelled can't be measured in miles, but I've been wondering if the north road didn't challenge that notion completely. Whether this 400-mile seam of experience and memory didn't serve as a kind of antithesis to the contrived look-at-me, believe-in-me narratives being peddled and postered around our streets. Whether, if uncovered and held up to the light, that unspooled reel of forgotten footage might not provide a different perspective.

Then this. This photograph with its blood ties to the highway and its rows of expectant faces. The revelation that beneath the old highway's black top, and its wild, littered edges, lies not only something of this country's story, but my own.

*

I make calls to my dad and his cousins. I should have expected it, but answers are partial, incomplete, half-remembered. Only one cousin, Jason Conrad (born Allan Turner), can bring to mind anything first-hand about Doncaster. Jay was born there, living his first years in the city as son of Ellen, the dark-eyed girl in the photo, third from left on the second row. In his eighties now, at the other end of a crackling phone line, he warns me that it's a long time since he tried to bring these memories to mind.

'They had a few businesses, Bill and May,' he says. 'After Bill came out of the mines. That photo would have been in front of one. Probably in the early 1920s? Number 16, French Gate. Yes. That was theirs. Near a pub, I seem to remember . . .'

'How many of these businesses did they have?'

'Nine, I think. In all. They worked hard. Bed and breakfasts, fish and chip shops, hardware stores, that kind of thing. Whatever made them money.'

'*Nine?* As many as that?'

'I think so. In the end. Before the Depression . . .'

'And where were they? All in Doncaster?'

'Mostly in the centre. On French Gate. Another one on North Bridge Road . . .'

As he talks, I scribble notes and pull over my laptop, trying to find the locations he mentions on Google Maps. I zoom in, zoom out, peering at the screen.

'You still there?' he asks. I am, but I'm checking something, because it looks as if North Bridge Road, like French Gate, was part of the Great North Road.

'Of course,' he says. 'They were all on the Great North Road. All the places they had. The A1 was the main highway through town then. Everything flowed through the middle of Doncaster, so it was the place to be. Especially on race days.'

'And do you know what they were called?' I ask him. 'These businesses.'

'Well, the shops were called *Cowen's*. I know that. They were all Cowen's.'

Cowen's. I shake my head at it.

'Do you remember any of the other addresses?'

'Not really. Not for the shops. I was very young when we left for London. I remember the houses.' Then he opens up: 'Mining terraces and their little front gardens, and backyards. Always flowers. That was the funny thing about miners, they all loved flowers. Something to do with being underground and in the dark, probably. They'd make a garden out of anything. Now, when Bill was down the mine, they lived at 71, The Avenue, Bentley. When in Doncaster, they lived in Bentley the longest . . .'

'Bentley?' I note the word down.

'Yes. But there are two Bentleys to look for. The old village, and the new. They lived up in the new village, which was built when they discovered the seam of coal near there. They chucked up a whole village around Bentley Colliery. Schools, pubs, shops, houses, tramways, churches, cricket pitches. You name it. They built everything . . .'

'And that was the colliery Bill worked at? Bentley?'

'Yeah.' A pause. 'But he didn't just work there. You know that?'

'What do you mean?'

'It was Bill and his brother and his uncle that dug the seam. They were the ones who sunk the pit shaft there that found the coal. That's what I was always told.'

'When was this?'

'Must have been around 1906, something like that. He was young at the time.'

'What do you remember about him, Jay? About Bill. His character.'

'Ah, he was kind, but strict too. You didn't cross him. I remember he was sitting in a chair once before the range in one of the kitchens. I was at an age where I was pushing boundaries, you know? I was running around screaming and he kept telling me to shush. After a while he reached into a drawer and pulled out a policeman's truncheon. The old wooden ones? As I ran past, he clocked me with it. Not hard enough to do damage, but enough to knock me flat and teach me a lesson. Granny May and Mum were livid with him.' He laughs. 'Yeah. He adored the family, though. He adored May, all of his children and his grandchildren. We knew he would do anything for any of us.'

'Do you remember anything about leaving Doncaster? Like why they did it?'

'Not really. But you don't get told anything when you're young, do you? It must have been desperate, because we all upped sticks. Just like that. My mum and dad too. Down to London where nobody knew anybody and we had nothing. That must have been hard for them. All those mouths to feed. I don't think they ever went back. To Doncaster, I mean. It's all a bit of a mystery. Wasn't talked about. I don't even know if there's anything left up there from those days. It's probably all gone by now.'

I bring the photograph up on my screen again.

'Then again, who knows?' he adds. 'There may still be a few ghosts standing.'

*

Later, while searching through online censuses, I realise something. Our name finally settled on its spelling around the same period Bill was painting it on those shopfronts. Perhaps one of the first times 'Cowen' was written anywhere, it was written there along the road. The call also has me flicking back through highway literature again, for I'm sure I've seen 'Bentley' mentioned in C. G. Harper's *The Great North Road* (1901).

As north road books go, Harper's is regarded as the Bible. Two huge volumes, bound in blood-red cloth, written in the late 1890s and reprinted numerous times. Travel writing was a profitable venture and Charles George Harper prolific in output. The man himself was problematic: an early book, *Revolted Woman* (1894), was an appalling diatribe against the emancipation of women. Absurdly out of step even with its time, it was ridiculed in reviews ('[as] worthless a piece of writing as we've ever had to denounce . . .'). Roads became his focus. He began penning mile-by-mile readings of many of Britain's significant highways, finding new audiences and peaking sales with the arrival of the motoring age. The tone tends towards the arch, the superior, an appeal to humour a class not his own, but as archives go, each is deep in its highway details.

I find the Bentley reference among a list of calling points and mileages. 'Doncaster (cross River Don) 162¼ / Bentley 164 / Owston 167¾ . . .' If Bentley village was on the road's route, then Bill's colliery must have been visible from the highway. Only a few years after Harper's book was published, every traveller arriving at or departing from Doncaster's northern limits would have seen the smoking chimney, the winding tower and the monumental pit-head wheel rising bold and stark against the sky.

Confronted with these proximities and still-active mysteries, rereading Harper's table of the Great North Road's calling points and distances from London laid out to the quarter mile, I feel the power and pull of the road and its potential to carry me somewhere. Like slipping your hand into a fast-flowing river. Broken into stages, its 400 miles appear immediately close and achievable. Explorable. It strikes me that this is the key to the highway. To be out there, experiencing it not just with foot down, speeding to the horizon, but via its first state: slowed to the speed of footfall, bringing into focus the horizons we've already reached. The Great North Road has always been a form of transformation and the act of walking the same. It is the means by which the past returns to us most easily. We can't help but cross our own inland peripheries and thresholds and find ourselves pacing down the back roads of memory. *So, bring these connections together then.* That's the thought. Go. *Go follow this line of flight. Go trace this ghost road from beginning to end. Go try to untangle, understand and come to terms with all of these things – a country's story, a family's story, my own story. Go bring up the bodies, the bones and the broken pieces. Go stare down the standing ghosts and take the hints. Take the road, and let it take me too.* Because it will anyway, let's face it. If this photograph confirms anything, it is that we're all tied to this highway one way or another, whether we realise it or not.

*

It's evening and we're driving home from the north-east coast, down the A1(M); the kids deeply asleep in the back. It's the outcome of every parent who's ever planned a day out with the hope of getting home and putting their children to bed. But suddenly Rosie and I find ourselves alone, amid this holy quietness, and with all the space it gives to talk. That rare kind of talking that only flows when you're close enough to feel the heat of the other's skin yet aren't looking at each other; when you've got the buzz of a day's sea air in the lungs and your eyes on a drifting horizon. I've kept falling in love with her over and over again all day. Her surprises. How she wraps her arm around me when I'm not expecting it or runs ahead to show Tom how to roll down a dune. The way she so effortlessly lives in time, unafraid of time. Unlike me, watching on, wondering when we might finish this thing and move on to the next; always wandering around a corner in my mind. Trying to keep a step ahead of myself to prevent thoughts from gaining ground. Aware that feeling like this isn't *me* at all.

I've been meaning to tell Rosie everything for months. Not just about the road, but all that unearthing this highway has been stirring up in me. I've been close to bringing it up numerous times, ever since I began to recognise the shape of this thing at my shoulder – but it's not easy to articulate to the person you love that it feels like something is stalking your steps. That even after sixteen years together there are chapters of your life you've never reconciled or really come to terms with, let alone shared with them. Chapters that now find their echoes in the present; that draw their own unnerving energies out of the happy life you're building. It's not easy to admit that memories that were lost to me have begun returning in the daylight and the dark.

With Rosie's hand resting on my knee and the horizon and the calm hum of the road, I'm desperate that nothing be concealed or left unsaid between us. I find myself beginning to speak about coincidences and connections, of the oddness of uncovering these family ties to the road and this sense that there are other stories waiting to be discovered. We talk about the way the past can shape the present, forming part of who we are and where we're headed. Then, cautiously, as if walking into an unlit room, come words it's harder to say. Things that are harder to confess – the fears and anxieties that have been surfacing. When her hand falls from my knee, I glance over, concerned I've gone too far. But she's not looking at me with hurt or anger or worry. Something else. She slips her hand behind my head and holds it there.

I don't know why it might surprise me that Rosie already knows. That she's always known and accepted these unquiet elements in me. That she's suspected my struggles with these things of late and been aware of my attempts to hide them. She's woken when I've stirred in my sleep. She knows there are times I don't mention. She remembers early in our relationship when I could suddenly be cold and distant. While she doesn't know the whole story, she knows enough to understand. As we talk, she explains that she read once how those events in our lives that define us, or that leave us less defined, can become a form of fastening, like a photograph. How they can hold a part of us locked in time until we find a way back to work through and loosen the bonds. To cut those ties that bind. Her understanding in that moment undoes me.

When we get home, the kids are – of course – wide awake and hungry. I play with them while Rosie runs a bath. Bea is toddling. She loves to run into your arms and to be lifted and kissed. Her copper hair is growing into curls. Her scalp sparkles this evening with fine, diamond-like sand. I'm warming milk and unpacking the bags, thinking about the things we've said when Tom bursts in, waving my phone, dragging a spade. 'Take a photo?' he asks. Then, seriously, parroting what one of us must have said at some point: 'We have to take photos, Daddy. To remember what's happened.'

*

You could go. That's what I'd thought last spring, before the dig. *Follow the road awhile. See where it leads. Not too long to abandon Rosie and the kids.* Now, over glasses of beer, it's Rosie suggesting that maybe I should go. Go stir the ground and see what comes up. Walk the near space where the mind slips gear and time becomes plural; where memories can surface and stories be spread out, pinned down and made visible. Where it might be possible to understand the roads taken and not. To unfasten the things that tether. And she's right, of course. It's all there. The place where all the veins meet. The way into everything. Only a few miles away. Proximity, *close*ness – these were part of the road's appeal a year ago; they remain so now. Rather than vanishing for months in some gruelling single journey, the north road is a line I might track a few days at a time through the seasons and the years. Somewhere to slip away to and return from between days like these, spent forging the ties that bind the strongest and matter most. For as this dog-eared photograph of my ancestors affirms, it is in these moments that we all truly live, and must learn to live well. So, go then, yes, but with this understanding: sometimes the urge to take to the highway is not about the leaving. It is about finding and following the road that may bring us home.

Walking Out

(London Bridge–Smithfield)

I

At first there was nothing. Then murmurs. Whispers. Surfacing from half-sleep in a heartbeat, I opened my eyes into darkness. From my bedroom I couldn't make out what was being said, only the muffled sounds of raised voices. Like words spoken underwater. Cries; suppressed shouts. The strange staccato rhythms of an argument when all emotional limits have been exceeded. When there's nothing left to say and nothing that could be said would change anything anyway. I lay there, still, waiting for the surge of adrenalin to subside, then did what I'd done for countless nights by then. I opened the door, crept on to the landing and sat with my legs through the banisters, my forehead against the cold wood. I stared into the stairwell's gloom and I listened. Though I knew it was wrong, that no good would come of it, I sat and stared into the dark and I listened.

*

It had been a year or more since tensions began to spark like static through the house and the rows and spells of not speaking became occurrences to be guarded against whenever coming home. Sixteen is a good age to adopt the armour of aloofness; to give an impression that you don't care what your parents think or do, or say. This was the tactic my older brother and I had taken. Ours was an unspoken agreement: ignore it. Pretend you don't notice. Don't talk about it. Listen to music loud. Drink. Escape the house when you can, but don't validate any of it with recognition. I thought I'd got pretty good at this – finding excuses to stay at school longer than required or holding band practices at mates' houses rather than mine. I could lose an hour tramping to see my girlfriend on the other side of the moor, and the same back again. I'd got good at all of these tricks until, a few weeks before that night, my brother had packed up and left for university. Then something in the method no longer seemed to work. I couldn't shake the feeling of emptiness and anxiety. My brother's absence – his bare room, newly unstocked shelves and cupboards – spoke to the inescapable reality I knew I'd been denying – that my home, my family, my life, was falling apart. My world was capsizing, and that the drama unfolding around me had but one inevitable conclusion.

What made things worse is that, sitting on that landing, the smell of our dinner still in the air, I couldn't help recalling the picture before it changed. How good things were. Memories surfaced, then slunk away. A long afternoon in summer painting with Mum when I was maybe three or four; the smell of her skin in the sun. Water fights on the lawn with old washing-up-liquid bottles; slipping, soaking, into the cool, open-door sanctuary of the house beyond. The way Dad would tuck me in when he got back from work late, jabbing the duvet in around me, mummy-like. How I'd fight sleep to try and catch him and then, as he crept out of my room, beg him to stay. How he sometimes did. The pair of them looking holiday-happy even after a week of rain lashing the windows of a tumbledown cottage in Northumberland. My brother and me at their feet building Airfix models in front of a three-bar fire. Fruit picking somewhere. Watching Mum driving there and back, singing along to an old tape of *Sgt Pepper's Lonely Hearts Club Band* with an overflowing box of raspberries on my lap. My first glimpse of the depth and despair of love the day I was nearly killed chasing a paper hat that had blown off my head across a road outside a supermarket. How, after the hiss of lorry brakes and the scream of tyres, Mum sat on the street, rocking me and crying as people gathered around us. Evenings kicking a ball against a garage door as Mum and Dad fed a bonfire with dead flowers and hedge cuttings. Christmases of sledging in bracken fields on the edge of town, and drinks parties when my brother and I would defy our orders for bed and creep out on to the landing, stick our legs through the banisters, and stare down into the light below, giggling along with the giddy laughter. I found my mind snatching at these memories as if engaged in a desperate act of recovery. Like it was going back, rescuing treasures from a burning house. Like it already knew what was coming next.

*

There was silence again. A long silence. Then the creak of the kitchen door. Footsteps in the hall. Purposeful, headed towards the stairs. The thought of being caught eavesdropping was unimaginable so I pulled up my legs and leapt back into my room, closing the door. Under the covers I breathed deeply to steady my heartbeat and give the impression of untroubled sleep, but the steps moved into the room next door. Through the wall I could hear the sound of drawers over runners, hangers, a bag being zipped open. Then the footsteps were outside my room. And with the sharp sting of tears, I realised why. Something to be said important enough that it required a moment's composure. The handle turned and Dad's silhouette was standing beside my bed. I acted as though I'd just woken. *Dad?* I said. But all pretence was pointless. He cleared his throat: *Listen. Mum and me, we're not going to be living together any more. I'm leaving now and I'm not going to be coming back.* He spoke it slowly and softly, the effort at controlling his emotion lending a formality to his voice. His words delivered as if to prevent misunderstanding. Maybe he sensed their effect because he also whispered: *I'm not walking out on you, OK? I'm not walking out on you.* And he smoothed my hair the way he did when I was little. I wanted to grab hold of him and ask him to stay, but I couldn't get my breath and, anyway, the moment was so surreal, the pressure so great in my chest, that I didn't want it to drag on any longer. He looked at me and I managed to steady myself enough to mumble: 'I understand.'

That was it. A few seconds and then he was gone.

I heard the front door being unlocked, then locked again. There was the slam of the car boot, the engine starting. I got out of bed and opened the curtains. Our house sat under a broad shoulder of Yorkshire moor. From my room, I could see the road snaking away into the valley, disappearing into the glow of town. I stood in the window and I watched the lights of Dad's car vanish down that ribbon of road.

II

Into a tunnel. Darkness. Out again. The slam-jolt of the train shakes awake a carriage of half-sleepers whose coffees from Canterbury West station have proved no match for the soporific overheating of the 06:01 to London Bridge. Snorts, coughs. The self-awareness that comes with waking among strangers; that shame of vulnerability. Blinking away the after-images of the dream, I lean against the triple-glazed safety glass, adjust the rucksack on my lap and find a new page in my notebook. Outside, a grey cowl covers the street-lit suburbs and towns. Smudged pewter Kentish fields. Bushes blurring past. Layered over it, the ghost-glow of the carriage's interior reflected in the window. I watch a projection of myself staring back, fluttering, flying, over the landscape. Thoughts flow out; thoughts flow in. *Where do you begin?*

*

The north road has always been as much myth as motorway. Like any myth, its origins are plural and difficult to pin down. The road has shape-shifted and altered over time, rearranging itself, coalescing, growing. Its creation wasn't like the predesigned, committee-agreed infrastructure developments of the modern era; it grew piecemeal fashion, finding its own ways, evolving constantly. Definitives are hard to discern; harder to prove. Take London. Points of departure abound, depending on which century you turn the dial back to. Pick any of the north road's identities – A1, the Great North Road, the Old North Road – each had its fountainhead in the City of London. Each, at some point, fed the surging current flowing north. 'But where is

[its] beginning on the time-scale?' asks Frank Morley, the American scholar and editor of T. S. Eliot, in his meandering psychogeographic 1960s book on the road. 'What was the original push? What caused this causeway ... to have been causative in the history of the English-speaking world?' The answer, he suggests, lies in that truism: *all roads lead to Rome*.

In 55 and 54 BC Julius Caesar made two landings in the south-east of Britain, an island regarded by Rome until that point as off the edge of the world. Britain: a synonym for wilderness, chaos. The effect of Caesar's short-lived, hastily concluded campaigns was to establish this 'northland' on the Roman map; to plant it in the Roman mind, even if nobody would return to fight for it for nearly a century. By the time of Augustus, Roman traders were making good livings in and out of Britain. Streams glittering with riches – tin, pearls, iron, silver, gold – ran back to Rome, rewriting the old 'wild' myths in the halls of power. Patronage and protection flowed back. Inroads were being made.

It was the emperor Claudius who saw the value of finally annexing Britain. The reasons were personal. With no military experience and plagued by tremors, tics, speech impediments, he was regarded as wholly unsuitable for office. Claudius was a historian, though. He knew Britain had proved too much for the god-like Caesar, his ancestor. Conquering it properly would win over the most sceptical of critics in the senate. In AD 43, he amassed more than 800 ships and a 40,000-strong invasion army. The stage was set for a theatrical moment of the highest order. His veteran general, Aulus Plautius, would do the dirty work, all but securing a victory before feigning an impasse. The cue for Claudius to perform a pre-agreed star turn, arriving from Rome on the back of a war elephant, flanked by his Praetorian Guard. Like some Marvel comic hero, he'd save the day, finish the job and receive the surrender of the Britons.

*

Through the train window, the land is coming into focus. The reflection of the carriage interior fades in the glass. My reflection flickers across the trackside scrub then vanishes into the middle distance of fields, pylons and full-flush copses and woods. It was out there, through that same undulating country, that Plautius's invasion army marched inland, following the dry ground and ancient trackways. The proto-road was touching down: all intent and kinetic energy, rumble and dust; horn blasts and gleaming metal. A spark chasing along a line of gunpowder. After making landfall at Richborough (Rutupiae), the army advanced along a similar trajectory to the train I'm travelling on, skirmishing eastwards through Canterbury, through Kent, along what would become Watling Street, before meeting the real British resistance on the west bank of the River Medway near modern-day Rochester. The low, beast-moan of the carynx sounding over the misty river. The howls and yells of the briefly unified tribes. Roman horns blasting back. A brutal two-day battle. The sources tell of a Roman auxiliary unit of 'Celts' swimming the river in full armour to assault the chariot horses of the Britons from the side. More units, one led by the future emperor, Vespasian, forded the Medway upstream to meet the tribes in open battle. The Britons, shattered, fled all the way back through marshlands and across the little islands and sandbanks of the River Thames. This was once the great tribal barrier, a natural defensive line. Not any more. The pattern repeated. Attacked in a pincer movement, the Britons were again routed in the marshy, muddy ground. The outcome was now inevitable and on the wooded slopes on the north bank of the Thames, Plautius dug in and plumped for political expediency. Word was sent back to Claudius: the time is right to make your move. Claudius arrived in the late autumn and marched on the tribal capital Camulodunum (Colchester) in a choreographed show. This was only some of the south-east of the island, and only really the beginning. The 'conquest' of Britain was only really ever partial and it proved in some places a struggle for the next four centuries. But in that moment, Claudius got what he needed: the propaganda coup. Camulodunum would be rebuilt as his city, *Colonia Claudia Victricensis*, the capital of a new Roman province: *Britannia*. At its centre, a temple in his honour where he would be worshipped like a god. The senate would grant him his triumph; the glory of this new colony and its riches celebrated across the empire. In a relief discovered in a temple in Turkey in 1980, the story is preserved for the ages. The stooping, limping Claudius reborn: airbrushed into a handsome, muscular warrior-hero about to deal a death blow to the bare-breasted form of Britannia, brought to submission under his knee. A Freudian field day in marble.

Legionaries and auxiliaries wasted little time in bulldozing into the territory, subduing resistance, strengthening Rome's claim, burning and building as they went. Wooden forts garrisoned at key strategic points; campaigns waged in a radial pattern outward. The consequences for the Britons were costly. The battles numerous, bloody, ruthlessly executed. As the columns probed and pushed deeper into tribal lands, they did so along networks of pathways and tracks, some of which dated back hundreds, even thousands of years. These were mostly routes that made sense from a local perspective – they were desire lines between settlements and religious sites or trade lines linking principalities with the coasts. But the old ways were changing. The new governing reality was a territorial totality. Province as a single body. The skeleton of Britannia was smashed and her bones reset in the Roman model: a series of wide, stone-paved roads purpose-built to carry messengers, soldiers, supplies. Direct lines, easy to map and memorise, marked with milestones (*miliarium*) every thousand paces. All along these highways, early blueprints of motorway service stations (*mansiones*) and posting places with stabling for the *cursus publicus* – the relay-rider communications and courier system that remained unmatched in its speed until the nineteenth century.

Road construction on a Roman scale was transformative, involving the scorching of large areas of ground and the mass felling of trees. Even routes that traced ancient, pre-existing trackways received the coloniser treatment – recast in service of imperial efficiency and authority. Courses straightened, adjusted, made *true*. The highways required quarrying and flanking ditches dug for drainage; pits for sand, clay and gravel. Streams and rivers were bridged or diverted. The new rectilinear web of rampart-roads followed a steamroller logic. Behind them rose interconnected districts with fortified centres from which Roman systems of control and exploitation could be administered. Mile by mile, they altered the geography, and psychology, of the island.

Camulodunum kept the title of capital of the province, but it wasn't the centre of the emerging radial road pattern. The dot in the middle of everything was an intersection sixty miles away; a junction of river and road that bloomed into Britannia's real nexus point and principal commercial centre. The ace in its sleeve being its situation. Here the river was wide and tidal, meandering into the country while providing access to open sea. Here, too, roads from the coast could be linked with the road to Camulodunum. The Romans knew this stretch of the Thames. It was the place Plautius crossed on the heels of the retreating Britons and they had set about consolidating its strategic promise soon after, selecting a bridging point where the river narrowed above a wide pool. At first, the connecting structure was a series of pontoons lashed together. Later, a timber bridge was built on colossal oak supports.

This crossing point marked the start. It was here that the Roman surveyors decided to converge all new military roads pushing out into the interior. Here, on the bank of the great Thames, at a crossroads just up from that crossing, that the notion of a road arrowing northward in a continuous line through Britain first took real, physical form. Like all of the highways being hammered out across the province, its root system reached back across the empire, back to the greed, insecurities and ambitions of Rome, but it was here that it broke the surface. Here that the notion of the north road was born.

The train whines as brakes are applied. The whirr of time begins to slow. A sense of falling. Outside, sun flares the windows of tower blocks and high-rises and the glass-flanked superstructures that form the geometric density of the city. Through the maze of buildings, a glint of river. Two notes, then an automated voice: *We will shortly be arriving at London Bridge where this train terminates. Please alight here and remember to take your baggage with you.*

*

Thoughts flow out; thoughts flow in. *Where do you begin?* There was not yet a Great North Road, but there was an ancestor – a great road heading north. Point of origin Londinium. Eye of the storm. A hub-hive settlement growing up around the bridge that would, in time, accrete into Britain's metropolis. Downriver, ships crammed with goods flooded the pool waiting for the tide. On the waterfront and the grid-structure streets, cultural flux. Races and languages intermingling; fashions, faiths, cultures. Points of origin unimportant. What mattered was where you were, and where you were headed.

Most of Londinium is buried below London, but its extents and edges, its ways in and out, leach through the layers. We know it more or less jigsaw-pieced into the City of London, the 'Square Mile', because its huge defensive walls built around AD 200 became the perimeter of the medieval city. The Roman gates, through which their roads rolled into the interior, evolved into the medieval gates whose names persist in London's *A to Z*: *Aldersgate, Aldgate, Bishopsgate, Cripplegate, Ludgate, Newgate*. The north road left via what became Bishopsgate. The first name given to this highway is lost. But it would have been functional – ironically, perhaps something like 'A1'. However, it is referred to now as Ermine Street, from the Saxon, *Earninga stræt* – the road of the Earningas – the post-Roman tribe that inhabited the area it carved through on its original course up to the military centres of Lindum (Lincoln) and, later, Eboracum (York).

Viewed on a modern map, the alignment of Ermine Street appears a direct continuation of the Roman bridge over the Thames, sited roughly sixty metres east of London Bridge today. It arrows up on an exit trajectory mirrored by the modern A10, through Shoreditch, Hackney, Dalston, Stoke Newington. From there it threads through Waltham Abbey, Wadesmill, Huntingdon, Alconbury, Sawtry and Stilton, all the way to Stamford and Lincoln. When extended beyond Lincoln, Ermine Street first struck out to a ferry crossing over the Humber, before swinging north-west to York. This route had its challenges, though. Boarding boats made travellers vulnerable; the tidal drag of the Humber was treacherous in winter. So, the Romans soon built a second branch of Ermine Street linking Lincoln to York via terra firma – avoiding the marshlands of the Humberhead, this traced a limestone ridge on the edge of the Vale of York over river crossings at Doncaster (Danum), Castleford (Lagentium) and Tadcaster (Calcaria).

The significance of Ermine Street can be seen in its size. Digs and accidental discoveries have unearthed widths of twenty metres in places. A road of three lanes: central section for military transport and six-abreast marching soldiers; lanes either side for local traffic. Material durability, solid construction and regular repair saw it outlive the end of Roman rule in Britain, around AD 410. Even as the province slipped back into a network of separate kingdoms and principalities and travel outside local areas became scarcer, this ghost road haunted the ground. From the early Middle Ages, Ermine Street and its northerly twin Dere Street – stretching from York into Northumberland and Scotland – provided a ready-made, north–south thoroughfare. Revisions occurred; deviations to post-Roman settlements; new trade routes and packhorse paths scratched parallels, detours. The old ribbon frayed and tore, but this roughly conjoined and fledgling north road evolved into a major ecclesiastical highway and bloodline of Britain – a mustering point for armies; a meeting point for nation-shaping engagements.

From early, the road was calling the shots, deciding everything, setting the agenda. Certain clashes stand out, their repercussions rippling up and down the highway, tweaking the direction of history. Catraeth, fought at Catterick on Dere Street around AD 600, saw a force raised by the Brythonic Goddodin people of Hen Olgledd (the 'Old North') meet the armies of the Anglo-Saxon kingdoms of Bernicia and Deira. We know this because a thirteenth-century Welsh poem, *Y Goddodin*, laments the fate of these elite, Old North soldiers, lyricising how they feasted for a year at Din Eidyn (Edinburgh) before taking the long road south to assault the Angle stronghold of Catterick. They were slaughtered, to a man. The Goddodin defeat opened up their territory, a foundational action in the formation of the future northern powerhouse, the Anglo-Saxon kingdom of Northumbria. Writing less than a century after the Battle of Winwaed (AD 655), thought to have been fought where Ermine Street crossed the Went River at Wentbridge, Bede notes that the victory of the Christian king of Northumbria, Oswiu, began the demise of Anglo-Saxon paganism, sealing the religious destiny of England.

The road flared with violence throughout the Viking invasions and migrations of the late eighth, ninth and tenth centuries too. One of Britain's watershed battles, Brunanburh, is believed by some historians to have taken place off Ermine Street near Doncaster in 937. This blood and guts meeting between Athelstan – credited as first king of all England – and a Celtic–Scots–Norse alliance would secure England's borders to the north and west, effectively creating the outlines for the nations of England, Scotland and Wales today. Later, Ermine Street was the 'herepath' Harold Godwinson charged his army up in 1066, raising the fyrd on a beasting route-march to meet Harald Hardrada at Stamford Bridge. It was the road he marched them down again, bloodied and hell-bent on exterminating William the Bastard at Hastings. Godwinson's dismembered body – or heart, at least – was ferried back up along the Roman stone for proper burial at Waltham Abbey. But we get ahead of ourselves. No one escapes the tangle of the capital so easily. The voice on the train was clear, unequivocal: *Please alight here.*

*

Baby-blue and cream-dollop clouds backdrop the city's skyline. I shoulder my rucksack and exit London Bridge station, baggage and all, heading over the river, looking east towards Tower Bridge. It's a scene I've seen a thousand times before: Thames TV's opening credits, early 1980s. Mirror images of bridge, sky, water emerging from a horizon line, accompanied by a brass fanfare. The title frame to that childhood triple-header of *Rainbow*, *Jamie and the Magic Torch*, *Danger Mouse*. Except now, this morning, the frame holds. This is weather made for walking, which is the idea. To roam around the north road's tangled origins and try to find a logical way out of London. To trace a tributary and follow it for as far as my legs might stretch in a couple of days.

It is still early. A little before eight o'clock, Saturday 30th April. Early enough that London trembles with that surreal sense of calm. Vastness and quietness. 'Unreal City', as Eliot, the great poet of the Great North Road, has it in *The Waste Land*. 'A crowd flowed over London Bridge,' he wrote in 1921, three years after the Great War: 'so many, / I had not thought death had undone so many ... And each man fixed his eyes before his feet / Flowed up the hill and down King William Street ...' And a crowd flows here still. A silent procession of finance professionals taking the weekend shifts in shirtsleeves, trainers; headphones clamped over caps, striding across the Thames.

Below, the river has lifted its hem. Mudlarkers pick about the sludge
and the stones for relics, tokens, totems. Boots clunky on the pavement, I move with the flow, north, on to King William Street, around
Wren's monument to the Great Fire of London, along Gracechurch
Street. This was once the beating heart of Roman Londinium, site of
its basilica and forum. Half a mile further on and I'd be past Bishopsgate and on to Ermine Street proper, feet already flying up the north
road. Pause, though. The north road, yes. But not the *Great* North
Road. As mentioned, points of departure abound and, down here,
strictly speaking, these two streams are distinct. They spring from
separate places.

Around the time of the Restoration, the stagecoach concept – a
coach travelling between pre-set 'stages' every ten or fifteen miles –
was evolving into a serious business on Britain's roads in a way that
it hadn't since the classical age. Other lines threading in and out of
London were starting to be favoured; alternatives to the Bishopsgate–
Ermine Street route. Among them, one serious title challenger. A mile
to the west of the older road, its origin was Smithfield Market. From
there, this road flowed north via Upper Street in Islington and Holloway Road, through Highgate, Barnet, Hatfield, Stevenage, Baldock,
Biggleswade and Sandy, before fusing with the old Roman road at
Alconbury in Cambridgeshire, sixty-eight miles north of London. By
the mid-seventeenth century, this route had already been a drovers'
track for 600 years.

Smithfield, from *smooth field*, was London's principal livestock
market. A wide area of grass on the bank of the River Fleet, just
beyond the northern wall of the city, it was ideal for the fattening and
watering of stock. A place of congregation and slaughter. Of true terminus and departure. The more direct route to reach it from Alconbury,
fringed with inns, grazing, stabling, provided a great northern bypass
to the old, beleaguered Roman road to the east. It never superseded
the original, however. Both would be continually used in the centuries
that followed. In fact, the first Turnpike Act, passed by Parliament in
1663, concerned a stretch of the older north road, between Wadesmill
and Stilton. This act would prove significant for roads everywhere,
shifting responsibility for repair and upkeep away from local parishes
to trust-managed toll businesses that taxed road users. That global

road-word 'turnpike' came from the resemblance of the newly installed wooden tollgates barring the highways to military methods of blocking routes with pikestaffs that could be 'turned' to the side for passage. The tollgates were similarly spiked to prevent their jumping by horse. After a slow uptake, the turnpike system, born on the north road, would revolutionise highways both home and abroad and pave the way for industrialisation and the coaching age. By 1730, every major route out of London had been turnpiked. A century later, they accounted for over 22,000 miles of British roads.

One question is where did the *great*-ness of this western branch's name originate? Around 1130, Henry, Archdeacon of Huntingdon, completed a history of England, *Historia Anglorum*, in which he refers, in Latin, to four major elevated roads. Nineteenth-century translators termed these the 'great highways'. Henry even listed them: *Ichenild*, *Watlingestrate*, *Fossa* and *Erningestrete* – roads we know today as the Icknield Way, Watling Street, Fosse Way and Ermine Street. The first 'great' reference in English, however, is perhaps in 1635 when a merchant, Thomas Witherings, was tasked by Charles I to set up and organise regular post services running day and night along the six 'great roads' of the country. Post-riders, often accurately described as 'boys', were employed to work their own stretches, passing the mail between 'posts' overseen by newly appointed postmasters. Certainly by 1675, with the publishing of the first real, usable road atlas of Britain – John Ogilby's *Britannia* – all the country's principal highways and post roads were routinely being termed *great*. But this was more in reference to length and historic provenance than condition or quality. In reality, at the time of Ogilby's writing, many stretches of high road were still little more than rutted tracks slipping and slithering through unenclosed countryside. Horsemen, drovers, wagons, carts, coaches – all were forced to wend and wander their way through mud and flood, straying into surrounding fields in search of passable terrain. An old advert discovered hidden in a drawer of the Black Swan coaching inn in York gives some sense of the treacherous and interminable nature of travel at the time. It announces a stagecoach service for 1706 from London to York in four days, with the telling addendum 'if God permits'. This experience needs to be imagined: four days shut in a wooden box with no suspension, where a window was a luxury; of being hurled about as the team of four horses strained with the weight and struggled with topography and weather; of being commanded to get out and walk up the steeper inclines. This was 'travel' in its original sense – from the Old French *travail*, meaning grim toil and labour.

By the latter years of the eighteenth century, things had changed. The 'great' roads began to be great in more ways than one. In October 1786, the first mail coach joined the stagecoaches on the north road, replacing lone post-riders, and kickstarting a succession of leaps forward in road building, engineering and infrastructure. Coaches became vehicles for cutting-edge design. Fifty years on, the London and Edinburgh Mail could cover the distance from London to York in twenty hours, averaging 10 miles per hour, five times as fast as that being prayed for in the old advert. Enter the golden age of coaching: 1780 to 1840. Short-lived but shining, when pioneering road-men like 'Blind' John Metcalf, Thomas Telford and John McAdam (fortune made from the spread of 'tar McAdam', or *tarmac*) were heroes. Highways of a quality unseen since the Romans. Sources of national pride. Wide, turnpiked, well surfaced, well drained, the great roads of Britain could now, indisputably, be called Great with a capital 'G'. Elevated to proper nouns. *Great* in that modern sense: *great* as in awesome and excellent. And queen of them all, the Great North Road.

In terms of routes in and out of London, codification, of a kind, eventually came in the pages of the road books, strip maps and to-the-minute timetables that serviced the stagecoaches and mails departing daily for every corner of the country. By the early 1800s, there was a general agreement on how the Great North Road entered and left the capital. Thereafter, the older, eastern branch via Bishopsgate was referred to as the Old North Road. If it was the *Great* North Road you were after, you needed to head west.

*

Thoughts flow out; thoughts flow in. *Where do you begin?* The road's sources are bubbling up through the ground. Each like a sign of the cross to be touched before the journey can begin. West, then. West off Gracechurch Street into Lombard Street, into a narrow fissure of fiscal dealings, of smoked-glass corporate facades. A deep, clear atmosphere. The City of London in its weekend repose: sober, quieter, populated by exhausted cleaners in rubber gloves carrying white bin bags. This shaded, sanitised ginnel – forerunner to the future capital cities of Wall Street and Canary Wharf – drifts with its deep mercantile mythologies. Walls sprout Hieronymus Bosch idolatry (a golden grasshopper; a cat playing a cello; a head with a crown and sun), remnants of a visual language that declared banking HQs, merchant houses, moneylenders, goldsmiths, insurance companies. Lloyds Coffee House, where the transportation of enslaved Africans was masterminded into a licence to print money, has a blue plaque.

The General Post Office (GPO) relocated to Lombard Street following the Great Fire of London, transforming this alley into a feeder stream for the north road. Over the next 140 years the importance and influence of the post office grew with the city's colossal rise, forcing the GPO's expansion into its neighbouring buildings. The swelling flood of postboys and, later, mail coaches leaving from here was integral to the apparatus of capitalism moving up the gears. Britain, the workshop of the world, needed rapid and reliable communications into its industrial heartlands, into the north.

In later life, Thomas De Quincey recalled the 'absolute perfection' of seeing immaculate long-distance mails departing in the early 1800s: the servants calling up the carriages, shouting the names of cities 'known to history for a thousand years'; the power of the horses plunging 'like leopards' in their harnesses. The night mails, lit by coach-lamp, were 'fiery arrows' arcing out into the unlit provinces. Faster and more reliable than a stagecoach, with right of way over everything, they were worth the premium to travel on. Four passengers could fit inside; one up top. The guard at the back was the rock star of the day. Think Mick Jagger, 1968, bedecked in scarlet coat with blue lapels, waistcoat, silk stockings, hat with gilt bands. They blew signature tunes on shiny post horns that let innkeepers, ostlers, turnpike gatemen know who exactly was in charge that day. Bagging an outside seat by the driver on these coaches as it tore up the highway was, in De Quincey's estimation, worth 'five years of life'.

Around the time of Waterloo, the congestion in Lombard Street saw it deemed unfit-for-purpose. Plans were tabled to relocate the expanding GPO to a specially designed site at St Martin's-le-Grand, half a mile west again, near St Paul's Cathedral.

Pull out the pin. Move it across the map. Walk on. This is how it is. This is how the weight and gravity of the road makes itself felt, underfoot and within the mind. London fully awake now, buzzing like a kicked nest. Inner London: London's innards, so obsessed with accumulation, with stocking up, stacking up and holding on. The accretion of memory is only to be expected. Memory palaces rise at every turn. Traffic rolls through a roll call of previous utopias: the Royal Exchange, the Bank of England, Mansion House. Classical columns, porticoes, friezes; stage sets from London's historic recasting of itself as the new Athens, the new Rome, the new Jerusalem. All designed to speak to the triumph of civilisation, yet founded on, and financed by, the horrors of the transatlantic slave 'trade'. Those long four centuries still unreckoned with when Britannia, born under the heel of empire, repeated behaviours ingrained in her infancy. When she became the driving force of the world, clutching whip and reins; eyes fixed on far-off lands, mind mad with desire for wealth, power and dominion.

Poultry on to Cheapside, moving parallel to the river. I'm searching for the sight of London's Calvary Hill: St Paul's epic dome and cross. The Great North Road's new beginning was fixed under its shadow once and for all in 1829 with the opening of a purpose-built General Post Office on a revamped St Martin's-le-Grand – a wide thoroughfare running north from the cathedral. This was intended as the course to eclipse all other claims. From St Martin's-le-Grand the road's trajectory crossed the site of what had once been the old Roman wall, up Aldersgate Street and Goswell Road to the Angel in Islington. When the Great North Road was reclassified as the A1 in 1921, its starting line remained the almost imperceptible point where St Martin's-le-Grand becomes Aldersgate Street. A century on and, officially, it still is.

This new GPO provided an excuse to tear down the area's notorious slums, poorhouses, brothels, drinking dens. Foundations were laid upon rubbled alleys that had names like 'Dark Entry' and 'Little Hell'. What emerged above was another icon of stateliness, 400 feet long and 64 feet high. The GPO's impressive facade featured three Ionic-columned porticoes and a huge timepiece, immortalised in

The Royal Mails Starting from
THE GENERAL POST OFFICE, LONDON

James Pollard's *The Royal Mails Starting from the General Post Office, London*. It's a painting intended to swell the breast of every Briton. An early brochure cover for future gentrification projects. Victorian London in full swing. Centre of the Earth. Sightseers in promenade-wear decked out to watch the grand depart. But stare at it long enough and a discordant note begins to sound. Something in the exaggerated, disjointed perspectives, the contrast. There is an Edward Hopper-esque washing of light and shadow. The peak of St Paul's looms over the suspiciously cleansed streets. And that moon. More a glaring all-seeing eye, complete with an encircling glory of clouds, than an astronomical body. A hidden Masonic message, maybe. The Grand Architect of the City of London surveying the great highway's new position and potential. A nod to God, perhaps, or the devil lurking in the detail, eyeballing us down the road.

*

Thoughts flow out; thoughts flow in. *Where do you begin?* Here, then. Technically. Topographically. Right here. This is the place I arranged to meet *A*, a good friend and foot companion for this leg out of London. Someone unfazed by the physical and psychological drift of walking, of sleeping rough in unknown territory. Infantryman, map reader, veteran of doomed tours of Iraq and Afghanistan, his modus operandi is the swift processing of information, the handling of chaos and the assessing of situations on shape-shifting highways. Skills force-learned on Red Routes in and out of Basra in 2007 when every road guaranteed fire-fights, ambushes, junctions loaded with IEDs. A second sense is rumoured to develop under such pressures. Certainly, with scant briefing, he'd perceived the notion of the north road as far more than mere infrastructure. He'd understood how roads can become borders to other places, other times. He hadn't needed to mention that he'd be walking with his own ghosts too.

My phone rings. He's on his way. 'Where are we starting from again?' It's a fair question because I'm having doubts myself. Something isn't right. For all the officialdom of St Martin's-le-Grand, there's unfinished business nearby. When *A* arrives, heaving kit and coffee, I suggest a change of plan. The place tugging at my sleeve is Smithfield. Identified, but not properly explored. Not paid the correct respect. Less than half a mile west again but a world away from the formality of the Great North Road's later starting gate. From 1829, St Martin's-le-Grand could claim to be the road's certified beginning, but it was a marriage of convenience. The queen of roads espousing new money. No concealing, though, the wilder past that the Great North Road could never live down or forget. In its youth, its heart had been pledged to another. St Martin's-le-Grand was Edgar Linton to Smithfield's Heathcliff and the influence of the old flesh fair, the ravenous mouth of the City, on the soul and spirit of the road is difficult to overstate.

Of all London's tributaries, most road books pin Smithfield – or to be precise, a spot on the market's northern edge known as *Hicks's Hall* – as the traditional origin of the Great North Road. Hicks's Hall, once home to a wealthy City merchant, Baptist Hicks, was a recognisable landmark and gateway for travellers. Even after it was pulled down, the ground where it used to stand remained the spectral datum point for the entire capital. When milestones along the north road read 'X' miles to London, this was the spot they were measuring to. Smithfield was London. And its business was blood.

Blood driven down from grazing lands in Portree, Dumfries, Carlisle, from as far as the Isle of Skye. Herds of horned walking dead. Future meat, tallow and leather head-bobbing the length of the country under its own steam, feeding on the hoof and on the road's long acres of verge, overnighting (for a price) in the pastures of gentry or on the common land they passed through. Experienced drovers – Cumbrians, Scotsmen, Yorkshiremen – were skilled workers on decent wages. Literate men, negotiators, security guards. The road's route, its terrains, towns and turnings, locked in memory. Many made their way south using a credit system built for the purpose, expensing journeys to the landowner-cattle dealers who'd commissioned them. Others were cheap hired hands; X-signers on bills who made little more per day than they did as labourers. The more senior-ranking drovers brought with them horses, trusted hounds. They put in at night at drover inns and bunk-barns where bed, bread and decent beer was bought on tick, while the hired hands slept in fields and hayricks. Once the cattle had been flogged for meat at Smithfield, younger drovers often stuck around for casual work in London and the southeast, harvesting, hop-picking. The more experienced travelled back via stagecoach or ship, selling their horses and setting their dogs free to find their own way home. There are remarkable accounts of these solitary hounds trotting hundreds of miles back to where they belonged, fed along the way at the same inns they had passed through on southward journeys. The proprietors kept tabs of each dog's dinners for the drovers to settle when they next came by.

The wave of beasts washing into Smithfield jumped from 75,000 cattle and half a million sheep per year in the mid-1700s, to three times those numbers a hundred years later. All packed into five acres in the heart of London. This flow of animals turned early stretches of the Great North Road into impassable amalgams of beasts and men, stagecoaches, carts, wagons. Cacophonies of drink-edged drover shouts and threats; animal moans, cries and screams. Holloway Road – a *hollow-way* being a sunken road recessed below the surface through usage – was worn into a deep, wide groove of filth. Its earth eroded by rivers of rain in winter and wet springs; baked dry as snuff in the summer and kicked up into huge dust clouds visible for miles behind the endless processions of lowing beasts.

Charles Dickens was disgusted by Smithfield's chaos and squalor. He penned essays decrying it as a shameful stain on civilised London and used what he perceived as the area's manifest greed and barbarousness as a narrative metaphor in *Great Expectations*. Other writers expressed similar revulsion. 'Many of the drovers we doubt not are ruffians,' Wynter wrote in his *Quarterly Review* of 1854. 'But the greater part of the cruelty is to be ascribed to the market place itself . . .' There's a hint of ground with form here. Possessed earth. But who'd be surprised? At this end of the road, execution and butchery before a crowd was not a fate reserved solely for animals.

Heretics, dissenters, traitors – if you were being dragged to Smithfield, insult was being preloaded to forthcoming injury. You were no better than a beast; unworthy of a death at the Tower or Tyburn. Of the many hundreds of slaughtered souls martyred here, most were selected on grounds of faith. Stubborn Catholics or Protestants caught under the wrong monarch and hierarchy. Refusals to recant meant being chained and roasted alive at the western edge of Smithfield,

The Burning of Master John Rogers Vicar of St Sepulchers & Reader of St Pauls in London.

facing the eastern gate of the Norman monastery of St Bartholomew, while its prior watched on. Damnation enacted before the gates of God. Political targets snuffed out in ignominy on this soil famously included William Wallace, the riskily fitting candidate for a King of Scotland in the eyes of the English crown and scourge of Edward I's attempts to seize control over a leaderless kingdom. After his capture, Wallace was rushed down the road for a show trial before being hauled naked from Westminster by horse and hanged. Cut down while still conscious, he was 'emasculated' and eviscerated, his intestines burned on a fire in front of him. His heart was cut out before the denouement: beheading and butchering. His limbs were dispatched to the four corners of Scotland as a warning to other rebellious-minded. His head tarred and displayed on a spike on London Bridge.

The date of Wallace's death – 23rd August 1305 – was surely no coincidence. It marked the eve of the Feast of St Bartholomew. Smithfield had been the site of the Bartholomew's Fair since 1133. London's biggest, most raucous roadshow was a riotous three-day festival of dealers, traders, sideshow entertainers, jesters, minstrels, prostitutes and thieves coming together to buy, sell, feast, drink, dance and fight. Smithfield was England's epicentre of carnival and mayhem, 'Bart's Fair' a brief respite from the drudgery and hardship of the otherwise strict codes of medieval feudalism. It was an annual release of the pressure valve, sanctioned and controlled by the City, and a time that the mob might be temporarily demobbed so that the rest of the year would pass without questioning of the established order. Wallace's hurried death on the day of this festival's beginning smacks of a PR stunt – a headline act designed for maximum exposure among crowds congregating from across the country. A message wrapped in the public gift of gruesome spectacle. Crown and the City speaking in one clear voice: *Observe what occurs to threats to our authority.*

Seventy-six years later, a similar lesson, meted out on the same spot. Wat Tyler, head of a wave of peasant protest besieging the capital, met with the Lord Mayor of London, William Walworth, and the young king, Richard II, at Smithfield. Draw the rabble out of the city walls. That was the strategy. Real deals were there to be struck; parleying to be done. Sensible mediation. Fair pay for the peasants and an end to a poll tax levied for foreign wars that was crippling the poor. Wat

Tyler had ridden out from his massed support and explained the logic of the case when Walworth, supposedly outraged that a churl might speak to a king in such a way, leapt forward and stuck his dagger into Tyler's neck. Disrespect was one explanation. The other is that Walworth acted pragmatically because the fourteen-year-old king seemed to be wavering. He'd appeared like he might actually concede to the people's demands. Wounded, Tyler was dragged from the hospital he'd been rushed to and beheaded at Smithfield for good measure. His killing an intervention. A teachable moment for a boy monarch on who held the true power and how that power was to be wielded. A reminder that the City of London was the true engine room of Britain and it depended on a populous kept in its place. A lesson that its knights were unafraid to step in whenever threats to interests materialised. Walworth was subsequently honoured and lauded as Protector of the City and its merchants and capital generators, its societies, guilds and fraternities. A verse in the Fishmongers' Hall today suggests the blood-coloured sword seen in the City of London's crest is actually Walworth's dagger, crusher of the Peasants' Revolt:

> Brave Walworth, Knight, lord mayor that slew
> Rebellious Tyler in his alarmes;
> The king therefore did give him in lieu
> The dagger to the city armes.

Maybe this is true, maybe not. But all of it is part of Origin Point Smithfield. All of it is *here*, bound up with the story of the Great North Road. These are the threads that maketh the highway – the exposed layers of memory and connections that conjoin the events of our history, revealing how things end up the way they are, why we live the way we do, why we think of the structures and systems we're born into as set and unchangeable. With each step a questioning and disassembling of received notions, such as the City of London as some all-powerful but ultimately benign entity. The elemental force but one that *surely* exists for the benefit of the whole nation and its people? The revelations that this may never have been the case. That it was always a dynamo driving the course and concerns of this country for the few. The pre-eminent centre of ethics-free enterprise and above-the-law dealings. An empire within an empire governed by secret societies offering fortunes for those prepared to sign up to its self-regulated, self-serving codes. How it might transpire that, with this as its founding ethos, the City of London could find itself in recent decades money-laundering for dodgy Russian billionaires and unscrupulous international financiers, washing corruption cash flowing in from tax havens and helping it flow out through offshore-owned property portfolios, apartment blocks, office complexes, media institutions, football clubs, universities, shopping centres. The very fabric of Britain.

These are the topics of conversation as, packs on our backs, we cut through the narrow streets around St Bart's Hospital, past the Wallace Memorial draped with its saltires and flowers, and wander into the architectural emptiness of Smithfield Market. The cast-iron, arcade-style Victorian reinvention of 1868 was a realised vision of a covered, *civilised* market. New Smithfield was ahead of the City of London in the art of burying, disguising, hiding its unsavoury activities. A million pounds-worth of Italianate glamour to still the pen of critics like Dickens, it was, crucially, serviced by underground railway rather than the Great North Road, which, by then, had married up and moved to St Martin's-le-Grand anyway. Subterranean tunnels and cold storage saw animals transported in on ice, already dispatched and dealt with. More a morgue than a market. The bloody business of slaughter out of sight, and out of mind. It is the same today. As we trudge the Grand Avenue separating the East and West Halls, what look like bloody puddles resolve into industrial-pink detergent slicks. Worn-out, white-coated traders brush down pavements, dragging on smokes at the end of shifts that began at 4 a.m. The stalls boarded up; the fleets of white vans gone. Business done for the day. It takes imagination to envisage what it must have been like standing here before.

*

Step out. Wait for eyes to adjust. A block-of-light street with bright building wedges; vistas topped with cuts of cloudy blue. Memories shift and settle again. Recollections of personal arrivals and departures. Smithfield Market, with all its daytime abandonment and cheap eateries, its confusions of smells and stacked boxes of produce being trolleyed into restaurant back doors, was the place to escape at lunchtimes during the first summer I spent in London in 2001 while a student. Weeks of bewilderment and *can I sleep on your sofa?* favours. A bedroom too small to lie flat in. Weeks when the worst thing imaginable was to be without a place to be. That enfant terrible of 1990s publishing, James Brown, had granted me a placement on his pet-project film magazine *Hotdog*, which had offices around the corner on Farringdon Road. He'd explained on my first day that my letter had been pulled from the pile not because of the promise of my writing so much as that it was postmarked 'Leeds', his hometown. It was here too, at Smithfield, that I would wash up on a July morning, 2005, with the dawning awareness that something terrible was happening. A resident of London for years by then, I was travelling to work late when I was kicked off the Underground (Northern Line) and sardined into an overfull bus being diverted east. It made it as far as Smithfield from where I could hear continuous waves of sirens echoing across the city. The judder-throb of circling helicopters. I remember someone shouting that there were suicide bombers on the Tube. A woman said it was the buses that they were hitting. The shock of her words: 'They're fucking blowing up double-deckers.' London locked down; no way in or out. The scrambled calls to loved ones refusing to connect. Panicked texts sitting unsent. Paralysis of disbelief everywhere. Hours passing in minutes until that eerie scene that everyone remembers so well: the long, straggly lines of Londoners drifting back home. That en masse exodus on foot and in a sombre silence. That moment the wounded city started emptying. When everyone began walking out.

Thoughts flow out; thoughts flow in. *Where do you begin?* It didn't register at the time, but when I wandered up to my flat that day it was the Great North Road that took me home. At the corner of Charterhouse Street and St John's Street, a parked-up taxi driver with his door open, cigarette and tea in hand, had lent me an *A–Z* to plot my route. I had set off that afternoon unaware I was inverting the north road's flow, the traditional direction of its footfall. I was following the herd *up* the old drovers' streets, away from the fresh blood and the butchery, the noise, the death, the turmoil. No, it didn't register then,

but it registers now. And as we're standing here, Smithfield at our backs, on the traffic island where Hicks's Hall once stood, the ear-burst scream of a siren erupts behind us with perfect timing. I turn, then take in the ribbon of road ahead.

'Are we lost already?' *A* is smiling at me, itching to move.

'No,' I say, taking a step. 'This is the place. This is where we begin.'

Escape Velocities

(Smithfield–North Finchley)

St John's Street encourages speed. You can't help but quicken your step. It's the release. Freed from the densely packed streets of the City, so squeezed by the weight of history and memory, there's a lightheadedness in heading true north at last. Even before the St Martin's-le-Grand relocation, the delirium of the Great North Road's beginnings became easier to follow from here. Like the album cover for Pink Floyd's *The Dark Side of the Moon* read right to left, the road's multiple lines of origin left the prism of the Square Mile to emerge as a single course pushing through what were once London's edge-lands, up to the outlying village of Islington. Until the mass architectural accumulation of the eighteenth and nineteenth centuries – storehouses, distilleries, breweries, stables, inns – travelling up St John's Street was a sharp transition from the urban into open country, into fields, woods and the estates of nearby religious houses. The street was christened after an adjacent priory: London HQ of the Knights of St John of Jerusalem, the 'Knights Hospitallers' – a military order tasked with readying and restoring pilgrims and crusaders hastening to, and returning from, the Holy Land. The haul is physical, a fast-track up a trench of discontinued banks, fine-fronted eateries, coffee shops and the hubs of Clerkenwell's creative agencies. Past insanely priced listings in estate agent windows and hoardings tagged with unwitting reminders of the street's historic trades: MONEY *IS* BLOOD / BLOOD *IS* MONEY.

A sets the pace, weaving between courier bikes and kerb-mounted delivery vans, snapping on his phone the street-side jostles of offices, old merchant warehouses, retired pubs. I leave him to it. After sixteen years of friendship, of carving out windows to escape up mountains and pitch tents on summits in all weathers, we've come to appreciate the space and quiet walking with one another brings. To not regard shared silences between conversation as a problem to be overcome. With A questions are direct. Answers always truthful. It's one of the reasons I wanted him here: a reliable witness to future memories. Someone to check my notes with further down the line.

There was another motive. As he walks ahead, name and number stencilled across his Bergen, I'm reminded that in counterpoint to the disorder of mine, A's life has been a tracer round in its trajectory: school, university, the army. Around the time we got the same tattoo on our shoulders, I'd toyed with the idea of following the same course. Lost and exasperated with the chaos of my life, I'd considered putting it into the hands of others to make something of. I chose the line to be inked on our skin because it was a soldier's protection prayer: IN MANUS TUAS DOMINE. *Into thy hands, Lord*. The last words of Christ on the cross; Van Helsing's outcry as he enters Dracula's tomb. At the crucial fork in the road, we took different paths, but A has always been that ghost double walking down a road not taken. Who knows? Maybe I'm the same to him.

Saturday-morning drifters amble south, meeting us head-on in straggling lines. The hungover: squinting, hunting for coffee and upscale breakfasts, lighting up, applying lip salve, yammering into phones. Following the old cattle trail the other way, there is a sense akin to taxiing on a runway. Doors closed and locked now; no going back. Half a mile further, the pavements widen. St John's Street's trench sides open up into sun-splintering high-rises, new university monoliths and the ship-bridge stacks of flats that have elbowed a little breathing room. I find my notebook. We're still so close to the source, but even this far out you start to appreciate the Great North Road as an organising principle. I underline these words: _An Organising Principle. The road is the 'event' behind which everything else fell into place._ Vapour trails scratch the blue above us. One silver line is stretching back. Lifting, shifting, my thoughts begin to follow it.

*

I've never really been able to sort the months after my dad left home into any kind of coherence. If I try, things get confused. Lots of spaces.

Moments that don't quite fit. Scenes that feel like they happened to someone else. Such are the imperfections of memory, especially memory forcibly unremembered for so long. But I can recall the feelings – an engulfing sense of going under, the collapse of what had been our lives. Mostly, the fear and frustrations of being trapped and left behind in the wreckage. From the night he left home, Dad was gone. He was renting a flat in another town, and it would be over a year before I would see him in person again. Suddenly I didn't know anything about his life any more, what he did, who he was with, how he spent his time. He became a stranger to me and I missed him. We'd always been thick as thieves. A running joke was how similar we were, how much of a 'father's son' I'd become. We looked like each other; we walked the same way. Now it was as if I'd been robbed of him and yet his presence was still everywhere. Friends and colleagues would ring up our house asking for him, thinking I *was* him, then quickly hang up embarrassed when I explained he didn't live with us any more. To hear his voice, I'd call his office, for we both knew that him ringing our home in the evening might create more upset and pain. But these conversations soon became pointless. Dad would make small talk, ask if I was all right and I'd tell him I was, but we both knew that I was lying. While I was sure he wanted to help, to make things better, there was no way of him doing that then, nor of things going back to how they were. So, after a while, it became easier not to speak.

It was a similar story with my brother. In the early 1990s, before mobile phones and email, students at university fell (ecstatically, usually) off the radar in their first years. Communal payphones in halls were ineffective ways to stay in touch, even if you wanted to. Arranged times got missed. The line permanently engaged. I knew deep down he'd already crossed a border. He was somewhere I couldn't follow. I wasn't getting him back. I didn't blame him for staying away any more than I blamed Dad for not being around. It was what it was. But the fact of it didn't make things any easier.

I remember Mum and me limping around our house on the moor like wounded animals. It must have been getting on for winter when it happened for there always seemed to be darkness pressing the windows. Rising in the dark, going to bed in the dark, short days of dim light between. I remember trying to pretend life was normal. I got up, got dressed; I got the bus to school in Leeds. I came home again. Mum made us dinner and we sat in the kitchen, attempting to talk about anything other than what was really happening. We rarely managed it for very long. I remember realising that my parents were two fallible human beings – that they were two people with emotions and nervous systems that were broken and hurting. I remember how disorientating and lonely it was to feel all sense of safety, security, of *home* vanish. Everything now inside out and sore. The internal wiring of my parents' marriage no longer concealed. It lay ripped out and exposed, delivering fresh shocks every time I came into contact with it. If Dad was brought up, I defended him. I did the same with Mum, but because she wasn't present at the time, in her eyes I became my father's proxy. The lookalike around the house. Rooms felt haunted, except Mum and me were the ghosts that couldn't move on. Reminders lay everywhere – innocuous things held newly profound meaning. I knew my mum felt the same anguish and loss that I did when we eventually cleared these things out. But I felt robbed of her too – the strong, funny, carefree, creative woman who knew everything about nature, who opened a lifelong love of the world outside. I remember the tension of hanging-by-a-thread days when if we got to bedtime without the reality of the situation bursting in, it felt like victory. I remember all the nights of crying and lying there listening and hurting, not knowing what to do. When I'd close my eyes and imagine I couldn't feel the sadness, willing it away, like a child.

I hadn't encountered grief like it before. Not then. Not the kind of unshakeable grief that alters people. It was alien to me and, at sixteen, I was as incapable of recognising it in others as I was of recognising it in myself. As the months passed things got tougher. We did our best, but the house was overwhelmed. There was no break from the engine-scream of us both being jammed in the wrong emotional gear. Trying to hold the weight of this and not let it show, my mind began adapting to the pressure. It learned to filter, and then to narrow that filter ever more until it shut down parts of me. It was a dangerous road to go down, but I remember being relieved and intrigued by the numbness, the sensation strong enough that, at times, it was like I was on the other side of thick glass, as if studying what was happening down the wrong end of a microscope. One night, when things had blown up again, I found my body was shivering and twitching uncontrollably. I hid in my room and sat on the bed. It was a strange out-of-body experience. I gripped my fingers tight and held my arms to stop them jolting and told myself this was *good*. This was the strong alternative to crying. Things couldn't reach me or affect me emotionally any more. Or that's what I believed.

I've read since that sixteen into seventeen is a formative time in adolescence. A time you're supposed to gather all you've learned in childhood and take tentative steps from the security of home towards building your own version of the world. But the inverse was happening. As much as I craved it, 'home' was gone. Rather than stepping out of it, I was stuck; caught on a threshold, looking back. For the first time I was acutely aware how alone we are in life and yet there always seemed to be some small emergency for me to attend to, some catastrophe that would spike the adrenalin again. The hardest thing was knowing that I wasn't going anywhere. Mum needed me and besides I was still at school. It wasn't like there was anywhere for me to go, or any money to go there with. It felt as if a decision about the rest of my life had been made without me. For reasons I couldn't fathom, the people I loved most had conspired to leave me standing in the ruins, trying to repair something that was unrepairable.

There was a change in my personality. The numbness was intoxicating and, like drunkenness, it was emboldening too. I knew it was altering who I was, but at that moment it felt exciting to be moving in any direction. I was intrigued by the confidence and edge it brought. Filled with anger and rough cynicism, I thought I could see the cracks in everything and I wanted others to see them too. I wasn't answering to anyone and I wasn't afraid. Soon it became clear that fearlessness could be attractive. It got laughs. It got you in places. It got you served alcohol in corner shops, off-licences, pubs. It drew friends around you and gave you the gall to speak to girls; to answer back. I found I could be loud and sharp. I could exploit weakness and insecurities in others while hiding my own. These were useful tools to have in a school where, on my first day, aged eleven, someone three years older had asked for my name in the corridor and then punched me in the face because they didn't like my older brother. They were useful tools too if you had the urge and idea to stand up in front of strangers and sing.

I'd been playing guitar for five years by the time my mum and dad separated. The band I was in had been cutting its teeth at gigs for about as long. We started young – learning chords and songs from a mate's dad on a Saturday morning, graduating quickly to playing 1960s covers – 'I Wanna Be Your Man', 'To Know Her is to Love Her', 'Chains', 'House of the Rising Sun', 'Twist and Shout', 'Please Please Me' – in church halls, youth centres and working men's clubs for pass-the-glass pocket money. We pulled poses and got featured in local papers under patronising headlines, YOUTH CLUB DISCO ROCKERS, but built enough of a reputation to play almost every week in our town. There was always someone looking for a group. In 1989, fifty years after the outbreak of the Second World War, we were onstage at an event in a memorial hall at ten o'clock at night, playing to a couple of hundred people. Outside, we drank warm cans of beer stolen from the kitchen. I was twelve. By thirteen or fourteen, we were already pushing ourselves towards harder-edged sounds. We began writing our own songs; some we thought good enough to sneak into sets. By sixteen, the band was my saving grace. A real world within my increasingly unreal one. As things fell apart at home, the ritual of practising one or two nights a week and gigging on a weekend was the only thing in my life that seemed to stay constant. I held on to it, grasping even then that it was about far more than just the reassurance of routine. For all my growing apathy towards everything else, I was well aware that music, books, poems, *art* opened me up in ways I couldn't explain. The power and potential of sentences and songs; the way they caught and conjured and could somehow provide a shortcut to the soul. The sense of a truth beyond what was often spoken. Absolute elsewhere. It was all bewitching and essential to me. I'd always written, sung and drawn, and these habits endured. When all else was broken, I could still shut the door to my room, find a notebook or a guitar and make something. Do something. *Go* somewhere. A pen skittering across the page was still movement. It was still escape and I felt it somewhere different than before, as if it was rising from, or engaging with, another part of my head and my heart. Whatever impulse there'd long been in me to be recognised and heard, to make sense of things, it was drawing from new wellsprings now. I knew that words helped me, and so I wrote them.

In 1992, inspiration was everywhere. Iconic albums seemed to drop out of the sky: Nirvana's *Nevermind*, R.E.M.'s *Automatic for the People*, Pearl Jam's *Ten*. Raw, true, urgent, yet also in the charts and on the radio. We didn't just listen to those albums; we became possessed by them. They were forty-minute transformative acts, each with an authentic language of its own, speaking, it seemed, directly to us. In an age before endless content streams and always-on entertainment, it's hard to overstate how culturally and socially essential the arrival of new music felt, yet simultaneously how close and touchable it was. Any week of the year, bands were driving up and down the A1 on tour in beat-up coaches playing circuits of small venues in towns and cities that a cocky grin, a few quid and the confidence to lie about your age might get you into. In 1989, Nirvana had played to a half-empty pub (the Duchess of York) in Leeds; now they were the biggest act in the world. In February 1992, I was watching Pearl Jam in a tiny hall in Bradford, a gig you can still see in all its low-fi grainy, jumpy glory on YouTube. Search for it and you'll witness a different era. There's no division between band and crowd. A mate of mine is caught by the wobbly camcorder stage-diving; people jump onstage drinking, smoking, singing into the mics. At home in our empty house, my headphones on, I would slip inside albums and go through the stacks of my parents' records and hide there. For the duration, I could be somewhere out of time. I was not beyond the feelings of grief, pain, stress and worry, but I was experiencing them differently. Everything smouldering within me was – if not exorcised – alleviated through some shared emotional bond with the band or the characters in the songs I was listening to. Springsteen's 'Racing in the Street' could put me in a trance. I was in it: the night, the cold, the heartbreak, the highway, the disappointment, the loss of faith in the drudgery. How that worked was a mystery, but it was a magic I was desperate to learn. I wrote to try to understand it: songs with teenage, grunge-angst titles that creak with the cliché of that era – 'Dark', 'Hollow' – but that, in hindsight, perhaps speak volumes too.

When we could afford it, we recorded in a tiny, damp studio in Bradford, then spent hours in the library getting record label addresses from directories and sending off demo tapes. Waiting for the inevitable rejection, we gigged anywhere and everywhere that would have us. There was innocence and ignorance in this determination. We believed if we pushed ourselves, wrote more, withstood the nights of playing in no-hope places, that we might break through the glass wall and be the band arriving on the tour bus in town each evening, not the kids stuck there waiting. It was *escape* we were chasing. I can see that now. There was escape in writing and gigging, but also in everything that came with it. Centre stage, the new numbness within me was at its most encompassing. I felt bulletproof, which was just as well because for all the thrills of playing, there were harder nights too: nights of fighting, mockery, gigs when things got thrown. A lot of hopefuls scrapping over the same plate. The same ticket out.

It was escape we were chasing, and there were always other ways to find it. By seventeen we were drinking every night we played. Rehearsals and shows. Before, after. Cheap booze. Cans of beer. Shared quarter-bottles of discount-brand whisky. Nothing so different from anyone else our age in the early 1990s perhaps, but a particular requirement of being in a band. Cigarettes and alcohol ubiquitous. Drugs too, if you knew someone and could afford them. Weed, mostly. The justification for intoxicants and music was passed down from on high. Look anywhere. Listen to anything. It was always there. Drugs shaped pain into art. That was the belief, the truth. It was there in the Rolling Stones, the Beatles. The whole, arch look-back-and-plunder movement that would soon become 'Britpop'. Lie your way into gigs or clubs and it was assumed you were eighteen. Drink subsidised as part of the ticket price. Rooms would become slippery, sweaty, smoke-filled, heaving with the power of a sea wave. Safer to go with it than resist. Safer to go with everything. So, we did, happily. On weekends, when not playing or writing or doing jobs, the band would meet by the river or up on the moor and get drunk, smoke grass, and plot the shape of our escape: the record deal, the studio in London, the breakthrough album, the *road*. Always that mythical end point – the road – that concept of constant escape with its promise of distance and possibility of remaking yourself. Where you might run and keep running.

There are blank spots. These are blurry years for all of us, but consciously calling them to mind again now as I walk, I feel afresh the vertigo of the highs and lows. The confusions, the tensions. Life as something raw and real and exciting, yet heavy and hard to bear at times too. A painful energy within me that I couldn't think about. The hardening of my heart against increasingly desperate emotions. I only remember a few times when they got the better of me. One day my art teacher asked to see me after school. He was a gruff and unimpressible man who kept order by unpicking my cockiness, who smoked a pipe and smelled of coffee. Four cans of beer a night, he told us once. That was the key to a balanced life. I liked him. I sat down in his office and he told me that he'd heard what was happening at home and that he was glad because it explained my behaviour of late. Waning concentration, disruptiveness. Then in a way I'd never heard him speak before, he said: 'You do know that you're not to blame for any of it, don't you? It's shit what's happening, but you'll be all right.' Just that. It caught me off-guard. Everything was instantly burning and catching light inside me before I could smother it. I recall the slam of all the held-at-bay pain, anger, worry and sadness kicking open a door in my brain. It was terrifying. I felt tears rising and a crushing ache in my lungs and heart, and, quickly, I assured him I was OK and got out of there. I was livid that someone had been able to do that to me. I was livid because a part of me had wanted to stay and tell him everything.

There was another who could see through the facade. I had a girl-friend who was older than me and had gone away to college. She came from a family that appeared to be everything mine wasn't. A unit of calm domesticity. We'd been together for more than a year and I believed that this was it – this was how I would put the pieces back together. Everyone remembers the intensity of first love. The world overloaded with meaning and magic. But when things began unravelling at home, the relationship was put under a strain far more psychological and serious than it could handle. I'd beg, borrow or steal money, skip school and take the coach six hours to see her. To try to hold on. The last time I did before we broke up, she told me that she was worried about me. We'd gone out with her college friends and I'd drunk too much, picked an argument with someone and woken up to find her looking at me like a stranger. When things ended, I pretended it didn't affect me. I was determined not to show what I thought must be weakness. But I missed her and her family, and I could feel the hopes of finding a home again slipping away. A couple of months later, I convinced a schoolmate to bunk off with me and take the National Express the 200 miles south from Leeds just to see her. We arrived at her door, stoned, to find she'd gone away with a new boyfriend. Her housemates let us stay and I slept in her bed. The next morning, I woke early to feel the weight of her absence, of all the absences in my life, more than ever. I looked at the spaces where a few months before photos of us had been stuck to the walls and wondered what the hell I was doing. I shook awake my friend and we left.

When she heard about what had happened, that lovely girl called my house to say she would be home for Christmas soon, and would I come around and see her? So, I did, fresh from playing a gig in town, late, dishevelled, wild-eyed, stinking of cigarettes and drink. Play-acting disinterest, I walked into her parents' home to find it decorated with lights and greenery and with a huge fir tree in the hallway. Her younger brothers were watching a film. All of them seemed delighted to see me. They hugged me. Her dad made me a cup of tea and gave me toast. He'd just retired to become ordained as a reverend and this was his first Christmas ministering. The subject of faith came up and, wounded, angry and flush with arrogance, I explained that I didn't believe in any supreme being that happily doled out pain as blatantly and cruelly as his God evidently did. I pointed out that my mum's long and dedicated faith had really worked out for her, hadn't it? It was childish, performative stuff. He met all of it with gentleness, assuring me that I wasn't alone, no matter what I thought. It ached to receive such kindheartedness and to see her, to think of her with someone else. I couldn't handle it – the warmth, the family, the affection. Ashamed, I made my excuses and left. As I closed the door, her dad pressed a piece of notepaper into my hand with a Bible verse written on it and asked me to promise to look it up. I walked home, around town, along the edge of the moor. When I got back, the house was dark. Mum asleep upstairs. I found her Bible in the kitchen and flicked to the passage he'd written. I still remember the line. Psalm 91:11: *God will command his angels to protect you wherever you go.*

*

I'm remembering these things as we pass under the first road sign marked ANGEL. Beneath this: THE NORTH. An arrow pointing ahead. A already has it framed on his phone screen. The north road has long had its own protecting spirits – those angel-named inns and post-houses that once appeared along its high streets before enforced revamps and change-of-use applications. That rusting iron giant, the Angel of the North, overwatching the A1 at Gateshead, arms open for embrace. The great archangel of the road, though, was always the Angel of Islington at the top of St John's Street. Originally, it was a modest hostelry on the drover track, but its position as a first stop and obvious pickup point for passengers outside London saw it expand and grow in the coaching age. Over two centuries, between the 1600s and 1800s, the Angel Inn transformed into one of the largest establishments in the country, significant enough for its name to double as a moniker for the surrounding area. As with most of the road's other angels, the nomenclature denoted the proximity of a religious house or a church, in this case Clerkenwell Priory. Nevertheless, encircled by wild environs, a gruelling mile up the rising ground from the last lights of London, for a long time the Angel stood as an outpost as much as an inn. Reaching it was a potentially lethal expedition at night. The risk real enough that, in the 1700s, armed patrols were commissioned by the City to escort evening travellers between Smithfield and Islington. Back then the appearance of its candlelit windows in the dark must have felt like encountering a holy presence.

It was inevitable the encroaching city would come knocking. Bricks laid over the intervening fields. The inn's spread intersected by roads. The untapped potential of *urbe in rus*. When the coaching trade was done for, the skeleton of the building was remodelled numerous times, becoming a Lyons tearoom in 1921. The last vestige of the Angel Inn is now an overdressed branch of the Co-op Bank, squeezed by RIBA award-winning modernist slabs, sitting formal and ridiculous in its High Victorian domed hat, overlooking the intersection of five of London's major roads: St John's Street and the A1 from the south, City Road from the east, west-bound Pentonville Road, and the onward trajectory of the A1/Great North Road: High Street, Islington.

We cross the five-way junction, hurrying through a gap in the onrush of engine noise, diesel fumes and rapidly accelerating metal. Filling the glass of the Co-op Bank's windows are colourful slogans: *For people who believe in the power of WE*. A tone at odds with the scene out front. A rough-sleeper with empty cans and a worried dog being unangelically evicted from his cardboard sleeping mat beside an unused, painted-in door. 'It's health and safety, mate . . .' the attendant PCSO is explaining. Given the building's history, there's irony to his words – as there is to the strapline postered behind the unfolding scene, stuck up apparently without any awareness that across the road, down a passage by Angel Tube, stands an obelisk asserting that Thomas Paine wrote his defence of *liberté, égalité, fraternité – Rights of Man* – while living here, at the Angel Inn, in 1791. Embossed on that monument is a quote that is more truthful and appropriate for any bank window today: *These are the times that try men's souls*.

I scan the first-floors on the high street's north side, looking for a sign. The Angel Inn possessed the brand equity, the name, but at the height of the coaching age it was a smaller neighbour – the Peacock Inn – that was the real nodal point of convergence for those with escape on the mind. I spy a green plaque marking the site set into the brick above a takeaway: GERMAN DONER KEBAB (The *Original* German Doner Kebab). Hemmed in next door, a better aide-memoire – a period slice of the Peacock's once-considerable stucco frontage. This houses its own ground-floor, fast-food confusion: TORTILLA (The *REAL* California Burritos & Tacos). We can still make out the old upper storeys, though, unchanged from their depiction in another of Pollard's many road paintings, called *North Country Mails at the Peacock, Islington*.

At the time of its painting (1821), there were fifty inns in London dispatching long-distance coaches. Every northbound service stopped at the Peacock. If you wanted to leave the capital you need not trouble yourself with the complexities of timetables at the city's many posting inns. You only needed to get to the Peacock, safe in the knowledge your coach would always stop there. Travellers from the Home Counties venturing up-country did the same, congregating at the inn to avoid the metropolis.

To pause on the pavement now (except to eat or drink), or worse – to be seen photographing something other than the self – is to arouse

suspicion, especially when carrying a rucksack. A man in a pink tab-arded uniform appears at my shoulder with a radio crackling: 'Can I help you?' Too firm. Too loud. Our motives for loitering register as improbable: enquiry, the road, history, the vague compulsion to try to make sense of things. Anything but shopping fails to compute. He scowls up at the green plaque. 'Nah. You're opposite a Tube station, mate. You can't photograph security cameras around here. I could call the police right now and have them come and take that phone off you.'

'Where are these security cameras?' I ask.

'Not gonna tell you that, am I? You just need to move on. *Now*.'

Hand on his radio. Fingers ready to squeeze out the emergency sequence.

Given the PCSO's performance six doors down, it's not worth the argument. In dirty boots and walking kit, we're masquerading as members of the great displaced that Islington has no use for. Vaga-bonds. Then again, maybe he's right. Momentum was always the raison d'être here. *Look lively, lads*. Go, if you're going. But keep going.

*

Islington remains a composite of times and traces. The view from the road, its constant through historic set changes, is the only one to be trusted. Up from the Peacock, just beyond where antiquarian prints reveal a tollhouse and a turnpike gate stretching across a muddy highway, is the tiny triangle of Islington Green. Here the high street from Angel splits into two: Upper Street and (what was) Lower Street, before the latter became Essex Road. Signs on railings read ISLINGTON MEMORIAL GREEN. Memorial *to* a green, more like; a flashback to the swathes of pasture and common that existed for centuries where drovers fattened weary, road-thinned beasts spitting distance from their slaughter. A hundred years after the Norman conquest, William Fitzstephen waxed lyrical about this area's natural riches in what reads like an early sketch of Xanadu. Sweet meadows, twinkling rivers. Arable land to rival the bounties of Asia. Barn-filling yields. Even its mills 'are turned about with a delightful noise'. Further up the (Holloway) road, a Norman wet dream: '. . . an immense forest . . . beautified with woods and groves, and full of the lairs and coverts of beasts and game, stags, bucks, boars, and wild bulls'. Later mandates insisted Cockney men hiked up the highway with yew bows for archery practice – warm-ups for inevitable wars with France. Henry VIII favoured Islington for duck hunting. Soon after, London's well-to-do began to colonise the territory: Sir Walter Raleigh took a timber-beamed mansion by the road and invested in a pub. Drink always the safe bet, even if there were still other, darker groves about – the haunts of coiners, footpads, rustlers, cut-throats. Workers of the rag-over-the-mouth economy: rifled pockets and purses; rings removed; fingers still attached. By the 1700s, the wealthy and fashionable were flocking to Islington's demi-vision of the English pastoral with leisure on the mind. Air, views, recreational booze. The thirst of through-traffic drovers and day-trippers saw businesses boom along the highway. In 1715, Upper Street had fifty-six alehouses. Twenty years on, buildings fronted the road all the way to Highbury Corner. Property the expanding industry. Developers speculating on fine resort architecture. Elegant grids, crescents, terraces, squares. By the middle of the 1800s, the largest city in the world had swallowed the old rural borough completely. As London's housing density and population increased, the city consolidated its space. While the wealthy rode the sprawl's wave off in search of new suburban Xanadus, properties from Angel to Archway began to be broken up and repurposed into multi-occupancy stacks and rent-by-room slum lodgings for working-class families and the immigrant poor. The Irish navvies brought in to hack out the capital's canals, railways and roads haemorrhaged earnings in down-at-heel inns and alehouses left floundering by the deaths of the droving and coaching trades. Though still a respectable street by day, noted for underclothes and trousseau, by the 1880s, Upper Street's night-time reputation for drunkenness, crime and prostitution earned it the name 'The Devil's Mile'.

*

Place/memory. It's a two-way relationship, each triggering and constructing the other. Even post-regeneration the past pushes through the fabric. It's there in the tramshed repurposed as a sofa warehouse; the faded adverts ghosting the sides of refurbed hulks; the notable high pavements, raised to keep the shit-splash of livestock from the good shoes of townsfolk, doubling as al fresco Pret benches. It's there in the off-street Agricultural Hall (1864), reskinned as the Business Design Centre, in the Union Chapel's Victorian Gothic harnessed as an intimate acoustic venue for big-name bands. And there in the old pubs, the brown, crumbling hangers-on, skeleton frames persisting through Thai restaurant and bank remodels. We pass the three-storey frontage of what was the Wheatsheaf, now rainbow-painted, top to bottom, in pastel stripes.

Gentrification didn't just happen here. The term was coined in Islington in 1964 to describe the influx of middle-class creatives, publishers, ad-men, journalists, teachers and social workers who (priced out of Hampstead) were buying and reconverting grand, dilapidated stock from the first property boom, edging out the working classes and – by then – largely West Indian population into new-build estates in the process. Inadvertently, the anarchists, Trotskyites, the aspiring liberal and left-leaning intelligentsia, began forging new enclaves of exclusivity. New 'villages' where a five-bed pile restored to former glories could be both lifestyle statement and lottery win. Islington morphed into Blair-land: home for a New Labour vision. Renewed momentum. *Things Can Only Get Better.* The Granita restaurant on Upper Street was the setting for Tony and Gordon's non-aggression pact in 1994, the gentleman's agreement to split future power. The restaurant is gone. In its place a marketing suite for ISLINGTON SQUARE – the elite, self-contained, total-living project housed in the old Islington mail sorting office. Beneath its luxury apartments, labyrinthine corridors to house retail and restaurant franchises: gallery-style clothes stores, wellness eateries, sterile cocktail bars. Yet outside the Farrow & Ball exterior with its photographic appropriations of the past, Islington's non-fictions continue to collide and contradict. The other half of the borough's population is among the poorest in London. Islington ranks third nationally on deprivation indicators for children. There are stories in the local press of nineteenth-century levels of occupation – six families cohabiting in tiny flats to make rents. Residents split between those rich enough to own homes here and the impoverished who've followed the money. *But what's the alternative?* defenders of gentrification ask. *Who's brought in all the cash, the cool eateries? Who's improved the streets and the services? Created better schools?* The road makes no judgement. It's not here to solve our problems. It's seen it all before on this stretch anyway. It has had a hand in much of it. It just rolls on, recording, remembering, reflecting everything back. The great, mirrored mother-river.

*

We go with the flow, up and on, but I'm walking with half an eye out for meeting myself coming back the other way. The long haul of highway here, Upper Street to Highgate, is familiar. Overlaid with my own story. The Devil's Mile reputation was still strong when I was packing bags for London in 2003. The summer stint at the *Hotdog* film magazine had opened a few doors. A newspaper prepared to listen to pitches. Before leaving Yorkshire, a friend had sent me off with advice: *It's all about Upper Street. The craic. Start one end, drink all the way down the road, wind up by the Angel at dawn. You'll get a gig somewhere there.* I'd taken him at his word, arriving with the aim of playing live again after a three-year lay-off while at university. I'd written perhaps fifty songs in that time but hadn't performed a single one to anybody. The first place I plugged in, the same night I reached London, was in the basement of the Hope & Anchor, Upper Street. A cellar filled with aura; a place to get hands dirty. A legendary 1970s sweatbox – Dire Straits, the Clash, the Police, the Stranglers, the Ramones, U2 – hosting unforgettable, cramped gigs on a tiny stage. The ambience I wandered into was very different. I opened for a Polydor showcase. A new, over-polished R&B talent playing five songs to an audience of distracted label staff. PR execs on the front row, swapping bags with surreptitious handshakes, ducking off to the toilets. Dead-eyed session players. I managed to get a good thing going at the venue, though. Billed once a month and first on the promoter's ringaround for no-shows. I could leave any temping job I was doing and be up at the pub in time for soundcheck. A good listing in *Time Out* could land other gigs. All along the runway of the Great North Road, old pubs were letting young promoters prospect start-up nights in empty backrooms. 'Nu-folk' all the rage. Rumours of record deals. A spawning ground of superstars and stadium fillers. Misspelt future household names on homemade flyers: Sheerhan, Marlin, Golding. You'd find strange crowds. Intoxicated city workers pub-crawling it home, slumming it for a 'cheeky one'. Locals guzzling post-work lagers, raging at big-screen football. Alternative and indie kids squashed next to the ghosts of navvies: grimy shadows, unshakeable from dark corners. Gigs were about road-testing material, writing and rewriting until things began to hook. Sweating out the urge and learning to craft stories and melodies that might win over indifferent faces by evening's close. Stick at it long enough and you begin to work out the shared secret: listening, noticing, paying attention. Being *in* the room you're in, alive to the energies of people and place around you. Working through your own narratives, but keeping an ear to the ground for stories coming back the other way. Giving form to wider feelings in the air.

A remembers a gig I'm struggling to recall at the Archway Tavern. The clock-topped, red-brick, Renaissance Revival roadblock of a pub (rebuilt 1886) that sits at the limit of Holloway Road. An open mic in 2004, he insists. I rack my brains but can't place it. Maybe it's the unsecured topography currently around the building: hoardings,

pneumatic drills, plastic sheets, lane closures, snarling traffic. Roadworks are underway to convert Archway's gyratory into a traffic-free
pedestrian plaza, which will be called 'Navigator Square' in honour of
the navvies and Irish immigrant families who made their homes here.
Odd timing, though, for overlooking it and also partly through a
transition is Archway Tower – a Gotham block built in the 1960s,
clad in ominous black. It's being re-formed into private rental apartments. Remodelled, reclad in peach, renamed: *Vantage Point*.
Complete with gym, winter garden, roof terrace and 'club room', it is
emblematic of the colonising of Archway by professionals no longer
able to afford to buy homes in the area; who are now coerced to buy
instead into an investment-owned, 'luxury lifestyle' rental narrative.
In a self-assured piece of wordplay, the developers promise 'better
horizons'. The question is always: *better for whom?* Certainly not
those whose extortionate rents line the pockets of super-rich owners,
or the remnant Irish community referenced in the plaza's new name.
We stop to speak to an elderly woman crossing the road, who tells us
she used to work as a nurse at the Whittington Hospital. London-
born, but with an inherited Irish lilt. 'It's like they want us gone,' she
says, pointing out the conversion of her beloved pub the Lion into a
Starbucks. 'It's a shame. All the places we used to meet, you know?
Three quid plus for a cup of coffee? They're turning them into places
we don't have the money to go.'

*

Having climbed steadily all the way from the City, the Great North
Road changed gear here. From 1380, the line of the road left the
trough of Holloway for the upward drag of Highgate Hill. At its
summit, the highway passed through the hunting estate of the Bishop
of London who set up a new road and tollgate in 1386, bestowing the
future village with name and identity. For centuries, in bad weather,
the gradient up to Highgate presented a 'ruinous' challenge for laden
packhorses, carts and wagons. Even so the village positioned on the
elevated, breezy, wooded lip of land above the Thames Basin grew into
a prosperous coaching stop and relay point. Only with the improve-
ments in speed and efficiency during the later years of the coaching

age did the notion of an ascent of 400 feet (higher than the cross on top of St Paul's Cathedral) followed by an immediate descent on the other side become an intolerable obstacle for the straining teams of the northern stages and mails. A solution was proposed in 1809: a brick-lined tunnel – or 'archway', in the parlance of the day – that would branch off at an old inn (afterwards reborn as the Archway Tavern) and drive straight through the hill, bypassing Highgate and reducing the climb to a gradual 100 feet. These engineering works on the Great North Road were being pre-emptively billed as the 'Eighth Wonder of the World'. The London clay had other ideas. The tunnel collapsed in 1812, forcing the project to be reconceived as a long cutting – a road gorge with embankments on either side. This severed the old hilltop route of Hornsey Lane, meaning a bridge needed to be built to carry it. A Nash-designed viaduct – a high, narrow tunnel for regulating passage and tolls with three-arched bridge above. It resembled a Roman fortress gate to London. It wouldn't be replaced until 1900 when the weight of traffic demanded the wide, iron-strut version that still spans the A1/Archway Road today. By then it had earned a darker reputation and nickname: 'Suicide Bridge'. During early road research, I bought a 1904 postcard of Nash's original on eBay that conveys its intrinsic gloominess in more ways than one. A

HIGHGATE. – THE OLD ARCHWAY.

dashed-out note overleaf reads: *The fogs are very bad here . . .* Look closely at the front and you can see Victorian anti-suicide barriers along the top. A pragmatic and necessary alteration to Nash's genteel balustrade. You see why this true vantage point, with its total view of London, endured as a place of escape for those desperate enough to try. Why it still does. Archway has always been the first fork in the road; the point for looking back before picking your route and pressing on.

Things might have ended here for me before they even began. A few months ago, I learned that, in the mid-1950s, my dad was knocked off a bike underneath Suicide Bridge. The bike was dragged one way, under the wheels of a cement mixer thundering up the A1; my dad thrown the other, delivered on to the pavement unconscious, coming around in the Whittington Hospital to find his parents and grandparents, Bill and May, gathered by the bed. The road enjoys such fates and coincidences. It is encoded with incidents loaded with potential significance. Collisions. Repetitions. Forty-five years on, yards from the same spot, a different fork in the road. I can give you the date exactly: 6th March 2000. An event scribbled down over pages in an abandoned diary I still have.

My brother had just returned from living in New York and was ensconced in a shared house on Harberton Road, under the shadow of the bridge. I was midway through the first year at university and visiting for the weekend from Leeds. On the Monday morning, with everyone gone to work, I found myself alone and locking up. As I opened the front door, I turned and caught a glimpse of a stranger with a rucksack on in one of the downstairs bedrooms, looking at me. It was an uncanny thing. The crack of the outside light flooding in; the noise of the rush-hour A1 at the end of the road and the jolt realisation it was, in fact, me reflected there in a mirror, tired, hungover, looking back. Me, yet somehow not me. Like a doppelgänger. It was a shock, and in that off-guard, unexpected moment, I saw it all in my face. Everything that I'd become so adept at concealing from others. Everything I'd been carrying and burying since I was sixteen. The creeping fear I couldn't admit to that, at nearly twenty-four, I was still on the outside. Still lost, damaged, unable to fit in. That time was passing and I had nothing to show for it. That as much as I loved studying – which I did, with all my heart – university served another purpose: masking a mess. I'd applied late after near expulsion from art college and three chaotic years of working jobs I hated while playing in the band. Three years of being told that the only thing I wanted to do (to *write* – books, poems, songs) was never going to happen. University's lectures and seminars a final roll of the dice. An expensive way of legitimising some last, longed-for days of reading and freedom. Of buying the time to try to make something happen.

My old English teacher, taken aback when I'd turned up at his door one night, had sold it to me over a bottle of wine: *you can feed a wounded soul with thought.* He'd suggested an art theory course rebellious to its bones that would challenge anyone to think differently and see the world in new ways. I'd filled in the forms on his kitchen table, there and then. He hadn't been wrong and yet, half a year in, here I was: drinking too much, smoking weed daily. Racking up debts. Still seeking escape. Still walking away from things I loved for fear of losing them. What made the doubts worse was that I was not only older than the students around me, and in a different place to most, but I was separated from the people I'd grown up with – all of whom were earning some kind of living. On the way down to visit my brother I'd bumped into an old acquaintance a year into a new job flogging computer software up and down the A1. Travelling for life. Easy fixes. Salary. A car thrown in. New mornings in new places: Peterborough, Newark, Nottingham. 'Quit the pretentious shit and I'll vouch for you,' he'd offered. A card with his number handed over. That weekend I'd fished it out numerous times, tempted by its possibilities, the promise of movement and money.

By Monday I was close to making the call, but something in what I saw in the mirror that morning stopped me. A brief coming-to on the threshold. A feeling of pause for a moment, of being present for the first time since standing framed in a different window on a different threshold, almost eight years earlier. This was long before I would come to appreciate that the past you leave behind travels ahead of you. That it is waiting to meet you. That maybe escape isn't always about running. But there was enough awareness even then to recognise a point of divergence. Two paths leading two different ways. It was a rare, fleeting feeling of control amid the confusion. *This is your choice to make.* I remember thinking this as clearly as anything. Standing in the doorway in Archway with the noise of the road, staring at my reflection in a mirror down the corridor. *What are you going to do?* What I did was curl up the card in my hand and leave it there. I cut that other notion of a life loose and sent it up the road.

It was the decision made that morning, noted across the pages of my diary on a delayed train home, that would lead me to Rosie. It would bring me back to London with the necessary dedication and desperation and the small hope that never gives up. In time, it would take us north again and gift us our children. And it would circle me back to stand here, sixteen years later, outside this same house and this same door. What I wonder now is, had I chosen differently that day, where I'd be. Who I would be, even.

*

A hundred metres away, back on the original line of the Great North Road, at the foot of the hill to Highgate, stands a monument to that most famous fork in the road of English folklore. A cat on a slab of stone marks the place where Dick Whittington, fleeing life as impoverished whipping boy in London, rested on his desperate escape from the capital. But hearing his name and the promise of future fortunes spelled out in the distant ringing of the bells of St Mary-le-Bow – *Turn again, Whittington, thrice Lord Mayor of London* – he felt the overwhelming compulsion to return. Through the canny loaning of his pet cat to a rat-infested country overseas, Whittington won wealth beyond measure and was rewarded with the high office he'd heard the bells foretell.

It's a construct, of course: a layered fable. The boy himself was born into a titled family in Gloucestershire in the 1350s. Richard's move to London was prompted by primogeniture, not poverty. A third son, Whittington wouldn't inherit. No scullery, though; Richard was apprenticed in the City – a promising position purchasable for a fee – before becoming a mercer trading in cloth. With wealth came the mercantile side-hustle: moneylending. In Whittington's case to nobility and crown. These twin earners paid dividends. Whittington amassed riches while achieving rare political and monarchical influence with which he could safeguard the City's liberties and reinvest in its activities, home and abroad. He was fast-tracked into the higher echelons. In truth, though, it was less a rags-to-riches story than a relatively well-off man becoming prosperous beyond his wildest dreams. Always a far more common and credible arc.

A century after his death, Whittington's life story resurfaced edited to fit later times. In came the childhood destitution, the harsh treatment, the destiny in the peal of the bells, and the cat – a mutated metaphor arising from the language of mercantile business. In Whittington's days, trading for profit was known by the French word '*achat*' (pronounced '*acat*'). Not hard to see how this shape-shifted into an allegory of a boy speculating to accumulate, loaning his prized asset to a trading ship, returning an enormous profit. This myth became a siren song for the rural destitute and dispossessed tramping the high roads, pouring into the cities desperate for work during the enclosures of the seventeenth and eighteenth centuries. It was an enduring folk-fable; a succour for the struggling and a powerful propaganda that promised social mobility, wealth and freedom might be won in the city through hard labour. The story would evolve again during the Industrial Revolution, reworked for another audience. Whittington's origins were relocated north. The road he tramped down to make his fortune the Great North Road. The place he paused during his flight back home, the slope of Highgate Hill. But none of this actually happened. He was never here. The Whittington Stone is an 1821 visitor attraction built on the stump of an old cross. The Harry Potter Platform 9¾ experience of its day. *Experience the magic.* As with any myth, the truth had long since become irrelevant. All that mattered was what people wanted, or needed, to believe.

We're standing by the memorial with its looking-back cat. *A* is making a portrait. I'm making notes, trying to stitch these turning points together, these forks in the road, toying with the idea that the location of the Whittington Stone served another purpose. A shadier art. Fable as psychological force-field. *Turn again, all ye disgruntled and destitute. Turn again! Make your fortune! Dick did it! You can too!* Myth-making to lure the downtrodden. A way to keep the city fed with the required quotas of disposable low-paid workers. Early proof-of-concept for this current Age of the Precariat's zero-hour contract Catch-22 – unpaid yet always on-call, struggling with the rising cost of living and the fact that any opportunity for enterprise has been eradicated below a certain social rung. The impoverished blamed, naturally, not the stacked system keeping them down. I'm trying to imagine how my great-grandfather would fare now if he was passing me on his way down the north road with his family. Penniless, pushing a barrow around the streets selling fish? The authorities would lock him up in seconds.

*

A slog of hill up to Highgate. Behind the high wall on our left, the stroll of Waterlow Park with its lawny grass and borders encircling the curio relic of Lauderdale House. For six years, Rosie and I lived in a shoebox flat on the far side of the park, beside Highgate Cemetery, in the Holly Lodge Estate. The five-storey, semi-communal, mock-Tudor stacks were built on land bequeathed by Angela Burdett-Coutts ('England's richest heiress') after the Great War, in the same year the Great North Road was being renamed the A1. Rooms were designed for single, young women heading to the city for work as secretaries and nurses. Our flat – a nest at the top of that nursing-home-scented building – was impractically small, but it had a tiny balcony and a view. The proximity/proximation of moor that is Hampstead Heath had been the real lure. It was a slow climatisation process. Part of a staggered escape from the capital, back to Yorkshire.

Highgate repays the climb up the hill, as it always has, with a nostalgia shot of eighteenth-century quaintness. The boon of the Archway bypass was the preservation of the village ideal. Shade-throwing trees, sporadic mansions, inns, a well-mannered square with listed fronts gave the great and the good of Highgate's heyday views back (and down) upon London. It was a magnet for the well-heeled and well-known – Dickens, Coleridge, Byron, Marx. Its stock trade remains its notables, both those venerable dead buried in its Victorian necropolis and its crop of more recent A-listers.

The Gatehouse pub is a black and white memory of Highgate's tollgate days – the spot where the Great North Road slipped under a pay-as-you-go arch into the Bishop of London's Park. Travellers wearied by the grind of the ascent from London could stop for a spirit-lifter while sorting out the fee for onward passage. A man unloading beer into its cellars has the stories. 'You're right on the old border here,' he says, pointing out that a dividing line between the boroughs of Middlesex and London once ran through the ground floor. He explains too that, at various times, the building also served as sessions house, courtroom, Masonic lodge. Tales abound of a ghost in a 'Guy Fawkes hat' in the upstairs theatre room. Unseen hands were once laid on a previous owner in a near-fatal shove down a flight of stairs in the dark. In the early 1960s, a fresh-faced Paul Simon played on the pub's stage. 'Homeward Bound', no doubt. 'But this place has been around since about the 1300s,' the drayman says. 'So, you've got to imagine the people that've passed through these walls.

*

Moving ever north we will at some point cross the last line of the metropolis. We'll exceed the city and be somewhere else. That's the theory. The eye of the storm, where all roads leave and return to, at our backs. Enough momentum to hit escape velocity. Half a mile down a tree-lined avenue of grand houses and Victorian villas (North Hill), we're crossing the A1 as it snakes west-north-west from Archway in a start–stop chain of traffic, and pushing along the line of the original road again. No need for maps. The familiar name resurfaces in a flicker of the old highway manifesting. There, bold in black and white, on a street sign: GREAT NORTH ROAD. A hundred metres on, it's gone again. We're on the HIGH ROAD, crossing a new border, into East Finchley.

At anything but walking speed, you might not notice. The drift of architecture, visual, aural, is unchanging. Pitched roofs over period facades face-off with beige post-war builds. Plane rumbles. Insistent sirens. The growl-hiss of stopping buses, cars revving at the lights, stereos throbbing. A revolving cast of shops: deli, Costa, hair salon, takeaway, off-licence, pharmacy and charity shop. The closed, redundant church.

Had we been here a few centuries ago, we'd have found a straggling hamlet fringing a great common. We'd be out of London, entering more risky territory for travellers, notorious for its robbers and highwaymen. In 1774, the Earl of Minto confided to his wife that he would not 'trust my throat on Finchley Common in the dark'. Local chancers robbed anyone they could, but the jackpots for the more professional gangs were the merchants passing over the lonely expanse. Its thieves and highwaymen were frequently caught and quickly strung up, jerking, gurgling, kicking out their last at the end of a rope at Tyburn, before a long leathering beside this road. On the exact spot where the gibbet stood is now a shop selling funerary sculpture: ROBERTSON MEMORIALS (est. 1876). In its window, awaiting the names, are gravestones, urns and pristine crosses. 'You couldn't make this up, could you?' *A* says.

The romance of the highwayman hasn't fully vanished here. Past a stand of horse chestnuts, by the turning into Oak Lane, we locate the place where a great tree once stood, named after that undeserving *Übermensch* of the Great North Road, Dick Turpin. Murderer, rapist and thief in life, Turpin was redrawn via Victorian melodrama and penny dreadfuls as a mob hero who stuck it to the man. Ainsworth's *Rookwood* fancied him as Jessie James in a tricorn, fabricating his record-breaking escape from London to York on Black Bess, leaping tollgates along the way, to secure a cast-iron alibi. The tree referred to as 'Turpin's Oak' was apocryphal. The furthest point from safety and light, its broad trunk provided cover for the nefarious. As a result, a custom developed for travellers to discharge firearms as they passed. A warning that they were carrying. When Turpin's Oak was cut down in 1952, blunted saws revealed a trunk infested with shot. The real dangers of the old highway readable in its ancient cambium.

To drift this far from the centre, to begin to approach London's outer growth rings, brings at last a growing sense of drawing closer to some other vision. Some other reality. The Smoke (proper) dissolving into its hinterlands. We pass the gates of that symptomatic feature of any city limits: a cemetery. The UK's largest. Known for 150 years as the Islington and St Pancras Cemetery, it has been re-envisaged as the 'Islington and Camden Cemetery Service'. A banner ad is plasticuffed to the railings: WE NOW SELL MEMORIALS. The reason the name of this million-strong city of the dead doesn't fit the East

Finchley location is because, by 1854, the ever-swelling populous of London had left the city's churchyards in an appalling state. Great, out-of-town spillover sites needed to be staked out; in this case, across the sprawling acres of Finchley Common. The Islington and St Pancras site was the first publicly owned, municipal graveyard. The authorities followed Roman fashion, laying out lost citizens beside the great highway, Bainesse-style. Respects to be paid by passing trade. In turn, the growing organism of the Great North Road would feed this graveyard. Within its walls is a memorial over a mass grave of human remains 'deposited' from St Mary's Church, Islington: 'in order to effect the widening of Upper Street'. For the first time since the plague, Londoners were being buried away from their homes and communities in a location they'd never lived in, or perhaps even visited. The departed, apart. Souls disinterred, shaken loose. A sign of the times to come for both the dead and the living. The old bonds severed. The urge to belong viewed with scepticism and distrust. The coming flux of future identities. The impending mobility and mutability of the self.

As we approach the torrent of traffic hurtling down the concrete gorge of the North Circular, I'm trying to follow that thought – to recall the Zygmunt Bauman theory of liquid modernity over the deafening onslaught of cars. The bones of his concept concern the shift from the rock-solid, unmovable (and usually oppressive) systems of organisation that once defined identity (place, family, school, work, class, church, state, nation) into our current high-consumerist, hyper-individualistic identities. His ideas explore the dualities of the 'freedoms' won via the dismantling of those old orders, boundaries and limits thanks to advancing technologies and free-flowing capital. On the one hand: unprecedented opportunities for self-empowerment, self-identity and autonomy; the potential to disassemble and reassemble ourselves and our reality as we choose. On the other: the total commodification of life. An obligatory locking into destructive cycles of consumption dictated by an ethics-free global market. Growth without limits. Debt, disposability, shallowness. The notion of self, of worth, predicated on public scrutiny, on being seen. Value based on owning with the repeated and privileged acts of purchasing our attempts to try to escape the uncertainties and insecurities of a world of constant flow.

It's a model with flaws. Bauman is, at times, reductive, technophobic, grumpy; he can be blind to the positives and potentials of liquidising borders and barriers, of self-forming communities and identities. Yet his thinking feels pertinent too as we stand midway across the flyover carrying the Great North Road over the North Circular. Out here, at the perimeter, we've walked into a vision of roads of the future. Howling roads indistinct from any other with an unending tide of traffic shining under sun and strip-lit dark. Roads that could be anywhere and everywhere. Roads with the same signposted turn-offs for fuel, McDonald's (24-HOURS) and identikit retail–leisure parks (Hollywood Bowl, Wagamama, Chimichanga, Pizza Hut, Vue, Nando's). Roads created for freight, not feet. Roads that only make sense when locked in a bubble of self-contained transit. Roads that the A1(M) project at Catterick aspires to. The perfect embodiment of Bauman's theory: roads of permanent and constant movement designed to service a high-capitalism so advanced that either side of this six-lane highway there's the need for colossal warehouse facilities (Big Yellow Self Storage) to house that for which there is no space.

Close your eyes and the sensation is that of being lifted, the body

being dissipated. *A* is standing by the bridge's metal railing, holding on. He's feeling the vibrations through his hands. The thundering pressures of the flow. The nearness of engines dropping gear, accelerating. The gale-winds of tyres whipping over the slap-back tarmac. Nine miles out and it feels like we're crossing a line. A border of noise and speed beyond which London's histories can't easily drift. Where its voices become drowned out in the roar of the present. And here, where memory is annihilated by the amnesia of real-time, two memorials have been intertwined in the railings. The reasons aren't immediately clear: accident, suicide; perhaps an act of remembrance left at this point of transition, akin to offerings placed beside, or cast into, the fast-flowing waters of a river. The first is a garland of sun-faded plastic flowers – gerberas, roses – formed into the words MUM and DAD. *NEVER FORGOTTEN* is just readable on the rain-swollen, browned note.

Further on, at the centre of the bridge, a white fabric lily has been tethered with a laminated card. It declares: 'You are free now / Gone to a better place.'

Crash

(North Finchley–Hatfield)

The sky is darkening. The last of dusk's half-light tipping swiftly into night. Along the back road, behind the Potters Bar industrial estate, we feel more than we see the shift underfoot – pavement into rough path – as we enter an unpeopled land. Fields. Overgrown hedges. Rooks. From the west, that long, breathy exhale of the A1(M).

The route ahead vanishes into a belt of trees. There is the acrid smell of wet woodsmoke. Branches lean in, scratching at our packs. The ground humps up, then – beyond a lethally spiked metal barrier – tumbles into a gully where a railway runs. Voices over this ground. Laughing, hacking up. Snatches of conversation. Rough-sleepers bedding down in London's margins. Those migrant workers rolling out mats beside campfires, pooling provisions, sharing cans of cheap beer. The old Hertfordshire parklands are a powerful draw. A sanctuary. Here it is possible to curl up and pass the night unmolested, away from intolerant, unforgiving streets of the city and yet still be in London on time for dawn clock-ins at billion-pound construction sites, cleaning and courier agencies, restaurants. We walk deeper into trees, across clearings silvery with moonlight. The air bitter, crystalline. Beside us, through a chain-link fence, the shingle mounds and shining rails of the East Coast Main Line. The scene is lit by halogens buzzing with the snap-hum of power cable, of static amplified through steel girders.

This major artery of British transport was laid down by the Great Northern Railway Company in 1850 during Britain's earliest wave of Railway Mania. Its job to link London and Edinburgh via new and previously unimaginable speeds, superseding the role performed for more than a thousand years by the Great North Road, lying 800 metres to its east. In time, the road would reappear: the A1(M) (the Great North Road bypass) tarmacked across fields west of the railway again, creating the three timelines that cut north–south through the once-grand acreage around Brookmans Park. It's odd, this territory between – parcels of woodland, fields linked by new-sawn timber stiles. Signage for suburban leisure walks through edge-lands jungled through neglect. Newspaper stories tell of local residents occasionally disturbed by disembodied voices erupting from dustbin lids, kettles and toasters, of hearing snatches of otherworldly conversations. Heated discussions in German. Faint bars of old songs. The explanation given is the nearby Brookmans Park transmitting station, a 200-foot radio tower built by the BBC beside the Great North Road in the 1920s, that has continued to broadcast ever since. This historic site of transmission and reception has latterly switched its focus to other realms of discovery and opportunity – engineered to become 'an earth satellite teleport' by its new, private owners ARQIVA (*Enabling a switched-on world to flow*).

We slip off rucksacks by the railway fence, layer up into jackets. The atmosphere crackles. A faint wind-whistle, then, suddenly, a train hammering down the track at a speed that dumbfounds the mind, putting everything in slow-motion. Close enough that it knocks the breath from us and yet my eyes fix on a man framed in a passing window – the light of the carriage and shape of him looking out, sipping from a cup. He is shaken free from the headlong rush of metal and held there for a moment.

A suggests we make camp further west, in a rectangle of wood halfway between the railway and the A1(M), inside a littery curtain of hazel and elder. Pitch-black now. Our breath blowing in clouds, fogging the light of our headtorches. The urge is to quickly get into sleeping bags, to rest legs and warm up, but I take a last stroll to ensure we're alone, that there's no risk of being moved on before dawn. Up a small rise, I'm scanning the darkness, the circle of my torch moving across ranks of beech trunks, when my heart freezes. At the same height as my head, the beam picks out a pair of bright red eyes staring back. A second later, the reddish form of a fox turns and bounds down off a stump and into a thicket. I return to my hammock. Possessing that superpower of all soldiers, *A* is already asleep under a low-strung tarpaulin. I check the map and my notebook. Nineteen miles or thereabouts since London Bridge. Lying in the cold listening to the road, I let its moans and half-word whispers speak me to sleep.

*

Progress from the bridge over the North Circular had swallowed the whole afternoon. North Finchley, Whetstone, Barnet, following the Great North Road (reskinned as the A1000) into London's suburbs within suburbs, trying to keep tabs on our location. Guesses, cross-checked, invariably under- or overshot. For five miles the road's retail frontage was a challenge: a corridor of local enterprises and global franchises running through linear ex-villages without discernible centres. We'd presupposed an alternative territory in the outer ring between the North Circular and the howling line of the M25, but found ourselves similarly guard-railed. On either side, a flick-book flurry of shops giving way to carpet stores, tyre warehouses, car-hire centres, showrooms and garages amid apartment schemes and council offices. Our constant companion a line of cars, vans, buses revving then sharply braking, occupants enviously eyeing our walking pace.

The old Griffin pub at Whetstone proved a useful feature. Somewhere we might actually pinpoint on a map, opposite a giant, grey sea-stack of a 1960s block. While A hunted for cold drinks at a newsagent's, I waited by the stone slab rumoured to have given the area its name. Where, legend has it, Yorkist soldiers marching north to fight at the Battle of Barnet stopped to sharpen blades. A good story, but a coachman's tall tale. The name already existed. The slab, outside what was the site of an inn on the main route to London for centuries, is likely the base of an old horse mounting block.

The battle was real enough, though. A brutal blood-letting conducted further up the highway on Easter Day, 1471. A revenge-fuelled clash. Family feuds. Chivalry at its absolute nadir. Scores to be settled on both sides with the sure and certain knowledge there'd be no mercy for defeated men. As the spine through body Britain, the north road was witness to more bloodshed between the houses of York and Lancaster than anywhere else in the three decades of the Wars of the Roses. The battles of Towton, Wakefield, Stoke (near Newark),

Hedgeley Moor, Losecote Field – all took place close to the ancient highway, but Barnet was unique in being fought right upon the road itself.

We'd gone in search of the site, up the long hill, ascending out of London into what was once a periphery town with open commons famed for horse, cattle and pleasure fairs. The Great North Road lifted us through Barnet's foothills into its urban uplands. Along the summit, roads span off in all directions, avenues, cul-de-sacs; a blue wall of container storage. London was a fading still-life at our back, glimpsed through the high street's vista of coaching inns, civic blocks and outer-rim retail offerings.

At the village of Hadley Green, a complete altering of outlook. Outlying period houses and genteel cottages bowed back to reveal a wide plateau of common. Across its swathe, low-branching oaks, ponds, hedges, ditches, banks. Just north of here two of Britain's great roads traditionally divided. The Great North Road plunging straight on; the Holyhead Road branching west, tracing, in parts, the Roman line of Watling Street to St Albans, Wales and the major port for Ireland. Near the old junction of these roads, we found the stone obelisk recording where the two armies of the roses met that Easter.

A had understood the topographical advantage immediately. Moving towards London to engage Edward IV, the Lancastrians arrayed a battle line east to west across the road, making use of high ground and cover. The Earl of Warwick, known as 'Kingmaker' due to his influence and power, took a central position with the reserves. Once a trusted adviser of Edward (his cousin) and loyal to the House of York, Warwick had swapped allegiances to the House of Lancaster and Henry VI, then imprisoned in the Tower of London. Fighting ahead of Warwick was his brother, Marquess of Montagu. To his right and left, the Earl of Oxford and the Duke of Exeter.

Recognising the Lancastrian advantage, aware he was heavily outnumbered, Edward IV rushed up from London to prepare his own battle lines. He took command of the centre. Edward knew the odds were against him, so he pushed for surprise – his army creeping closer to the Lancastrian line under the cover of darkness and the strict order of silence. It meant the Lancastrian barrage of Yorkist positions overshot. At four o'clock in the morning, in thick fog, the fighting began. Cannons, arrows, then men in armour hacking through the hedges; the crash-crush of fine steel crafted in Milan and Germany being uncrafted with poleaxes, maces, halberds. The aim to get the man down, then pierce seam, joint or eye slit with the murderous fifteen-inch blade of a rondel.

The Lancastrians broke the deadlock. The line gave. Yorkist soldiers on the left fled south to Barnet, some as far as London, pursued by Oxford. By the time he could rally his troops from looting and steer them back to battle, the press of the fighting had rotated the front line from east–west to north–south, exactly along the Great North Road.

When Oxford retraced his steps, he unwittingly advanced on Montagu's men, his own side. In the fog, confusion reigned. Oxford's banner was mistaken for Edward IV's and Montagu unleashed arrows on his ally. Crying treason, assuming Montagu had defected to the Yorkists, Oxford's men attacked back. Disarray spread through the Lancastrians. Men panicked, fled. Seeing what was happening, Edward capitalised and sent in his reserves. Exeter was wounded. Montagu killed. Witnessing his brother's death, Warwick tried to retreat to his horse, tied up behind the lines at Wrotham Wood, but was cut down in the rout that followed. The battle was over in three hours. Estimates of between 3,000 and 10,000 dead and dying before nine o'clock in the morning.

In his book on the Great North Road, Frank Morley is dismissive of Barnet. He describes it as an 'unusually nasty street accident', suggesting that, by the time of the battle, the title of 'Kingmaker' was anachronistic anyway. Other governing forces had taken power, namely Parliament and the City of London. *Who* sat on the throne was academic. Money was the true authority. 'To the City of London, it did not matter so much who happened to be king as it did that the wool-trade could support his expenses,' Morley concludes. 'Any Crown could be supported if there was foreign trade in wool.'

The implication is a hierarchy between those privileged enclaves of Crown, City and Parliament with one superior body having influence over the others. Rituals and traditions still enacted today only seem to reinforce where the real power in the country has lain for the last six centuries. Consider the way permission must still be sought by any reigning monarch to enter the boundaries of the Square Mile. Or the role of the mysterious 'remembrancer' – the City of London's official lobbyist in the Commons – whose purpose is to ensure the will and policies of those elected by the people don't impede or impact upon the rights, privileges and interests of the City. Consider too the fact that there is no reciprocal arrangement – that the City of London remains the only place in the UK where Parliament holds no authority. Perhaps Frank Morley's words – *any Crown could be supported* – hint at the real dynamics at play, both then and now.

Beside the monument to the battle, under a sky shifting with late afternoon, I found myself imagining what those people believed they were fighting for as they began mustering before first light, strapping on armour, pushing numb fingers into gloves, working ornate rings painted with family mottos over their knuckles, preparing to slaughter one another. Honour? Duty? Money? Power? God? Land? And what of those men simply caught up in it all, conscripted by the fact that they had to work the earth owned by those noblemen? What did they pray for on that Easter dawn? The chance to get home to fields, families and fires? Delivery from a slow, painful death?

I knew *A* had an answer, just as I knew his picturing of the chaos and confusion of that morning came with an empathy far deeper and darker than mine. But you don't need to have witnessed combat to comprehend the ways we're still conditioned into fervent beliefs, into allegiances, into taking stands and fighting for what is handed down to us and what we think we believe. We're still born into organising systems and structures that we accept without question, without challenge. It left me wondering as we'd walked on – *how much do we truly comprehend the forces that govern our lives?*

*

I wake in the wood with the uneasy feeling that something is approaching. The long howl of a motorcycle carried from the A1(M). I open my eyes as it hits the high whine of its engine's limits and the first thing I do is check there isn't someone standing beside my hammock. We brew tea and pack up damp kit as the low mist over the fields lifts and the white noise of the road is drowned in a swelling sea of birdsong. The weight and distance of the previous day is felt in the legs, but in our heads too. We both slept heavily, but with strange dreams. In the part of mine I can recall I was standing on a road at night, unable to move. Cars slowing as they passed, drivers demanding to know what the hell I thought I was doing. Though I tried, I couldn't speak to them. Eventually a car stopped and out climbed my great-grandfather. He told me I had to stop standing about and keep going. I heard my voice enquiring of him: 'Where?' And he gestured up the black road. I asked him: 'Where are you?' And he handed me a book and said, 'You know where I am,' but when I opened it, it was too dark to read any of the pages.

We cross fields away from the A1(M) towards the old route of the Great North Road, hopping fences, soaking our legs with dew. The sun up and dazzling, dappling the copses we're hacking through. There are bluebells in the woods. Roe deer scatter through undergrowth a split-second swifter than eyes can fix on them. When we reach the road – still the A1000, but now re-street-named *Great North Road* – we trek north on pavement. There is a drowsy, dreamy, forlorn atmosphere: a Sunday two-lane fringed with trees that almost intermesh overhead. Sweeps of crops and concealed housing estates emerge and disappear. For a couple of miles, if you were to snap what lies before us and overlay a sepia filter, the image would be indistinguishable from the kind of photographs taken by camera-wielding coach-road Romantics in the 1890s. In creams and burnt-browns, the postcard would show a strip of pale highway curving around a bend, shaded by overreaching drapes of foliage and dark recesses of bushes. Consciousness connects to the place you are. To slow and walk into such a picture is to feel time slipping. Memories forming, fading. Moments finding themselves recalled.

What happens next is neither expected nor immediately processable because of its peculiarity. On the approach to Hatfield, on an amended loop of the Great North Road diverted from its original course by the then Lord Salisbury to force its course around the town's famous stately home, *A* is firing questions. Direct, as ever. He is ruminating on the intensity of yesterday's miles and pulling at the threads of my dream. 'What I want to know is how the story of your life connects with the story of this road? I mean how does that *work* . . . ?' He is mid-sentence when the curtain of greenery on our left is drawn back to reveal a manicured rhododendron bank underlaid with wood chip and edged with spring flowers. We look down a neat, narrow path into a beautifully tended space built-up with railway sleepers. At its entrance a brass plaque: *This memorial garden has been created in memory of those who died in the Hatfield rail tragedy, 17th October 2000.* It takes a second to read the sentence, and in that second, all the brightness of the morning, its colour and song, has gone. I'm somewhere else.

*

The facts of that day are well documented; details pored over and presented in the reams of accident reports, investigations, High Court hearings. At 12:10, a GNER InterCity train left London for Leeds. It was travelling along the East Coast Main Line at close to 115 mph. At 12:23, just south of Hatfield, where the railway comes to within touching distance of the Great North Road, the train was thrown from the track, sliding a thousand yards before stopping. The cause was identified as metal fatigue on the left-hand rail. Tiny stress cracks that fractured as the train passed over. The crash lasted seventeen seconds but by the end of it there were four killed and more than seventy injured. All those that lost their lives were in the restaurant car. The carriage hit a gantry and was almost destroyed by the impact. I know this because the name of one of those men was Peter Monkhouse. He was fifty years old and he was the dad of one of my best friends, Nick. I remember that day. I remember the call from another friend and being told that Nick was driving down to Hatfield, to the crash site. I remember not knowing where Hatfield was. I remember the days and the weeks that followed and Peter's funeral in Headingley. All of us gathered in a state of disbelief. I remember the glow in the nave as Nick and his sister, Claire, delivered their eulogies through tears. I remember the family in the front row, their arms around each other as the coda from James Taylor's 'Shower the People' echoed around the church. Its message: show love. Show it to the people you love, unreservedly.

I remember walking back to my flat, to what I thought was a normal life. Since curling up that card in the doorway of my brother's house in Archway seven months earlier, I'd been industrious in my studies at university. I'd tried to deepen my thinking, opening myself to new ideas, critical theories, philosophies. I had found the way that these texts refigured ways of seeing and understanding addictive. I understood them, applied them. What hadn't changed were the destructive traits that had been hard-coded in the years after my parents broke up. Through school, art college, through the years of playing in a band while working in shitty jobs, drinking and drugs had become an increasingly necessary means of escape. I don't want to misrepresent anything – I *loved* the feeling of being six or seven drinks in and seeing the way people change and open up. I loved that feeling of edge and slipping, of going further, that sense of danger and chaos, the freedom. I loved having my perception of the world altered and the way that drugs created a hyper-reality where you saw more, understood more, heard more, laughed more, yet didn't feel anything. So, I smoked grass when I woke up, quoting that Peter Fonda line from *Easy Rider* should anyone look at me askance: 'It gives you a whole new way of looking at the day.' For years my friends and I thought nothing of going out three or four nights a week drinking hard until everything was closed. If mates couldn't make it because of money or work, I'd find someone who could, or go on my own and meet people in pubs. If you were skint, you'd get drinks bought for you as long as you were good company. Because this was what people all around me were doing, because it was part of the culture in Britain in the 1990s in the north, and because I kept up the supremely confident, cocky, all's-fine-with-me facade, none of this seemed particularly out of the ordinary. Inwardly, though, I was sensationless. There had been danger signs that even I couldn't avoid seeing. In the final days of a term at art college in Dewsbury, south of Leeds, the year group had taken a field trip to a gallery in Halifax. On the way there, at nine in the morning, I'd smoked a joint and then dropped LSD with my housemate. It's often said that you only need to take LSD once for it to alter the way you perceive this world forever and I believe that. The first time I ever took it, one summer evening, walking into town down the moor road, everything suddenly appeared flooded with light, heavenly. I could taste hyper-saturated colour and see connections between things as never before. I saw trees; I saw birds in three-dimensions as if Cubist paintings; I saw the landscape, every atom of it. I could feel living presence like an immense force, as well as the aura of people I knew weren't really there walking alongside me. I could hear on a different frequency. When a crow cocked its eye at me, I felt the enormity of the universe in its shattering, fractal glare. A wasp landed on my arm and I watched it crawl up and down it, as if reading me through the hairs on my skin, its movements vibrating ecstatically through my body. The intensity of that drift into town on that summer's night changed what and how I saw. It left a kind of empathy that I can still feel; that is still accessible when I put my mind to it. That last time I took LSD, though, in Halifax, it was totally different. It was wintry and dark. The world immediately scrambled into a nightmare from which I couldn't wake, flee or make any sense. Everything freighted with fear. Human faces masks of pain or threat. By the time we got back to our student house, things were really bad. Rocking on the sofa, I wasn't there at all but locked in my own head standing at the edge of a precipice with a great void beneath. There was something within me willing me forward – go, take a step – but something else resisting too. Like it knew for certain that if I did, I wouldn't be coming back again. The hours of struggle it took to come out of that place, not knowing if those feelings would ever end, were terrifying.

No more acid, then. I made the rule there and then, aged nineteen. A boundary I believed showed that I was responsible, sensible. Recalling that horror over the following years I even convinced myself that it was just a bad trip. Still, I shivered whenever I thought of the darkness that had surfaced that day. The power of it and how uncontrollable and yet all-controlling it had been. It didn't change my reliance on other intoxicants, though, and they worked just as well to keep me shut down and emotionally distanced. But after the Hatfield crash and Peter's funeral, after watching a family so devastated and raw with the shock of suddenly losing someone so loved, something had altered. Part of me was sharply aware that things weren't OK. I went to lectures, I read set texts. I composed questioning, deconstructive essays and handed them in on time. I wrote songs and I signed up as an arts journalist for the student paper, but I found too that hours might pass where I'd be staring at a blank wall. Every now and then, when I wasn't concentrating, the distance from my own emotions and the loneliness of my life – my brother in America, my dad on the way to moving there too, my mother remarried, the damaging cycle of falling in love, then pushing the people I loved away – arrived in a flood of despair. I fought it. I started smoking a new, stronger weed with a more powerful, psychological high. I drank more nights than not. This was easy to disguise among the excesses of a student lifestyle, but I was twenty-four. It had been going on for far too long. I maintained that life was good. I was in control, on-track, but I was speeding up wildly and dangerously. What followed seems, in hindsight, inevitable.

It was a Saturday. I'd been drinking all day. I was in my hometown with a friend and we ended up in the only nightclub for miles around. I don't remember much, but about 2 a.m., I could hardly stand. Staggering down the stairs, opening the door, I walked straight into a fight on the street. There were four or five men, all strangers to me, all bloodied with their shirts torn, grappling and punching each other as if fighting for their lives. I remember something heavy hitting the back of my head. Someone grabbed me and I swung at them before fists smashed me from the side and I was on the ground. A bottle shattered by my face, then the kicking started. Then blackness. I remember coming to and coughing up blood as two people dragged me out of the road. I remember the inside of the ambulance with a paramedic trying to keep me conscious, and waking up in the semi-dark of a hospital ward with an alarm ringing. In the bed next to mine, an elderly man was still with his eyes and mouth wide open. The monitor he was hooked up to emitting a single high note. It dawned on me what was happening and I began shouting for help. As a nurse hurried in and pulled the curtain around his bed, I dragged myself up and stumbled down the corridor until I found the exit. A taxi driver agreed to take me home, but it cost me all the money I had. He kept checking me, asking whether I didn't want to go back to hospital, or if there was anyone else who could look after me. I shook my head. In the bathroom mirror, at the sight of broken front teeth, black eyes and a swollen face bleeding from open cuts, I barely recognised myself.

When I woke the next day, my body ached and I couldn't move without pain. I rolled and smoked a joint with shaking hands.

Stubbing it out, there was the sensation of something cold rising up within me, like terror. I doubled up, holding myself, waiting for it to pass. Instead, the room vanished and I was looking down from that precipice again. There were no hours of struggle this time. I was over the edge and into the void. With it came a heavy gripping sensation like a clawed weight, pressing down hard on to my head and shoulders. Everything was there then and it wasn't going away. Every buried emotion; everything I'd numbed myself against for years. All I'd worked to hide came rushing in at once. I was sick with it. I lay on the bathroom floor for a day. I climbed into bed and tried to rest, but nothing changed. It was there on waking and there when I went to sleep. A noise dialled up to full and a desperate feeling of panic. When I closed my eyes, I could see the poor man dying in the hospital bed next to mine. I could see him lying there, alone, in his tie and woollen tank top. I would dream of him passing away alone. I would rehear the things my mum and dad had said to each other in those months before they'd broken apart. I'd feel anew the tension, sadness and stress. I would relive the worst moments of the years that followed again and again, only there was nowhere to run to. No escape. Walled inside my brain, not seeing anyone, I was hardly looking up, never mind leaving the flat. I was confronted with all of it. I wasn't drinking anything. I'd thrown away the last of the drugs, but when the horror didn't budge after two weeks, I went back to the hospital. My injuries were assessed and scanned. Bloods tested. Painkillers prescribed and taken. My busted teeth were fixed. Nothing changed. Then, after another sleepless night, I found I was crying.

It says something about how we construct ideas of masculinity that to admit these things still feels difficult for me. It's tough now; it was tougher then. It would have been shameful to tell anyone that a man of my age couldn't stop crying for days at a time, or that I was experiencing breath-robbing spells of fear. Shameful to confess that I sat inside for weeks with the curtains drawn or that I begged to stay at my mother's house because I was too scared of what was in my head to sleep on my own. Things had stopped making sense. There was an unliftable deadness to the world. Friends who dropped in wondering where I'd got to wore looks somewhere between bemused and frightened at the changed person they found. *What's wrong with you?* the common question. But I knew if I tried to explain it would have only driven them further away, as it would have done with me before. So, I retreated. I stopped seeing anyone, until one morning there was a knock at my door. When I opened it, Nick was standing there.

In the time since the Hatfield crash, Nick's world had been unimaginable. Not only had he been dealing with the searing grief of losing his father, but he'd been forced to endure repeating reports, comments and newspaper stories on the details of the disaster. Full-page spreads appeared for weeks with pictures of his dad and the other victims alongside that haunting image of the shell of the wrecked train. He was trying to cope and help look after a distraught family while caught in the middle of public investigations and court cases that sought to apportion responsibility or shift blame for what happened. Frequently mentioned was the 'misfortune' of the four men who'd died because they'd been queueing up for a coffee. Had they not been, the chances are they would have survived. Chances are. *Chance*. It was an impossible thing to deal with. The world was making less and less sense to Nick also, and when I opened the door that day, we only needed to look at each other to know we were both in pieces and barely hanging on. I'd not spoken the truth of what I was going through to anyone. Nick hadn't either, but from that point, in desperation, we began talking in ways that would have been inconceivable before. Every week we'd loop the woods behind my flat in Leeds covering mile after mile, trying to chase to exhaustion the energy that was fuelling our waking nightmares. Nothing was all right, but we were able to admit that to someone and that helped. We could shine a light into the recesses of our minds and talk through what we found there. For me, it was the inescapable sense of ending. In the months after hitting the wall, the thing with its claws in me had resolved into something singular, into an unshakeable presence gripping my thoughts. Death. The pointlessness of everything in the face of its sure and certain ending. *Why get up? Why do anything? Look at that man dying alone, dressed smartly for hospital. Look at Mum and Dad. Look at Peter.* This was the running dialogue I couldn't quieten.

It was Nick who eventually suggested I speak to someone. He told me about a brilliant counselling psychologist and hypnotherapist he'd been recommended. I had scrutinised the certificates hanging on the wall while I waited outside his attic office door, but despite my fears, I was able to open up to this stranger. The inner stories and struggles unravelled. With calmness and reassurance, he mentioned conditions I'd never heard of: post-traumatic stress disorder, acute stress disorder. He said that these things were natural and normal given what had happened to me and what I'd been living with for years. He told me that this new horror could pass, just as sharply as it had come. I've never forgotten his metaphor for human experience as a TV with fifty-two channels. Some channels are happy, some tragic. Some show us horror, some comedy. Some are boring and mundane. Some are sheer ecstasy. Some are death, of course. He told me that our minds can usually process all of these without thinking about it, but sometimes, especially after trauma, the mind gets stuck on one channel and you can't switch over.

The hypnosis wasn't profound but it took me out of the world for a while. Long enough to breathe. It lifted me from my own head and showed me that I could, in fact, switch off that channel. When I left the counseller's office, it was with the awareness that there might be a way out. After six months, things weren't about to change overnight, but I understood it was possible to rekindle that inner fire. The hunger for living. There was a road back. Slowly, Nick and I took a step. Then another. Slowly, we began to remember who we were. Our walks became about noticing the world around us, about plans and new horizons – not escaping the confines of our minds. Slowly, as we got busier, they became less frequent. Slowly, we returned to ourselves.

*

A passing train sucks the energy from the air, arriving with a sound like a sharp, loud inhale in the ear. Deafening for a second or two, then gone. My mind snaps back to where I am, back to the little garden of remembrance. I hadn't noticed when we walked in and sat down how close this oasis of memory is to the railway, to the place it happened. I'm metres away. The only separation a screen of mahonia erupting with flowers. A high, wire fence. As the noise of the train fizzes north, amid the quiet and the birdsong that descends, I whisper

In memory of
Peter John Monkhouse
A wonderful husband and father
his life cut tragically short in the
Hatfield rail crash
October 17th 2000
your gentleness was your strength
your family your life
a true gentleman loved and admired
by all who knew you
we shall love and miss you always and forever
Sue, Nick, Claire and James
xxxx

a few words for Peter under my breath. Then, using a T-shirt from my backpack, I clean the dedication left by his wife and children.

A has been silent throughout. He knows this story and he'd realised immediately what we'd stumbled upon. Besides, he has endured enough flag-draped repatriations of soldiers, funerals held for even younger lives tragically cut short, to know how such things are best handled. A calm presence. He sits, cross-legged, eyes closed, face turned towards the sun. Only after we leave the garden and begin our progress north again does he admit to being unnerved by the coincidences. Not one for superstition, he can't quite reconcile the fact that he was asking *that* question about how my life might connect with the road at *that* precise moment. 'Explain it to me,' he says. 'It's too bizarre.'

All the way to Hatfield I'm walking with one foot in a different time, with the rawness that comes from unforeseen remembering. The sudden lurching back to a younger version of myself brings feelings that are hard to loosen and to shake. Retracing those steps again, recalling those months, complicates my memories. It forces me to confront something. The dread and fear that gripped me; that questioning of everything in the face of our inevitable end; the constant voice pointing out the bleakness, the unfairness, the *chance* of it all – this shadowed my life for a long time. Even all these years after the slow recovery, of learning how to switch between the channels, I remember the darkness of seeing everything through that filter. I'm still aware of its presence at the edge of my life. But what I have to appreciate too is how much this has shaped my life. I've made choices and taken chances I wouldn't have because of this awareness, and because of what happened to me in those years. I've learned that it's only when we accept this shadow, when we are made to live with its weight, that we perceive with absolute focus the briefness and preciousness of our time on this Earth. Only then do we start asking questions and looking for answers that might fulfil us. Those things that might still our unquiet hearts and settle our unquiet minds.

At the time, I rationalised the fear as a fear of dying. The shock of the Hatfield crash, of seeing my friend and his family broken into pieces, and then sudden proximity of death that came after that night outside the club. Thrust back into that place again, though, I understand what I couldn't then. That it was a fear of all endings. The grief that comes with life moving on. Of change. It's a strange thing to leave the box that contained you as a child, and those months were an outpouring of the hurt, loss, stress and anxiety I'd been internalising for years. The processing of pain that had come with one profound change and an ending that has both damaged and driven me in ways I've never fully appreciated. Now I find myself wondering again – *how much do we truly comprehend the forces that govern our lives?* We're such complex and fragile systems, storied with, and steered by, our experiences. While we can't go back and choose a different life, we can perhaps try to reclaim those parts of us we've struggled to live with. For had I never been through that time, had I never drunk destructively or taken drugs, had I never known the hard limits of human emotions and felt the weight of the world so early on, had I not messed up and made mistakes – would I see and think the way I do now? Would I have been compelled to enquire and understand? To try to make sense? To make the choices I have? Would I have tried to live as deeply and as lovingly?

*

The curve of the Great North Road sweeps us into Old Hatfield. Mirroring the line on a parallel trajectory 600 metres to our west, the A1(M). In between the two, viewed on the map, Hatfield's New Town appears a slab of development tissue, marbled with roads.

With the ambition of quickly rehousing the bombed-out populations of London, the New Towns Act of 1946 designated swathes of Hertfordshire to emerging post-war urban visions. Hatfield was the ninth 'New Town' to be created. The plan: neat terraces (grey fronts/ white windows/red doors) with impeccable strips of baize lawn; a few high-rise tower blocks (then the model for progressive, single living) and smart, utilitarian neighbourhoods surrounded by pristine fields and woods. Nearby industries would provide bomb-proof jobs – aerospace, weapon systems, automotive, retail – with employment centres linked by smooth highways, shopping parades and precincts. A digs around YouTube and turns up a few incredible minutes of the concept in 16mm colour footage from the late 1950s or early 1960s. Hilltop, one of the new suburbs of south Hatfield, appears like a self-contained colony on another planet. People in sharp uniform suits, hats. Cars with fins and spaceship trims. One after another, children run into shot and disappear behind a colour-coded estate map/bus shelter. Not one reappears on the other side, giving the impression they're being teleported. St John's of Hilltop is midway through being roofed. It is *all* roof, in fact: a giant aviation wing of a church. A wedge of strut and beam with strangely patterned windowless gables. You'd be forgiven for thinking you were looking at a radar station for the Nuclear Age.

The centre of Old Hatfield is a different world. We're greeted by houses and shops clustered around the heritage core of Fore Street. Bleary-eyed dreams of Georgian England. New-builds nodding along in nostalgic reverie, aping the vernacular, but with cheap materials. Replicas on a developer's budget. Ten-year guarantees, max.

Old Hatfield grew up around the Great North Road. It was a day's ride (horse or coach) from London and a convenient bag-drop for the bishops and clergy of Ely Cathedral en route to and from the capital. Their old digs were seized by Henry VIII in 1538 and converted into a nursery palace for his royal offspring, most notably Elizabeth I, who spent her childhood in the house. It was in these grounds, under an oak, in 1558, she would receive word of her accession and in this house that she held her first council. Later, when the inheritor James I expressed a preference for the house of his chief minister at Theobalds, Robert Cecil found himself embroiled in something like a pilot of the BBC's *House Swap*, becoming owner of this estate instead and financing its crowning glory: the great Jacobean landmark of Hatfield House. Although nibbling away at Elizabeth's childhood home, harvesting its nicely matured brick wings, Cecil raised his new, grand design in the shape of an 'E' to commemorate the past queen's connections. A prescient move that pre-empted the tastes and aspirations of Hatfield's visiting public four centuries later. The enduring pulling power of royalty and (live-in) nobility, open to scrutiny. A place for the grey-haired to potter (men in burgundy cords, blazers with handkerchiefs/women: Country Casuals merino cardigans, pearls), hammered on history, picking about the gardens of Tradescant, angling for specimen cuttings or the chance to roll out an encyclopedic knowledge of the dynasties of English ruling families. Fifty quid for a family ticket with the chance of bumping into relics of the landed gentry, conspicuous in down-at-heel gardening kit with their wild eyebrows and thick heads of white hair, among oblivious parents carrying coffees and toddlers.

I know all this because I was given a tour a year ago as part of the speaker's privileges that came with a talk delivered at a book festival hosted in the house and grounds. It was an eclectic line-up: Will Self, Chloe Aridjis, Simon Jenkins. I'd arrived by train into curious juxtapositions: Will Self exhaling vape clouds into the Old Palace during a panel discussion on *Candide*; Richard Mabey waxing lyrical on moonflowers with a portrait of the Virgin Queen glowering over his shoulder. I was underprepared, a stunt double of myself, sleepless from sitting up with Bea the night before, still new to the circuit and its unspoken rules. The surrealness was exaggerated with an invitation to a champagne reception with the Marchioness of Salisbury. At ninety-four, she was aristocratic Englishness distilled: redoubtable constitution; patron of the arts; a 'high priestess of historic garden design'; custodian of unmentionable wealth. In jeans and a T-shirt, I queued behind dinner-jacketed notables, waiting for an audience in the King James Drawing Room. Perhaps because I was so unsuitably dressed, she made a beeline for me and began picking over my talk on edge-lands. Before shaking the next hand, I brought up the Great North Road and the roads that lead us to where we find ourselves. She recalled a 22-foot illuminated scroll in the house's library, created to affirm Elizabeth's right to rule. Ancestries mined and explored to prove an unbroken line back to Adam and Eve. 'Quite a thing, really,' she'd said. 'Rather a road in itself.' I'd seen out that night in the Eight Bells pub, the same place that the highway deposits us now, at the foot of Fore Street. A squat building crouched on a bend.

Inside, *A* spreads the OS map over a table, using fresh cups of tea to hold down its creases. Above this landscape we see the contrasting, juggling visions vying for space along the road. The great, green bulges of country houses and parklands: Hatfield, Brocket Hall and, further up the highway, Knebworth. The spectacular current and ex-domiciles of the ruling classes – of queens, prime ministers, statesmen. Hotbeds of scandal too.

Brocket Hall was home to Lady Caroline Lamb, author, poet, lover (and literary poker) of Byron. Shaper of his reputation; coiner of that 'mad, bad and dangerous to know' line. Already vulnerable and obsessive, scarred from a childhood of abandonment, her tempestuous affair with Byron in 1812 led to spells of manic behaviour. The harder she tried to rekindle his affection, the more her reputation was tarnished. Affairs were one thing in high society; public displays of uncontrollable, damaged emotions – breaking a glass at a ball and 'scratching' at her wrists – something else. Revenge came via a thinly veiled attack of Byron and the society that rejected her in her Gothic novel *Glenarvon*. Further alienation followed, including from her long-suffering, publicly embarrassed, husband: the prime minister to be, William Lamb. She steadied herself enough to write songs, other books. *Ada Reis* (1823) pre-empts Dickens with its questioning of power and patriarchy and its asking whether the fortune to be well born or wealthy qualifies anyone to lead. Yet 'Caro' was already doomed to be a side player in the myth-world around Byron. That 'mad, bad and dangerous to know' line thrown back at her. Her work rubbished by critics with agendas. Then the old highway would serve up a last, cruel shock. In 1824, leaving the gates of Brocket Hall, Caro met a funeral procession on the Great North Road. Enquiring whose it was, she was told it was Byron's. Returned from Greece, his corpse was being taken to Newstead Abbey for burial. It was said she fainted on the spot and, in that moment, reason left her. Sickening, medicated with laudanum and alcohol, Caro died just four years later.

These great country houses were conceived as closed-door estates of power and prestige. Everlasting worlds-apart for a class that believed itself exceptional. After 1945, changes that had once been inconceivable, then stoically withstood for decades, became unavoidable. Family fortunes evaporated in death duties, post-war tax rises, the shrinking empire. The doors of many houses had to be thrown open to the public and estates sold off, demolished, repurposed into anything from hotels with golf courses (Brocket Hall) to open-air gig venues (Knebworth). Up sprung those newer realities – the futuristic worlds of the New Towns with their soft-socialist roots. Model houses and gleaming infrastructure optimistically concreted around Hatfield, and further north, Welwyn Garden City and Stevenage. Places that also struggled to live up to utopian masterplans. That were soon derided as sterile outlying colonies stripped of culture and history, bereft of centre and soul. Places that have suffered in the decades since with poor construction, joblessness, crime. That have rallied behind new forward-looking identities, yet remain, in terms of concept, works in progress. This is the collage spread out on the table before us: a legacy landscape of historic estates and brave new worlds. Visions tempered and mutated. Monuments only to change and the flux of history.

The unfolded map also reveals a problem. The Great North Road surrenders its identity to the thick blue line of the A1(M). Google Maps confirms a frenzied six-lane hemmed in by crash barriers and sheer verges of impenetrable bushes and trees. Nowhere to walk.

'We've lost time too,' A says, checking his watch. His suggestion is the train. Whip north to Stevenage and try to catch up with ourselves. I'm not about to argue. I'm still feeling blindsided by the earlier encounter; still trying to process the fact of that memorial appearing when it did. A dissolving together of inner and outer worlds. That double exposure of place and person overlaying in the same frame.

*

The train arrives at the platform and I slide into a table seat by the window. A takes the four opposite and, arms folded, falls asleep in moments. My tea from the station is too hot to drink, so I open my notebook and begin to write. As we slip away, I feel a sudden pull. The sensation of leaving something behind. I squint through the glass into sun and glimpse, for a second, a man standing in the fields staring back at me.

Mayday

(Stevenage–Ickwell Green)

I

Across the fields it comes. Conjunct voices carried on the evening breeze. We freeze, midway through putting up our shelters, and stare at each other. It isn't me who first says what it sounds like, but when A does, I know he's right. It is children softly singing.

'*Arise, arise, you fair pretty maid . . . and bring the May tree in . . .*'

Young voices fading and swelling with the ebb and the flow of the wind. A loose union. A church-like chorus following a lilting minor to major to minor tune.

'*For the life of a man it is but a span and he's cut down like the flower . . .*'

We have walked to the edge of the wood to listen, puzzled and unnerved, for we're too far from anywhere here for the singing to be as close and clear as it appears.

'*We're here today, tomorrow we're gone. We're dead all in one hour . . .*'

Beyond the wood, dark land blurs darkening sky. There is nobody there.

*

Hours earlier, outside the Standing Order in Stevenage, the Alpha of the pub table – decked in red short-sleeved gingham button-down, wraparound shades – is rocking, holding a half-guzzled pint of Strongbow in a Stella glass. He's yelling: 'I was fucking drinking gin with Carol at one-thirty this morning, mate! Straight back on it, mate!'

Light rakes the ensemble gathered around him. His audience, hungover faces already nappy-rash-red from direct sun, sits in awe or fear of the brash patter being barked out without any break. A young boy fidgets on a separate table, peering at an iPhone screen, watching *Thomas the Tank Engine* on full volume. His quiet questions – 'Mum? What am I doing today?' – are shushed or ignored as the repartee continues.

'So, yous know I went to see him, right? They takes out his tubes and I *swear down*, he fucking wakes up!' An inhaling of cider. 'Next thing, he's fucking *dead*!'

Laughter. Lung-clearing coughs. Fresh rounds. He lights a cigarette and in that tiny moment of quiet, he searches around for something new to fix on to, to riff about. We know what's coming: 'What yous two doing with all that gear? On the run, are you?'

*

Finding a pub in Stevenage had been more complicated than we'd considered. I'd used the downtime on the train to investigate. The bio of the first I found – the Marquis of Lorne – read like a thinly veiled threat: *A traditional pub with traditional values*. Scrolling PDFs of out-of-print highway books on my phone, I'd tried to work out which coaching inns had survived from the old days. The Swan used to be the premium establishment. Samuel Pepys recorded overnighting, enjoying games of bowls on the green opposite. It's now a million-pound private residence. Other possibilities along the line of the Great North Road (aka Stevenage High Street) appeared just as elusive: the Yorkshire Grey now a branch of ASK Italian; the White Hart a Spice Rouge curry house. The Old Castle Inn is a shut-up and shuttered ex-branch of NatWest bank.

In my searching, I'd read again C. G. Harper's introduction to the town, his focus falling on a place called 'Six Hills': '. . . a series of sepulchral barrows of prehistoric date, beside the highway . . . they were once remarkable enough to give the place its name, Stevenage deriving from the Saxon "stigenhaght" or "hills by the highway".' Historians have cast doubt on the prehistoric date: the mounds are Romano-British. The result of a prestigious family of the new province choosing to be buried along the Roman road in the ancient Bronze Age style. Emerging from Stevenage station, *A* had discovered on a blown-up town map that Six Hills was not only still visitable, but only a few hundred metres to our east. He suggested that it was a fitting place to try to rejoin the old highway. Somewhere we might make contact with the Great North Road again.

We'd cut across estate roads from a leisure park (Hollywood Bowl, Mr Mulligan's Lost World, Cineworld) into a business park. The New Town narrative writ large: Americana retail, entertainment, home improvement. Giant steel-frame warehouses. CCTV. Aerials. Offices islanded by car parks crammed with glinting vehicles. Small, sickly patches of green. Distribution centres flanked by lorries. The grassy domes of Six Hills were dwarfed by a colossal building (ex-Fujitsu) midway through conversion into new apartments. The prospect over the burial mounds – now scheduled ancient monuments – leveraged by developers in their sales pitch. No mention, though, of the even larger Asda 'Supercentre' in full view behind them.

Within minutes the burial mounds, tufted with wild grass, buttercup, forget-me-not, interspersed with bushy elms, had brought us back to the old highway. Looking north, zooming in on vintage photographs scoured from local history websites, we could orientate the road's previous position running just left of the barrows. A shred of its former self, but enough to get a scent. The same websites were useful repositories for stranger Six Hills origin folklore. A read aloud a tale of their making that involved Satan jealously flinging six great shovelfuls of earth at passing travellers on the Great North Road. Other testimonies included the many sightings of spectral black dogs as big as donkeys materialising from the tumuli, barking, then bouncing off into thin air.

The sign said OLD TOWN. After entering one enormous car park we were up an access road (KEEP CLEAR) into another; this one in front of a sports centre. Striking along the approximate route of the ancient road, we arrived at our third car park in ten minutes. This one the largest yet, servicing a Tesco Extra; a sea of cars idling, waiting to exit, boots filled with bags of barbecue supplies. The high street, when we reached it, was another shift. A footbridge launched us over a tangle of weed-grown concrete flyover into a pretty, lime-tree-shaded strip of shops. Dickens described Stevenage High Street as 'like most other village streets: wide for its height, silent for its size and drowsy in the dullest degree . . .' Nothing drowsy about it today, though – not at lunchtime on a Bank Holiday Sunday. A-boards out. Sky Sports blaring. The first two pubs rammed. Five screens of live football but the kitchens closed ('We do crisps?'). Ex-coaching inns only teased us with pictures of their ranges of unavailable fry-ups and *MAIN'S*. Spice Rouge closed until 5 p.m. A few doors up, the Standing Order (ex-bank repurposed into a Wetherspoon's) was our last hope.

*

'I said . . . on the run are you, lads?' It falls to me to answer, so I do. We're not on the run, no, but we are on the *road*. The Alpha laughs. Coughs. Raises his glass. A cabbie working in London, he likes the concept: 'Love old roads, mate. The stories. All that.'

He's not the only one. Inside the pub, ordering burgers and beer, I pass a Hogarth illustration from the coaching days with a potted history (title: *The Great North Road*) included in the frame. It is flanked with other descriptions of the local area and black and whites of ex-notables: the actor Denholm Elliott; the composer and writer Elizabeth Poston who lived at nearby Rooks Nest – childhood home of the author E. M. Forster and setting for *Howards End*, his defining condition of England novel.

Stevenage has the only memorial to Forster in the world. Half a mile east of the Great North Road is a stone that has, carved within its centre, that famous line, theme and subtitle of *Howards End*: ONLY CONNECT. At the time, Forster was exploring the juxtapositions of the dull, ordered, ordinariness of external life in Edwardian England with the transgressive erotic desires and passions of the inner self. The phrase has since bloomed, been co-opted. Found its own meanings, relevancies. Appearing on posters, T-shirts, in countless GenZ tattoos, it has become a rallying call about the need for connection between all humanity, across barriers of nationhood, class, race, sexuality. *Only connect* is a marker of a mindset seeking to move on from differences.

Outside, by the Alpha's table, a group of men have colonised the corner, paunches bulging band tees, arms blotched with green-grey tattoos, eyes smudged behind photochromatic lenses. The boy watching *Thomas the Tank Engine* has been evicted. Before long, Brexit is being debated. Surprisingly, it's the Alpha, looking every bit a nationalist poster boy, arguing the counterpoints – shouting back about how he's always picking up late-shift NHS workers in his cab: 'Most of them aren't English . . .'

'Yeah?' comes the menacing reply. 'Well maybe *that's* the problem.'

More drinks arrive, interrupting hostilities, easing the heat. Watching the men seething in their corner, I'm wondering what potted histories are pinned in the interiors of their minds; what current condition of England they represent. The unredressed, unaddressed narratives of imperialism, colonialism and world wars passed down through the generations. Living proof of how unresolved trauma gets twisted into anger and indignation that gets aimed in the wrong direction. An urge to find blame and difference where it doesn't exist. To seek *dis*connect. The antithesis of Forster's phrase.

The irony being, of course, that I watch each of them order curry and rounds of Belgian lager. But it is a debate not worth having. We eat quickly. Before we leave, the Alpha, perhaps seeking allies, staggers by on his way to piss. Shades off and slurring, he offers cigarettes, lighting one up as we haul on our rucksacks and drain our beers.

'Where you headed, then?' He's swaying. A steadying hand laid on our table.

I tell him we'll follow the road as far as we can before nightfall, then play it by ear. Find a pub, maybe. Make camp. Let the road dictate the movement and momentum.

'Well, if you're going *up* the road, you gotta get to Ickwell Green.'

'*Ick-well* Green?'

'Yeah. Get up there tonight. About twelve mile north of here.'

'Why?'

'May Day tomorrow.'

Now he's whispering, dragging on his smoke, muttering: 'Used to go up there with my dad when I was a . . . my sister too . . . wish I could go up tomorrow but fucking working, aren't I?' A slow blink. Another wet drag. A long cough. 'But it's fucking madness on May Day up there. Swear down. Nowhere like Ickwell Green on May Day.'

*

Clear blue skies. Screens of hedge, fresh-flush trees. The odd Scots pine. Pink-beige 1970s cul-de-sacs. The Lister Hospital. Stevenage's limits. We're back on the road, listed here as North Road. Old coach track, Roman street. Stopping for water, I find a little bird midden of Roman snail shells under a hawthorn. It's open-stride walking, stripped to T-shirts and army-issue bucket hats, bodies and minds slowly realigning with the bleached surface of the highway. Into a deep gorge of deep green; song thrushes, chiffchaffs, great tits. Dog walkers nod as they pass, intrigued by our overstuffed rucksacks, the sheen of road grime on our sweaty skin. Through the gaps, fields, pylons. A low hum that can't be distinguished. Contrails. We're on the old A1; visible to our west, the A1(M) and its blue signs. Lorries glint and glide silently in the distance over a foreground of emerging crops. The village of *Grave*-ley, once a busy stop for fast coaches with two coaching inns, was left marooned decades ago by the shift in flow. It's a haunted stretch. Another ghost place on the ghost of the great northern highway.

For a long time, Jack's Hill prided itself on its transport café. It was a favourite refuelling stop for long-distance drivers. Soldiers in the last war, hoying up and down the old A1 on troop movement or manoeuvre, took advantage of its free 'cuppa and sarnie' policy for servicemen. Post-war, those same men dragged families on detours during holidays to revisit and reminisce, smoking in silence over their egg and chips, listening to voices only they could hear, frustrated by giddy offspring and their own inability to explain. We approach the place, set back from the road, to find it is 'the Highwayman' – a single-storey pub with a play barn attached. Rendered Daz-white, it has the Union Jack bunting out. St George's flag tacked to its wall. The car park is full.

A pushes us on, leading us down a time tunnel. A paint-by-numbers May Day scene: spring into summer, sometime pre-industrialisation. Gouache greens and blues. Hockney iPad stuff. Heaped blossoms, the swelling earth, spluttering thrushes. The quiet, open road running dead ahead through England's sun-struck, stirring dreamland.

*

In 1955, Ted Hughes was working near Baldock, turning the earth and tending flowers. He was for a time a rose gardener, camping each

night behind a pub near an orchard. His letters home describe a sub-
urbia so picture-perfect it feels unreal. Roads abutted by lawns. Great
houses, prized livestock, golf courses; cricket pitches and pools. The
pursuit of rare flowers, immaculate borders and beds. His summa-
tion: 'Very strange!' The over-tweaked has the same effect on us:
perfection and strangeness. Like white-picket-fence America with a
Twin Peaks undercurrent. Something unsettling and unsettled beyond
the surface. Footsore, we reach Baldock's high street to find it dressed
in more bunting. More St George's flags. The town is deep into the
Baldock Festival (mascot: a Templar Knight, red cross on his shield).
A local historian is doing a free walking tour for genial folk, explaining the origins of the name: Baldock from *Baudac*, the old French
name for Baghdad, bestowed by the Knights Templar who founded
this market town in the 1140s, hoping it might one day emulate the
fortunes of a city that was then known as the greatest market in the
world.

North of the town, beyond a kinked double-turn bemoaned in all
the old coaching books, we step over the X where the Great North
Road intersects the Icknield Way – the time immemorial trackway
running along a chalk escarpment from Norfolk to Wiltshire. Centuries before the Templars developed Baldock, laying down streets in the
shape of a cross, there was a thriving settlement and three temples
near this crossing. It was a transitional point in more ways than one.
Prehistoric traces, including a narrow Neolithic cursus, have been
found close by, but nothing compares to the number of Roman burial
sites. Thirteen areas uncovered so far. In a report in the local paper,
the council archaeology officer, Keith Matthews, describes it as 'the
largest collection of Roman burials found anywhere outside Egypt'.
He draws attention to the curious lines of posts unearthed around the
graveyards, marking – it's believed – a symbolic boundary between
the living and the dead. 'We think this was a cult centre,' he explains,
the finds seeming to point to the worship of a kind of hunting god or
goddess. Offerings were made. Pledges. Curses were written on wax
and wood, nailed shut, then buried.

Under a rail bridge. Scrappy, fox-tang pockets of road-front edge-
land. Razor fences. New-builds. Streaks of sun; cool pools of shadow
cast by ragged hedges. A rabbit road-killed – entrails intact and spread

out for inspection, for divining. Things take on a different meaning when you are walking over boundaries to other worlds, when you're treading cult ground. When you are being watched by ancient deities.

Although written before the majority of these discoveries, it's intriguing how much of this atmosphere leaches into the 1969 Kingsley Amis novel, *The Green Man*. That strange, comic-sexual ghost story was intentionally set on an old road near Baldock (somewhere 'between Stevenage and Royston'), a mythical sub-artery of highway but one that Amis must have modelled on a redesignated stretch of the Great North Road, left stranded by bypasses and A-roads. In the novel, the coaching inn of the book's title is haunted with spirits. A previous owner who dabbled in the occult becomes a controlling phantom that takes over the narrator: 'But yours was the hand that writ, mine merely the hand that guided yours.' Time freezes as God appears in the form of a suave young man, drinking whisky, warning the narrator of the dangers of allowing this body possession. The whole book is sexually charged and filled with metaphorical battles. A crucifix becomes a weapon against an ancient fertility figurine. Everything builds up to a denouement involving the Green Man manifesting and hunting down the narrator's daughter. He is the conjured spirit that the narrator has to confront: 'I saw its face for the first time, an almost flat surface of smooth dusty bark like the trunk of a Scotch pine, with irregular eye-sockets in which a fungoid luminescence glimmered, and a wide grinning mouth . . . that cry as of wind through foliage issuing from its mouth, exultant as much as menacing.' It is through the lens of Amis's novel that the area begins to make sense. Ancient gods lurking in the earth. The crucifix over the cult. Maybe it isn't pure metaphor. Maybe it isn't author imagination. The book appears to call out things that feel truer the further we go. Old roads lead to uncanny places. Time does stand still. The enormous past can possess the present.

Biggleswade is the culmination of seven miles of trespassing, of cutting along the ankle-sprain terrain abutting the dual carriageway of the A1. The 'M' suffix of the A1 is absent here; road signs returned to the colour of footpath markers: yellow on green. Great sky views over farmland to western horizons. Conversation whipped away by thundering-past projectiles; moments of quiet between. A single sky-lark. The name of the roadside spot 'Topler's Hill' betrays the gentle gradient. At its crest, a farm engulfed by trees was familiar to coach travellers – Dickens among them – as 'Bleak House'. No credit ever given. Before us, the flat expanse of Bedfordshire.

The walk into town almost finishes me off. The sky clouds over; the heat remains. We pass a retail park, out-of-town stores, Biggleswade's suburbs. We find the coaching inn, the Crown, with its arched entrance, has gone to the wall. Down the street, the owner of a curry house sees us coming: 'Table for two is it, lads? And two beers?'

After fifty miles in two days, the hardest thing is to rise again, to leave the high-back leather chairs and dishes of fragrant biryani. But the evening sun is breaking through, flooding the window, luring us west. Consulting the map spread between the bill and a dish of mints, A fixes our destination with a finger: 'Ickwell Green. It's three miles maybe, but it looks like it has a wood to its south. Good as anywhere for pitching tonight.' My smile is more of a grimace. Three more miles. It sounds nothing, except for the fact that I could happily close my eyes and fall asleep exactly where I'm sitting.

Outside it is finally growing cooler. The evening aroma of lit stoves. Blackbirds fluting from aerials. Dogs nosing at fence gaps. At the edge of Biggleswade, the cold-steel, weedy stink of wild water. The south-flowing courses of the Lea, Mimram, Beane and Rib lie behind us now. For the next hundred miles, the rivers that meet the road will drain east to the Wash, not the Thames. Crossing the little bridge that spans the River Ivel, a different temperature again. A new weight to the light. Something present in the deserted fields. The silence is like that pause before somebody speaks. There is a sense of expectant story waiting to be disturbed, dusted off, wishing to push through.

The road, never missing the chance to get personal, serves up another sign. On a nettle-infested verge, a tree trunk has been sawn into a seat. Peering at the crumpled, rusted, faux number plate screwed into its backrest, I can make out the name: *ROSIE*.

But I'm already thinking of her, of Tom and Bea, of home. My heart aches for the children after hearing their voices, their bath-time joy-screams, during a call as we waited for dinner. Rosie had wanted to relay her newly hatched plan – an impromptu visit to her parents'

house. *Let's make the most of the sunny weather and take the kids to Kent. Work from there for a few days. Take advantage of an actual garden.* She is setting off early the day after tomorrow. It makes sense to pick me up along the way.

Now it occurs to me what this means – that I will be reversing the journey just taken. Winding the road back to its start. Closing a loop, of sorts. As we leave the lane and push into the evening woods, I begin to do the same in my mind, unspooling the already printed footage, the ground covered, retracing steps back to the man staring at his reflection ghosting over the ghostly, pre-light Kentish landscape on the early train from Canterbury to London. Back to somebody who already feels like somebody else.

A tawny's tremble-call. Rooks yak. A breeze in the canopies. Dog's mercury, wild garlic, wood anemone. Patterns of prints pressed into muddy earth. We squat to study them. A man's boots interlaced with the splayed two-finger tracks of a deer.

*

Across the fields it comes. Conjunct voices carried on the evening breeze. We freeze, midway through putting up our shelters, and stare at each other. It isn't me who first says what it sounds like, but when A does, I know he's right. It is children softly singing.

'*Arise, arise, you fair pretty maid . . . and bring the May tree in . . .*'

Young voices fading and swelling with the ebb and the flow of the wind. A loose union. A church-like chorus following a lilting minor to major to minor tune.

'*For the life of a man it is but a span and he's cut down like the flower . . .*'

We walk to the edge of the wood to listen, puzzled and unnerved, for we're too far from anywhere here for the singing to be as close and clear as it appears.

'*We're here today, tomorrow we're gone. We're dead all in one hour . . .*'

Beyond the wood, dark land blurs into darkening sky. There is nobody there.

II

Birds sing. Cold on the face. Dew dampening the sleeping bag. May Day light between the trees falling in great golden shafts, like sheets of sugarwork. That ecstatic feeling upon waking that is hard to put in words: everything coming to life, and you part of it.

I heard animal shrieks in the wee hours. Something moving by my hammock. It shook me from another dream of my great-grandfather. This time he'd been walking on the road ahead of me but I couldn't catch up with him. He was in a suit I recognised from the cache of photographs I was sent months ago. I'd shouted out to him and he'd stopped and turned, his face a mask of coal dust, as if he'd just emerged from the mine.

A yawn. The zip of *A*'s softie jacket being done up. The rattle of cooking kit. 'So, what was making all the noise in the night?' he asks. 'Must've been right by us.'

He is silhouetted by the glow of morning, sitting on a log.

'Fox? Or a badger? Maybe that deer?'

'Well,' he says. 'I asked it to kindly fuck off and come back in the morning.'

I laugh. 'Did it?'

'No.'

A dries his things as best he can, folds them away. He is catching a train later, returning to barracks. I hang my damp sleeping bag between the trees in a bit of sun, and leave the hammock up. I'll be staying another night in this clearing ahead of meeting Rosie and the kids tomorrow. With black coffee steaming in mugs, we begin cooking porridge on the stove, using a pan lid to fry the last of our bacon, when the singing starts up again.

'*Oh, what verdure clothes the ground ... oh, what fragrance breathes around.*'

Children's voices in loose unison again, fading, swelling. Except it's different now. The inevitable feedback howls and squeaks and the bass-boosts of volume give away microphones and a PA being tested. Someone tweaking the sound, getting levels. This is amplified singing drifting from distance, and it isn't what we heard yesterday.

'*See the grain is waving high ... beneath the blue and cloudless sky ...*'

'OK, thanks,' a voice says into the mic. 'Good for me. Try another?'

*

He tells us that we should call him 'fool'. Or 'the liar that tells the truth'. He's smiling but there's something about him that's wilfully slippy and dangerous. The air of mischief. A face you'd be pushed to pick out later. Maybe it's the rags and riches together: the faded, threadbare Union Jack draped from the pocket of a morning coat; the straw-man badge; the spotted neckerchiefs tied around neck and waist; the high boots and ragged bloomers with silver bells. The top hat garlanded with pheasant feathers and flowers: bluebells, self-heal, hawthorn blossom, a sprig of rosemary.

Upon questioning, a woman (ex-May Queen herself) had forcibly explained with a smile that never dimmed that the souvenir pro-gramme (£1) had *all* we needed to know. The meeting point for the procession is *always* the car park of the Crown in Northill, the vil-lage up from Ickwell Green. On the walk to the pub, we'd glimpsed the procession's eventual destination: a great maypole, striped red and white like a candy cane, in the middle of Ickwell's expansive green. A fixed monument in time pinning this place to the map. The stage behind and its golden throne were being decorated to receive the May Queen and her entourage of 'maids, pages, attendants and dancers'.

We're at the Crown too early. The pub is still reeling from the night before. We're immediately accused, albeit with a smile, of having slept in their beer garden. 'Don't worry, *we* won't charge you. But you know what happens to those who wake in the dew, don't you?' The fool is moving between people, teasing, working up his audience. A presence that evidently carries more weight than any badge of author-ity. Drinks are brought into the sun as the Bedford Morris Men go through their paces. Their caller is dressed as a court jester. Sticks, shouts, bells. Local ales are seen off by the pint. The fool pretends to trip and fall over in front of children and they belly-laugh and run off. Then he's up in our faces, prodding with his stick, asking if we're 'good stock for the good ladies later' and 'all right downstairs'. Are we *up* to it? is his question. Or do we need a little help? If so, he says, leaning in, tapping his pocket, he always packs a few Viagra. People laugh. When I turn around, someone's drunk my beer. More morris men arrive. The car park fills with competing noise, claps, yells and ribbons. Joining us on our outside table is a roofer in an own-brand hoodie. Prime piss-taker, I assume, here to mock the skipping men. That is until I hear him mumbling into his mobile, lambasting his mates for their lateness: 'You're missing the bloody Bedfords.'

*

May Day is alive with subtle switches. With double-takes. Normal into abnormal. Folklore and echo-memory surfacing in rural villages and towns; the embedded narratives of place, belief, superstition, all stirred up by the yearly enacting of the old rituals over old soil. May Day was traditionally the celebration of the return of spring, of fecundity and reproduction, of the resurrection of nature after the death of winter. It was deep-rooted in Roman and pagan festivals of feasting, flowers, dancing, merrymaking. The centrepiece: the phallic maypole. Once this was the tallest tree of the forest, cut down, trimmed of all its branches (only its 'crown' left) and woven with ribbons. Held. Then released. The symbolism is congress with the fertile goddess: the May Queen. Mother Nature. Later, the Virgin Mary and Maid Marian in the Robin Hood myths; Guinevere in Arthur. The maypole, decorated with flowers and greenery, including hawthorn – or *May* – would have carried the 'carnal scent'. The tang of sex.

Perhaps this is why Philip Stubbes refers to it as the 'stinking idol' in his pre-emptive Puritan pamphlet of 1583, *Anatomie of Abuses*. Stubbes dedicates an entire chapter – 'Against May' – to decrying such practices as immoral, lustful and ungodly.

> ... *the young men and maids run gadding over night to the woods, groves ... where they spend all the night in pleasant pastimes ... in the morning they return, bringing with them birch and branches of trees, to deck their assemblies ...*

He may have been describing Ickwell Green. The first written records of May Day ritual in the village date from 1563, but it's thought it was already ancient by then. After its banning under Cromwell in 1644, May Day everywhere re-emerged semi-neutered, Christianised. Men and maids segregated. Children as the main participants; young(er) girls as May Queens. 'The Lord' – a masculine God – the focus of the songs. But the open rift was never closed. The conflagration of centuries of rural customs and characters erupted in its yearly dance. It still does, even if no one is sure of the origins. Received memories are respected. The gods and goddesses of the elements appeased. Recalled. Embedded in the psyche of communities like Ickwell Green is an unshakeable conviction that sensible women and men must take up these roles and re-enact rituals. We see that switch.

That double-take. And in certain places, behind the comic dress, the Bank Holiday drinking, the primary school parades, the cake stalls, the charity collections, there's something distinctly unmentionable in it all. A respect, or a fear.

*

The procession is ready. More pints swallowed. Ploughman lunches finished, and plough boys – middle-aged professionals in rough smocks, hobnailed boots, fake earth daubed on office-soft cheeks – have been lined up. Mary (she says, or *Merry*) is our own self-appointed guide. She's here every year, brings her own folding chair, her own sandwiches. A potent hedgerow gin. The fool knows her. He doffs his hat. Bows. Steals a nip. She points out he's really an interloper, a figure amalgamated from the medieval April Fool's festival. His job is the trickster – the embodiment of an old inversion of order, that flipping of status that occurred when master would wait at the servants' table for a day. When the rural labourers got to air their grievances without recourse and (in disguise) beg for pennies, illegal at the time. It's hard to know what to believe. Mary tells me that his neckerchief is also a reference to itinerant 'gypsy' workers; the seasonal labourers who would travel to the rural areas in spring and summer for employment. Another man with an 'Ickwell Green Committee' badge is wearing a badly fitting floral frock and boots; a crocheted shoulder throw, a wig. He is not – it's stressed – trying to pass for a woman, but as *a man dressed as a woman*. The distinction seems important, but this isn't what shocks. He is also in blackface – white holes left for his eyes and mouth. My question as to why gets batted away. A no-go topic. Murmurs made from some of those in earshot about it being 'harmless tradition': Molly gangs, mummers, maskers. Just a legacy of when May Day dances were performed by trades such as chimney sweeps. Sweeps (the totem for good luck) were unemployed in the summer. May Day was a chance to dance, parade, pass a collecting tin to see them through the lean months. They bestowed luck with a black smudge on each coin giver's cheek. But I'm not entirely convinced. It's Jim Crow too. Minstrel show. A knowing flashback to the days of crude, dehumanising racial caricature, to the mocking and the mimicry that was all-too-common in the May Day pageantry of the nineteenth century. But either way, the modern connotations of black-face are well known, making attempts at indemnification via historic justification irrelevant. Especially when a blacked-up, middle-aged white man appears to be the only non-white face in the crowd. Amid all the heady atmosphere, the joviality, it's easy to forget that these kinds of heritage traditions can also, often, be hijacked by those who want to parade murkier, jingoistic narratives: *to hell with your political correctness. The past had it right. Britons never, never, never shall be slaves.*

Turning away, I glimpse someone who passes for well-kept topiary. Entirely green tree-costumed, flower-headed. Elsewhere a pair of antlers hovers above the heads. Then a shout goes up. With Mary, we jostle to the front to follow a procession of trailers festooned with greenery and flowers, pulled by tractors. Schoolkids dressed as maids and ploughboys; in white dresses with velvet cloaks and flower crowns the attendants and the May Queen herself. She is being lavished with attention. People pinch-zoom photos on phones; toddlers stare open-mouthed, ice creams melting over fists. A protective guard of honour walks behind her trailer. More men in floral dresses and wigs. Nothing comic about it. Stern faces set for duties, as if about to defuse a bomb. Here is where the echo hits. That double-take. The darker rites of spring: a chosen girl led through the fields by the elders of the village in the faith that the land will grow rich with corn, wheat, barley. An exchange for her blood. The symbolic white and red.

Half a mile on, at the maypole, the crowning ceremony begins. The mob gathered around the green numbers in the hundreds now. All join in the quivering singing: '*Oh! The lovely, lovely May . . .*' The fool gads about, making his rounds. The collecting buckets rattle in the hands of the old maids. Flower garlands are presented, a sceptre too, before the newly crowned May Queen rises and processes around the green to cheers, signalling the start of the dancing, the intricate maypole plaiting, the crossing, uncrossing morris men. The children twirling to 'Boys and Girls Come Out to Play'.

The sky has become ash grey, pregnant with what might turn into rain.

'A lovely English day, folks. Please don't forget to take photographs,' the announcer jokes over the PA. 'You can always Photoshop the sunny weather in later.'

More drink taken. For those not wielding sticks or handkerchiefs, not plaiting the maypole in smocks and straw hats, not doing the 'goddess' folk dance, this is the quickest route into the revelry, into the trance of this Middle England voodoo. Men and women of Ickwell Green's surrounding villages – Northill, Southill, Broom, Upper Caldecote, Hatch, Moggerhanger – indulging in convivial competitive boozing. Glazed expressions, the sour-sweet scent of beer on the breath. The cricket club bar is doing great business and A points out that it's my round. Inside, the fool is temporarily out-of-character – his morning coat slung on the back of a chair, hat off, bolting a sandwich and a pint of John Smith's. I pay my dues and set him up with a fresh beer. In the conversation that follows, he asks what I'm doing down here? So, I give him the story, the road so far. He nods his understanding. As he puts his hat back on and picks up his stick, he says: 'And I bet you wouldn't have believed any of it before you started out?'

'No. I probably wouldn't.'

'No. See? That's the trick with these things. *Gotta* give yourself up to it. *Gotta* step out of your skin a bit. Do that and you'll find that your whole perception changes.'

*

Heat clamped under overcast skies. Families flopped in lush grass. Drums and fiddles. The foxy smell of skunk from behind the Porta-loos. Between the rounds of beer and tiredness my sense of reality begins to wear away with the drowsy afternoon. I'm ordering again in the clubhouse when a barman, mad hair, early twenties, remarks how it's nice to see me back. 'You must have enjoyed yourself last time.' It becomes clear he doesn't mean earlier. He's talking about last year. He insists I was here, at this bar, last May Day. *Don't you remember? You bought me a drink? We talked about music?* I don't know how to tell him that I'd never even heard of the place until yesterday, so I go along with it, offering for him to pour himself a pint out of the change this time too. It's only when walking away that I wonder whether it's a ploy tried on everyone.

When the presentations and songs are done and the last, looped-arm Circassian Circle performed, the crowd begins to thin. Revellers start to disperse or stagger off towards the Crown. *A*'s time is up too. He has to get back. At the corner of the green, I watch him heave his Bergen into the boot of the waiting cab and disappear east, towards the A1. He texts me from the road: *I feel like I've been through some initiation.*

My mind is following a similar trajectory to his taxi, over quiet fields of cereal crops, down the long lane edged with hedges, back towards the highway. In this fever-vision of the late May Day after-noon, I'm gripped by the notion that we were meant to reach this place, this fold, where narratives are replayed over ground; where the past arrives like a wave, washing stories into the present. As with the road, this is a ritual space chasing us back to questions of subjectivity and identity: *Who are we? Where have we come from? Where are we going?* I think too of how, in times of schism, such traditions can be perceived as providing a kind of a solid, untouched continuity through history. Or, more dangerously, used to bulwark notions of an unchanging 'native' identity. Get close enough and you understand the opposite is true. Like the north road, they are testament to a wild, unfixed reality. Not a constant line, but a collective dream, thick with narratives and counter-narratives. A poem still being written by many hands.

*

The stage is packed up. The stalls taken down. The blurry melancholia of light fading down over empty land. Everything at once posthumous and filled with potential. I walk back towards the woods, the hammock, the sleeping bag, keeping my distance from a couple making for the treeline themselves, garland-crowned, bottles in hand. Something catches my eye: metal screwed into a stump. A plaque. Engraved into it is a poem by local writer, Ed Burnett. A man who *knows* this ground, it asserts. I read it, frozen to the spot. If it wasn't for the rusted screws and the algae, if I didn't know better, I'd think that the words had just been put up. That they were left here for me:

> You, who walk to think / May seek your path in life . . . / Be wary, you may stumble like me into the spell of a mighty Queen. / She'll whisper you scarlet secrets, to set alight a jubilee sunset / Hope you do not find what you seek / For those who search all their lives / Are blessed with a welcoming road.

Liquid night. Dark shapes stirring in the darkness. No singing, but there is movement. Out there in the trees. And a half-call. Human. Deer. It's hard to say. But it is coming closer. *Well, let it come,* I think. I shut my eyes and lie suspended between the trees, waiting.

II

Open Road

That was the moment the road entered us,
winding and unwinding
down the center of our lives.

Susan Mitchell

One can call spirits from the vasty deep with which to
people the way. No need to ask, 'Will they come?'
They cannot choose but do so; they are here.

C. G. Harper

The Hind

(Ickwell Green–Huntingdon)

Go back.

Again? To the Beginning?

Aye.

Very well. The candle a little nearer then, if you please. And I read . . .

Indeared Countrey-men,

Whereas there hath been sundry and various Relations of the
proceedings of Capt. James Hind, fraught with impertinent stories,
and new-invented fictions; I am desired by the said Mr. Hind, to
publish this ensuing Declaration, for the sattisfaction, & true
information of the People . . .

Hold there. See, I care not for the sattisfaction of the People.

Aye, perhaps, but . . .

I hath say'd I wish to tell the Truth plainly. This is all.

Sir, if I may; I write for the People. I understand the People . . .

'Tis over-salted, Mr Paxton.

Nay! We might not but begin in such a manner to appeal to the People's hearts. To make them for *you*, Sir. From the very beginning. For it is the People that will carry you hence and judge you in time, not Lawyers or Council of State, or Parliament.

God and my master the King will judge me, Paxton.

God's Will be done, aye. Even so, the People will judge you. They will come to know you; and in these words, *your words*, we may lay a foundation on which your Principles and Deeds and Honour might endure, whatsoever fate decrees . . . Will I continue, Sir?

As you were.

And I read ... *for the sattisfaction, & true information of the People; together with a Narrative of his Travels, which I shall impartially represent, as followeth:*

Whereas the Heavens are doomers of men's deeds, and God holds a ballance in his hand, to reward with favour, all those that walk uprightly; and to revenge with justice, all those that steers their ways to the contrary; even so may the life of man well be compared to the Ocean Seas, that for every calm hath a thousand storms; for a little pleasure much pain; and for high desire, much discontent: For as folly perswaded me to lead a sinful life, so at length Justice may bring me to a sorrowful end; (but God requires Mercy in the midst thereof) Yet notwithstanding, I am confident, the wrongs which I have committed doth not cry aloud for vengeance; but rather the Mercy that I shewed in all my Designs and Actions, may plead an acquitment of punishments ...

Acquitment of all punishments.

Forgive me ...?

An acquitment of all punishments.

Ah, very well. I see.

... an acquitment of all punishments. However, Gods Will be done; for while I live my heart shall not faint me: I sorrow not to die; neither shall I grieve at the manner of my death, though it be never so untimely. For every wrong I have done (called now to remembrance) wrings drops of blood from my heart. But never did I take the worth of a peny from a poor man; but at what time soever I met with any such person, it was my constant custom, to ask, Who he was for? if he reply'd, For the King, I gave him 20 shillings: but if he answer'd, For the Parliament, I left him, as I found him. As for any other Exploits since 1649. I am guiltless of: For in the same year, May 2. I departed England (as appears by my Confession to the Council at White-Hal on the 10 instant, 1651) and went to the Hague; But after I had been there three days, I departed for Ireland, in the Vessel that carry'd the Kings Goods, and landed at Galloway: in which Kingdome I staid three quarters of a year; part of which time I was Corporal to the Marquess of Ormond's Life-Guard:

And being at Yonghall, when that was surprised by the Parliaments
Forces, was there wounded in the right Arm and Hand with Halberts.
After which (making a narrow escape) I went to Duncannon; but
because of the sickness, came thence to Scilly, staid there eight months;
and from thence I came to the Isle of MAN, staid there 13 weeks; and
went thence to Scotland, arrived at Sterling, where I sent a Letter to his
Majesty, acquainting his Highness of my arrival; and represented my
service, &c. Which was favourably accepted of; for no sooner had the
King notice of my coming; but immediately I had admittance into his
chamber, and kist his hand; and after some discourse, his Majesty com-
mended me to the D. of Buckingham then present, to ride in his troop
because his Life-guard was full. I came to England with the Troop, was
in the Engagement at Warrington, also at Worcester, where I kept the
field, till the King was fled, and in the evening, the Gates being full of
flying persons, I leapt over the Wall on foot by myself only, travel'd
the Countrey, and lay three days under Bush and hedge, because of the
Souldiery, till I came to Sir John Packington's Woods, where I lay five
days and then afterward, to London . . .

And here, Sir, we arrive at the place. A fresh candle if you please,
Keeper. Aye and let me fill your cup anew. Now, and in your time Captain, I beg pray proceed.

*

We must go back again, Paxton. For tho I am call'd a *highway*-man I
am no highway-man. Let it be known I Robb'd the rich but I gave to
the poor Moneys as I hath say'd or the freedom to pass unmolest'd.
For they were ne'er mine Enemy. You ask'd last time we were here
what truth lay in that rumours of the inn in Warwick where I Robb'd
a bayliff. Well, 'tis true. It grieve'd me to see the Landlord there so
harras'd by officials so I pay'd them off in full and then follow'd them
on the Road. I swapp'd jacket and don'd mask and Robb'd them for
my 20 pounds returned. I gave the Landlord 5 pounds for good measure and told him I'd ne'er done badly by lending honest men Money.
'Tis true. Robbery, aye, but ne'er did I anything to a man who didn't
deserve it. I once Robb'd a poor old man with children on his way to

buy a cow of 40 shillings, but I promised to meet him at the same place at night-fall and if he spoke not to anyone between, I would repay him more than that which he had outlay'd to me. This I did. More besides; double, with twenty shillings more to sweeten the lend. But I swear, Imprisoned as I am in Custody, that since '47 I hath been engaged in God's Bidding.

Be not deceive'd as to why I am here. 'Tis simple Politik. And Faith. For when Compton made me Captain in '47 at Colchester I swore Oath to my Majesty and issues. I swore to ne'er end this fight nor give ground to those rebellious who hath so grievously brought these civil woes to this Goodly land. Who hath split it asunder. These fanatics and usurpers who hath Murder'd our Rightful King and latterly chased his kin to Foreign shores. I made Oath, understand, and enact'd Revenge justly against these Regicides. You ask for Evidence? Well, I will tell you all and you may Publish what you see fit to further the Virtue of my Deeds. But remember that you hath sworn to Publish in my favour, Sir. These words must be True and your Oath kept for I entrust my life to these words, and I have known enough Treachery of late among my friends.

After they shamefully behead'd my King outside his gate and Banquet Hall, you may recall how the crowd cry'd out when his head still a-crowned was held aloft. I was sore maladied and I made Oath to ne'er spare a Regicide and I hath made good that Oath yet, with-out blood-shed. Write that for 'tis important. *With-out* bloodshed. With-out a single drop. Indeed, know this: outside Battle I hath kill'd no man e'er but one and he was unintend'd. He was a servant who rode the Road too swiftly and by chance rode on my heels with a good horse as I fled from the Robbery of that Regiside Colonel Harrison for 70 pounds. By *chance*. He rode too close and fearing him a Souldier I turn'd and shot him through the forehead. He died lamentably on the Road. That was a misfortune but a Self-Defence. I carry it with a sad heart for I learn'd later that the man was only seeking his Master and I was sorry for it and I am sorry for it now. Nay, I made good my Oath without bloodshed even though I could have kill'd a great many of the Bastards. In the months after they kill'd my King, I made discourse at

inns and wherever possible and you would be surprise'd by the Good
feeling among so many along the Roads for justice, and not all were
Kings gentlemen neither before that murder. Many women too. Poor
landsmen and labourers with ready ale mugs, a few even who'd fought
for Parliament and were wounded and never pay'd and had been
misuse'd and that curse'd their fate in throwing their lot in with that
stinking Rump. It committed me to be more diligent to promote the
Cause wherever I encounter'd it and I encounter'd it everywhere. I
declared often to full rooms that I hath live'd Extravagantly but, as
I certified, Honestly and I beseech'd them trust not these men who
claim'd to Serve them. Who sought to break up our content'd Countrey with poisonous words for these are our Arch-Traitors. For they
Serve nought but themselves. Trust not these men's Oaths for they are
empty. Trust not their false Gods but trust a just Cause and in the
Glory of the World to Come and pox take all Turn-Coats. This talk
was how I heard of that villain Huw Peters being on the north-Road
without Guard and I rode to him at . . . was it Enfield Chase? I recall
not but I commanded him release all he carry'd and beg forgiveness
for the abomination of Murder. He began to quote me Scripture on
the immorality of thievery. The pride of him, Sir, was so astounding
that I dug the barrel of a pistole into that Presbyterian's face and
made clear that I would hear no reflection on my profession and that
Solomon also plainly say'd 'Despise not a thief'. I told him: 'Deliver
thy money presently else I shall send thee out of the World to thy
master in an instant.' Thirty broad pieces of gold did he serve up to
me with shaking hands. As he depart'd he warn'd me a fate await'd
me. That I best repent or I would hang by this Road longer than I
wish. I decide'd I was not done with him. I rode after him and
brought the horses to slow and I say'd to him: 'Sir, I am convince'd
this hath all happen'd because of thy failure to obey the words of the
Scriptures, which sayeth "Provide neither gold nor silver nor brass
in your purse for your journey" whereas it is evident that you hath
provided a pretty deal of gold unto me. It is in my power, then, to
ask ye to fulfil another command. Give me thy cloak.' Which he did.
Then I say'd: 'Did our Saviour not command that if any man take
away thy cloak, thou must not refuse thy coat?' He gave that up too.
Then I made him strip to his skin and kneel before me. I put my

Pistol against his head and then I bade him better mind his Scripture next time.

From thence I went to London. I heard that most wicked High Judge of my master the King and the man who pass'd grievous and unjust Sentence upon him, Bradshaw, would be returning on the Road from the south to Shaftesbury. I rode down and staid at an inn to wait for him. Of all robberies this was the sweetest, Paxton. Bradshaw seethed with rage when I got to him and he was all hot and red and snarling, e'en though it was still that cold March. I told him: 'I hath now as much power over you as you lately had over my King and I should do God and Countrey Good Service if I made the same use of it. Yet I desireth you to live, whore's-son, to suffer-thee the pangs of Conscience till Justice lays her Yron Hand upon thee and requires an answer for your Crimes more proper. You, Sir, are unworthy to die by any hand but those of the common hang-man.' He made to spit at me. I say'd 'Unworthy or not, be assure'd that lest you deliver Money to me now you will indeed die in a way that will pain you greatly.' Then I whipp'd a man of his crew with my Pistol butt. With rage, Bradshaw did bile at me and so I bade him 'Open thy mouth.' I stuck the Pistole into it and bade him bite on its barrel with his teeth. He gave up forty shillings in silver then. But this game was poor and I knew. I made him climb down and kneel in the Road-mud like Peters and I put the Pistole to his bald head and told him to consider finding coin of another species lest I spill his hot brains in the shit for his crew to shovel back in. He found a purse of Jacobuses. But I dislike'd the Expression on his face in its reviling of me, so that I couldn't leave without more sport. I took his Pistols and shot each into a horse's head until his Coach-team were dead and his men strand'd on foot. You may write that better in your pamphlet, but the sweetness of his sore Lament as I rode off remains with me.

Now, you mentioned Cromwell. That was different. Cromwell was no Robbery and I mean to talk plainly about this for many inventions came about after Bradshaw's Robbing concerning me. The name Captain James Hind was on the lips of many on the north Road and in the inns and many fictions were invented of which I had no part. I rode the Road then with burnt-face Tom Allen. A man of the True Faith and as sick as me of this false Government and all usurpers doing the willing bidding of the Anti-Christ. When in London we heard from other sympathisers with the King that Cromwell would arrive in the place of his Nativity. That being Huntingdon. That was in the April '49. We rode in advance up the drove-Roads for the north-Road was heavy with Souldiery. We came past Hatfield and Stefenhage to Balduc. At the inn there, Wilyam Kennette was a friend to our Cause. It was Kennette that told us of celebrations in contrivance of the orders of Parliament for May-Day at a place called Ickwell-Greene which Tom and I were desirous to attend. Being banned by order, these celebrations were held early to fool the Patrols and having days at our leisure before Cromwell was due at Huntingdon, he being delay'd in the North, we rode to the Village where word of my treat-ment of Regicides was known. The people were in Great spirit and receive'd us as friends. After two days a woman, Mary, did confide to us their Activities. That was the fairest Spring I hath e'er known, Paxton. The May full and bright and all the land Godly. As Mary say'd, the village folk went into the Trees. Maids and Yong men. There was singing and merry-making and devotions to Our Lady. Hidden in the Woods they had made effigy of the Blessed Mother from branches; the green boughs were gather'd and the May woven into Crowns. When the byrch was cut and hung with blooms, a cup was passed around and filled again and passed freely around many more times in the darkness and a great fire blazed. A maid groomed my hair and crowned me with May and kist my head and Blessed me. I laugh'd and cry'd. I saw Tom Allen before the Virgin and I swear there were tears in his Eyes. Now I mean to tell you that what came to me that night in sleep was a Prophecy, Sir. Write this. Eyes full of wonder, I beheld things that Our Saviour was desireth of me to see. I saw the Green running as a River from the Land like blood from a grave-wound. I saw the withdrawing of God's spirits from our Godly World to leave all places Barren and I saw wells be-Devil'd by Drought. I saw deer stand on their hind legs and walk as Men over hills and all the birds silence'd and vanish'd. West, I saw the Road glint like blade-steel in the Sun and heard it howl as if lamenting. I walked in fields poisoned, which groweth only poisoned corn, and with not a soul working them. Not hare nor Curlewe nor child could I root up or behold. When I awoke I knew that the murder of Our King had commenced an ushering in of Hell in Our Land and that the prevention of this grievous Vision was my sole Cause; no matter the expense to my own Person. This was God's Bidding. He hath delivereth unto me Cromwell, not for the Robbery, you understand, but for the Killing.

Huntingdon you know is about a day's ride from Ickwell-Greene but we had to be cautious then and keep to Woods and Rivers. Saint Neottes, once loyal to Our King, had been lately in the hands of mine Enemy. The Bishop's Palace at Bucden had been Seized by a similar Plague. Yet we were able to pass through narrow streets and bye-lanes to avoid Troops of Roundheads, retiring into the Woods and by traversing Encampments. It was fair and warm and Tom Allen good Company. He was alive in spirit and similarly stir'd by the necessity of our Cause to rid this Countrey of its fate and calamities. Our Path was the River Ouse and when we found it running as with Green blood it forcibly call'd to mind that which I'd seen at Ickwell-Greene. I told Allen this was a Sign. I was infinitely concern'd that we met Cromwell alone and we got to a fitting place upon the Old London-Road outside Huntingdon on a Common beyond a Bridge where word was among the River vessels that he would pass in a day. As it transpire'd, half a day was all but we were Ready and glad-hearted to see his Coach turn the corner alone. Tom Allen rode hard from one side and attack'd and Shot into the lead horse but without killing it. I came upon the other side at a gallop but 'ere I was beside the Coach than a great shout from behind rose up and I saw the mounted Guard turn the corner onto the Common rising in their saddles. Thirty-horse I reckon'd and I call'd to Tom to press on. *Press On.* But he stall'd and made to turn his horse which did for him. I caught the Coach and put through its shutter and saw Cromwell flinch and duck at the Pistol-flash. But as I fired I fear'd it was adrift. Then the Roundheads were upon us. I rode my horse hard for the woods. I saw Tom Allen cut down and torn to pieces by their blades. After that I rode for a full day until my horse gave in. I left her foaming and heart-burst in a cornfield and escape'd on foot. In a few days, I made my way to London and took a Boat to The Hague, it being May 2 '49.

The rest as you have it is the Truth. Yet mark, what I say: there hath been no Robbery since. Nay, no blood spill'd that was not in Honourable battle with mine Enemy. I reside here because of Politik. I hath been true to my Honour and Consciense and ne'er betray'd a man or my Cause and now the Rightful Yong King has fled once more and I am proud to declare with my Help. I care not for the threat of the Scaffold. I hath given my life and I would so again. All I beseech is that you write this *Honestly* before this trial for there is no Sin committed, Sir. Nay, there is nought but the Honourable Service of a man to his God and his Rightful King. If what you say is true and the People will judge me then let this be my Declaration: With Heart I did God's bidding.

*

To Mr G. Horton
London, 8th September 1658

Sir,

I reply to your Enquiries relating to Capt. Hind and Enclose the full transcript of his (and mine-own) words I took in the Gaol of New-gate for your Consideration for inclusion in the reissuing of Mr. Hind's Declaration pamphlet. This, as I am given to understand, is his only true Testimony about his Actions and all that was declared and confessed by him; I am sure it will furnish new Editions with the Narratives that we were unable to be Published before his trial at the sessions house of the Old Bailly and later at his Arraignment at Reading. I believe all within to be The Truth. You ask also, Sir, for my opinions of the man in-person: Quick-tempered, he was, undoubtedly, yet notwithstanding, a Man of Honour and great bravery, Resolute on the legitimacy of his faith and the King; You asked of me also about the wisdom of reprinting the pamphlet and I concur that with the Magesterial funeral of Our Lord Protector now done, there is unrest among the People; and a Regret and Shame for the Treatment of the King that will see Hind's Declaration well received publicly. Regarding the Postscript, I concur. And I offer my final Recollections as they are:

One Gentleman I recall came to Hind in New-gate whilst I was in his company a third time, born in the same Town that he was, viz. Chipping-Norton; who took acquaintance of him, and saluting him, said; Truly Countrey-man I am sorry to see you in this place. He answered, that imprisonment was a comfort to him, in suffering for so good and just a Cause, as adhering to the King. His Countrey-man reply'd, that tomorrow he was to return home, and that if he had anything to recommend to his wife, or friends, he would communicate it: I thank you Sir (said Hind) Pray remember my love to them all, and certifie them, that although I shall never see them more in this world; yet in the world to come, I hope we shall meet in glory. Then the Gentleman took a Glass of Beer, and drank to him; which he pledged about half; And filling up his Glass, said; Come (taking the Gentleman by the hand) here is a good health to my Master the King; and God bless and preserve his Majesty: But the Gentleman who was worryed to drink the same upon such an account before the Keepers, moved Hind to passion, who said; The Devill take all Traytors: Had I a thousand lives, and at liberty, I would adventure them all for King Charles; and damn all Turn-coats. Forbear Sir, replyed one of the Keepers, and be not in passion. Not in the least (said Hind), I am free from Passions now; but I could wish more love and loyalty amongst you all: As for my own part, should I live a hundred years, I would not flinch from my principles; and then immediately he spake as followeth: I desire all men to be true to their Trust, and to stand firm & unmoveable to their Rightful principles; and those that have laid a foundation for their King let them endeavour to raise it; and those that are on the contrary party, let them strive to level it. And indeed, this likewise is a supportment to me, that I have taken from the rich, and given to the poor; for nothing doth more impoverish the Cottage-keeper, than the rich Farmer, and full-fed Lawyer. And far worse is to come.

On the last day I visited Him, in Worcester Gaol in September 1652, a Gentleman came, importuning him to petition the Parliament for life, and to impeach and make a discovery of all his Associates, perswading him in so doing, the Parliament would be merciful to him. No, no, Sir! (said Hind) I defie such treachery and persidiousness: no man living shall be by me impeached; if I die, I'll die alone; I am resolved to keep my Conscience clear and untainted of that bloody Fact, or guilt of Sin. At that time, he stood accused of High-Treason which was the sole charge that could be brought and two men did watch each night with him, burning candle night and day.

As a matter of resolution and accuracy, Hind was Hanged, Drawn & Quartr'd, with as much Honour as might be mustered, on the <u>24th day</u> of September at Worcester 1652: his head display'd on the Severn Bridge; his quarters upon the City Gates where they remain'd, in my understanding until wind and rain destroy'd them.

I remain, Your humblest servant,
William Paxton

Leave/Remain

(Huntingdon–Stamford)

I

Consciousness lurches forward. We carry the eyes of the dead in our eyes for miles. Cromwell's face is just inches from mine: that skewed nose, Caesar-ish in profile; the famous wart on his right brow. Eyes closed. Slack-skinned. Preserved in a waxy, death-mask replica. I can read his flourished, dried blood-brown scrawl in a letter dispatched on the eve of the Battle of Naseby. I can see his sword, felt hat, spurs and leather gaiters, shrunk-fit by weather and the heat of him, arranged in display boxes. What there is not is a clear or guiding narrative. No A to B with a neat conclusion. The museum dedicated to Huntingdon's most notable son is housed in the building he, and later Samuel Pepys, attended when it was a grammar school. Before that, it was part of a road hospital and stopping-in place; an infirmary and dorm for pilgrims and travellers, slap-bang on Huntingdon's high street – the Roman line of the Old North Road. The room is claustrophobic with atavistic energies. Portraits cover walls; the space crammed with the complicated detritus of history impossible to sort into simple story. Lessons are difficult to learn. Walk loops of the room's exhibits, relooking at the same relics, and Cromwell's character becomes more unfixed with every cycle: gentry, yeoman farmer, general, Lord Protector, mercantile-class hero, empire builder, perpetrator of unspeakable atrocities. The museum is not prepared to make any judgement beyond suggesting that safe word of our times: 'controversial'. I pass a grey-haired volunteer seated in the corner, who asks me to forgive him as, shaking, he leans forward and tries to press a fan of local-attraction flyers into my palm. 'Parkinson's, I'm afraid,' he says. 'A bloody pain.' I take the literature offered so he can sink back into his chair. He smiles, surveys the room. 'A very interesting time to be alive, though. Don't you think?'

The question is non-specific. As I leave the museum, I'm asking myself: *Did he mean then or now?* Either works. It's 11th February 2017. A late, limp, winter day. To reach Huntingdon, I've already trekked the hard shoulder and slipped over wet footpaths bordering barren fields, past spent cereal crops and skeletal grasses shivering under skies of grey. It was like being lost in a cloud. A fitting season for the current national stasis – this new and undiscovered limbo landscape of post-Brexit Britain.

I should have known what was coming back in June. All the signs were there. Around the same time votes were being cast, our house had begun to manifest worrying symptoms: constant damp; wallpaper unscrolling from the walls; a pervading stench of cellars; patches of dangerous black mould blooming through the skirting. A burst mains pipe on the road, unnoticed for months and seeping into the foundations, was identified as the culprit. The insurance company took the financial hit, but we were uprooted; forced to move out as remedial works began. Our house designated 'uninhabitable'. For the first time in two years, Bea had just settled into a regular pattern of sleeping through the night. Now we had to get used to a new reality of unfamiliar rooms; used to living with a terrier barking constantly through one wall and waking at 3 a.m. every night to a voice of rage coming through the other – a teenage lad screaming into a gaming headset.

*

Huntingdon was the obvious place to return to the road. A nexus point where the River Great Ouse threads beside the Old North Road, three miles east of the Great North Road (A1), and four and a half south from the wishbone junction where both north roads from London flow into one. A countryside where the present tense and its mirroring of past tensions might be explored. Where the touching folds of time might be made visible.

Cromwell is the inescapable phantom of the region. The old estate boundaries of the family seat, Hinchingbrooke House (belonging to his uncle, Sir Oliver Cromwell, before bankruptcy forced its sale in 1627), sprawl across the triangle of land between the two north roads. Hinchingbrooke was a rarefied world. Royal favour and patronage. Sir Oliver's hosting of James I on his journey down the north road to take possession of his kingdom in 1603 featured the most lavish feast ever given to a king by a subject.

Born nearby in Huntingdon in 1599, Sir Oliver's nephew and godson (named after him) lived with one foot in this world and one foot in another. Stories persist of a young Oliver playing in the grounds of Hinchingbrooke with a young Charles Stuart, yet Cromwell was also son of a second son. Brought up in a modest town house, educated (and chastised as a 'splenetic dreamer') by his puritan headmaster, he was twenty-eight when the incredible debts incurred by his uncle finally caught up with the family. Hinchingbrooke House was ignominiously sold off to the highest bidder. A year later, the younger Oliver Cromwell was venturing down the London Road himself as a freshly elected MP for Huntingdon. This stab at respectability in the capital quickly collapsed after Charles I dismissed Parliament in 1629. Over the following months, a further series of calamities occurred, which eventually forced Cromwell, his wife and their young children to sell everything and take a lease on a farmstead in St Ives, just east of Huntingdon. The fall was dramatic, transformative. Earth-work a cure for the bouts of 'melancholia'. For years, Cromwell toiled the land alongside hired labourers, speaking in their tongue, understanding what made them tick, building an empathy he would later use to mobilise the same kind of men into an undefeatable army in the civil wars. Those sodden soils of below-sea-level fenland were a proving ground and a fertile space in which his radical faith and pragmatic political beliefs could grow among the crops. Letters reveal his repulsion towards a church still filled with what he regarded as myth and popish magic. He found sin everywhere and yearned for a place the gospel could be proclaimed unadorned. He demonised bishops, preached at illegal assemblies. In 1636, and with no prospect of Charles calling another Parliament, Cromwell's name appeared on the manifest for a ship bound for America, seeking a passage for his family to the Massachusetts Bay Colony. The reason given: '. . . disgusted with government'.

The authorities intervened. Permission denied. Too many radical Englishmen with intent already fleeing to foreign shores where they might freely devise and design. No matter. Cromwell's fortunes were about to change anyway. First with a timely inheritance of land and properties, then the restoration of Parliament in 1640 in which Cromwell was returned for the town of Cambridge as part of a Puritan caucus. Scorching with the flame of conviction and spiritual awakening, he saw it all as part of his own pilgrim's progress. God had a purpose for him. Emerging from the wilderness, from his smallholding life of chickens and sheep, he was reborn with an inner fire. But surely even he couldn't have imagined where the road would lead.

*

Across from the museum, the sixteenth-century Falcon (inn, tavern, hostelry – pick your own descriptor) is open for business. Refurbed and lease-held after its own spell of years in the wilderness, it's billed as *a slice of history on Huntingdon's market square*. A building-wide coaching arch resembles a grouper's mouth; a black cave leading back along a stone-flagged carriageway. Inside, locals are hunched over tables under the period beams, working through lunchtime stacks of onion rings and burgers. The only woman present is keeping the flow of ales coming, her hands a gallery of henna tattoos.

The Falcon doubled as Cromwell's recruiting office and headquarters during the most intense years of the civil wars. 'His presence is strongest in the top room,' the woman behind the bar explains. 'It's closed at the moment. They're turning it into a Victorian tea room.' After some enquiries about my notebook and a conversation about her own ambitious and unwinding writing project on India ('I'm saving to get out there again'), she relents: 'No one's up there today. Have a nosey if you want.'

Sloping stairs, warped floors, fleur-de-lys carpet; the creak of old wood. Tilted corridors. Low lintels. Picking between piles of board games, air fresheners and toilet rolls, I'm stepping into a room with a fireplace in its wall that distorts with its sudden flood of daylight, its odd, heavy pressures. The window, from where Cromwell addressed his army mustered on the market square below, is a curiously haunted

frame. Approach and you can almost hear the noise. The roar. The stamp of horses. You can almost sense the massed rabble in their Venetian red coats and bandoliers. A step further and it bleaches away. Up close the frame is rotten, blown. The square is empty. The window is an old aperture, left open, over the ancient road. Stand long enough and your outline is imprinted on the air. When I zoom in on the photograph I take from outside, there appears to be a figure looking down at me from the window.

*

Land re-remembers, even as we forget. One of the most striking disclosures from the Brexit vote has been its sporadic echoes of the civil wars. Not just the familial rifts, the splits down fault-lines, incredulous arguments over dinner tables, the storm-outs and slammed doors, but the geographical parallels. The voting map revealed regional support for Leave and Remain that uncannily mirrored support for King and Parliament at the start of the wars. The regions that were for the King turning out to be unassailable enclaves of Leave; those that were for Parliament, Remain. Economic assessments since have suggested that this signals a return to divides from the seventeenth century between traditional, closed-door conservatism and globalised, open-door liberalism.

Although it was ultimately the issue of the divine right of kings, feverish religious convictions, fears of an English counter-Reformation and anger at the crown's arbitrary use of power that lit the fires of the civil wars, it was all carried on the wind of globalisation, advancing technologies, expanding interests abroad, and a new, rising merchant class hungry for the opportunities of a free, open market. Many of the ruling elite of the City of London – those merchants of the old cloth: wealthy landowning gentry with interests overseas in Europe, the Mediterranean, the East – were Royalist. Yet a newer breed of merchants – householders with smaller property interests, domestic traders, shopkeepers, artisans – became the militant and dominant force behind the Parliamentary cause. Sons of lesser gentry or yeoman farmers, these were men in the Cromwell model. Men who were similarly 'disgusted with government', meaning, at the time, the king. On one side an older order's interests remained in the chartered monopoly companies, a restrictive feudal system and the reinforcement of the socio-political structures that kept them at the top. On the other, a new breed of colonial trader-merchant whose entrepreneurial zeal pointed it towards projects such as the Massachusetts Bay Colony in America and the Caribbean as the expanding territories of opportunity. Goods were made and exported out to these burgeoning colonies, plots and plantations; tobacco and slave-worked sugar sent back. The profits astronomical. The new colonial merchants were made up of – and bound up with – the middling classes of shopkeepers, ship captains, craftsmen and small producers in cities like London and Bristol. It was from this devoutly Puritan middle class of gentry and merchants that the opposition in Parliament drew most of its support. They despised the king's interference and they resented being cut off from England's religious, political and economic decision-making by what they saw as an increasingly despotic crown and a popish ecclesiastical hierarchy. Citing Magna Carta, evoking their *freedom* as

Englishmen, they were open to political–religious action and radical new departures.

In the years leading up to the first engagement of the wars, the Battle of Edgehill, other parts of the country were less convinced. Unlike thriving, dynamic London (connected; buoyed by foreign trade), areas of advancing production in the south or the busy ports and cathedral cities, the rural heartlands of the north and west of England and Wales were more marginalised, poorer. With minds harking back to better times in the shires, the often-Catholic gentry and nobility in such areas were uncomfortable with the new Parlia-mentary puritanism – especially its encroachment of the monarch's absolute power, its persecution of traditions and the persistent demon-ising of all traces of the old faith. Even those inclined to consider some of the demands of Parliament reasonable believed a line was being crossed when it came to the question of the king. Agonies of alle-giance erupted. Families, friends, communities that had shared land, customs and beliefs for generations turned on each other. Bonds frayed, then tore irreparably in 1642, when Charles raised his stand-ard in Warwickshire.

Unquiet history stares us in the face. Brexit burst into flame from sparks struck over similar tinder: half a century of rapid modernisa-tion and accelerated globalisation, new technologies replacing once-great regional industries; uneven and unfair recovery from reces-sion. Instigating it, a prosperous elite grown rich from the privileges and opportunities offered by global trade and the EU's single market (largely centred in and around cosmopolitan cities such as London) unable to comprehend the concerns and simmering anger of the 'left behind' and disenfranchised rural communities in the north, the west, and Wales. Throw in the inflammatory propaganda, the fresh, home-spun scapegoating of immigrants and the young, upstart city-dwelling 'winners' of globalisation (with their new views on politics, sex, gender and identity); then inject a particularly murky strain of false memory into an ageing and fearful generation and it's little wonder that we have seen the same patterns of allegiance and division repeating.

*

It's been nine months since I last saw *A*. After Ickwell Green there were foreign postings, operations. Unanswered texts on both sides. He was unreachable. The road had stayed with him, though. When I'd messaged to float the notion of walking some more, he'd replied immediately: *I'll be there*. Timings were fortuitous. He would be returning from a recce in the Kuwait desert, flying in the night before, ahead of returning again to the Middle East to train local forces in repelling attacks from Islamic State. Drills, assault tactics. Overspill from the continuing mess over the border in Iraq.

At the agreed rendezvous, we slip into step, reconnecting to the original north road, Ermine Street. *A*'s face betrays exhaustion. The weather and the rain hood don't help, but he looks older, drawn, wearier than I've seen him before. More than once I catch him, chin up to the grey sky, eyes closed, letting the drizzle streak down his face.

From Huntingdon, the line to Alconbury Junction is Roman in design. No nonsense; no meandering. The area is set-dressed with a vehicle-part warehouse, offices, a Homebase, a 'glazing solutions' site resembling a moon colony; car showrooms. The drizzle waters down the taste of diesel on the tongue, transforming the sound of tyres on tarmac into perpetual hiss. Beyond the spin of the A141 roundabout and the in-flow/out-flow of the Ermine Business Park, both road and landscape open up. Sights are truer to a legionary's view. Raw, rough-worked fields to the west. A wet treeline shivering on the horizon. The sudden heavy silence of the quietened highway.

It was along this road, across these fields, that Cromwell trained his New Model Army, drilling cavalry and infantry in the mud and sleet of the early months of 1645, shaping the formidable and disciplined force that would win the decisive battles of the wars. Three years before that, along this same road, Charles had fled north to set up his court at York after the London mob became too dangerous for him to remain. Both men cantered over first-century workmanship, horse-shoes clattering on ancient strata. When, in the 1700s, Daniel Defoe noted how a section of the old road a little to the north was still 'paved with stone', he was referring to the enduring mid-layer of Roman construction. Our highway is shining wet, blue-grey, smooth as Lakeland slate. The tone along tarmac different: hoofbeats replaced by the slap-back of a plane echoing above. Disjointed bursts of engine noise moan through a muffling, sodden-fleece sky. RAF Alconbury, the airfield sprawling beside the road, is the obvious contender, except that we learn that flying ceased there in 2009. Still the spectral sounds continue. Acoustic replays of the waves of Flying Fortresses and Liberators that took off from here to wreak fire and destruction on the factories of German industrial cities. That limped back home flak-punctured to land in the darkness, or never returned at all.

Our search is for an old totem and road guardian. The hand-carved, seventeenth-century milestone further up the road at Alconbury Hill. This tombstone-like limestone block, with its plinth and cornicing, traditionally marked the merging point of the Old North Road into the Great North Road on their routes up from the capital. Its hand (period, frilly shirt-cuff visible) points out the way(s) back: 'To LONDON 64 miles through Huntingdon, Royston and Ware / To LONDON 68 miles through Buckden, Biggleswade, Hatfield'. For centuries this sat in the middle of the Great North Road. We track it to a spot concealed by thickets between the eastern carriageway of the new A1(M) and its abandoned predecessor on an adjacent line, classified now as the B1043.

We stick to this B-road, following the monument's direction onwards: 'To STILTON 7 miles'. The cloud lifts in a quick flare of light. *A* snaps a thin starling murmuration knotting itself over the

fields. Not a single car. The eight-lane A1(M) is screened by thorns. Unseen, but constantly heard. If that is the living highway, we're on the ghost road. Desaturated, wintry, unerringly straight, it resembles a monochrome photocopy of a Midwest highway – an infinity line disappearing into the horizon. Perfect for the coachman or the cruise-controller; frustrating for the walker. Distances don't seem to diminish. That horizon never gets closer. The road books describe the long descent from Alconbury as 'Stangate Hill', from *stone*-gate, referring to its once-visible Roman paving. The dip at the bottom was 'Stangate Hole' – a lethal haunt of highwaymen and thieves, a flow of whom ended up suspended in the gibbet on Alconbury Hill. Suspension remains the overwhelming sensation here. A suspension in time. With its traffic transposed and its sporadic enterprises (a Pace petrol station, window smashed; a Spiceland Indian Buffet with a vacant car park) appearing on the verge of collapsing, the road imparts the feeling of being between. We're pacing an empty corridor somewhere that travellers have been moving through for 2,000 years.

T. S. Eliot knew this atmosphere well. He knew what it was to be in places and moments where you encounter the eerie interrelation between time and timelessness: 'The intersection of the timeless moment / Is England and nowhere.'

'Little Gidding', the title of the final of his *Four Quartets* and his swansong as a poet, refers to the religious community and chapel set up by Nicholas Ferrar in the 1620s, just west of our position on the Great North Road. Now so close to its orbit, I locate an archive audio of the poem, read by Alec Guinness, and play it on my phone. I've been reading this poem for twenty years, but listening to it out here, against the shuffle of our footfall on asphalt, it strikes me how much *Four Quartets* is a highway hymn. A meditation on time, history, memory as well as a record of Eliot's own inner struggle towards some homecoming. It is a road poem that must be read – or travelled – in its entirety before those famous conclusionary lines can be understood:

> *And the end of all our exploring*
> *Will be to arrive where we started*
> *And know the place for the first time.*

As with the north road, from its beginning 'Little Gidding' delivers up interstitial spaces: 'midwinter spring is its own season ... suspended in time'. Seasons, centuries, past, present, future, all are interlaced. Intriguingly, given the ground we're covering (Huntingdon to our south; the old airfield to our east), the whole movement hovers between two dark and calamitous moments in British history: the civil wars and the Second World War. Eliot overlays events of the 1640s and the 1940s. The 'broken king' he describes in the poem arriving at nightfall is Charles I who fled to Little Gidding after his crushing defeat at Naseby. The dove with its tongue of fire and the 'Dust in the air suspended / Marks the place where a story ended. / Dust inbreathed was a house ...' speak of the Battle of Britain and the devastating bombing raids on London in 1940–1941, which Eliot witnessed in his role as a fire watcher when working on the verses. Against these backdrops of destruction and death, the narrator follows in the footsteps of Charles I to fall at the foot of the cross, envisioning these cataclysmic 'world's end' moments as profoundly connected. Moments of 'refining fire' in the cycle of civilisation. Purges that may lead the soul towards eternal places like Little Gidding where 'prayer is valid', where the voices of the dead are heard, where the ultimate, inexpressible, mystical experience of God is realised. Where redemption is possible.

Eliot travelled up the same road we are walking to visit Little Gidding in 1936, his pilgrimage recalled in the lines: '... when you leave the rough road / And turn behind the pig-sty to the dull façade ...' During the first hopeless years of the war that followed, Little Gidding shone in his memory, coming to symbolise a conjunction of the personal, spiritual and historical. Ferrar's semi-monastic community with its staunch faith and quiet devotion existed in defiance of the storm of radical Puritanism sweeping the land. Dismantled by Cromwell's forces, its chapel was rebuilt in 1714 and 1853. A metaphor that mattered at another point of national peril. Moreover, Eliot's own Anglo-Catholicism was informed from the same old faith rootstock as Ferrar's community. In *Four Quartets*, the poet declares himself part of the cult of King Charles the Martyr. 'Little Gidding' is awash with allusions to the Royalist (Anglo-Catholic) cause, evolving themes of fallen humanity wandering lost in the desert explored in *The Waste Land*, towards a religious, metaphysical destination.

Integral to Eliot's faith was the notion of enchantment. The idea that the natural world is interwoven with the supernatural; that the world material is enhanced, enriched and given meaning by the world spiritual and that the two together find a symbiosis and harmony. Enchantment is at the root of many pre-modern cultures and fundamental to early faiths and founding deities, such as the mother goddess. Spiritual power manifesting through sacred sites and sacramental practice underpins Greek, Celtic and Roman religions. It *is* animism – the reverence of place and nature, of springs, rivers, wells and woods. And it was at the core of faith, myth and superstition in this country.

Things changed with the advancement of science, reason and logic in the sixteenth and seventeenth centuries. During the Enlightenment, ideas of enchantment began to be viewed as primitive, childish, dangerous even. Enchantment was abuse – the spell of Popish bewitchment and superstition cast over people. So began the long process of *disen*chantment. In the mind of the Protestant and Puritan, the material world was not imbued with any mystery or spirit. God created it for mankind to exploit in His name and in the name of establishing a dominant, productive and God-fearing civilisation. The same base justification for all that would follow: colonialism, industrialisation, capitalism. Throughout *The Waste Land* and *Four Quartets*, Eliot bears weary witness to the results of taking this road: conflict and a deep despair in the heart of humanity. He paints a vision of a secular world-gone-wrong where enchantment has been diminished and corrupted, displaced into an insatiable lust for money, pleasure, the want of things. Gains aplenty perhaps, but at what cost?

Ironically, a direct descendant of Nicholas Ferrar, Ted Hughes, would highlight the effect of this displacement on our natural, living world once held so sacred. In his 1970 essay, 'The Environmental Revolution', he argues that the founding principles of western civilisation are set against conservation because: 'They derive from Reformed Christianity and from Old Testament Puritanism ... [and] are based on the assumption that the earth is a heap of raw materials given to man by God for his exclusive profit and use ...' With the twisted outcome of this 'exile' being a '[P]rogressively more desperate search for mechanical and rational and symbolic securities, which will substitute for the spirit-confidence of the Nature he has lost'.

And how are we supposed to react now? That's the question we're asking ourselves as the rain begins again and we stop to pull back on waterproofs and blink up at the ton-weight heavy sky. Now, in this path of coming extinctions, of ecosystems ravaged beyond repair, of communities fracturing into tribalism once more, of war. Now that our consumption runs ever wilder and we become further distanced from the earth, from the land, from the rivers and woods. Now that Eliot's God, like all gods, is missing, presumed dead. Is it not to try and restore some sense of enchantment that we are out here walking this road? Not with the intent of returning to naivety or to escape, nor to regress our scientific knowledge, but to experience something of what Eliot did that day in 1936 at Little Gidding, just over the fields from here. To find those interstitial spaces, those gaps, those places that possess an aura where time falls away and we enter a present that reminds us that the universe is vital, rich and unexpected. That it is alive and animate in ways we are only just starting to (re)discover. Where we meet ourselves, others and the past in that manner Edward Thomas described: 'Going up such a road ... worn twenty feet deep ... we may be half-conscious that we have climbed that way before during the furrowing of the road and we move as in a dream between this age and that dim one which we vainly strive to recover ... we are aware of the passing of time in ways too difficult and strange for the explanation of historian and zoologist and philosopher.'

Yes, T. S. Eliot knew this atmosphere well. The potency of such places. He knew that to move through them was to open doors. March on and you find you are dragging a crowd of voices with you. The presence of the vanished *there*, through the dark hedgerow. You are aware that history's ghosts are interacting with us constantly.

*

At home, when I'd been plotting the route for this stretch of road, an email had landed. A 'new record' alert from an ancestry site. Attached, I found the scan of a front page from the *Leeds Mercury* dated 7th

September 1923. I zoomed in on the newsprint looking for my great-grandfather's name among the archaic articles ('Birth of a Crown Prince' / 'What Leeds Thinks of London'), the reports on Western Front battlefield crosses, and the telling adverts ('GET GRANITE: for your imperishable memorial').

Word was out among the family that I was on the trail of Bill Cowen, as much as he seemed to be on mine – permeating my dreams; a near constant presence on the road. What I was seeking from him, or what he wanted of me, as yet unclear, but older first and second cousins were now raiding memories, opening boxes, trying to plot various disparate scenes and handed-down stories into logical sequences that might make sense. Most promising of all was news from a cousin of Dad's – John (another grandson of Bill and May) – that he'd unearthed an aide-memoire: a diminishing memory diary, complete with photographs, written by his late mother Ellen (Bill and May's eldest child) in the 1970s. He was now intending to transcribe the lot. What John could already confide was that he'd turned up the earliest mention of Bill anywhere, well before any fortune-seeking in Doncaster, when he was a young boy living in the mining slums of Old Radford in Nottingham. Written by Ellen about her father, it must have been a received memory given to her, possibly by her grand-mother: 'One day a young lady called at a little house in Nottingham to thank a small boy called Billie Cowen for saving her son from drowning in the canal. Sally, Billie's mother, not knowing anything about this but aware he'd been swimming, which they did naked, gave him a dunking under the tap for being near the canal. He was a hero, but so small.'

An origin story with a whiff of fairy tale. A dunking punishment for a hero boy who risked his life to save another. Nothing more yet from this emerging cache of snapshots and memories on the enigma of the family's penniless flight from Doncaster. Nothing on the imperative to leave a hard-established mini-empire of shops – Cowen's – along the Great North Road and head south to London. My ancestry site search had been an attempt to cast the net wider. To mine the public records as well as the private.

Dragging the cursor around the wall of news type, I found his full name – John William Cowen – under an unexpected headline:

GASSED IN BED ... NIGHTDRESS SLEEVE THAT MIGHT HAVE TURNED TAP. It was a brief, disturbing report on a coroner's inquiry held in Doncaster. No chance of mistaken identity. John William Cowen was described as a 'fried fish dealer' and employer of three girls – Agnes Bolton, Emily Loughton and fifteen-year-old Doris Coles – at '16 North Bridge-road'. I remembered mention of a shop at that location and that North Bridge-road *was* the Great North Road.

The report stated that on the preceding Friday, the girls, who lived above the shop and café and shared a bedroom, were up talking until after midnight with a gas lamp on. Bill was making his way upstairs when he noticed their light under the door. In her testimony, Emily said Bill had knocked and called out: 'Now, Emily, what about that light?' Doris Coles was already asleep, so, reaching over Agnes, Emily had turned the gas lamp off. Or believed that she had. When questioned, Emily stated she thought she may have caught the gas tap in the cuff of her nightdress and, in the act of pulling away, had inadvertently opened it up again. When Bill knocked on their door early the next morning, he found all three unconscious 'snoring and breathing very heavily'. The room full of gas, the window open a crack. The article gives little beyond the fact that Agnes and Emily recovered, but Doris never woke up, succumbing to gas poisoning that afternoon. The closing sentence: 'A verdict of "Accidental death" was returned.'

The first thing I did was search through the repository of photographs I'd been sent of Bill and the family again, to look into his eyes. For what, I'm not sure. A sign? Something registering? The weight of a tragedy carried in his face? There was nothing. A couple of emails and phone calls later, I'd ascertained that no one alive in the family knew about this. No relative had ever mentioned it. There was shock all round. The article mentioned Doris's father, George, had been a joiner in the Bentley mine, meaning he and Bill would have known each other. Putting the kids to bed that night, tucking up Bea, turning off the little lamp by her bed, it flashed into my mind again just as it must have done with Bill for the rest of his life. The funeral, the guilt, seeing Doris's father daily on the street. *Were these part of the reason for leaving Doncaster?* Only the dates didn't stack up. The accident was 1923, but the family didn't flee until more like 1936. Even so, it was a lesson. Dig the seam and you best be prepared for what appears.

It's not all fairy tales. Lives get lost as well as saved. We can't be sure what these ghosts we summon might want to show us.

*

Stilton is the archetype road story. A small village along the great highway that boomed between the seventeenth and mid-nineteenth centuries, finding itself, at one point, with fourteen pubs and inns servicing the coaching and posting trades. In the 1830s, forty-two coaches and mails, plus innumerable post-chaises, surged down Stilton High Street every twenty-four hours. At its peak, postmasters would forgo a wage and pay a £40 levy just to secure a position in the village, knowing the potential for earnings. The main drag is a time capsule of old cottage, grand house and coaching inn sealed up and buried with the overnight rise of the railways (two miles east) then reanimated again with the dawning of the age of the motor car. Now it finds itself off-highway once more, bypassed by a bump in the line of the modern eight-lane motorway, unseen to drivers gunning for refuels and refreshments at Peterborough Services four miles to its north.

To reach it we cross a bridge over the A1(M) in an intensifying downpour. Darkness closing in like Indian ink poured into the dank sky. The zip, sigh and frenzy of speeding freight and cars; blurs of white headlamps and red brake lights streaking by. The grey road a snowmelt river thundering beneath the trembling gantry.

The Bell Inn is Stilton's real museum piece – a building dating back to the year the civil wars broke out, with a painted sign on a wrought-iron bracket, mullioned windows, a frontage of buttery stone. All work to prevent the erosion of memory. So too the tattooed arch that picks up distance duties from the Alconbury signpost: 'To LONDON 74 / HUNTINGDON 12 / BUCKDEN 14 / STAMFORD 14 miles.' Through the glass entrance, over strains of Cliff Richard's 'Millennium Prayer', smartly dressed staff are busy servicing nostalgia seekers in the know who like their hit of the coaching age with a hint of luxury. The literature, available on request, details the litany of famous ex-guests: Dick Turpin (obviously, complete with a fabricated escape from a top window) and Clark Gable and Joe Louis sneaking out for whiskies when stationed at nearby US airbases during the war. Darting straight to their bedrooms is a smattering of suited road professionals with no interest in the place beyond its AA three-star-rated dining. In a quiet corner, an elderly couple that used to stop here in the 1950s smile at younger lovers who've made the drive into the dark countryside from Peterborough. After grimace-smiles at the sight of our waterproofs dripping on to the carpet, a room key is found with an apology – the restaurant is fully booked tonight. No tables available. No chance to try the inn's famous export. 'No. Sorry. Not unless you have it for your breakfast?'

The export in question: Stilton cheese. The Bell is no stranger to its hard sell. In the 1740s, the landlord was the man who first began buying a blue-veined matured cheese for his dining room from a 'Mrs Paulet' in Wymondham in Leicestershire. Noting its popularity, he had the idea of offering it to passing coaches from outside the inn. Before long, it was flying off the dairy's shelves. Although the cheese was made elsewhere, it was Stilton – its place of sale – that stuck as the name. The rival inn opposite, the Angel, wanted a slice. In the early 1800s, a Miss Worthington is recorded as pushing the product harder. Her angle being that hers was the genuine Stilton cheese. A stab at authenticity that backfired when a coach passenger, who was local and knew the story, asked if her cheese was, in fact, *real* Stilton. She confirmed it was, saying it was made right there at the Angel. The trap was sprung. Stilton came from Leicestershire; whatever aberration she was making wasn't worth considering.

We duck out of the Bell to try our luck on the other side of the Great North Road at the Angel, reborn now as the 'Angel Spice' Indian restaurant. Curry is the road walker's preferred sustenance anyway. It's what the body craves. Spices and chilli to cut through the tongue-coating of exhaust fumes; rice to replenish expended calories. We fall into conversation with two women on the table next to ours who immediately tell us they're not on a date. 'Although I've given up men,' one says.

'Bollocks you have,' her friend counters. 'You're only thirty.'

'It's true. I'm thinking of trying a dating site. Would you two go on one? The big problem for me is that I don't, *I can't*, love anybody as much as I love my dogs.'

Her tone is funny, full-throttle. She fires questions at us. *What are you doing? Why? Where are you from? Are you two married? To each other?* Her accent is strong, local. Over pints of beer, she tells us she was born in Sawtry, the village we passed a few miles down the road. I hear in her pronunciation two words: *salt-tree*. 'That's what it was!' she says. 'Sawtry was where they brought the salt from the fens to the road to sell. The wagons and coaches picked it up and took it off everywhere.'

A is listening, plate still full. His eating speed, always a thousand chews per mouthful, has slipped down another gear. But it's difficult to resist her energy, her burst-epiphanies: 'D'you know what?' she says. 'I think every problem in my life has been because I overthought something. I went with head, not heart. We all overthink everything. I genuinely believe that. Then those safe choices take us down wrong turns where we don't want to be. And then *they don't even work out.* Ha! You take the safe route and *wham*; life fucks you anyway. So, what's the lesson? In the end, we might as well go with our hearts and take the chances. I wish I'd taken more chances.'

She slips out to the toilet. Her friend leans in. 'She is the best. She was with a man who . . .' A shake of the head. 'He was an abusive shit. Put it that way. Took a long time for her to leave him, but it can be hard to move on sometimes, right?'

When her friend returns, she has news. They are going out in Peterborough. Right now. The bill paid. Taxi booked. No arguing. 'It's Saturday night and it's *your* two's fault anyway,' she says, thumping my arm. 'I want to do something now. Maybe we'll do a Thelma and Louise. Maybe we'll just ride off into the sunset . . .'

'Yeah?' her mate interrupts, pulling on her jacket. 'And what about your dogs?'

'Fine. Peterborough it is, then. But tomorrow? Who knows?'

In our room, I can't sleep. I lie listening to 'Little Gidding' again on headphones, my mind filling with thoughts of the ghost road, the civil wars, where our current situation may lead. I close my eyes as Alec Guinness intones: 'If I think of a king at nightfall / Of three men, and more, on the scaffold . . .' The king is Charles Stuart, but when hearing this line on the road before I'd failed to consider the others. Now it occurs to me that they must be Cromwell, Bradshaw and Ireton.

The men whose corpses were dug up and hanged in chains at Tyburn in 1661 during the Restoration – when crowds were kneeling and raising their hands in blessing at Charles II's victorious return and crowning. Those scaffolded three were posthumously punished for their parts in the king's beheading. Yet when Charles I's head had been lifted from its bloody basket in 1649, no one could have imagined events turning out as they would twelve years later. Isn't this the cycle of things? Political experiments falter and fail. Ineffectual leaders fall away. The public grow to resent false promises undelivered. A new generation emerges eager to overturn the decisions made by the previous one. Repeats and echoes.

Listening to 'Little Gidding' again I hear something else in Eliot's words too – the reminder that we are all united in time. 'These men, and those who opposed them / And those whom they opposed / Accept the constitution of silence / And are folded in a single party.' The line hangs in the darkness. Pure memento mori. Cromwell, Stuart, insert any name – we're all ultimately destined to become the past, the dead. Whatever our oppositions in life, our earthly differences evaporate once we're laid in the earth. We're all pressed together into the same pages of history. And suddenly I'm thinking of that newsprint of the *Leeds Mercury* – of scanning for my great-grandfather's name. Of that poor girl, Doris Coles, who fell asleep and never woke up. And I'm thinking of my own children, of the way they reach up to hold my hand.

An early milk-haze morning. Grey, damp. A February, but not our February. A February forty-two years earlier in 1975. A man is walking through a ploughed field near the village of Water Newton. The A1, upgraded in 1958, rushes past in intermittent crescendos just beyond a belt of hawthorn. Glancing at a furrow and a freshly dug rabbit hole, he spies something. A black pot that he takes for pewter. Crouching, investigating, he begins to uncover what will turn out to be a hoard of Roman treasure: silver bowls, plates, flagons, a chalice and numerous votive triangular plaques with nail holes in their centres. Many are engraved or embossed with a symbol. An 'X' intersected by the letter 'P' – the 'Chi-Rho' monogram formed from the first two letters of 'Christ' in Greek.

The hoard sends ripples of excitement through archaeological circles. Engravings whisper through time of offerings made, vows fulfilled. It will soon be recognised as the earliest Christian silverware discovered in the Roman Empire. It was buried at the bottom of one of the defensive ditches encircling Durobrivae, the walled town that grew up around a fort built early in the Roman occupation at the point where Ermine Street crossed the River Nene. The town's footprint spread beyond its walls. Wealthy farmsteads, villas; the hinterlands to its north developed into ironworks facilities. To the west, potteries, kiln sites – centres of production for a ceramic known as Nene Valley Colour Coated Ware that was exported all over the empire. That same style of pottery that I'd seen hand-drawn depictions of back on the dig near Catterick.

Durobrivae was long-known to be a transport hub in the east of England, listed under 'Iter V' in the Antonine Itinerary, the part-surviving second-century register of distances and stations along Roman roads. But it would be aerial photography that really showed its bones. Fields disclosed the polygon shape of a fort, the extents of its town, its districts. Look at satellite imagery now and you see it, faintly, there, like a shadow town under the land. Through it all: the long, straight thread of Ermine Street.

*

Our February. Dull, grey. A thundering highway slick with freezing rain. Mud-field under a cloche of pale glass. We beat the bounds of the A1's roadside pastures to reach Water Newton. On the map it is little more than an exaggerated layby. Its only thoroughfare ('Old North Road') a strand of fibre connected at both ends, worked loose from the thick rope of the dual carriageway veering west to avoid the river. Step away from the pull and push of the trunk road and a preserved village emerges. Drowsy, quaint stone houses with small windows; numb lawns, weeping willows. Rooks cawing in morning mist. A snapshot England cut from a vintage motoring annual. We skulk along a hedge using satellite imagery to try and find the location of Durobrivae. There are no footpaths. It is fence jumping or nothing. Muck, rain, wet grass, sprays of thistle; stands of dripping blackthorn. Cars swishing past, north and south. 'We're here,' A says, slipping his phone into his jacket. A grassy bank and ditch are all that can be determined of past habitation. The brain has work to do to imagine the lost shapes of architecture, the high town gates and enclosing walls packed with travellers, livestock, wagons and soldiers – to conceive of a sprawling mass of stink, smoke and fire, of out-of-town warehouses and gleaming villas, of street after street of workshops, homes and inns, built and rebuilt over four centuries.

The deep, glaze-green River Nene is bordered by thick beds of head-high rushes. To cross it we return to Water Newton and chance a lane leading down to water meadows and an old mill near a Norman church. Sheltering inside as another fenland monsoon erupts, stories bubble up from the walls and floors. The slab to one native son of the village, Edward Edwards, catches A's eye. He sits in a pew, opens the laminated folder of church history. Edwards was baptised in this church before leaving for the saltwater of the sea and the navy, aged seventeen. In 1790 he was appointed captain of the *Pandora*; the frigate tasked by the Admiralty to pursue and round up the mutineers from the *Bounty*. By anyone's standards, it was a failed mission. Trawling the South Seas and the Pacific islands he'd captured just ten of the crew when his ship foundered on the Great Barrier Reef and sank with four of the mutineers and thirty-one of his own men drowning. Like Captain Bligh before him, he faced an arduous open-boat voyage of survival before making it back to England with seventy-eight of his 134-strong crew and four hostages remaining. In the court martial that followed, Edwards was exonerated, but no other ship would be trusted to him. He took desk jobs, rose to the rank of admiral and died in 1815, his body returned to this church on the banks of the Nene to be buried.

Crossing the water on a lock gate, we pick up Ermine Street again. The Roman road is a laser-line from Durobrivae north-west to meet another fenland river, the Welland, before bending north for Lincoln. Writing in 1724, Defoe described the visible 'Roman causeway' between these two rivers. Though much reduced and buried, it remains evident: a long, low ridge under a patchwork of fields and woods, like an arm thrust under a duvet. Our intention: trace it all the way to Stamford.

The cancelled road is a path through middle distance, but you need to hold your nerve. It requires an indifference to fences, the clambering over barbed wire. Beating through bushes, we ford the panic-rush

of the A47. The hump of the track becomes a rise again, then a dark stain in soil. The whole exercise is a rerunning back of time. The Roman causeway cuts through woods that are clones of the woods that were here before the causeway was constructed. We cook up lunch – soups, ration packs – on stoves among the dead winter trees and wet leaf litter, then follow the undeletable line onwards again across the open fields.

This is the mission: *follow*. After a good sleep in a real bed, *A* is trying to get a fix on a wider potential project he's been mulling over. His notion is a pragmatic one: the whole scramble up the highway from London to Edinburgh, the sheer experience of it, should be made accessible. A right to roam meets a rite of passage, for anyone with the mind to travel it. Or not. 'It could, *should*, be the new national service,' he suggests, 'and a compulsory requirement for every politician seeking power. Think about it. A modern pilgrimage through home soil. Nobody returns unaltered.'

I know what he means; what he's hoping for. The heightened senses when taking the road; the self-induced derealisation. The enchantment that comes with it. A sense of being embodied and embedded in a bigger world, of being part of a strange, living, complicated history that works on and through us. Empathy and connection.

Transformations don't happen overnight, but gradually, subtly, they can occur. It might even take others to notice them. I tell *A* about how, over the months since we were last on the road, it's been pointed out to me that I am sharing things I didn't talk about before. One evening, in the midst of boxing up our things and moving the family from our flooded house, I began recalling for Rosie the night my dad left. In all our time together, I had never done that. But that night, as we wrapped the contents of our cupboards in paper, I recounted everything that I remembered, walking her through the dark details and difficulties of the years that came after with Mum on the moor. How it felt. How it still feels. Another time, I brought it up with a friend that I know went through similar experiences, but who's never mentioned them. I was shocked at how easily his memories and emotions had arrived afterwards. How cathartic it can be to break the codes of silence and give voice to denied years. Harder was to raise these things with Mum and Dad, but it also felt important to try. I've always been worried about upsetting them, yet both listened as I stumbled through my words. I shied away from the tougher stuff, but a door was opened a little. A conversation begun. One I know I've needed to have for a long time and one I'll be having for the rest of my life. It's exactly this potential that *A* wants to explore. The way the road can shift set patterns and our ways of thinking and being. The way it seems to erase and remake who we are.

Mist closes in like smoke, growing denser with the afternoon's plummeting temperature, creeping over the muted fields, curtaining the spectral extents of Ermine Street. On the outskirts of Burghley Park, the shadow of the ghost road morphs into footpath, track, then a broad weave stitched through sheep pasture. The worsening weather reveals vague approximations of estate walls, scraps of game cover, streams and bare oaks. Further on, we're aware of moving through equestrian plains. Looming out of the fog come Land Rover-sponsored jumps, fences, water barriers. All are revealed, then immediately cloaked over again by the leaf-rot, fire-scented whiteout.

*

Burghley is John Clare territory. England's peasant poet and mad wanderer of the Great North Road was born and lived in Helpston, five miles east, but he was briefly apprenticed at the big house as a gardener. Significantly, it was here that the Damascene moment struck, that the yearning to scratch out verse took hold. Cutting back homeward from a bookseller's in Stamford, lumbering along the same vanished road we're on, Clare jumped the estate wall to lose himself in a newly purchased copy of James Thomson's poem *The Seasons*. This would be, in Iain Sinclair's words, 'the fatal book'. The hook. The pact. Clare was, in his own words, lured 'into a strain of descriptive rhyming on my journey home' that would split his soul and seal his destiny as (firstly) an effortlessly gifted labourer-composer – one of a sheaf of erstwhile, dirt-under-nails rural poets fashionable among the book-buying public and London's literary elite – and (later) as lunatic pauper-poet. A stranger to his own life writing verses for loose change. In his monumental shadow-study of the man, *Edge of the Orison*, Sinclair captures him up before the dawn, tramping the miles from Helpston to Stamford along an echo-line imprinted with his own previous drifts:

> *He overtook earlier selves, plodding ahead of him. The village boy on his errands, seeing shapes in the dark, Fen spirits, soul stealers. The drunken youth returning to Burghley with fellow labourers, wall at a tilt, to sleep under a tree ... Clare is the supreme articulator of the mundane. Self-appointed laureate of a corner of disputed land. His accounts of Helpston's flora and fauna become a series of brief lives, genealogies of lichen, snail shells, stones. His separate existence, divorced from these things, is an unstable fiction.*

London drove a wedge. Clare left his disputed land and took the long rattle down the Great North Road on the Regent coach, climbing aboard at the George in Stamford. A necessary journey for the poet whose *Poems Descriptive of Rural Life and Scenery* (1820) was peaking in sales, but a wrench in his sense of self. Quoting Clare biographer Edward Storey, Sinclair notes the road's on-rush of sensations, the altered perception, the shift: '[H]e fancied that he'd changed his identity as well as his occupation, that he was not the same John Clare but some strange soul that had jumped into his skin.'

Such is the tension of the highway – the interspace somewhere between leaving and remaining. The overlaying of inner and outer maps. The coach wheel liberated Clare from his place of birth, but the landscape that knew him and gave him meaning was an immovable filter. It was a prism through which he measured and understood. He began to live between two selves and two places. In one slide: the peasant with an ever-growing family to feed, picking over once-familiar fields, harvesting newly enclosed land. Then click: the poet, plucked from soil, exhibited, wined, gawped at like a curiosity. Wide-eyed, green as his trademark jacket. In subsequent journeys to London, between ego-meets with his publishers, awkward afternoons with patrons, visits to theatres, churches, fights, the wandering, drunken nights and stumbles to bedrooms through forbidding streets, he projected Helpston over London, attempting to merge the two maps into sense, walking the streets in the same tramping circles of enquiry and discovery he had as a lad at home. By the time of his fourth trip, in 1828, he'd been chewed up and spat out. The fashion for him had passed. Mental illness and depression were plaguing his days. Drink was always the poison of choice of the dispossessed – a suspension state for the mind that can't fully go back, or move on. Clare took to it, driven to despair trying to square that circle: a need to earn money versus a need to write.

His identity became less certain as his sense of self slipped further. He was possessed by people, none of them much good to his wife, Patty, and his seven children at home. Interned at the suggestion of his publisher in a private asylum at High Beach in Epping Forest in Essex, Clare believed himself a prize-fighter, then Lord Byron, whose funeral cortège he'd seen in London (two days before Caro encountered it at Brocket Hall). He also declared that he'd been Shakespeare, but 'I'm John Clare now'.

In 1841, homesick, he absconded and walked the eighty miles back up the Great North Road to Helpston, returning (he thought) to Mary Joyce, his first love, whom he believed his wife, but who'd actually died three years earlier. It is this desperate Clare that stalks the highway. A warped reflection of the man who left Stamford heading south. A ditch-sleeper, chewing grass to stave off starvation, begging for bread. A man who would soon be committed to the asylum at Northborough for the rest of his life.

This Clare was a returning spectre in a different sense: the ghost of the sixteenth-century rural poor of the north road that had their own connections to Burghley. The great house was built by William Cecil, chief adviser and treasurer to Elizabeth I and co-orchestrator of the Elizabethan Poor Laws. Unease about 'idleness' and concerns about money was rife among the queen's Parliament and in the City of London. Poverty becoming endemic. Following the dissolution of the monasteries and the outlawing of pilgrimage in 1538, the roads had been left to rot. Gone the intricate networks of rural employment and any duty of care to travellers. Twinned with the pressure of Tudor land enclosure for wool, it had resulted in huge numbers of the poor hitting the roads in search of any kind of work or relief. Fearing the mob, rebellion, disease, Elizabeth and Cecil had launched a punitive response in 1572, branding the jobless itinerants as vagabonds and rogues to be whipped away from parish boundaries. A second offence for beggary could see a hole burned through your ear. A third, death.

One route left open to the destitute was to leave for the sea. South-wards lay the shipyards and recruiting offices of new merchant companies and privateers. To the north, displaced labourers and land-workers could turn their hands to the ocean's bounties. In the words of Frank Morley, the Great North Road became 'a spillway', its wandering ghosts siphoned off into crews for fishing fleets at Hull and Whitby. Encouraged by Elizabeth's subsidies and declarations (no one to eat meat on Wednesdays, Fridays, Saturdays), these boats worked the watery commons offshore. Others began to venture further into unchartered seas (Greenland, Iceland, Spitsbergen) after a greater prey – the whale. In the centuries after, it was oil rendered from the blubber of these whales that would light the lamps of writers like John Clare and turn night into day in cities the world over. It would be the proto-industrial hunting of the whale that would usher in new levels of exploitation of nature by mankind. And it would be the sight of a sixty-foot right whale, stranded and then slaughtered on the shore at Deptford near London in 1658, that even enlightened folk took as a portent of the death of Oliver Cromwell, who died in the September of that year. One leviathan coming to pay its respects to another, as one biographer put it.

*

Evening closing fast. A security lamp is diffused into a misted moon at the edge of Burghley's parkland. We hear the Great North Road again through the saturated gloom. The line of the Roman road con-joins the highway in a long curve down into Stamford, towards the river. When we reach the George, night has fallen. This honeyed town – described in road books as the 'finest on the highway' – with its clusters of churches, squares, mazy passageways; its twisting, tip-ping, rising thoroughfare – will have to wait until morning. The full reveal is always Stamford's preferred introduction anyway. Off-A1 detours shock by delivering up an ancient inland port and road cross-ing, a medieval university town with all the accoutrements: fine architecture, resentful locals, the binge drinking. A condensed Oxford or Cambridge transposed to a leafy fold in Lincolnshire.

The George provides a shortcut through Stamford's history. Less a place than a portal to be moved through. A feeling amplified as you pass under its eighteenth-century 'gallows' sign stretching across the road, doubling as both welcome and warning to travellers, depending on intentions. Within the building, shape-shifting walls, rooms and halls are composites from millennia of use. Stone-still, still moving. Remnant features from its time as a hostelry and hospital for knights and pilgrims making for Jerusalem, grudgingly accept re-imaginings as the 'Garden Room' or 'Business Centre'. Given the right mix of gut-tering candles and good wine, guests still get glimpses of cowled shadows staggering ahead of them as they climb the stairs.

Cromwell is rumoured to have overnighted here following the siege of Royalist positions at Burghley, 1643. Charles I's stays are more formally noted: 23rd August 1645 – a year before he returned to town as a hunted man. His last evening of freedom was spent in Stamford; the next day he met the Scottish army he hoped would support him, but that sold him to Parliament. A century on, the 'bloody' Duke of Cumberland, Butcher of Culloden, took dinner here on his way down the north road after mercilessly routing the army of Charles I's great-grandson, Bonnie Prince Charlie, on a Scottish moor. Tonight, tired and packed into the heat and din of the dining room that hosted them, we feel the crowding-in of connections. The temptation is to wonder: *What is going on? Surely there must be some meaning to it all?* The answer is always more prosaic: survival, conviction, the chaos of his-tory. More than anywhere, places like the George testify to the truth of that Eliot line about being folded 'in a single party'. We who remain will join all of those who have left. Each of us is only ever passing through.

*

At the entrance, two rooms either side of the corridor. Legacies of the coaching age. One titled LONDON for those, like John Clare, head-ing south; the other, YORK, for the north. I have a cheap room for the night in a different pub. A needs to hurry to make the train back to Salisbury, back to the desert. Then another long posting abroad. The next time we meet, A will be in a hospital bed recovering from a tumour the size of a fist being cut from his liver. Surgical punctures like bullet holes across his abdomen; the consultant commenting on his tattoo. '*In manus tuas domine*? What does that mean?' We do not know this now, of course, but we both know that we are at another fork in the highway. Shouldering packs, we shake hands between those rooms. South and north. Taking opposite directions, opposite roads, we walk off into the dark.

Genius Loci

(Stretton)

The road wanted to live. It envied the deer, wolf, snake and spider; it envied the trees and the grasses. It envied the wind and fire, the stars. It envied, most of all, the river. Earth-bound, land-locked, the road groaned under the thickness of forest, it struggled under tussock and bramble and stone. It raged and cried. It pleaded to enter the world. It tore at the underside of things, yet it could not be born. So, it bided its time under the skin of the land, among the atoms, among the dirt and death. Imprisoned, it imagined itself: blood-black, smooth-skinned, hissing louder than the snake, flowing more mightily than the river, devouring grass and forest, humbling the wolf with its skill for the kill, feeding on Earth's minerals and materials, hacking back up what couldn't be digested. It imagined power the way a child does. It saw itself shining, spreading in every direction as spiderlings hitch infant webs to the wind. And as it dreamed it felt a foot, then another, pressing down upon the ground above. A host. It sensed the light and it smelled dawn; it suckered to a sole, bit, and slipped into the open wound, taking root in the blood and brain. Taking form in the forming mind.

I was here. I saw everything. I lived for a long time as the breeze. I had no history, no tangible existence. Then, suddenly, I did. Like all places I was conjured into being. I remember three men and four women, survivors of death, one of whom the others feared was cursed for she could *see*. She knew that I was here. They lit a fire and made a clearing. They put up their smoke and cut timbers. Before walls and roof were finished, the woman with foresight stole away from the camp as the others slept. She was the one who kneeled and petitioned me; who willed me into being and asked that I protect this place. She made offerings, burying them in the mud. Coin. Eggs. Elder. Yarrow. The road was already old by then and it watched my becoming.

Spin the world. Forests grow and shrink. Sun and moon slip through changing skies. The nodding wheat and barley noses up and then is cut. Snow blankets and melts. The road remains. The road and its souls. Someone always arriving. Someone always leaving and never coming back. Someone trying to find a way home. Some kind, some cruel. Most indifferent to anything more than staying fed and warm and alive. I never forget the faces. They move through here for ale or to collapse into a bed or the barn straw and pass the night in safety. People live and die; someone takes over. They build and change. Lime plaster to stone. Thatch to slab and tile. Pigs in the yard; ale in the store. Some know I'm here. They speak to me at night. Some pray that I will disappear.

Spin again. There are crops burning. A church on fire. Men mad with God feed the road with blood. Smoke, black, vaulting the horizon. Farmhands in soldier cloth, soon to die, eyeing maids as they pass. One child I recall was a gift of a boy. Thirteen. Hands too small to wield a pike. I tried to speak to him as he filled up on water. My voice was the creak of the well's wheel. The slam of the shutter. The crow of the cockerel. I tried, but he wouldn't hear. When they rabbled back again, those halting men, limping, thinned, they couldn't look the maids in the eye. And the boy was not among them.

I have no sense of time as you do. No fear of time. Time is not as you understand it. But there is a great emptiness for many seasons. The roof falls in. Timber is wormy, rotted. The barn burns. Stone is hacked out, lifted into carts and taken for houses in Stretton. The sundial lies upturned in the yard. One afternoon I watch a man arrive by horse. Batting away flies, cursing the stench, he carefully scratches numbers in a ledger: *1703*. And beside them, *Winchelsea Arms*. He stands for a long time looking up and down the road. He comes back with others. They dig out the well and clear the orchard. They rebuild walls and make new rooms with new stone. As he digs into the earth floor, one of the workers, a lad with pox scars who cannot hear, finds the muddy old coins buried by the wall. He slips them into his clothes and in that moment becomes aware of me. When he returns the next day, he is afraid. When no one is watching, he buries them again in the same place asking me to forgive him. When he cuts his arm, I save the wound from festering. I show him the yarrow patch and he binds a handful of the feathery leaves into his opened flesh. A shield with arms is painted and nailed over a new oak door. Meat roasts over charcoal.

I see light. Candles, whale oil lamps. The glow of fires. The shapes and sounds of souls fill the parlour rooms. Sodden shadows from the coaches bundled up against the cold. Staggering fieldhands in summer sup hard on harvest pay. The noise is laughter and gossip, parley, threat. The smell is meadowsweet and straw strewn over wet floor, beer and sweat. And horses. Beneath the pomades, the caps, lavender wigs, the clinging smoke of damp wood, horse-sweat in the seams, the leather, in the pores. My voice is the rattle of harnesses, the mew of kites, the tick and spit of fires, the barking and singing of the tavern at night, the heavens hammering the stone road, the wind rattling the panes of glass. I see light and dark, the darkness of the highway made deeper by the night-glow of the windows. I see on a cold, rainy night the men drift in from the darkness shouting out for the keeper to be woken and the groom to attend. The pale girl who sleeps by the scullery does not heed my warnings: my rising howl in the chimney, the stoneware I push off the table. They beat her in the mud and straw until the keeper opens the doors to the cellar, and empties the coin drawer. She dies lying in the rain and mud, but she does not leave. There are many who will come as these men do and many keepers who will become allies, stashing coin and jewels under boards, making it their own when those road men are hanged and gibbeted.

The road brings them all. It brings a short man with broad shoulders, a keeper who walks with a limp. I glean from his memory that he was once an officer's servant to a son of the Earl of Winchelsea in India. And that after nursing his master back from death he was promised a position. I know he can sense me. Pushing open the door, his eyes become accustomed to the dark and he says loudly: 'May I enter?' A maid frowns, bemused. She answers, not realising he's speaking to me. I notice the way he concocts spirits in the cellar, his sleeves rolled up, mixing the egg and rum and sugar; how thirstily it is drunk in the parlour. When she asks him, the man tells the maid to call it Ram Ján for it is the name of the Indian servant who brings rum to the officer's table. 'Or Rum Johnny,' he laughs. 'For they call them that too.' She turns on the stair and grins, arms full of bottles. 'Ram Jam is more favourable to my ear, sir.' By the time they are married the next summer, all that come here call this place the Ram Jam House.

Then they are gone, and their son too, becoming part of me like every soul passing through, like the passageways and walls and rooms that appear and disappear. The nests in the eaves. The hollyhocks that rise, die, seed and rise again by the door.

Spin the world. Dawn after dawn. Sundown after sundown. The road is alive. Light on coach brass. Lanterns approaching out of pitch-blackness. Postboys leading shays. I could give you names, secrets. Like Mary Hobbs, her back still smarting from the buckle of her husband's belt, dragging a blade over his throat in the smallest bedroom. Waiting in the parlour below are Tom Moody and Sarah Storing and Jane Lister. See Jane hide the razor and wash her sister's nightgown clean of blood. See Old Moody burning and burying the body three miles away. Not one of them regrets it; not one of them will be discovered. See all of it. The laughter and the crying; the gatherings and farewells. The dancing, the fucking and the fighting. See the souls that become aware of me on their creaking way up the stairs. See how I show them shapes in the shadows. The way they learn to hear my voice in the clatter of horseshoes on the turnpike, the slam of glasses, the fiddler's bow being drawn across the string.

A cold dawn brings no light. No lanterns in the dark. No postboys. No shays. Slow, blue, mist-mornings give way to empty days. Shabby traps and dog carts. Most souls that come traipse over the fields from Stretton. The *street*-town. Born of the road too. Stories are told by the fire that have no truth in them. Mouths that talk of the Ram Jam Inn talk of things that never happened. Memories are fictions. The keeper, a widow, lights a pipe each evening by the wall. She watches smoke billowing on the horizon. She tells me that I'm a figment of her imagination. So I show her the maid who was beaten in the rain and still runs down the passage. The next morning, she packs and leaves. The hollyhocks topple and don't grow any more. Dock and nettle forest the yard. The road refuses to die; it only sheds one skin and then grows another. It knows what is coming.

Spin the world again. A hard, black river. A trickle followed by a flood. The tang of tarmac. And passing over it, the high-whine engines and hum of rubber wheels. Gummy lead-air sticky with summer honeydew; the dirty wet highway spray of winter. The parlours are full, so the walls move. Rooms change shape. Teams of men who think of France and howl sometimes in their sleep build huge stone gables, bars, lounges and kitchens, new buildings, chimneys, corridors, cupboards. Mullioned windows. Leaded glass. I read the intent in their minds to create a past that never was. I try to show them true images, but the one who is the most susceptible dismisses me as fatigue. Hallucination. Just the whisky he stashes in his tent. He says nothing. Garages are riveted over the orchard. A name, RAM JAM INN, is lettered in stone and set into a wall above the old sundial, discovered under an uprooted elder. A sign is painted and hung.

In the clouds, I glimpse patterns. Vapour trails. Along the road, I watch the flow. The waves of moving metal. The fur-splatter of beasts torn open across the tarmac. The crows, kestrels. My voice is Adele Dixon singing 'The Magic Rays of Light' on the radio.

I see change. The air bursts with fire, smoke trails. Then clears.

Seasons turn. Spring warms the slates; winter powders them. Snow muffles the steps. Once the fields and woods made the loudest noise. A thousand voices in the trees. The wind hissing through the wheat. Now the front windows rattle in their frames. Vibrations shiver shelves of glasses over the bar. The keeper wears a badge: MANAGER. He has ideas of a swimming pool, a conference suite. He instals velvet curtains and clears room for a dance floor. He opens late for bands travelling the highway and stands, a silhouette in the doorway, watching for lights approaching in the darkness again. He serves them egg and chips, pints of Courage. They are road souls. Someone always arriving. Someone always leaving and never coming back. Someone trying to find a way home. Girls with nothing and everything money could buy that have the highway within them. That hate their prescribed paths. Boys, raving and drunk, unsure of what they seek, and don't know how or who to ask. I sense their emptiness, their loneliness, their stasis, like they've just been born. They sit and they watch the cars hammering north, south, waiting for meaning to descend, feeling their disconnection like grief. I speak to them but most cannot hear me. My voice is the pitch of motorcycles, the sea-roar of passing cars. It is the sound of slamming doors, a shout, an engine revving and the squeal of tyres. It is a man sobbing in his room alone. It is the jukebox in the lounge playing Geno Washington and the Ram Jam Band's 'Black Betty'.

Spin the world once more. Three men and four women wait for fish and chips. One of them came here as a girl. I remember her face; how she counted cars with her father and noted the colours down in thick crayon. The men drink and type angrily on their phones. *NO STARS. Sh*t hole* and *Gone to the dogs.* When they leave, the manager reads what they've posted on the back-office computer. The road moans through the dirty glazing. By the winter, there is no one left. Boards screwed over the windows. Fencing across the yard. Steel shutters mask the door. A curling calendar hangs on a peeling wall with HAPPY 2012 on the front. A young man and his girlfriend break in one night and sleep in the east lounge among scattered chairs and litter. She knows I'm here. They buy food and beer from the petrol station next door and they eat it under the unbroken stained-glass window. In his sleep, he holds her belly.

I make the lights flash and music sound in the lounge. There is no one to hear it. I watch the maid hurrying down the passage and the yarrow, ragwort and elder colonise the car park. I see the boy with a pikestaff too big for his hands walk past the door with his eager face. I hear the fiddlers and the horses. Rooms disappear; the walls pour with rain. My voice is the sigh of collapsing floors. The traffic through broken windows. The shatter-crack of bricks brought down on sinks.

Road souls still pull in to sleep in their lorries. Others come with headtorches and cameras to pick about the mess. They spray symbols on the walls, words: URBAN EXPLORER. They talk down a lens and say things like 'shame' and 'disgusting' as their beams touch upon piles of wet books and abandoned leaflet stands. They peer into holes knocked by men who came here to strip copper and roof lead. Wet ceilings cascade on to floors. Some sense I am here. One man rushes out moaning and swearing when, in an upstairs room, I paint images of John Hobbs with his throat slit in his mind. He sits in his car and fights the urge to be sick when I give him the feelings of emptiness so many have brought here. He doesn't know that you leave something of yourself everywhere you go. He doesn't understand that all of it remains. That just because you can't see something doesn't mean it isn't there.

The road changes. It grows wider, thicker. It watches my slow decay. Not with satisfaction or sadness, but as a rock watches a tree fall and fade into earth. In bright sunlight I see contrasts. Shadows upon shadows. Forms slip free. I can't tell if the world is spinning forward or back. I see things I can't be sure of. Flashes. The road overgrown. Crops burning. Smoke on the horizon. Survivors making shelters. I have no sense of time as you do. No fear of time. Time is not as you understand it. I wait. I wait for the coins under the wall to be found. I wait to become the breeze again.

Gravity

(Thistleton Gap–Grantham)

THE BATTLE between CRIB and MOLINEAUX, fought at Thisfeleton Gap in the County of Rutland Sept. 28.ᵗʰ 1811 for 600 Guineas. it was terminated in
11 rounds, fought in 50 Minutes, in which Crib was Victorius. the Moor was carried off senseless, with a broken Jaw, Crib was but trisling hurt.

I

Enormous skies. Cloud-occluded sun. Stubbled barley, wet with rain, crackling in heat. And stillness. September stillness beneath open blue. The curve of cut fields like a golden coverlet, like a new canvas. Two huge barns. One is an open hangar. Under the remains of a roof, bees drift about slumped hives. Not a soul to be seen anywhere.

A few minutes after twelve o'clock, they mounted the stage (25 feet), CRIBB springing upon it with great confidence and bowing to the spectators ... The Moor *followed and jumped over the railing with considerable spirit. Both the combatants looked well; and Molineaux, for a man of colour, might be termed rather good-looking. The* Moor *seemed disturbed ... [t]he combatants were soon brought to the mark by their seconds.*

A track through stems and scattered-flint soils, towards a farm marked CRIBB'S LODGE. Boundary hedges are three- or four-metre-high impenetrable walls of life. Entanglements of hawthorn, blackthorn, bramble, maple, crab apple. Thrushes. A buzzard feather beneath a toppled oak. My map, its white paper veined with fine black field edges, is like a bee's-wing. Wrong turns are a mile in the correction; a mile through flat expanses of harvested cereals. No way of pushing through.

[B]lows were exchanged. Molineaux received a hit in his throat, which sent him down, though not considered clean. The claret *was perceived to issue first from the mouth of Cribb ... [Then] a most terrible rally took place by mutual consent. The superiority of the Moor's strength*

*evinced by his grasping the body of Cribb with one hand, and his sup-
porting himself by the other ... and threw Cribb completely over on
the stage. To those not* flash *the appearance of things was in favour of
the* Moor ... *Seven to four.*

Intersecting the fields is a disused railway line thick with undergrowth.
A steep shingle bank. It will get me closer, so I hack up its jungle flank
and crawl and climb along. Skin nicked, legs bleeding, I kick up
scorched middens of gravel, logs, farm litter. A dog barks. Jabbing
branches of hazel; skull-knocks from arms of beech.

Molineaux commenced a rally and the punishment *was truly dreadful
on both sides ... Cribb now gave the* Moor *so severe a blow to the
body that it not only appeared to* roll him up, *but seemed as if it had
completely knocked the wind out of him, which issued strong from
his mouth, like smoke from a pipe. The champion pursued him around
the stage ... and concluded the round with a full-length hit which laid
the* Moor *prostrate.*

A tangle of wire pinned down by a riven ash. Heartwood exposed;
branches split open. Beside it, across a gate, the inscribed words:
CRIBBS MEADOW. A rise into high grassland. A glass bottle, semi-
buried in the earth, contains a curl of dandelion on a mat of roots.
Midday. Pure sun now. Sweat. The crowd-roar of the road from
the east.

Molineaux, quite furious, ran in on an intemperate rally ... Cribb
punished *him as severe as can be described, about the neck and jugu-
lar: after the expiration of a minute, the* Moor *fell from weakness ...
It was so evident which way the battle would now terminate that it
was* 'Lombard Street to a China Orange' *Cribb was the conqueror.*

A sea of grasses, thistles. Crickets. Oaks roping a rough boundary.
Gates swung open under silent power cables. This must be the place.
A small box has a strange triangular symbol. Written above, white on
blue, the words: PROTECTION / GROUND BED / *LOCATION.*
White on blue: two clouds over the meadow in the blurred form of

hunched fighters approaching the centre. A fingerpost in the corner reads: DEAD END.

The Moor, in running in, had his jaw broke ... he fell as if dead, from a tremendous left-handed blow ... Molineaux did not come to his time by full half-a minute, but Cribb wished the spectators should fully witness his superiority in giving away this chance, dancing about the stage when he should have been proclaimed conqueror ... the Moor, still game, made a desperate effort and fell from great distress.

There is a stage still where meadow meets B-road. A square of metal security fencing surrounding an electricity substation. Road litter carpeting couch grass. The striking yellow signage: a figure struck down, thunderbolted with the warning DANGER OF DEATH beneath. A roe buck leathering on its side, eyes gone, jaw hanging wide.

Cribb had given another chance *away respecting time, but the* Moor *was in a state of stupor, his senses having been completely* milled *out of him; and upon receiving a* floorer, *he was unable to be got up. Cribb ... beat the* Moor *in* nineteen minutes and ten seconds ... *The hardiest frame couldn't resist the blows of the CHAMPION; and it is astonishing the* Moor *stood them so long. He was taken out of the ring senseless, and could not articulate ... [H]is jawbone and ribs were fractured.*

*

Stories roll beneath old roads, under ancient soil. All you need to disturb them are rough coordinates; the spare time, a willingness to wander. To keep an eye out for happenstance repetitions and echoes. Even buried narratives replay in small, strange ways. Just west of the Great North Road, amid industrial-scale fields where the counties of Lincolnshire, Leicestershire and Rutland conjoin, there is such a place.

Two hundred and seven years ago to the day that I'm standing here, the scene couldn't have been more contrasting. Contemporary estimates put the crowd at 15,000; others, of which the sportswriter Pierce Egan is the most trustworthy, over 20,000. Surviving etchings show masses vying for a view, people standing on coach roofs or 'circus style' on the backs of horses. It was said that a bed could not be bought for twenty miles up or down the highway the night before the fight.

The draw: an all-out, bare-knuckle blood spilling. The dishing out of unchecked punishment between the two greatest fighters of their time: Tom Cribb and Tom Molineaux. Cribb, Bristol-born, a reputation for being able to 'punch the bark off trees', was an ex-bell hanger and coal lugger in the seamier parts of London who'd fought his way to professional and become the undisputed British 'Champion of Champions'. The challenger: young, up-and-coming, American, had already disfigured the faces of some of Britain's most respected contenders to earn his spurs. Molineaux's backstory is more uncertain. A former enslaved person born in the plantations of Virginia in the 1780s who'd won his freedom in brutal slave-on-slave fights, before making for England in a quest for glory and renown. He came to London in 1809 and met his future trainer, Bill Richmond, while drinking in a Leicester Square pub, the Horse and Dolphin, which Richmond owned. Like Molineaux, Bill Richmond was also American, also ex-enslaved, and a man who'd first attracted the attention of Lord Percy, Duke of Northumberland, while brawling with British redcoats in a tavern during the American War of Independence. After making money organising bouts for him, Percy had arranged for Richmond's transportation to northern England in 1777 and set him up with an education and an apprenticeship as a cabinet maker in York. Relentless racism, exacerbated by his marriage to a white Yorkshire woman, led Richmond to brawl for his honour many times, defeating all challengers and earning considerable purses in the process. Notoriety followed. He moved to London and took up more lucrative prize-fighting in his forties. What Richmond recognised in the young Molineaux the night he walked into his pub was raw, pure potential – an unshaped, staggering strength and power. He saw too a chance for vengeance. For all his victories, one fight still plagued him: a counter-punch grudge match he'd lost in 1805. The victor's name: Tom Cribb.

Fights were gruesome spectacles of punching, milling, wrestling, head-butting. Rounds untimed; each lasting until a man was knocked, or thrown, down. He then had thirty seconds to get up again and present himself at 'the scratch'. Hence the idiom: *up to scratch*. Endings only came when one man was physically incapable of rising again. Even by these standards, the first Cribb vs Molineaux meeting in 1810 was reported to have been particularly 'ferocious and sanguinary'. Thirty-nine (ish) rounds; both men battered beyond recognition, mauling in the mud, their own blood and freezing sideways rain; dead on their feet, yet just alive enough to keep swinging before the baying mob. When Molineaux mumbled, 'I can fight no more,' his eyes were swollen shut, his nose split in two places and part of his ear was hanging off. The crowd erupted.

The problem was Cribb didn't win. Not honestly. In the nineteenth round, Molineaux had him pinned on the ropes in a hold he couldn't escape from. With Cribb's strength slipping, the mob surged the stage. Men shoved and clawed to engineer his release. Molineaux's fingers were dislocated in the melee. Then, in the twenty-third round, Molineaux flattened Cribb, leaving him pawing uselessly at the ropes. All knew the champion was done. Thinking quickly, his second, Joe Ward, jumped into the ring, accusing Bill Richmond of concealing pistol balls in his fighter's hands. Nonsense, but the investigation that followed dragged well past the thirty seconds allowed, buying time for Cribb's team to get him up to scratch. It was, by anyone's definition, cheating.

Pierce Egan's writing speaks with the tongue of its time. Prejudices, untruths. His throwaway asides, like Molineaux being rather good-looking 'for a man of colour', aren't the only racism. Yet even he would later write: '[Molineaux's] first contest with *Cribb* will long be remembered by the Sporting World. It will not be forgotten, if Justice holds the scales, that his *colour* alone prevented him becoming the hero of that fight.'

His 'colour'; his country too. Engaged in the Napoleonic Wars, the Peninsular War, the Anglo-Russian War, racking up colonies as it went, and rapidly expanding its industrial, manufacturing and military power, the United Kingdom of Great Britain and Ireland was not in the right place to begin to entertain the idea of a black American ex-slave as a national champion. Worthy adversary, brave challenger, celebrity even, perhaps – but not a *superior*. The American War of Independence had ended in defeat only twenty-seven years earlier and as a beleaguered but cocky Britain changed up the gears on its way to developing the largest dominion in world history, it would have been unconscionable to lose to a man who was formerly the lowest ranked in the new republic. That first fight had been front-page news everywhere and was easily the most high-profile international sporting event ever held at the time. The massive crowd was in no doubt whatsoever that the bout was political as much as personal. Cribb, the double of John Bull with the fighting heart of Nelson, facing down the 'foreigner' foe who'd already battered the best of the competition. The stalwart champion lured out of retirement to restore some national honour. The narrative written and concluded before it began.

Although, perhaps, a more fitting metaphor for Britain's imperial activities, the shamefulness of Cribb's first 'win' that day played on the conscience of more than Pierce Egan. Decency, fairness, sportsmanship – the nation's favourite myths about itself – were called into question. When Molineaux's team published a plea in *The Times* for a rematch, referencing the racially motivated loss, Cribb had little choice but to accept. A date was set, 28th September 1811, when it would be decided, as Egan put it: '[W]hether OLD ENGLAND should still retain her proud characteristics of conquering, or that an AMERICAN, and *a man of colour*, should win the honour … and carry it from the shores of Britain.' The place? Beside the Great North Road.

The harvest in. The fields stubbled. A farmer paid £50 for the loan of his land. Twenty thousand descending on that September morning, including 'principal CORINTHIANS of the state'. MPs, military heroes, other notables fresh from fighting campaigns; all the aristocratic gamblers, such as the Prince of Wales's agent and bet placer, Sir Charles Aston. From first light, a jostling for position. Peers taking to the roofs of their four-in-hand with wine; ale-drunk ploughboys crowding the ropes in clouted boots. Thistleton Gap not only abutted the main highway of Britain, but it was the meeting point of the county lines of Rutland, Leicestershire and Lincolnshire. This mattered. Despite its popularity, the pedigree of its attendees and the vast wagers laid on by royalty, bare-knuckle boxing was technically illegal. These travelling attractions still had to bob and weave with the letter of the law. At Thistleton Gap, if one county official took it upon himself to be difficult, the stage could easily be carried a few yards over the border and the bout restarted. As it happened, all three local magistrates closed court early in order that they might attend the fight.

Cribb spent the night before at the Black Bull at nearby Witham Common. The building is still there, if you look. Now the 'Black Bull Lodge' – an eighteenth-century doll's house sitting at a right angle to the A1 south's hard shoulder. Molineaux took rooms at the New Inn, Greetham. The two men were unrecognisable in condition from their first fight. Cribb, serious, disciplined, mindful of his controversial 'win', had enlisted the help of the Georgian celebrity, Captain Barclay. An amateur boxer and renowned *pedestrian* – when that word still meant an athlete of the feet – Barclay had famously walked a thousand miles in a thousand hours. He held training camps for Cribb at his family's seat in Scotland; stamina-building hikes up and down the north road. Strict diets; a strict regimen. In contrast, Molineaux had revelled in his fame. Prizes, lavish dinners, sparring for cash. Women and drink. His guineas were squandered in brothels, bars. There were rumours of dalliances with high-society wives, actresses. Richmond's daily training a hangover nightmare.

On the morning of the fight, Tom Molineaux devoured a whole chicken, an apple pie and draughts of porter. Hair of the dog. When he made his way through the crowd and climbed on to the stage to see Cribb's hard, muscled frame, he became visibly shaken. As Egan relates in his round-by-round account, the bout was short. Nineteen minutes in total. For all the hype, the months of scrutiny, the money, Cribb hammered Molineaux. A little blood and a swollen eye were nothing to Cribb who danced a hornpipe around the stage while his opponent floundered. Molineaux tried to rally until Cribb broke his jaw. Forced up by his corner, by a furious Bill Richmond, Tom Molineaux staggered forward into a hard left hook. He didn't get up again.

'All the towns upon the North road gained considerably by this contest, particularly those of Grantham and Stamford. [The champion] was cheered through all the towns he passed, after the manner of an officer bearing despatches of a victory, so much was it felt by the people of England.' Egan paints a lurid picture of the aftermath, inserting his own 'impromptu' verses on Cribb's brilliance, mocking Molineaux's enslaved origins. He describes a nation ecstatic; superiority restored. Towns bringing out bunting and beer. Bets cashed. Captain Barclay pocketed £10,000 alone. Cribb was presented with a silver cup and lauded at celebratory dinners.

In the following years the old adversaries Tom Cribb and Bill Richmond would grow surprisingly close. Bankrupted by the Molineaux fight, Richmond was forced to sell his pub and get back in the ring to face men half his age. He trained amateurs, including Lord Byron, and became much-respected among that fight-fancying bastion of privilege: the aristocracy. So much so, in fact, that in 1821 he was chosen to be one of the twelve pugilists ushering at George IV's ridiculously flamboyant coronation. Hamming it up in a Tudor costume, guarding the new king, he stood beside Tom Cribb that day. Eight years later, Richmond spent his last night on earth in Cribb's pub in Piccadilly. Although he couldn't attend because of an attack of gout, it was Tom Cribb who wrote the heartfelt eulogy for Richmond's funeral.

In contrast, Richmond and his protégé's relationship disintegrated after the defeat at Thistleton Gap. Richmond threw Tom Molineaux out of his gym in disgust at his squandering of his once-prodigious talents. Molineaux was forced to travel up the north road to take bouts below his grade in Scotland; he worked a speaking circuit, fought in fields, fairs and squares chalked on the ground. Increasingly booze-ravaged, suffering from consumption, when he crossed the Irish Sea to rinse the last from his celebrity, he was penniless and broken. Collapsing in 1818, he was pitied and nursed by three black drummers who were serving in a British regiment in Galway. But his body was done. He died soon after in the band room of the barracks.

All this, here. The story of a man who, for a time, was as famous as Napoleon. A man who, rightfully, should have been declared the first black heavyweight champion of the world, but who found himself not just competing against another man, but coming up against a nation. Impossible odds. Here, in that last round, slipping his tongue over his broken jaw, dragging himself to the scratch, the desperation, the *great distress* that Egan notes in his demeanour, was the realisation that his chance was gone. Maybe that it was never there. No plaque; no silver

cup for poor Tom. Only strange echoes in this rough meadow. The metal stage of an electricity substation. The coincidence of a DANGER OF DEATH sign. Its man, forever thunderbolted, stricken, is Tom Molineaux who fell here and kept falling.

*

Dead north. Up the narrow, foliate corridor of English pastoral that connects Thistleton Gap with Colsterworth. I'm off-road. Or off-A1 at least, moving along a narrow, western parallel: the 'Old Post Lane'. English elsewhere: prickle-field panoramas fading into hanger woods. Horizons tethered to sky by pylons. The subliminal hum of earth. Chemical sweetness on the lips. Sun reddening the neck.

Walking alone, the nudge of ghosts is inexorable, even in this atomic brightness. Chief among them, my great-grandfather, summoned by all the fighting talk. The discovery of Doris Coles's death under his roof had brought everyone in the family up sharp. A fracturing of the picture. The dirt and grunge of a lived life in all its messy, chaotic, constituent parts. It confirmed what all of us already knew: history,

233

even our own history, is indefinable and slippery. But the shock waves have washed other things to the surface. New evidence to be considered, explored. Old memories to be reappraised.

Bill Cowen was a fighter, literally as much as metaphorically. Weekends in his teens and twenties were spent playing Division III football, but he boxed also. Skills that evidently came in useful. Further passages from his daughter's remembrances have worked their way down to me and include a description of him storming out of the back of one of his fish shops when a customer got 'too saucy' with her at the counter. A beating administered in the street. This was on French Gate in Doncaster; the Great North Road itself. Ellen writes that her father hit the man so hard 'he was still spinning when he reached the other side of the road'. The shop was opposite a police station, but blind eyes were turned. Ellen reveals existing quid pro quo arrangements with the local constabulary. When things kicked off at the station, an officer would often be dispensed to fetch Bill. 'He'd do three rounds with the violent or troublesome in the cells,' she writes. 'To quieten them down.' Whether there was any payment is unknown, but court reports I've managed to track down from local newspaper archives hint at a man working angles. Fighting for everything. In a brawl in his restaurant on North Bridge Road involving two Arksey miners, Bill's false teeth (a present from Doncaster Rovers after his own were knocked out during a match) got cracked. His claim was for a staggering £7 7s in damages. He was in court twice for speeding offences – one being a side-on collision with a corporation bus, with the force of impact overturning it. No injuries; considerable costs. The reports note that an RAC scout (proto-traffic cop) 'happened' to be in Bill's passenger seat. He happily vouched for the defence: a slip of the foot; a greasy road. A small fine.

In the 1920s, fresh out of the mines with fledgling shops along the Great North Road, Bill certainly had means beyond what might reasonably be expected. He drove down the (recently renamed) A1 from Scotland in a newly bought custom Arrol-Johnston costing £850. Silver piper mascot on the bonnet. A decent car forty years later would set you back half of that. There are suggestions of gambling money, side hustles; ready cash made in ways not obvious or declarable. A week ago, I found him under the 'dissolved partnerships' section of

the *Daily Telegraph* for 1929. He is listed as 'dance hall proprietor' of the Empress Hall in Doncaster. No one had the faintest idea.

As with everything, context is important. A second-generation Irish immigrant working in the coal mines from eleven years old, he knew what it was to grow up poor in late-Victorian Britain. The struggle to survive, hunger, exhaustion, daily danger. The family archive has served up scenes. On 31st July 1915, the day my grandfather, Bartley, was born, Bill stayed at home with May who was then in advanced labour. His hewing partner and best friend, Thomas Burbanks, was 'ripping coal' as usual that morning at the face in Bentley Colliery when there was a collapse. Burbanks was killed instantly. Soon after, Bill too was buried in the pit. A scrape in the seam he'd been hacking at saved his life when the ceiling of the chamber fell in behind. He waited in the pitch-black, folded into that airless cave, as miners tried to find a way to him. Working open a gap, they began to pull him through when there was another rockfall. Digging to reach him again, they found Bill's eyes and throat filled with a fine black dust that had to be scooped out. As his daughter recollects in her diaries: 'He told me once that thoughts of his life, his wife and his new baby flashed through his mind.' Freed and then stretchered the half-mile under-ground to the main shaft, Bill was said to have screamed and sworn the entire way. Most remarkably perhaps, he was back down the mine again the very next morning.

Tunnels through or up and out of this world and this existence weren't cut without wits, risk, some inextinguishable inner fire. They had to be fought for. Once carved, they were held fast, protected. My suspicion is that Bill saw opportunities and took them without think-ing, battling for every yard of life without fear of authority – or rather, with the canny understanding of how to use authority's duplicities and hypocrisies to his end. We know too that he encouraged his chil-dren to fight the way he had. The story goes that Bartley, my grandfather, had real potential as a boxer in his youth in Doncaster – better even than Bill. The problem was that he hated hurting anyone. To force him into the ring, Bill had to agree to pay his opponents 'a few bob' at the end or Bartley would refuse to fight.

Ironic, then, that when Bartley enlisted to fight at the outbreak of war in 1939, applying to be a pilot in the RAF, he was denied. Classed unfit to serve. The medical board that assessed him diagnosed the per-sistent swelling and aches and sensitivities in his wrists and ankles as early rheumatoid arthritis. A condition that would shorten his life and render him – as he was informed at the time – a 'cripple' in a matter of years. While his brothers fought overseas, Bartley remained in London where the entire family had relocated only a few years before. Helping to run fish shops for Bill and May in the day, he volunteered with London's Fire Service at night. In 1940, during the Luftwaffe's most intense period of bombing, Bartley was digging for survivors, pulling people from rubble, fighting fires – including, as my nana once told me, during those desperate hours when tidal waves of flame threatened to torch St Paul's Cathedral.

In the decades after the war, Bartley's condition deteriorated. He lived in pain. To move was to feel the grind of broken glass against bone. The medication prescribed had a terrible side effect: cancer. Reduced to walking with sticks, the fight and inner fire instilled in him in childhood endured. When I was young, his surviving siblings, my great-uncles and -aunts, and my dad, shared with me that he never once complained. He brought laughter everywhere. He remained gentle and kind, proving to all those who loved him that not all fights are with other people, nor true strength necessarily physical. It was this that they remembered and celebrated about him.

Thoughts crowd in again on the approach to Woolsthorpe Manor. How does what we receive shape our lives and understanding? How does what is passed down to us govern the way we navigate this world? What is it that we, in turn, pass on?

*

Phil, the tour guide, is at pains to point out that the apple tree is *still* alive, even if the original trunk was felled in a storm two centuries ago. This Flower of Kent sprang up from its antecedent's roots to grow again and bear the famous fruit that still falls thickly on the grass, less than a mile eastward of the A1(M)/Great North Road. He asks for a show of hands: 'Who's heard of Newton being hit on the head by an apple?

'OK ... good. Well, that almost certainly never happened.'

With more than seven miles under my belt, thirsty and hungry, I'd entered Woolsthorpe's idyllic, time-freeze Lincolnshire setting, surrounded by garden, orchard, barns and outbuildings, to find nobody around. Two cars in the car park. No sound, save for the rusty handletwist of birdsong, the hum of wasps drunk on rotting apples. The place possessed a solemn air, even under the flawless sky and high sun. Wondering if it might be closed, I'd walked through a gate and up past a kiosk to the limestone farmhouse with its little windows and squat entrance to try to find someone to ask. A volunteer with a bleeping walkie-talkie had opened the door with a shriek at the sight of me standing on the threshold, looking up, reading the inscription carved into a stone tablet positioned above the lintel: *In this Manor House* ISAAC NEWTON *was born 25 December* AD 1642. My eye had been drawn to bones; the two human femurs arranged in a 'X', giving the impression there was a gravestone over the door.

'This is actually Newton's coat of arms,' the volunteer explained. 'But if you're interested, there's a tour in ten minutes. Go back to the shop. Ask for Phil.'

Phil is steeped in the subject matter. He wants our little group to understand the significance of this place, the meaning of what happened here. Newton's father – also Isaac Newton – sickened and died just three months before Isaac took his first breath in a small bedchamber at the top of the stairs. Christmas 1642: barely a year since Charles I had hurried his retinue up the north road, along the Roman highway at the edge of vision; two months since the first engagement of the civil wars at Edgehill. This was the land he was born into. At war with itself, with its beliefs.

When Isaac was three, further upheaval. His mother, Hannah, accepted the hand of a wealthy rector, Barnabas Smith, leaving Isaac at Woolsthorpe with his grandmother to relocate to a new life a few miles down the highway. Isaac would hardly see his mother again until the age of ten, when Smith died and Hannah returned to Woolsthorpe with Isaac's stepbrother and stepsisters in tow. In those patriarchal times, Hannah had little choice but to agree, yet this abandonment would scar Newton for the rest of his life. It was a darkness and emotional trauma that couldn't be remedied. He detested Smith and he could not hide his resentment towards his mother for leaving him, cataloguing later in a list of sins committed in childhood: 'Threatning my father and mother smith to burne them and the house over them'. And: 'Wishing death and hoping it to some . . .'

Newton's was a distracted mind. Distracted, troubled, brilliant. Its relentless focus fell on the workings of the world around him: questioning, experimenting, puzzling always: *Why?* He was fascinated by the way the sun shining through windows projected light upon a wall. He tracked the paths of the celestial bodies and crafted sundials, charting not only the passage of the sun, but of time itself. Time not as some mysterious or mystic influence, but measurable. Duration visible in the length of an arc. Small yet interconnected pieces to what was the great puzzle, the great *design*, of the universe.

Evidently unsuited as a yeoman farmer, Newton was sent eight miles up the Great North Road to the free grammar school in Grantham, before securing a place at Cambridge University. Solitary, driven, his notebooks were overwritten with his workings-out: critiques of theories, ideas, remedies, cures, chemical properties. Scribbled across those same pages were flashes of deep despair and loneliness. Doubt

and depression: 'What imployment is he fit for? What is hee good for? I will make an end. I cannot but weepe. I know not what to doe.'

Phil is sorry but the video in the parlour can obviously only show so much. What it shows is a boy out of place ambling around Woolsthorpe's rooms and grounds, Keats-like. Charcoaling the whitewashed walls; conducting experiments. Newton appears surreally handsome; a soft-focus sheen to his face and Jim Morrison locks. The young actor playing him is delivering it in a bewildered style: a lone dreamer in the orchard, in the garden, his eyes fixed up to the cosmos. Troubled genius is so hard to unpack in six minutes. We are left with the impression of the place much more than the person.

Place, though, is significant. In 1665, the Great Plague forced Cambridge to close its doors. Newton returned to Woolsthorpe for his *annus mirabilis*, or 'Year of Wonders'. It was here, in solitude, close to the Great North Road, freed from the restrictions of the university curriculum, that his thinking intensified. *In utero* theories for what would become world-changing revelations on light, motion and gravity. Newton would later describe the incident at Woolsthorpe when he caught sight of an apple falling from a tree being the inspiration to wonder why it fell straight down to the earth – at the nature of the force acting upon it and, by extension, upon the orb above it: the moon. Published twenty years later, his laws of motion and gravitation defined in *Principia* would transform knowledge and steer the course of history, unlocking the language of the universe and providing the method to understanding it.

We're led into the kitchen. Phil asks that we conjure a noisy, busy space. Meals being cooked for farm workers. Field medicines, tinctures and exotic spices being prepared in a pestle and mortar. I smell thyme, woundwort and cinnamon.

'Just imagine,' Phil says. 'Straw strewn across this floor. Isaac walking through, thinking about these huge puzzles, asking that monumental question: *Why?*' As Phil talks, the group studies the props on the table – distillation apparatus, scales – but I find my focus settling on the rectangle of sunlight falling across the white wall behind him. That drift stare descends; tired eyes becoming fixed to a point. A dissolving of the periphery. Suddenly, I am in the inverse of the scene Phil is painting. I am alone in a dark kitchen. Winter. Night. A low ringing in my ears. There is something unbearable about the deadness of this space and in the faded bunches of scentless lavender hanging from the beams gathering dust. Something terrible about the silence, the empty chairs. I have the sickening feeling of being forgotten, of waiting hour by hour for something or somebody to arrive, and it fills me with such an awful sense of loneliness and sadness that I struggle to stand there. When Phil asks the group to step into the next room, I slip the other way, outside.

*

That space, that feeling. These moments still arrive sometimes from somewhere unexpected. They are present then gone before I can take hold of them, shake them out. I stand in the brilliant sunlight for a while, then walk back to the shop to retrieve my stashed rucksack. I check my phone. A missed call and two texts from Dad.

All summer my father and his wife, Karen, have given over a day each fortnight to looking after my children, with my mum doing the same the alternate week. The kids are those utter-joy ages now: nearly six, and three. All questions, gleeful discoveries, earnest conversations, comedic meltdowns. Dad has loved every second of it. Grand days out to museums. Adventures. Indulging ice-cream requests. Whetting their tastes for history. Screening afternoon Westerns far too old for them. These arrangements have come to an end, but the texts are enquiring about when they might have them again. The sign-off: a photo of the kids. An admission: *We miss them!*

I love seeing Tom and Bea with Dad, but it can ache too. Some of my strongest memories from childhood are the days when he wasn't working and his focus fell fully on me. A beam of undiluted attention. The warmth of it. Dad was always a rock in my eyes: experienced, knowledgeable, funny. He seemed a doorway to a bigger world, to the arts – to literature, poetry, great albums, great painters. Someone who seemed to possess the keys to the highway. Someone who knew how the world worked and had the answers to its technicalities and confusions. The first person I'd seek the opinion of. Love was not a word spoken freely or directly, not to my brother or me in the way we both tell our children now, daily, repeatedly. But it was implied by his presence, in how he looked after us and provided for us – in that way that was far more common between fathers and sons back then.

The depth of this connection, this love, was obvious when it wasn't as strong. After the rift of the divorce and his leaving home, it took time to repair. When it became possible for me to see him again, I was hurting in ways I couldn't appreciate or understand. I wanted him to *know* and acknowledge how things were, what I was going through, but he was already living another life. Sometimes promised calls were missed. Plans had to be cancelled last minute. Our stories had separated and we were in different places. I had to remind myself that he did not possess the memories I had of the last two years and there was no way I could begin to explain the sad honesty of them. Not then. It took a long time for me to realise this and to move on from it. After my disastrous stint at art college, we would meet up in Leeds and he'd buy me lunch and books. He'd take me to the theatre, or out with his friends. He helped find me a job so I could earn money while playing in my band before going to university. After a while, I started visiting him at his new flat, fitting myself into his altered world. Bit by bit, things eased. We fell back into being how we had been before – that same closeness, that similarity. I think there was some self-reflection on his part too. Where words failed us, we managed to say what we needed through our joint obsessions with novels, films, songs. Even if we couldn't express our emotions directly, we could recognise and be absorbed by those same emotions expressed by others. We could let them flow through us at the same time in the same room, always with that silent assertion: *You can make something beautiful, worthwhile, valuable, out of pain.*

I was picking up the kids from Dad's house a few weeks back and I found myself smiling at the sight of Tom holding his hand in the garden, inspecting the hydrangeas. Later, Dad told me that he remembered doing the same with his grandad, Bill. How, after school, he would walk up from Chalk Farm to Bill and May's home in Hampstead, past mounds of bomb rubble, to spend time with them while his parents were flat-out working a fish counter. There would be the same inspection of the garden, the flowers. A coin slipped into the palm. The spoils always afforded by a generation once removed. That undiluted attention. As we were about to leave, Tom suddenly hugged his grandad and told him that he loved him. Then he looked up at him expectantly. I watched Dad pause, stumble. He laughed, glanced over at me with a grin, like he was waiting for me to bail him out, but I shook my head. *This one is on you.* Dad stroked Tom's hair behind his ear and he said: 'I love you too.'

Memories still rise from nowhere. We carry these spaces, these feelings inside us. They arrive without warning and perhaps they always will, but I can talk to Dad nowadays about those harder days because when I look back, I know that he was there. He looked after us. He made sure we were OK. These were things, I believe, passed down to him from his father, and from Bill. Even when life was at its messiest, when I was most lost, when everything was hazy and shape-shifting, he was still a rock. It was just that sometimes I couldn't see it. I have learned more about freedom and responsibilities, about adulthood, from him than I have from anyone. There are friends of mine who have no relationship with a parent because of divorce or things that happened. For me and Dad, the story changed, but in the end, we have grown stronger because he has always kept that promise whispered to me a long time ago: *I'm not walking out on you.*

*

A last look at the apple tree takes me past a signboard affirming Woolsthorpe's hoped-for takeaway: 'INSPIRATION for a GENIUS'. The focus here is less on other parts of Newton's character. Although he lived to a great age in great wealth, holding positions of great power, Newton remained solitary, disconnected, difficult. He is believed to have never held a relationship, or a lover. He pursued vendettas against (wrongly) perceived enemies or colleagues, manipulating events to do them ill. These behaviours perhaps also have their roots at Woolsthorpe, in his mother walking away. In a perceived rejection. In a little boy left to believe he was unloved and unlovable.

Finding a bench in the corner of the orchard, I remember that Ted Hughes line in a letter to his son: 'Behind the most efficient seeming adult exterior, the whole world of the person's childhood is being carefully held like a glass of water bulging above the brim.' How true that is. There is complexity to the fact that Isaac Newton achieved what he did partly because of the adaptive responses to trauma hardwired in him here. There is an irony that many of the qualities we associate with his 'genius' – being distracted, inquisitive, competitive, isolated, obsessive – were, for Newton, coping mechanisms. Behaviours that would ultimately drive him to open the door for much of human knowledge, but also prevent him from knowing and experiencing much of what being human is really about. An irony, too, that he should be remembered for discovering the nature of the force that one body exerts over another.

II

The Great North Road splits from the Lincoln-bound line of Ermine Street (known as High Dyke hereabouts) at Colsterworth, close to a lorry park (McDonald's, Greggs, Travelodge). I tell Marie that she can leave me here if it's easier, but she's heading further north anyway. Edinburgh, eventually. We'd got talking in the orchard. Her father died unexpectedly two years ago. A physics teacher in Australia all his working life, he had been fascinated by Newton. Marie's visit was a pilgrimage made on his behalf. She'd unfolded her waterproof jacket close to the Flower of Kent, laying it beside its low, elliptical fence, installed – as Phil explained – in homage to the ever-falling path of the moon and 'to protect its roots'. After sitting alone for a while, Marie had quietly explained to me Newton's theories on the gravitational fields of planetary bodies and slingshot trajectories. How they were still in use by NASA and how they'd helped put humankind on the moon. How, in recognition, the shuttle Atlantis had carried a piece of this tree into space in 2010. I suggested she should take a windfall apple home with her and try to grow a descendant in her garden. She'd looked nervous about the idea, so I reached over the fence and sneaked a couple, pocketing one myself. We left the orchard grinning, stolen apples and all. Her offer of a lift was a gift in kind.

She drops me on the Great North Road (B1174) to Grantham. A long, grey line. Fall-aways of the lush valley of the River Witham to the east. I'm thinking of Newton and that falling apple, of something Marie had mentioned in the car about Newton's story likely being self-mythology. The apple, the discovery, all of it. Too perfect to be believable. Too much of a parable. What's often misunderstood about

Newton's work is that it sought to show the plans of creation; nature was, to his mind, a 'cryptogram set by the Almighty'. His work was about understanding the language of God, not disassembling or *disproving* the notion of a deity. In later life, while considering the settling of his accounts, did he switch the truth of decades of restless puzzling, of dead ends and wrong turns and his manic obsessions, into a simple story that was beautifully simple and biblical in style? A man in his little Eden; an apple (the symbol of knowledge); the moment the harmony of the universe suddenly arrived in his mind. Voltaire was the first to report this story. Then others – including Newton's biographer, Conduitt. Most claimed to have heard it directly from the old man himself during his final years. But suffering with uncurable pain, was Newton carefully arranging a remarkable yet disordered life into something with semi-religious meaning? Did he know full-well how he wanted to be remembered?

It was a story the Victorians lapped up. Divine genius. Inspiration granted to an Englishman; further evidence that God was on their side. Newton was a hero. His view of a mechanical universe powered the mechanisation of human activity. Buried and ignored were Newton's more intellectually embarrassing views – his enchanted beliefs in a world governed by spirits and occulted forces. A reigning animism in nature and through the universe. In the decades after his death, what sprang from his learning and laws was a distinctly disenchanted vision. Britain became the first country to industrialise because it was the first to disseminate and apply Newtonian culture; to open it up. His work was made available to engineers, entrepreneurs, manufacturers decades before other countries did the same, narrowing the space between theory and practicality, between scientific progress and production on the mill, factory or shop floor. This charged atmosphere of technological advancement, of tweaking and improving, gave the Industrial Revolution its lift-off. In 1858, Victoria thanked Newton's hometown for its brilliant son, donating £100 towards the effigy of him that stands in Grantham, the bronze coming from melted-down Russian cannons seized in the Crimean War. At its unveiling, relics – Newton's telescope, his prism, an original copy of *Principia* – were paraded on cushions before the statue. It was a national as well as local moment. Science as a new religion. Newton as prophet.

＊

His gaze still glowers out from that same statue in front of the guild-hall on St Peter's Hill. A place to pause for anyone passing through. To reach it, the Great North Road runs like a groove through Grantham's outskirts, into its heart. I follow it to find a core sample of a particular parochial British history. Market towns are often deep records of epochs. Places ever coming to terms, putting on a brave face. Grantham: handsome, exhausted. A Saxon river village with mythical origin story; a wool and leather centre. A place of grey friars with a stunning church, a Knights Templar hostel. Road-town, coaching-town. Even if Dickens hadn't overnighted at the George Inn, you'd believe that he had. A town that hedged its bets, swapping by-highway privileges for the promise of rail, ushering in a new era of heavy industry. Agricultural machinery, ploughs, carriage repairs, steam engines, breweries. Expensive villas popping up amid the rows of red-brick, back-to-back terraces; retouched Georgian high-street facades. Later, tractors, cranes, cannons for aircraft would roll off the town's well-oiled production lines. Shift-workers were rehoused in neat, post-war suburbs. The boom, then the inevitable bust. Factories knocked out like rotten teeth as post-war decline bit and then held. Boarded-up buildings looking for a purpose. The old road clogged with cars. A groove can so easily become a rut.

One girl who passed by the statue of Newton more often than most was Margaret Roberts – daughter of an alderman and mayor of Grantham who regularly visited the guildhall for civic duties and took his younger daughter along with him. Early conditioning in what it meant to lead. Dunks into the acid tank of politics. Lessons in how to strip empathy from decision-making. The conviction that people have no idea what's good for them and an ambition to bloody well tell them. All elements of the future Iron Lady were crafted in a flat above the A1/Great North Road on North Parade, where her father kept the grocer's shop below. Alfred Roberts: stern, overbearing, controlling. Master of his own domain. A small-business owner who liked to make a show of picking out who to serve from the queue. Unlike other shops, he flatly refused credit. A strict, authoritarian Methodist and preacher, he made his daughters attend the chapel around the corner four times each Sunday while street rumours circulated of his own ungodly habits. Girls banned from working in the shop for fear of wandering hands. Local gossip still holds that Roberts intentionally kept his chosen daughter separate from other children, feeding a contempt for the community she grew up in; that Margaret had a habit of spitting at kids from her window. Retrospective pantomime myth maybe, but it was true that Thatcher worshipped the ground her father walked on. She incubated his hatred of collective society ('there's no such thing as society') and state – of the left-leaning, the bolshy, the unpatriotic. The nuisances that asked for credit at the counter. No excuses, no pity.

Those questions surface again. How does what we receive shape our lives and understanding? How does what is passed down to us govern the way we navigate this world? What do we, in turn, pass on? Thatcher was a gravitational force that pulled the alignment of British politics, and the road ahead for the country, firmly to the right. Britain became her de facto grocer's shop; her apartment above Downing Street a facsimile of the north road flat. Being peddled this time was an experimental ideology to arrest Britain's decades-long decline and rocketing inflation: the promise to Make Britain Great Again. A dousing of petrol and a struck match for the Keynesian consensus, workers' rights and trade unions. Everyone for themselves on a trajectory of liberal free-market capitalism with the unfettered, deregulated City of London as its beating heart. Foreign coin flooding in. No questions asked. The tipping of the island towards the south, towards the *capital*. Towards new, glittering temple-like superstructures being stamped over London's post-industrial docklands. Manufacturing obliterated in favour of swelling financial and service industries. The privatisation of any publicly owned institution that could turn a profit – the slow choking of those that couldn't (health, education, prisons). Along the way, Britain reinvented itself as nostalgia brand. The Union flag flying over Port Stanley in 1982 was an unplanned global activation. A forced launch that worked very nicely, thank you: 'The house meets this Saturday to respond to a situation of great gravity . . .' The real enemy, though – as Thatcher insisted – was *within*. Mining and the NUM. The proxies for the Labour men who had driven her father from his aldermen's bench in Grantham. Fifth columnists. Their destruction was a personal matter, brutally overseen. Hit the power base. The poisoning of the well. The strangulation approach to negotiation. Communities torn apart, humiliated. Surging unemployment. Dole offices heaving. The fit and able forced on to sick-pay lists to keep the numbers down. A hard recession. Picket and protest beaten into submission, outlawed, as taxes were slashed for the highest earners. Like her father, Thatcher knew who in the queue she wanted to serve. Behind it, the flawed reasoning of trickle-down economics. Where you wound up on the inequality divide was positioned as your own choice. The poor only had themselves to blame. No ambition a disease. No excuses, no pity.

The north road became a line linking divided nations: London and the South East ('The South') and everything north, east and west of Watford Gap ('The North'). You can sense the shifting temperature in Paul Graham's incredible photographic record *A1 – The Great North Road* (1983). Post-Falklands. Thatcher in power for four years; the miners' strike coming. There is something in the air. Stark colour images. Saturated, weighted, freighted. Beginning in the financial district in London, we see bankers in Thatcher-blue ties laughing. Views back over the city from Suicide Bridge. Out beyond the borders, the road runs north into the industrial badlands – lamp-lit eateries set against colossal blue-black night. Fires in fields. Men in overalls over fry-ups, faces blurred by movement. Vermeer-esque portraits of truck drivers, waitresses. A young, tired salesman in an out-of-fashion suit standing in a car park at Leeming Bar Services. The fags, the hairstyles, the clothes, the glasses – all fix the shots in history; each keeps its cast present, and weirdly ageless. We identify with those trapped in a point in time looking forward at us *through* time. The north road – as always – is readable, eye-opening, revelatory; reflecting everything into the lens.

Graham's odyssey pre-empts the car boom of the late 1980s – part of the Thatcher government's materialist-individualist growth drive: 'the great car economy'. Own your own home and a car, or two. A white paper of 1989 was called *Roads for Prosperity*. It promised the

largest UK road-building scheme since the Romans. A pastiche of the US model of a road-retail two-step. A turbo-charging of the consumerist habits ingrained in the 1960s. More motorways; more out-of-town malls. High-street consolidations and conversions into shopping centres. In 1984, Grantham opened the Isaac Newton Centre, complete with a replica Newton telescope in the foyer. The shopping centre is still here (Morrisons, Costa, FoneDoctor, Cashbrokers, A1 Security Services), opposite St Peter's Hill and the Newton statue. The old coaching inn along the road, the George, has been tweaked into the George Shopping Centre (Pizza Express, Benetton, Tropicana Tan). To suggest that Grantham might be any town or every town along the highway is no insult. Give or take some specific architecture, some unique legacies of its location, it is a simple statement of fact.

We are all here now, in a Britain where these neoliberal legacies – adopted and democratised by successive governments – are inescapable. High-street oblivion. Bargain fashion and furniture chains, discount supermarkets, factory outlets – all enabled by low-wage manufacturing and climate-destroying fossil fuel industries. Growing inequality, debt culture. Over-mortgaging against unsustainable house prices. The struggles of soaring rents and food prices. A financial sector with a death grip on the economy. A welfare state unable to cope. An NHS against the wall. Council budgets eviscerated. Those communities hit the hardest in the 1980s and 1990s remain neglected. Ex-steel towns. Ex-coal towns. Places like Bentley where my great-grandfather dug the seam, and where the colliery was closed forever in 1993. Speaking at the pit gates, Bentley's vicar Bob Fitzharris summed up the community's mood: 'We are being held hostage to fortune by this evil Tory administration that worships the false god of the marketplace . . . this is a sad and black day for Bentley.'

Nobody believed British coal mining could go on forever. Few would argue either that the disastrous economy of the 1970s and Britain's reputation as the 'sick man of Europe' didn't require reform. What they wonder is whether there was another way, both back then and now. Another door to be pushed open to a different future.

*

In 1992, when Baroness Thatcher requested that her newly created coat of arms featured Newton, it was not the crossed bones over Woolsthorpe's door, but a cartoon Isaac in frock coat and wig. Now, on St Peter's Hill on the Great North Road, spitting distance from the statue she walked past in her youth, there will soon be an effigy of the Iron Lady too. Some residents look forward to paying their respects to one of Grantham's own; others await a £300,000 target. The chance to spit at the figure they maintain spat at them. To dress the girl from 'up the road' with their eggs and paint.

Up the road: North Parade. I find the Roberts's flat from a plaque identifying it as 'the birthplace of the first woman prime minister of Great Britain and Northern Ireland'. The shop below is now *Living Health (Feel Your Best)*. Its business is wellbeing, health, beauty. Natural remedies. Massage. Aromatherapy. Hypnotherapy. Antidotes to alleviate the malaises of this modern world. Taped inside the window, an advert offering Maggie's old bedroom for rent to 'any professional counsellor'.

From the moment we're born, we are bodies being enacted upon by forces. Our parents, our families, our neighbourhoods, friends, schools, streets. The circumstances in which we find ourselves growing up, time and place. Good or bad, attentive or traumatic, whether we are blessed with love or wounded by rejection, these forces set us on our motion through life – our movements: who we are, what paths we take, what roads. Whether we're fully aware of them or not, they drive us. But what I'm beginning to understand is that there is always room for manoeuvre. We can alter the path and try another road. We might still fall at times, but we needn't keep falling. We live in an age that better understands the human mind – an age when we are encouraged to be aware of these driving forces, to draw from their positive aspects and to work through the destructive parts. To be conscious of what we're leaving behind and handing down.

*

Out by the highway, where Grantham loosens its grip, the sky is indigo. The season is turning. The air growing colder. I'm walking to a bed in the A1 Travelodge, figuring I'll get a drink from somewhere. The road is a flickering strip-light flaring with headlights; the dark deepened by the sporadic glare. It's hard to distinguish much else but the moon. Pushing my hands into my pockets, I find the apple from Woolsthorpe and think of what Marie said. How five miles above in the heavens, inside the International Space Station, a sliver of bark from that same tree span in zero-gravity.

After three miles, a sense of weightlessness descends along the road too. That same peculiar, familiar sense of suspension felt before at Alconbury and Ickwell Green, wrought again by the effect of floating through night fields on the old road. The tide-flow river of time coming in too fast, rising, rushing at the heels. Caught in its current: people, places, plans, possibilities. The fractured memories. The shadow selves that stalk the dark. Those discontinued selves that were us before we took a turn – that appear in the mirror sometimes before slipping away elsewhere. They arrive, overlap and overtake me now, moving past like fingers drifting up a spine.

In the strip of parking in front of the motel, a car waits. A man sits stalled in the driving seat, his face half in shadow. As I walk past, something about the way the night encloses the car's interior light; something in the deathly stillness of the service area and the tyre-howl hum of the north road beyond makes me afraid to look at him.

One Last Look

(Gonerby Moor–Barnby Moor)

In the night's quiet she comes to him. He knew she would in the same way you know a phone will ring a second before it does, or you can smell the coming rain. He'd known it when he'd checked in, key-carded his way into the room and closed the curtains. He'd known it as he'd showered with that sand-timer sensation in his sternum, then emptied two whisky miniatures from the minibar into a plastic bath-room cup to speed his mind and body across the border to sleep. He'd known she would come to him and she does. This time looking away. He calls her name and she turns, taking his hands in hers. A half-bite of her lower lip. Then the scene changes; her hair falling loosely around her shoulders. He sees her crooked smile and the white thread-of-cotton scar on her chin. Around them, the clamour of a party. Wild comings and goings. That moment they'd met, in 1996. His friends half-drunk, barrelling on to a lawn. High summer. A stranger's house. The day half-done and him only half-invited. Broken glasses scattered in the grass. Her, there, leaning against a wall in a silk skirt. Their eyes meet and she looks away; then she looks back again. Drink-emboldened, he asks for a cigarette and she sparks a lighter for him. Then everything changes once more. It is weeks later. They are some-where else. Her mother's kitchen. She's standing on a chair stealing from her brother's multipack of Silk Cut hidden in a cupboard, open-ing red wine that neither of them needs. Now it's night, cold. She's zipped into his jacket on a rocky edge of a black flank of moor. Far below, the lights of town are fire embers raked along a canyon. In that moment, there's nothing else. Only the two of them and her whisper-ing words to 'Suzanne' in his ear; whispering about rivers and lovers and spending the night beside her. In the muddle of this dream, he's

255

pleading with his younger self to just stay and keep his arm around her. Instead, the slow fade begins. The sad transition. Then he is awake and blinking in the semi-dark of the hotel room. Slipping from the tangle of the sheet, he opens the curtains and listens to the melancholy moan of the road through dirty glass. He boils the kettle, shakes out instant coffee into a mug and watches the sun slowly rise over the horizon. The highway is a finger-smear of gold traced through the tarry dark.

*

This is how it is. Days arranged in advance from head office. Where to go and who to service. Alerts arriving in a digital calendar. Links automatically embedded into a schedule that governs the shape and journey of his waking hours. His is the paradoxical independence that over-regulated days can create – his is the freedom of always having somewhere to go and an excuse to disappear. Of never having to think or plan. He can look the part. That's why they like him. Swapping into a white shirt and tie he keeps stowed in a black carrier in the boot of the silver Volvo, hanging his suit in the shower overnight to straighten the creases and slipping on the lanyard and laminated ID. Most of the time, clients don't really care. It's surprising how many doors you are waved through if you just look like you know where you're going. Appointments rarely last longer than an hour or two. Almost always everything could have been fixed on the phone, but when a business signs up for the premium package promising all-round protection and maintenance, he and the eleven others like him across the country represent a big chunk of value in the chargeable retainer: a fleet of dedicated support managers delivering a 'guaranteed in-business presence within _two hours of call-out_', as the contract has it. Technically, his area is North Lincolnshire, Nottinghamshire and South Yorkshire, but borders don't mean all that much if one of his colleagues gets overrun. Reassignments happen at any time at the drop of a hat. Hence the high staff turnover and why, despite what they all promise in the interview, anyone with commitments (newly-weds, first-time mothers and fathers) rarely sticks at the job for more than six months. Even with good money, few can stand to be on the road for long.

One exception: Meena. She has been in place for three years now, maybe more. Like him, she knows the secret; the trick to inverting and using the corporate power dynamic. How to play it smart and tick boxes. Punch the clock, do the work, flatter the egos of the directors and, in return, coast for most of the time. Get it right and your mind is your own to drift elsewhere. The compromise being you don't complain when called.

The afternoon before, he had received a late request. Meena was stuck in Cambridge and someone had to make an appointment to an accountancy firm at the Ermine Business Park on the edge of Huntingdon. Arrival no later than 3.45 p.m. It was an hour and a half south on the A1, but he'd taken the request, pulling in at a brick, two-storey office with a line of executive-class cars nosed up to a bank of grass. On with the jacket, the lanyard. The problem was something and nothing; an operating system update. A desktop in the network had failed to upgrade before its user logged off for a week in Cancun, sending the error reporting haywire. Done and dusted in twenty minutes, including the tea. He'd stretched it to an hour, because *value is always measured in time*. He'd learned that from the man who hired him. Efficiency was all well and good but what people remembered was the time you spent with them. Afterwards, patting a pocket for his key, he'd watched a pied wagtail leaping in little bounds over the box hedging and across a bonnet, its tail bouncing like a wind-up toy. Sliding into the front seat, the key had automatically prompted the stereo into life, shuffling a playlist at random. A slow, heartbeat bass; the rim-click of a snare. Four bars before the soft, reverb piano refrain, that ghost voice: *When I lost you, honey, sometimes I think I lost my guts too.* Music: that skeleton key to all of memory's doors. Driving away, out on to the old highway, swinging the car north towards Grantham, he'd already known she would come to him.

*

The highway is a finger-smear of gold traced through the tarry dark, then all the night-silt is being rinsed away by the dawn. Gonerby Moor kindled and afire; horizons of beaten bronze and pale, smoke-blue milk trees. He leans, hands on the glass, forehead on the pane, and stares into emerging morning, watching the road as some people watch a river. It takes time and two more packets of the bitter, burnt-taste Nescafé to come back to himself. To find the energy to face the lukewarm shower. He brushes his teeth in water that won't drop below tepid. In the breakfast room, the coffee machine stirs and hums with the same noise-note-word opening as Leonard Cohen's 'Sisters of Mercy'. *Oh* . . . *the sisters of mercy, they are not departed or gone.* It plants an earworm that replays through the palaver of checkout, of minibar tallies and interacting with someone who doesn't want to be there but has no choice and who didn't sleep well because their youngest is sick and who's flustered because Kirsty's away and this is supposed to be her job and they're only a week out of the probation period, you know? He knows. Still, he's on the road by eight. North. His calendar shows no new updates. Service checks only. A print studio outside Tuxford. Newark Castle and Gardens. Newark Waitrose. Newark Asda Supercentre.

He searches for the song to stop its inner repeating, wondering if it might conjure her with it. There were times – months, years – that he struggled to place the features of her face. His mind only served up a blur. Her mouth. Grey eyes. The curve of a naked shoulder. But he'd learned that the oblivion of the highway sharpened the picture. The road-delirium of driving for hours on end somehow wiped away the fog. She would sometimes appear right there, every bit as real as she was in his dreams.

Ahead is nothingness, endlessness. Two highway lanes of pitted grey running north; two mirroring them in the other direction. Faded white lines, arrows. The central reservation's unruly overgrowth. The solitude of fields either side hidden by thorn. Signs for vague, off-highway villages: Foston, Marston, Barkston. The huge, weed-threaded parking of the boarded-up LJ's American Style Diner. The weather-faded FOR SALE sign. It hits him that no one will remember it when it's gone; no one will remember that it was once a motel, then a Little Chef before this doomed diner with its 'motsarella' and 'jalopeno' starters and discounts for Triumph Motorbike Club and National Hot Rod Association members. He thinks of the time he stopped one evening in winter, mid-January. The weather worsening. Lorry drivers parked up for the night with their engines running. The snow falling silently in the glittering dark, muffling the road. The Slovakian lad hurrying in and asking the waitress, loudly, if they had a condom machine in the toilets. He thinks of the time not long after when it was warmer and he was the only customer except for an elderly woman sitting on her own, reading by the window. The way she ate so slowly and turned the pages of a threadbare, cover-torn book with all that road framed behind her, flowing forwards, flowing back.

This image lingers like a sun-glance on his retina as he drives towards Newark. Thoughts muscle in before he can stop them. Home. The sick-stomach horror of wasted years. Guilt. His mother. He'd meant to return her calls days ago. He pushes it all down and draws a deep breath, forcing his focus on to a road bridge, then squinting at the line of pylons rising up in the fields to his left. The Leonard Cohen album cycles back to its beginning; the song once whispered to him on the moor begins thrumming through the speakers again. That finger-picked guitar. E. Esus4. E. The pre-seance sense of anticipation; a familiar feel of slipping. Gaps opening and widening. The highway falling away. *And you want to travel with her*. And then he is.

Twenty-two years ago. That summer. England waking up to that newly minted caricature of itself. 'Britannia' finding her feet once more. Union Jack skirts, guitars. Liam Gallagher's Churchillian fuck-off victory salute, right down the camera, right at you. The scenes flicker through his head all at once: leaving art college for the last time on a bright morning. Making his way home, skint and hungry, to an empty house. Odd labouring jobs. Hay baling on farms for beer money. The overspill of pubs at night. Kappa tops. Carling Premier. Cheap speed and teenths of gold seal. Pulp's 'Common People' on every radio. The poster in the station for *Trainspotting*. Choose Life, it said. 'Born Slippy'. Escape, escape, escape. Walking home through bewildering birdsong dawns. That party at a stranger's house. The day half-done and him only half-invited. That moment she looked away, then looked back again.

She said come over, come over / She smiled at you boy.

Was it the September that she left? That would only mean they were together from that June until August. It seems too short for the fierceness of the love he'd felt. Love unlike anything he'd known before. Altering love. Desperate love. An every-moment-beside-her love. The intensity of it was like being scorched by flame and then left gasping in a bed of salt. Every nerve on the outside of the skin. Uncontrollable love. Like they knew each other from somewhere else. Like they'd always known each other. He tries to force his mind to remember more, but nothing comes. Just the same brittle ash shapes of moments gone; the burn-on-cloth imprint of days lived too close to the light. The smell of her neck. A dinner somewhere where he met her brothers. A family wedding where he made a fool of himself. A drive north into the fells and lakes. The feel of her hand in his. The songs. This was how memories were formed and forged. Experiences etched into bones; things bored into the cells of being. It was the same for the whole of that ragged tribe lucky enough to be young and alive that year. A last generation to live eyes wide-open, utterly in the present. Nowhere to go or to be but *here* and *now*. And all those nights she told him that she loved him, and he believed it was true.

*

Return. Escape. MEMORY FULL. DELETE? Confirm. Escape. He waits, checks his calendar. No new updates. One text. From Meena: *Thanks for yesterday.* A groan-face emoji. *You're a STAR.* He taps a reply: *No worries.* A thumbs-up and a car. He unplugs his laptop and gives Helen, the office manager at Newark Asda, a smile.

'All good?' she asks.

'All good. I'll be back in two months.'

'See you then, then.'

'Any problems in the meantime, just . . .'

'I know. I'll call them in . . . sorry. Need to . . .'

She holds up her buzzing phone, smiles and answers it. He makes his way into the corridor and pushes through the door to the toilets by the lifts. He takes off his suit jacket and hangs it over the hand dryer, then washes his face in the sink. Pale grey bathroom walls, lurid green edging. Empty soap dispenser. He catches himself standing in the middle of it, face wet, and wonders who he is and what he is doing there, coming down so hard again. The forsaken sight of limbo. The price paid for the choices made. It will be days before these feelings recede again into numbness.

No new updates. An 'X' in his messages from Meena. He sits in the car and watches a woman loading bags of shopping into a boot as a toddler kicks his chubby legs in a trolley seat. He tries to stop imagining the home they'll drive back to. No new updates and a few hours of daylight, so he makes for where he knows the last of the late-September sun shines on water. The old road out of town: glimpsed side streets, a man with a look of horror in a white vest with a can of beer; the red iron bridge over the Trent. On this road, driven a thousand times, a between-world: road-houses that are forever for sale, roundabouts with yellow DIVERSION signs, such and such tribute act postered on a lamp post; roped, somnolent horses tugging at tufts of highway verge grass. On this road: the light-industrial estate and the WELCOME TO BRITISH SUGAR (NEWARK FACTORY) sign, then open road again. Mile after mile of anonymity where the desire to disappear is stronger than the desire to live.

That September, she had something to tell him. Could she come over? There was no one home but him, and he'd lit a fire. She was going away, she said. Six months. Volunteering. A children's hospital in South America. The travel paid by a charity. She hadn't wanted to mention it in case ... well, it had been organised before they'd met, before all of *this*. There was something else too. She was late. He remembered how she'd looked as she said it. The way she leaned close and laid her hand on his. 'Don't worry,' she said. But he wasn't. Not at all. Now on the stereo, the shuffle clicks into a song that, if he didn't know better, he'd think was no coincidence – that almost convinces him there is something bigger to all of this. He turns up the volume. The strummed, clean, electric guitar. G to Gsus4, and back again. 'Stolen Car'. That descending piano. Those words: *I met a little girl and I settled down* ... He'd written to her every week, recording mixtapes, walking into town between shifts to package up and send them. Her letters back were intermittent; the postal dates sometimes stamped weeks earlier than he received them. Some letters never arriving. Her voice on the page was already a voice from the past, asking him why he wasn't writing. A voice that seemed to be growing quieter. Another month passed and then came a letter about seeing a specialist doctor in Mexico. She was still late and worried. The doctor had suggested an injection that would help, but that cost hundreds of dollars. He'd tried desperately – letters and calls – to dissuade her. To beg her to speak to someone else. The only phone number she had given him rang out endlessly. *In the end it was something more, I guess, that tore us apart* ... Then the spring she came back, she wouldn't see him. Messages went unanswered. At the front door of her mother's house, her brothers said she wasn't in and, anyway, he shouldn't come round any more. Didn't he know there was somebody else? No. No, he didn't know that. Those haunted harmonies. The cave-thud of tom and drum, the sliding bass.

The spin-out of those last years of the 1990s. The great end-of-century party was winding down. Living for weekends, hard drunk into blackness, hoping to see her; to just have the chance to talk to her. But whenever he did, it was always the same. Too much drink for any sense to be spoken. Her taking his hands in hers. That half-bite of her lower lip. Eyes blurring. The war in their heads. Questions always unanswered. That night, after closing, when he walked around the corner and found her being pulled into a taxi. Half-in, half-out, with three men trying to shut the door. When he'd run and dragged her free and as it sped away, she'd screamed at him. That night years later amid the squeeze and singing of a midnight pub at Christmas when she'd slurred that they should have run away that summer. Taken her brother's car and just gone. Followed the road to its end. He'd left the girl he was with just so he could walk her home, waiting in the hallway as she'd called her boyfriend from the kitchen. And when she'd started crying down the phone, he had quietly let himself out. That was the last time he saw her. How could anyone understand the weight of it all? The weight of living each day knowing it was a rehearsal for a life already gone.

*

The road is the place all lost things go. He knows this. Before the last of the sun disappears into Smeaton's Lakes, before it is swallowed by the tops of trees, he is accelerating on to the Great North Road again. No updates. The calendar shows service checks only for tomorrow.

Four offices in Retford. A system check at Worksop Asda. Prospects widen as the tributary of the old highway pours into the four-lane of the A1. The hurtle and brake-flare of gleaming lorries; the weightlessness of unimpeded flow. Gold skies fiery with coming evening; gold-edged clouds shining over flat, featureless fields. In a little while he'll be checked in at the hotel on Barnby Moor, seated in the same dining room taking advantage of its midweek meal deal on steak and red wine. Listening to the same cycle of tinny music in the restaurant. 'Freefallin'' by Tom Petty. 'Walking on Broken Glass' by Annie Lennox. M-People's 'One Night in Heaven'. Pissing in the toilet with its glass-floor cutaway showing the worn cobbles of the original stabling. Age-stained horse-racing prints on the walls of the corridors. Undressing in an overheated bedroom. Trying to sleep. To recall.

He indicates and steers into the BP petrol station at Cromwell for coffee, stopping beside a dirty-white block next door, once called Café Amore. Lorries parked up for the night are like reef-struck shipwrecks. For a moment, with the engine fan still whirring away, he stares at the trees behind the building. A ragged strip of torn plastic sheeting flaps and snaps among the branches. Rising and falling with the wind and the backdraught of vehicles, it curls and fusses at where it's caught.

On the forecourt there is a queue at the pumps. Doors open on a Highways Agency truck: three men in high-vis climb out and amble over to the sliding entrance of the services. He lets them pass. 'Ta, mate,' says a lad with a cigarette behind his ear. In that moment of waiting, in a glance back towards the highway, he sees her.

A car door open. She is crouching, searching for something in the footwell of the passenger seat. He watches as she curls her hair behind her ear, leans into the car and speaks to someone in the back. Then the view is lost behind a plumber's van as it inches forward. A woman in glasses touches his elbow: 'Are you going in, love?'

It can't be her. That's what he tells himself as, over in a corner, he waits beside the Costa Express coffee machine, eyes flicking across the covers on the magazine rack. This is still the grip of the dream. It has to be. A remnant drifting through his conscious mind, attaching itself to someone with a passing resemblance. How could it possibly be her? Coffee in hand, he joins the back of the queue to pay when he recognises with another jolt the way she used to stand, her exact posture, three people ahead of him. When she moves back along the line to leave and catches his eye, that rising blush he'd forgotten. She looks away, then looks back again. With a quicksand feeling filling his chest, he half-smiles and watches as she does the same.

Outside she is waiting beside the sliding doors. He hears his name with a question mark attached and turns to find her standing there in a roll-neck black sweater and jeans. He hadn't noticed what she was wearing before. Her hair tumbling to her shoulders. Thinner, with lines about her eyes, but otherwise it is *her*, just as she was. She holds her phone and her purse awkwardly. She finds the words.

'I wasn't sure . . . I thought it was you –'

'Hi –'

'It's so weird to . . . I mean –' She shakes her head.

'I know. Do you live around –'

'No, no. I'm just driving back . . . I moved home a year ago, so –'

That word. *Home.* 'Oh, OK –'

'About a year ago, yeah –'

'Oh, right.'

'What about you? Do you ever go back –'

'Sometimes, yeah. Some Christmases, you know –'

'Yeah.'

She sweeps her hair behind her ear; stands on tiptoes to look past his shoulder over the forecourt towards the highway. 'Sorry. My kids are in the car. I'm just . . .'

'Oh, wow.' A pause. 'How many do you –'

'Two. Boy and girl –'

'How old are they?'

'Five and three. Yeah, they're –'

'That's great. I bet they're . . . great –'

'They are. They really are. And you? Did you ever –'

'Errr, no. No kids, no –'

When she glances again towards her car, he follows her gaze. The queue at the petrol pumps has grown. A van on the road is waiting to pull in. Evening light across the highway. Traffic as loud as thunder. He turns back.

She smiles. 'Sorry. It's so weird, this. I just wish I had more time –'

'I know. Me too. How are your –'

'I just wanted . . . I've wondered where you might be sometimes and –'

A car horn sounds at the pumps behind them. She looks over, frowns, sweeps her hair behind her ear again. 'I mean, I've wondered if . . . are you all right –'

'Yeah, I'm OK. I'm good. Thanks, though –'

'Because we never . . . you know. *I* never –'

'I know, but it's OK –'

'No. It's not. Not really. I feel like there are things I never –'

'No, no, it's all right. You don't need to –'

'I should have told you –'

'It's all right, honestly –'

'I –'

'It's OK. I know. I'm fine . . . I –'

He looks down, away, and then they are looking at each other. Eye to eye. The car horn from the queue sounds again. Longer this time. Another chimes in.

'I should go –'

'Yeah, of course. I hope . . . It is great to –'

'I wish we had more time.'

'It's OK –'

'It is so good to see you –'

'Yeah. And you. Take care –'

And then she is walking, turning. 'I will do. You too, OK?'

He doesn't see her leave. He takes a breath, steadies himself, then heads over to the old café building where he's parked, feeling in his pocket for his keys. As he rests his coffee on the roof, he hears quick footsteps behind him. She is half-biting her lower lip and, without a word, she wraps her arms around him. He feels the air leave his lungs. He embraces her back, resting his cheek on her head. When they separate, she reaches up, kisses him on the corner of his mouth. Eye to eye. This time he watches her go. One last look. She pulls away and is lost in the frenzy of the highway.

*

A song starts, but he reaches for the dial and switches it off. Drive far enough and the road starts to sing your stories back to you. He sits staring with his head against the headrest feeling the gentle rock of the car from the passing lorries. The torn plastic snagged in the branches still dances with the wind. What the hell was God thinking when he made life so short, so irredeemable, so sad? Two new updates sound. He doesn't look at them. He steers the Volvo towards the road and merges into its flow, putting his foot down, heading north. At Barnby Moor he ignores a turning for the hotel and presses on towards the horizon, towards a place he doesn't remember.

Leave/Remain (Reprise)
(Barnby Moor–Bawtry)

I

What you'll read is that there was a violent argument. Two men. A Nottinghamshire inn on the old highway. A June day, 1721. You'll read that an officer in a company of guards was returning south with his regiment from fighting the Jacobites in Scotland and that this officer, a Midford Hendry, stumbled into the inn, removed his hat and took refreshment. Exhausted to his bones, Hendry drank freely, indulgently. In a corner sat a local gentleman by the name of John Baragh, a name already nubbed with earthy inflection and associations: barrow, burial mound, spoil and bones. Words were exchanged. Inquisitively and then, as the drink flowed, carelessly. Meanings became confused. Courtesies ceased. Inferences were made. Words came back. Misconstrued opinions sounded like sympathies for enemies. Voices were raised, chairs overturned. The innkeeper and others drinking in the parlour rushed to intercede as the two men rose, before Hendry stepped back a few paces, drew a sabre and ran John Baragh through his heart. What you'll read in the old road books, in the county histories and local websites, is that there was a disagreement and a man killed unnecessarily. You'll read a road warning: a drinker's parable rolled out through the eighteenth and nineteenth centuries about the dangers of discussing politics in taverns. But what you'll read is wrong. For while these men would meet along the highway and there would be a murder, the circumstances and reasons – the how and why – are not the tale told. For three centuries the truth has been unknown.

*

Three north roads meet at Elkesley, just south of Barnby Moor. The A1 is the dominant party, winding thickly west and north, distinct from the Great North Road's passage up through Gamston, Eaton and Retford. Less well known and far less travelled is the original road – the 'Old London Road' – which threads, narrowed, silent, between the others. This is, by any classification, a lost highway. At its southern end, close to where it once ran into Elkesley's high street, I am kneeling by the highway again, searching for the dead. Hoping the ground might give up its ghosts.

The graveyard at St Giles' is, this morning, like the village: still, empty. The church locked. I try three numbers on the noticeboard, nobody picks up. A quick circuit of the streets reveals no one to ask for help. So, I search again. Names, dates, inscriptions, pocked and pitted with weather. Tiny grottos of sandstone hollowed into over-hangs. Then a small headstone with a curved top. I run my fingers over its words:

> *HERE lieth intered the body*
> *of John Baragh Gent*
> *who was murdered by*
> *Midford Hendry, officer*
> *in the Guards, on the 24th*
> *day of June 1721; aged*
> *29 years.*

C. G. Harper records this headstone in his book on the road. Drawing on older retellings he sites the killing at the 'Jockey House' – an inn less than half a mile along the Old London Road at its crossing with Jockey Lane. Gamston airfield has since erased the direct route from the church. Reaching it means a traverse of the multi-lanes of the A1.

Riotous wild flowers, grasses; spurts of ragwort, thistle, dock. Thick-leafed young hazel and orange-berried rowan. New planting for the adjusted road system. A tarmac-enclosed nature reserve of a central reservation. Pollinators baffled into loops and spirals by the traffic. 'Loony Juice' and ubiquitous Red Bull cans. Flattened McDonald's burger boxes. A solitary slipper with SUPER DAD printed across its top.

The Jockey House is now a private home, hidden away by hedges, by the crossroads. A stone pillar, inscription eroded, is unreadable, save for: 'Coach Road / Work/sop Mannor ... 176 ...' It is only from Harper's notes that I know to check for the words: 'Keys in the Jockey House' on the side. A memento of when the unmanned turnpike gate stood here with the business of payment being conducted from the pub.

Harper's story of Baragh and Hendry goes cold at this point. A body lies on a parlour floor. A gravestone inscribed with an unusually accusatory message. The questions left – *why would an officer in the Guards leave his company to drink alone in a roadside inn?* – become loose threads; nothing more. Other writers attempted investigations, before and after Harper, but gave up. Too many dead ends. Records too-long-lost to recover. Descendants of witnesses, participants, mouldering in the earth. Such is the way. Stories slacken and get re-spun for new times with new narratives. Truths buried. What actually happened, what might have happened, become indistinct.

The breakthrough was accidental. Good timing on my part. Accessible sources made available for the first time in more than 250 years at the same moment I was hunting for them. The key to it being the digitisation of stacks of records from the Nottingham assizes, including a review of 'the STATE TRIALS' of 1721. A casual search in the new database had returned two names. Altered, but unmistakable: *John Barugh* and *Mitford Henry*. Evidence, testimony. The whole truth, before God.

*

Let me tell this again. The 22nd of June 1721. John Barugh lifts his hat in a farewell to his aunt and trots up the drive of Apethorpe Hall, riding six miles on country lanes before turning his horse on to the Great North Road. Midsummer. Young hazel; rowan. Wild flowers in the meadows and verges. Grasses, thistle, dock. Skylarks rising into blue, their songs cascading over ripening wheat and barley. Barugh is in high spirits. His aunt, housekeeper to Lord Westmorland, had summoned her nephew from London to her Lord's seat near Peterborough for the purpose of naming him her sole heir. Barugh's plan was to return to his wife in London immediately afterwards, but he'd changed his mind. With matters concluded favourably and the weather beautifully clement, he declared his intention not to turn back for London straight away, but to travel onward, to visit another aunt who lived further up the north road, near Doncaster.

The stay at Apethorpe Hall with his aunt has been an enjoyable one. Members of Westmorland's household will, in time, from the witness stand, recall his character and behaviour. Servants and gentlemen of the estate describing him as an honest and 'timerous' man with impeccable manners. They will relate how Barugh was invited to various nearby estates belonging to 'Persons of Quality' to view collections of paintings and curiosities because of his keen interest in such things. They will share that the evening before he departed, concerns were raised that he would be taking to the highway alone and unarmed, carrying nothing more than a horse whip. One gentleman of the estate, a Mr Wardman, will later go on record as being so perturbed at Barugh's lack of pistols and sword that he offered him his own blade to carry, but Barugh refused.

What follows is unsure for Barugh travels alone. Assumptions might be made, however. The place he joins the Great North Road is not far from Wansford. It is a broad, well-worn yet relatively dry highway at this time of the year. He breaks for victuals at the George in Stamford, then pushes north again in the afternoon to make the most of long hours of daylight. Where he spends the night is unknown, but at a decent lick on a good horse, he could have covered twenty-five miles a day. There is no rush, though. Equally as likely is that he takes his time. Perhaps he visits the churches that may be glimpsed from the road, indulging his interests as his horse is rested and fed.

The journey opens up parts of England John Barugh has never seen. On either side a shifting prospect of sunbaked crops dotted with workers' cottages and the remnants of once-wide, unenclosed commons. Now and then, rest is taken at the little clusters of roadside buildings where beer, bread and cheese may be bought. But there are stretches where verges are high as a traveller on a horse and close over him. Spells of woodland where the bushes in the thickness of the season transform the road into a tunnel of darkness. Where the words of warning from Mr Wardman come back to him.

Wherever he goes, he is aware of being watched. On him, the eyes of the farm labourers and ostlers, of serving maids and carters, of

cartwrights, woodcutters, blacksmiths, postboys, of passing coachmen, walkers and beggars, and those other kinds of road men. The
sort you never see, but that see you well enough. You wonder if, after
two days, this begins to get to him. To gnaw at that 'timerous' soul.
You wonder if he begins to sense a malevolence to the highway and
realise the danger he is in, like a swimmer too far out in open sea. You
wonder if it infects his mind, for he rises early on Midsummer's Day,
24th of June, breakfasts and sets out at first light, heading north.

Enter the scene Mitford Henry. No company of soldiers. No regiment returning from Scotland, but a captain of the Horse Grenadier
Guards nonetheless. Henry is heading north, not south. He has travelled from London to Cambridge via stagecoach, arriving on the 23rd
of June, carrying warrants for post-horses and guides that will see him
all the way to Durham where he has business to attend to. By noon on
the 24th, he is in Tuxford where he requisitions a thirteen-year-old
postboy by the name of William Glaseby from the Tuxford postmaster. The boy will lead him as far as Bawtry, just inside the border
of Yorkshire. Knowing the way well, young Glaseby rides ahead of
Mitford Henry with the officer's portmanteau strapped to the back of
his horse. The jurors will hear tell of the captain's temperament this
day: distracted, impatient. They will hear of a previous incident where
he'd threatened to 'stab' a postboy who took him along a road he
disliked, and of how, on this journey, he repeatedly left his meal at the
post-house in Tuxford to check on his belongings, which contained
loose gold, a fine watch, a diamond ring and a considerable amount
of money. Two hundred pounds in notes. Riding on the Great North
Road, Henry takes comfort from having his portmanteau in sight, a
good horse and his sabre at his side. He possesses an instinctive knowledge of how to wield it in lethal fashion. He is a worldly man who
knows and fears the open road. Not for a second would he dream of
travelling it alone, or, God forbid, without a weapon.

What happens to John Barugh the morning before he encounters
Mitford Henry is a mystery, but they meet on what is now the Old
London Road, north of Elkesley at around 1.45 p.m., near to the farm
that will become the Jockey House Inn. John Barugh appears riding
fast 'on the gallop' in an agitated state. Pulling alongside the young
postboy, he asks if this is the road to Doncaster and whether the boy

and the gentleman were headed there themselves. He is spooked, wide-eyed and so unlike the shy, well-mannered man of Apethorpe Hall two days previously that the only conclusion to be drawn is that something has occurred. Panic, disorientation. A belief, perhaps, that he is being followed, for the postboy hasn't given an answer before Barugh is turning his horse in a circle and riding off some distance in a different direction. After seeming to change his mind, Barugh turns back again and returns once more at a gallop. In the time between, Mitford Henry has shouted up to the postboy, asking whether the stranger might not be a highwayman. Glaseby's reply is incredulous, throwaway: 'He is but a little one, if he is one!' Yet Captain Henry is not amused. He is twitchy. As Barugh passes him a second time to confer with the postboy again, Henry kicks his heels and closes the distance on his mare, drawing his sabre as he rides. Before Barugh can speak, Mitford Henry charges and thrusts his blade so forcefully into the left side of Barugh's back that most of it bursts out of his breastbone. Withdrawn, it is bloody from its tip to 'a hand's breadth from the hilt'. Grievously wounded, John Barugh clutches at his chest, exclaiming: *Lord have mercy on me.* Then, desperately: *What shall I do now?* He slumps, then slides off the still-trotting horse into the dust of the road. The injury is catastrophic. No surgeon, then or now, could prevent what follows. As Mitford Henry, his blade still bloodied and drawn, screams at the postboy to *ride on, ride on,* John Barugh lies alone on the old highway, coughing up his black heartblood, his eyes searching the blue; blinking, then stilling. With wild flowers and willowherb shushing him in the summer breeze and the skylarks burbling on above, the road absorbs him.

*

It is Midsummer's Day, 2019. A line of horse's prints in the mud of the verge. A black rider sign with a red margin. The road undulating with the land. Pencil-scratch wires disappear into distance. As far as I can estimate, I am standing where John Barugh met his fate. Nothing stirs in the film I record on my phone, but the calls of skylarks and yellowhammers burble over the distant, low hum-chorus of the A1.

The coroner's report detailed Barugh's wound as half an inch across and eight inches deep. A puncture through his torso. A real highway-man's farewell, which is exactly how Mitford Henry and his counsel tried to spin it. There had been, they maintained, a series of unfortunate events. The dead man's erratic arrival and his challenging (Henry claimed in court) of the postboy 'to a race'; his whipping of the lad's mare; the boy declaring that this stranger was surely 'a rogue'; Henry's concern for his all in the portmanteau; a riding whip in Barugh's hand that resembled a pistol – all grounds for action. The deceased had given the impression of a highwayman and it was this that drove the lethal charge, the death blow. When cross-examined on his actions and why he had fled from the mortally injured Barugh, Henry claimed that he had glimpsed a confederate – another man he said was half-hidden in the hedgerow.

The testimony of the postboy, William Glaseby, disassembled this. No pistol. No danger. No quarrel. No 'other'. After the killing, the captain's scream to *ride on* was made sabre-in-hand. As they galloped, coercion was attempted; warnings issued. *Barugh was a highwayman with a weapon, wasn't he?* When the boy disagreed, Henry threatened him: *If you do not say you saw a Pistol in his Hand, I will stab you wheresoever I meet you.* Glaseby's testimony to the Justices of the Peace in Bawtry initially backed up Henry's story, but this was the statement of a terrified boy made in front of the man he'd just witnessed kill another. Glaseby would swear later, when not 'under Terror and Surprize', that Barugh had possessed no weapon and posed no risk; that he *had a Mind to ride with them to Bautree, he being a Stranger to the Road.*

Nowhere is there mention of a Jockey House Inn. Barugh's body, found by field workers, was laid in a barn. Another inn makes the testimonies, though. A 'little House' up the road called *Russia-Inn* (later the Rushy Inn). Vintage brick, low and gabled, the place was already centuries old at the time of Barugh's killing and the mail drop point for Retford before the new line for the Great North Road was established in 1766.

Two miles of walking along the revoked high road to reach it is time enough to consider the case again, the closing arguments. It seems incredible, given the evidence, that Mitford Henry could be found anything other than guilty, but to become an officer in the

Horse Grenadier Guards required considerable wealth and social standing. Ranks closed in quickly. The defence produced a clutch of 'Persons of Quality' (including the Earl of Lichfield) to testify that Henry was a sober, modest, peaceable officer. Summing up, the judge, Mr Justice Powel, conceded the stabbing was rash, but was at pains to describe Barugh's actions as 'imprudent'. When the jury unanimously returned a guilty verdict for the murder, Powel stepped in to overrule it, prevailing on them that this was now a matter to be decided by judges. Sides had been chosen. A way out found to save face. Powel instructed that the guilty charge should apply to the lesser crime of common manslaughter, with 'benefit of clergy'. A piece of legal loop-holing that not only 'brought off' Mitford Henry from the indictment, but ensured the immediate appeal lodged by Barugh's widow couldn't stand either. The trial papers don't record a fine or punishment, so it's unlikely the captain faced any. In light of this, the pointed headstone in Elkesley churchyard starts to make sense. Its words deep-carved into durable stone. A lasting voice of anger and injustice defiantly describing a crime for what it really was: *HERE lieth John Baragh . . . murdered by Midford Hendry.*

The road I'm treading this late afternoon feels contemporaneous. More hoof prints; more black rider signs. The spirit of place comes sniffing. The judge described Barugh's behaviour as imprudent. Innocent is another word. What caused him to act the way he did will never be known. It is the bit of tape missing from the recording. Centuries later, other names would be assigned to a similar condition of disorientation and disconnection among travellers: road madness, the highway blues. A mind cut loose and floating, turning inward. The great everything pouring in. The thrill of imminent possibility, of encounter, counterweighted by the crush of unrelenting loneliness and loss. What sticks with me is the haunting image described in the post-boy's testimony: a worried stranger lost in a threatening place, trying to make his way back to safety. That, and the way truth gets overridden to serve self-interest, to get away with murder.

Evening light. A beech wood straddles the road. On its western edge, in a dip, I clear a small space for a fire. Through the trees, I can make out the warm lights of what was once the Rushy Inn, now converted into cottages. The great beeches stand watch here; their trunks have human eyes. There is the sense of being observed – of this wood looking back down the old high road to where the murder happened. Of witnessing. Tying up my hammock, wrapping the cord around a trunk, my fingers brush a letter 'J' carved repeatedly into the bark, like a word trying to be recalled. I trace its pattern, then pull my hand away as I touch and read the name bladed deep into the cambium: 'John'.

II

Pull on my boots, pack up my bed. First-light coffee while listening to the roll of road-thunder in the distance. I open maps, consult the sources. *Where does the highway go from here?* The multiplicity of roads encountered at Elkesley continues to loop and chase, sometimes coalescing; sometimes splitting into two or three. Ancient road, old road, motorway – it's the same all the way to Edinburgh: variations with one great split north of Doncaster that is a legacy of the coaching age. An eastern branch through Selby, York, Thirsk, Northallerton; the other, to the west, through Aberford, Wetherby, Boroughbridge and Catterick. Both becoming one again at Darlington.

I fold it all back together and stow the maps in my pack. It is seven miles straight from this dawn beech wood to Scrooby. A long march in silence. No digressions along the name-change track: the B6420, Green Lane, then the Old London Road again. A perma-tunnel of chlorophyll; strewn about sporadically fly-tipped mattresses, fridges; a post-apocalyptic bus shelter (TRUST NO ONE sprayed in blood red). Through the riotous undergrowth I glimpse razor-wire security fences and flashes of HM Prison Ranby. Then Ye Olde Bell on Barnby Moor appears, huge, white, at the point the older highway rejoins the later course of the Great North Road.

The Bell was once the greatest posting and coaching business outside London. Farms, paddocks, 200 horses, dorms for its postboys. There is still a suite named after Queen Victoria who overnighted here with her mother. Aura and nostalgia remain the potent welcome cocktail. Records are viewable on request. A distinguished visitors' book houses signatures of future ghosts. Among its twentieth-century celebrity scratches is the name Bing Crosby who stayed numerous times at the hotel in the 1950s during golfing tours of Britain. Unrecorded is how much of a notion Crosby had of his own connection to the north road – of his in-the-blood link to this highway. But what we know now is that Crosby was a descendant of William Brewster, the ruling elder of the Pilgrim Fathers who left this land for America on the *Mayflower*. Brewster was, for years, the postmaster at Scrooby. His beat: the drag between Tuxford and Doncaster, including this spot his nine-times great-grandson returned to.

The Great North Road bypassed Scrooby after 1766; part of the same realignment that consigned the older high road on which John Barugh was murdered to a backwater. The village now lies east of the later highway, quiet, unpeopled. Builders' vans half-parked on kerbs. A place of road-fronting cottages, bungalows, tidy gardens. A leafy eddy off the main river. 'Low Road' is the primary candidate for the course of the older line when it came through the village, so I follow it towards what is marked 'Scrooby Manor' on the map. Given the numbers of American tourists that must descend each year, everything is surprisingly uncurated, unscathed. A TripAdvisor link – 'What to do in Scrooby' – opens a blank page. Only one pub: the Pilgrim Fathers (once the Saracen's Head). No museum. No shops peddling *Mayflower* souvenirs. No statue of Brewster reciting the Compact. Manor Road promises, then deposits me at a locked gate. No admittance unless part of a guided tour, so I double back for a view over the fields at all that remains of the once-considerable manor: a pretty farmhouse of age-skewed pink brick and orange pantile roof. Virginia creeper softening its corners. Ecclesial windows. This remnant is believed to have once been part of the manor house's chapel. The rest of the estate – originally a timber-framed medieval palace built for the Archbishop of York – must be imagined.

Imagine again too that unsure, volatile world – those same shifting religious and political sands on which Cromwell and Charles Stuart found themselves. The lingering aftershocks of the Reformation, the lurches between Protestantism and Catholicism; heretics aflame at Smithfield. Foxe's gruesomely illustrated *Book of Martyrs* an enduring bestseller up and down the north road. Faith held firmly in the heart. Faith not a lifestyle choice, but law. Life dictated by the church courts. Local church attendance mandatory – no 'gadding about' allowed, as visiting other churches was described. Punishment for attending the wrong church. Punishment for preaching if not ordained.

William Brewster took over the role of postmaster at Scrooby in 1590. Duties were set: aid passage of the queen's mail. Organise and maintain riders, postboys and horses to cover the twenty-four miles under his jurisdiction. There were side hustles in food, drink, lodging and road guides for travellers, as well as the movement of private missals. Brewster had been exposed to reformed religion as a student at Cambridge, but it would be during his years as 'Master of Poste' at Scrooby that everything changed; here, on the Great North Road, that the course of history would once more be altered.

*

William Brewster's radicalisation came from the pulpit of Richard Clyfton. In Clyfton's hand while he preached, the illegal Geneva Bible – the first mass-produced, mechanically printed word of God made available to the common people, with its woodcuts, annotations and study aids. Unadulterated, unadorned, it was translated 'purely' from Hebrew and Greek origin texts and it flooded the north road after its first printings. It remained the dissenter's choice. Inspired to live by what they held to be its truths, men like Clyfton believed that Puritanism – with its wish to rinse away popery and ritual, but its ultimate compliance – didn't go far enough in removing Rome from the Church of England. Clyfton's separatist congregation followed the word of the Bible literally. They believed in organising themselves and condemned the church as filled with anti-Christian corruption. The only righteous road was a total break from the Church of England. This presented a direct challenge to the church's newly crowned head, James I. A crackdown was inevitable. In 1605, radical ministers, including Richard Clyfton, were removed and replaced by the episcopal hierarchy. In defiance, William Brewster opened up the doors of Scrooby Manor to secret, Nonconformist meetings. Clandestine gatherings on the Lord's Day saw Clyfton still preaching to the faithful. It was the ideal rallying place, and Brewster the perfect host. As postmaster, he had his fingers on the pulse. He knew the word on the street, the *strata*, outside his door. Scrooby Manor was a place to exchange secret letters. A liminal space for outside thinking. But the movement of people each Sunday to this new church was bound to attract attention. Royal spies were everywhere. Brewster too high-profile to ignore. By autumn 1607 the net was closing. Brewster resigned his commission as postmaster. The congregation was broken up by the authorities: fines, imprisonments, houses ransacked. Remaining in England became untenable. The separatists fled to Holland before entertaining fantasies of the New World – of establishing their own Promised Land.

What might be said is that, as well as its local deviations, the north road branched at Scrooby and, in 1620, the *Mayflower* carried it over the ocean, rooting it again at Plymouth Colony. Every Pilgrim, as the separatists came to be known, needs a road; every road needs its pilgrims. Bankrolling the vision of a heaven-on-earth elsewhere was the City of London. Joint-stock companies and merchant adventurers drew up patents to claim and colonise the east coast of North America as a way of expanding commercial opportunities. The success of Jamestown, founded in 1607 in Virginia, acted as inspiration and reassurance for investors. In the City's eyes, such settlements were risky ventures but potential gold mines. Future bastions of high-yield trade and footholds into new markets for English goods. All they required were willing colonisers, preferably family units, prepared to cross the ocean, facilitate the land grab and do the dirty work of surviving and negotiating for life and livelihood with the native populations. Financing was available for ocean crossings, but the terms onerous: seven years to repay the debt. The *Mayflower* Pilgrims went all-in, investing in their own enterprise, holding stock in the same companies that were lending them money to leave.

This was never a New England, or a 'new' anything. Not really. European traders, explorers, settlers and fishermen had been making contact with the indigenous people of the north-east coast of America well before the *Mayflower* docked. Slaves had been taken, blood spilled, viruses circulated. When the Pilgrims waded ashore, the Patuxet village they chose as a new Plymouth had been abandoned because of an epidemic of disease that tore through the Wampanoag tribal federation, decimating, in places, entire populations. Mortality rate among the Patuxet was 100 per cent. No one left, even, to bury the dead. The first act of the Pilgrims was to shovel away drifts of human bones bleached by the sun. *Providence*, they believed. This was God clearing the path.

Their survival, in fact, depended on the last remaining Patuxet. A man who'd been transported as an enslaved person in 1614 (thereby escaping the epidemic), but who'd found his way home with a grasp of English. 'Squanto', as the Pilgrims would call him, was their intermediary and oracle. After the winter of 1620, during which half the colony had died from sickness and starvation, Squanto showed them how to plant and grow the 'three sisters': beans, maize, squash. He set up trading arrangements with the Wampanoag – alliances of necessity that saw the reduced tribes and thinned-out Pilgrims strike deals of protection and partnership. Seeing out another year became possible; farming and a trade in furs might allow them to begin paying back their debts.

By 1623 William Brewster was the senior elder of the colony, preaching with a Geneva Bible brought over from Scrooby. His friend from just up the old highway at Austerfield, William Bradford, was at the colony's operational helm. For two years, systems of production and distribution were collective. Fruits of labour pooled and shared between the families. But the Pilgrims were unable to shrug off the want in the belly, the lingering threat of starvation. At Bradford's suggestion, an overhaul: each family would have a plot to cultivate, from which they would solely reap the rewards.

Working in isolation, the Pilgrims became newly incentivised. The shift dramatic. By 1624, in his *Good Newes from New England*, the Pilgrim Edward Winslow was describing the colony in Plymouth as a place where 'religion and profit jump together'. It was the City of London's vision manifesting: nascent venture capitalism. Up and down the north road, word spread about the success of the colonists and their religious freedoms, autonomy and opportunities. Waves of Puritans and separatists felt inspired to follow, including, as we know, a disgusted Oliver Cromwell in 1636. Frustrated in their bid for ecclesiastical power, these faithful had, with their everyman, easy-to-understand bibles, driven a cultural shift and birthed a new kind of Englishman. An Englishman that Roger Sharrock in his introduction to John Bunyan's *The Pilgrim's Progress* (itself set along the Great

North Road) describes as: '[E]ndowed with an earnestness and sense of mission not present in his medieval ancestor but familiar in the evangelical rebels and pioneers of the eighteenth and nineteenth centuries ... [L]ife was ... the adventurous journey of the armed and vigilant Christian through hostile country.' For 'hostile country' read both Old World and new. The expansion of the Virginia and Massachusetts colonies and the demand for more land to increase profits quickly brought the colonists into conflict with native populations. Deals were broken; promises on both sides ceased to be honoured. Alliances only held for as long as the colonisers needed them to. In the 1670s, a war broke out that saw the Wampanoag federation devastated. Lands were seized by forces of the combined colonies for further settlements. Metacomet, sachem to the Wampanoag, also known by his adopted English name 'King Philip', was killed, beheaded, drawn and quartered; his head spiked at Plymouth Colony's gates. The road, growing from New England, had seen it all before. Annexation; possession. The shadowing of an advancing column like a trail of blood.

We know what followed. The devastating fire that would be kindled and carried on the wind. The repeating pattern. From the vanished timber manor house across the fields at Scrooby, from the Great North Road, came the momentum for the great drive westward. It beams from John Gast's *American Progress* (1872). Columbia, spirit of the United States (upscaled Britannia in a Roman toga), is a celestial being bearing the star of empire, carrying in one hand telegraph wires; in the other, a good book. The painting seeks to be read right to left, east to west: the suggested direction of progress across the American landscape. From the coast of the first colonies and city successors drifts a goddess-angel of enlightenment bringing dawn to the treacherous, storm-dark lands of The West. Cowering, fleeing, falling out of frame, are buffalo, bears, indigenous people – signifiers of barbarism, wildness. On their heels, colonisers arrive via wagon, stagecoach, train. Beneath Columbia, pioneer-pilgrims walk a new road.

Heaven-on-earth came at a heavy price, paid by the native population. What we know of the Wampanoag and their ancestors before the arrival of the *Mayflower* speaks of thousands of years of symbiotic existence with the natural world. An evolved, living-in-tune with

nature that followed the migratory patterns of food sources. It wasn't all Eden, but as skilled hunters, farmers and fishers, the Wampanoag lived inland in the winter and by the water in the summer in homes befitting weather and climate. They had effective governing structures; matriarchal (and matrilineal) societies with leaders who were answerable to their people. The notion of pilgrims bringing over civilisation, advancement and salvation to the 'savages' would prove the enduring myth. It was the settler-colonialism logic rolled out across America but ruthlessly road-tested and enacted all over the wider world by Europe's burgeoning empires. Here was the real savagery. Exploitation, destruction. Mastery and control. A kind of perceptual narrowing that, over time, legitimised, even celebrated, the prolonged, systematic eradication and annihilation of indigenous peoples, cultures, learnings, religions, languages and, by default, ancient ways of existing with, and *within*, their environment. Acts that continue to have profound consequences on the way that all of us live today.

*

I follow the course of Low Road, twisting and lifting through Scrooby, to rejoin the Great North Road again. A passage of peaceful road walking beside tall fields, amid the scratch-drone of crickets, along a buffer of wild flowers, grasses, undersown with decaying road junk: plastic sheeting, farm sacks. Cans and bottles. On this road between Scrooby Manor and Austerfield, between the homes of William Brewster and William Bradford, the temptation is to imagine an undoing. The rolling-back of the road to its root. Gast's painting reversed. The shrinking of everything that came after, back to this old highway running through these fields. *What if?* I'm thinking of how complicated it can be to try to consider the motivations and attitudes of another time through the lens of our own. History is always more chaos than design. And although the road branched here, what might also be said is that the intent of Pilgrims like Bradford and Brewster was not to usher in what followed. They sought a New Testament and a mutuality and social perfection where people might go about their daily lives in holiness and purity. From the very beginning, this was tainted. Half of the Plymouth Colony was less than godly. The 'Strangers' to the separatist 'Saved', as Bradford described them, were those who'd come for other reasons – because they were seeking a better life, because they were running from crimes. Among this multitude were numerous 'wicked' and 'profane' who crept into the colony's corners and whose misdemeanours sickened and shocked Bradford. Punishments were handed out, a semblance of order restored each time, but the hoped-for vision of perfection was soon fading. What remained was a notion of religious ideals to be aimed at and (purportedly, at least) consulted and followed, but that went from jumping hand-in-hand with enterprise and profit to mattering far less. Both in America and England, the desires and intentions of the earthlier multitudes for land and plunder powered the Pilgrims' progress in America. It was something William Bradford would come to realise and lament in his own lifetime, writing of his beloved church in 1644: 'Thus she that had made many rich became herself poor.' As the poet Baron Wormser observes in his essay 'More Money than God': 'The immaterial longing evinced by the Pilgrims for a true church of true believers descended into material success: farms, houses and money. Moralizing habits remained ... but the animating power became mere covetous assertion – clear more land. The forests must have seemed endless.' And through them, a road. That tunnel vision.

Ours is, I tell myself, a prejudiced perspective, enjoyed with all the benefits growth and progress has brought. Ours is the luxury of hindsight. But what cannot be ignored is where else this road has led us – an ingrained belief in human exceptionalism and anthropocentrism. The dominance of individualistic commodity culture. The fixed notion that competition beats cooperation; that the environment necessary to our survival only exists to serve us. That it can be abused to the point of total destruction.

I'm thinking about these things along the Great North Road into Bawtry as shadows lengthen because the news carries two starkly relevant stories that seem so interlinked. One is about the UK Parliament becoming the first in the world to declare an environment and climate emergency. The other concerns SpaceX – the company of billionaire Elon Musk with its objective to colonise Mars. In reports of the latter, the *Mayflower* is evoked as evidence of humankind's thirst for freedom. We're told Musk's plans represent the '*Mayflower* moment' for space exploration. Words like 'mission' and 'destiny' are sprinkled through the writing – mentions of new frontiers, new worlds. The year 2050 is ringed as critical. Everything points to that being the achievable moment for touching down on Mars and populating a pre-built, life-sustaining colony on the desert planet. 2050 is also the critical date for the other story. It is the year by which the UK Parliament has committed to reach net-zero on greenhouse gas emissions. The imperative being to prevent global temperatures from reaching 2°C above pre-industrial levels by 2100, and no more than 1.5°C by 2050. Even if successful, which appears less than likely based on current trajectories, we must prepare for unprecedented ecological and environmental impacts: sea level rises, displaced populations, floods, more extreme weather, food and water shortages, the increasing risk of global conflict over resources. It is alarming the ways the powerful and those in power can close ranks and rewrite the truth. The way facts still get overridden to serve self-interest, to get away with murder. I'm thinking these things as I work out that in 2050 my son will only be thirty-eight years old and my daughter thirty-six. Both will be younger than I was when I began exploring this road.

*

It may be problematic to second-guess motivations and decisions made in history, but it is suicidal not to criticise, challenge and change our consistent failure to heed the warnings that history reveals. Even though we know they are not, we still behave as if the forests are endless. We pursue a path of limitless covetous assertion, of competition over cooperation; of profit over everything. Our restlessness means we still ache for new frontiers and promised lands and we stake fortunes on the dream of reaching them. We do it in the name of destiny, and in the name of God. What we seem unable to do is to make work the heaven-on-earth we have. Our perceptual narrowing continues to tunnel our vision. The only meaning, we assert, is the meaning that we make for ourselves. The meaning that *we* bring. There is an irony to the fact that the community and mutuality William Brewster sought to exist in was staring him in the face when he arrived in America. Looking down the road now, we must try to see what he could not: a people existing with and within their environment. A people resigned to the influence of the Earth. A people who believed they shared a consciousness with everything they encountered and that lived as part of a reciprocal system. Looking up the road to what's coming fast, we might then demand that the countless billions due to be spent on devising ways to leave this world are spent instead on saving it for our children. On learning how we can unblind ourselves and find ways of remaining here.

III

One more tale from this stretch of highway. This one known and still repeated. What you'll hear is of a man tried for murder sometime in the 1700s. A saddler from Bawtry, the coaching town on the north road just south of Doncaster. You'll hear that while the man protested his innocence and pleaded for clemency, he was sentenced to death. That in the tradition of all condemned men, on the way to the gallows he was offered a chance to remain a little longer, to take a measure of strong beer at an alehouse before he took to the scaffold. A last long drink before the long road out of this world. You'll hear that, raging at the fate forced upon him, the saddler refused, damning what was held up to him, demanding that the cart's course did not deviate from its ultimate end. You'll hear that, as he jerked, kicked and choked at the end of the rope, he saw the messenger desperately fighting through the crowd, waving a piece of paper, screaming that he held the saddler's reprieve signed by the judge that morning. But by the time they cut the condemned man down, they couldn't bring breath back to his broken body. The proverb is an old one. A Yorkshire folk tale slurred in pubs with a beer-skewed grin, warning about how you should never turn down a free drink for it might save your life. At its core, though, another haunting image: a man seeing that messenger, knowing he could have been saved, but that it was too late. The desperate realisation that had he only made a different decision and done what was suggested, he would have survived.

III

Road Home

It was in me, burning
like a coal-seam fire.
The Road.

Robin Robertson

Someone I loved once gave me a box full of darkness.
It took me years to understand that this too, was a gift.

Mary Oliver

Mine

(Doncaster–Catterick)

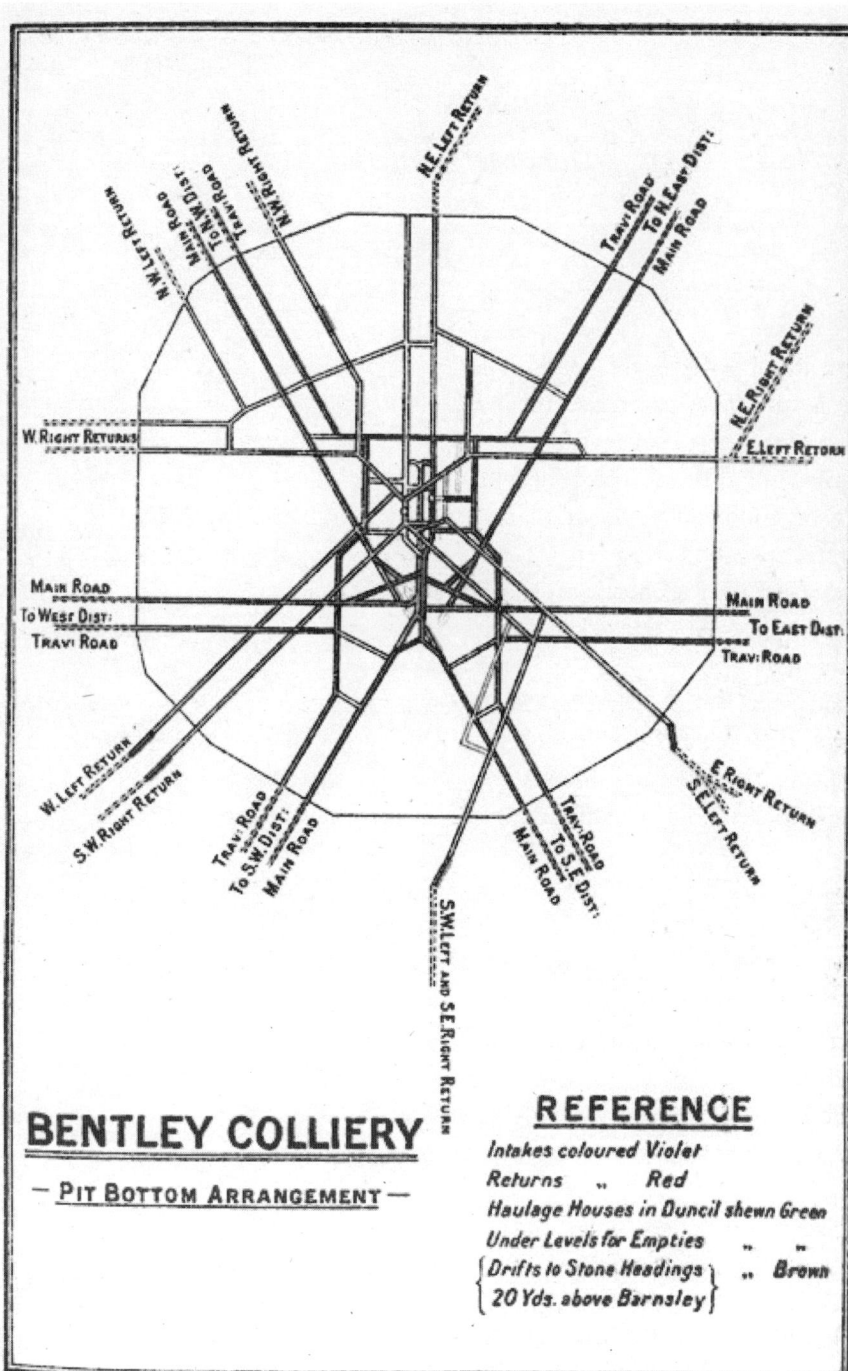

BENTLEY COLLIERY

— Pit Bottom Arrangement —

REFERENCE

Intakes coloured Violet
Returns   „   Red
Haulage Houses in Duncil shewn Green
Under Levels for Empties   „   „
{ Drifts to Stone Headings }   „   Brown
{ 20 Yds. above Barnsley }

I

Beneath me there are roads. Half a mile underground, below the birch- and pine-furred rise, this burial mound of a back-filled hill with its paths, open spaces and its views over Doncaster, a network of roads runs through the bedrock. While they can't be accessed, they can be followed. A 1924 plan of Bentley Colliery strips away the layers, revealing a pattern of roadways ribboning out in black, red and violet lines from the pit shaft to the coal faces and back. Tonight, here in the silent dark, I find the map on my phone. I zoom in and trace its lines, reading the names: the Main Roads, the Travelling Roads, the Returns. I see again the strange shape they form as they cross, then recross each other. Yesterday, when showing it to my son at home, it had resembled a star. Now it appears different. More clearly, I see a figure. A human body lying in a hole in the earth.

*

At the start of all this, the old photograph of my ancestors lined up along the highway had acted like a medium, establishing a point of contact. Its rows of expectant faces had raised questions. The dark, half-smile stare of my great-grandfather was a challenge to follow. The road beneath his feet a leading line. Not much to go on, but always that one clear destination, at least. Somewhere it felt like my duty to reach:

The Cowen Family. 16 French Gate. The Great North Road. Doncaster.

Earlier. Crossing the border into Yorkshire at Bawtry, I pick up the Great North Road northwards. I'm carrying a printout of the family photograph folded in my pocket; locations of the known places they lived and worked bullet-pointed in my notebook. Easy walking at first light under grey, ruffling skies split by occasional strafing shafts of sun. The tall, budding trees enclosing the broad strip of highway briefly catch the glow before being snuffed out again by the sudden squalls of a biting wind.

The news, like the day, unsettled. The virus that has been hacking, sneezing and sweating its way across Asia and Europe is now doing its damage on these shores. Government bluff, bluster and attempts to evoke British stoicism as a workable defence against infection have become layered with more practical advice. There is a fresh look of fear in ministers' eyes. The men (and it is always men) taking the questions at the lectern are beginning to look like worried boys in borrowed suits too big for their bones. The message has been: *business as usual*. Yet those really in the know (the epidemiologists, virologists) suggest a better use of the days before the coming storm might be to get our affairs in order. To attend to any loose ends. Taking their advice, I'd brought forward this planned day of walking over old ground in search of clues and cues – a searching of the territory for the possibility of meaning or explanation. Just enough time to get out under the wire and bring back some closure to these nagging preoccupations.

The world uncertain and anxious, and yet this leg of the highway unusually unequivocal, sure of itself. I can follow the exact route listed at the front of C. G. Harper's *The Great North Road* with its list of calling points and distances measured to the quarter-mile: 'Bawtry 153½ / Rossington Bridge (cross River Tome) 157¾ / Tophall 158¾ / Doncaster (cross River Don) 162¼'. This is the old Roman way that once connected colonies at Lincoln and York, noted in the Antonine Itinerary. It was that second branch to Ermine Street built soon after the first, west of the original, providing an all-weather, non-ferry alternative to the perils of crossing the Humber.

Doncaster grew out of *Danum*, the Roman fort and later village (*Don ceaster*) built to guard the meeting point of this inland road and the River Don. In his old age in the 1880s, the ex-coachman Tom Bradley recalled the nine miles leading to Doncaster from the south as the 'finest road in England'. A racing road in its heyday. Wide enough for six coaches abreast. He painted a vision: the likes of the *Highflyer* stretching her legs. Chestnuts in bloom, groves of purple beeches, laburnum; the scent of wild hyacinths and lilac. Remnants form strange juxtapositions today. Sweeps of sprayed-dead winter weeds ready for ploughing next to neat areas of cultivated grass dotted with broad parkland trunks. Stray copper beeches looming over signage for local ventures. BAWTRY PAINTBALL offers 'Archery / Axe-throwing / Zombie Paintball'. Other activities advertised on its website are darkly relevant: a game of trying to outwit and survive against a lethal, unseen predator – an experience endorsed by One Direction.

For miles, traffic is constant yet thinned, already distancing. Ahead, the land widens. Fizzes of chiffchaff, blackbird drowned out by the drone of a roundabout and the four-lane cutting east–west. I pass under the yellow, nine-metre-high letter 'Y' (signifying the 'Gateway to Yorkshire'), with its own parking for passing selfie takers, then drift along the old high road through Doncaster's southern suburbs to Town Moor.

Those coachmen rattling at full lick, whipping their four-teams to best each other, were only the warm-up. The real racing took place on the horse track. Back when the road was wider, unrestricted, un-kerbed, when the 'moor' of the racecourse's name was still undeveloped, this was a Great North Road institution. An unmissable feature. The big race days, the St Leger and the Cup, saw north–south coaches caught in riptides of visitors. Easier to stop in the city until races were over than fight your way through to reach already full hostelries and coaching inns. In the early 1800s, racegoers flocked to Doncaster by hoof, coach, foot; in the later Victorian period, when Doncaster was the industrial hub for the Great Northern Railway, iron rail shipped them in by the hundreds of thousands. On Leger Day, 1887, Sir William Acworth observed: '82 train-loads of excursion passengers from every part of the country, not only from London, Birmingham and Liverpool, but Barrow, Carlisle and Newcastle, from Chester, Bristol and King's Lynn.' Along the sidings he counted thirty-four trains drawn up, side by side.

Fortunes were made and lost in moments. The town turning a profit by turning itself over to gambling and hard drinking. Pickpockets dressed as clergy; clergy in the habit of locking up the parish church and making themselves scarce. In 1815, Sir William Maxwell celebrated winning the St Leger with his horse, Filho da Puta, by smashing every mirror in the Reindeer Inn with his walking stick, only expressing regret there weren't more to destroy. Forty-two years later, that road-scribe Charles Dickens visited with Wilkie Collins during St Leger week and captured the heaving mass from his bedroom window: '[A] gathering of blackguards from all parts of the racing earth. Every bad face that had ever caught wickedness from an innocent horse had its representation in the streets . . .' His night was spent listening to the shouts and groans of a man comatose in the corridor who'd lost 'two thousand' and drunk himself into oblivion. The next morning, from the same window, Dickens noted long queues for the chemist shops; the sobering and sick begging for relief from dispensers: 'Give us soom sal-volatile or soom damned thing o' that soort, in wather – my head's bad . . .' Half a century on again, little had changed. C. G. Harper notes St Leger week as when 'all the brazen-throated blackguards of the Three Kingdoms' descend upon Doncaster's streets. One street in particular. It's no coincidence Dickens witnessed the noisy congregation of the drunk from his window at the Angel on French Gate. French Gate was glitter and gutter; a fine coat with a dark underbelly. A cluster-strip of coaching inns, hostelries, taverns. The 'French' from its Norman settlement after 1066; the 'Gate' from *gata*, Old Norse for 'street'. French Gate: a later compounded nomenclature for the Roman line through town over river. The line that became the Great North Road.

*

With the photograph in hand, I look up the street. *16 French Gate*. A tangible event at an exact location, but it's harder to locate than it might seem. When my great-grandfather set up shop here the street would have been unchanged from Dickens's and Harper's times. They will have known the same facades, the same race crowds, the same roll call of inns. By my best estimate, after consulting a century-old OS map, number 16 was on the west side of French Gate, sandwiched somewhere between the Bay Horse and the Mail Coach inns. The location works too with Ellen's written testimony about Bill being called on to take the fight out of the more violent detainees in the police station across the road. A few doors down on the east side stood Doncaster's Guildhall. Columned, classical frontage; an echo of the GPO at St Martin's-le-Grand. As well as a court and sessions hall, it housed twenty-four cells. Being any more precise is tricky for the western side of French Gate was abolished in the 1960s. All traces of the medieval burgage plots that evolved into a run of small, roadside trades parasitical on the great highway were cleared off the map. The spine of Britain, the A1, kinked in 1961 in what was the original A1(M) upgrade. Doncaster's centre was bypassed by one of the first stretches of motorway built in the country. French Gate was suddenly open to new investment – new layout schemes and transport–retail concepts. The Guildhall pulled down in 1968; the opposite side razed to make room for the new brutalist architecture of a fast-spreading, US-style, mall concept: the Arndale Centre.

Its successor, the Frenchgate Centre, as it was rechristened in the 1980s, has been revised, enlarged and upgraded numerous times. Millions poured in. The remaining trace of the old road is a lime-tree-planted pedestrian walkway running alongside. An artery severed at both ends to through traffic. A shaded, open-air recovery zone for those exhausted by the franchised labyrinths of the retail colony within. Spray-down metal bench seating, limping pigeons; street lamps with cutaway lettering spell: FRENCHGATE. An attempt at appeasing the spirit of the original, the namesake – that place of genuine gathering that was so comprehensively erased. The question is what to do when even these investment-buoyed retail megaliths begin to doubt their own existence; when there are more discount stores appearing (and disappearing) in the shopping centre than hoped-for high-end brands attracting a hoped-for high-spending clientele? Under the shadow of the Frenchgate Centre's grey and glass exterior, a litter bin has NO MORE DREAMS scrawled on its side in silver marker. A street statement reflecting a tension felt throughout the town centre. Walking the north road continuity of High Street into French Gate is a reminder of once-moneyed townsfolk, of boomtown industries before their systematic disassembling. Of a time when citizens had cash to spend. The run of classical banks, public meeting rooms, places of assembly, Georgian shops, a gilded Mansion House are hollowed out or encroached by more recent realities of post-industrial and austerity government decline: spectral stores; sticky-carpeted betting outlets; empty banks; ex-charity, furniture and footwear shops with washed out TO LET signs. The noise and energy of the road emanates from Merkur Cashino, a 24-hour gambling arcade (free drinks and snacks for punters), with security to bar the rough sleepers. In light of this, NO MORE DREAMS reads like an emphatic response. A refusal to entertain any more plans to raise investment and inject developer collateral or to subscribe to the latest CGI visions of clean, green (-washed), tree-lined avenues with smoked glass, multinational branded stores beneath timber-clad apartment complexes. The same parachuted-in solutions that have folded under the weight of actuality before.

Who is going to live in these places? Who can afford to shop at these luxury stores? Speak to the remaining shopkeepers and they know the problems. The same factors (road and rail) that made Doncaster the perfect spot for Victorian industry have made it the ideal place for Amazon distribution depots the size of fifteen football pitches. Three, at the last count, dotted around its motorway outskirts. The shift online has left the town centre with no workforce, no passing trade, no footfall. No people. Younger idealists recognise the required pivot: smaller, independent stores, restaurants, bars – places that foster again Doncaster's sense of community, of congregation. Hand-crafted fabrics. Recycled clothing. A focus on the sustainable and the made-to-last. Council budgets spent on discounting rates for young, innovating start-ups. NO MORE DREAMS. No. Rather, a waking-up. That which was once here but was lost, restored.

Only one of French Gate's pubs has survived. The White Swan is the fixed point from which the old map makes sense, even if it is now the sliced-off end of French Gate, rather than halfway down. On the benches outside the pub, I fall into conversation with a man in his late seventies who is waiting for his wife. He sits under a newly erected sign, cuffed to a pole: KEEP YOUR DISTANCE. 'My memory is not what it used to be,' he tells me. 'But I remember before they built the shopping centre. The pubs on the street in the late 1950s. The shops. It's this newer stuff I struggle to keep hold of.' He taps his temple. A proud Donny lad, born and bred, he tells me he was an engineer for half a century at the same firm. He loves this place and would never move away, but it's heartbreaking to find it stuck in this constant minor key. To witness the loss of pride. 'It's the kids I feel sorry for. There's nothing for them now. Nothing.'

When his wife arrives, she confides that, with his memory going, he has got into the habit of photographing places on his phone and posting them to Facebook. Altered streets, the abandoned market, closing shops; impractical cycle lanes. Collisions of old and new. He documents the disappearance of places he knew, and that knew him. What this man is able to do, though, is give a good indication of where number 16 used to be.

The family story goes that French Gate was the last *Cowen's* concern to be lost in the Great Depression. The one they fought desperately to keep hold of. All through town, I've been trying to imagine my great-grandfather's arrival, his beginning – the way his eyes must have fallen upon the same details of the same buildings as mine. It occurs to me now that I should've been trying to picture it the other way: the end of his story here. That time in the 1930s when this high street was first a busted flush without an economy to support it. When the value of British exports halved and Doncaster, like all industrial and coal-mining areas, found itself devastated. When staff were laid off overnight and wages cut. When small shops went out of business daily. The French Gate property was the last of the nine businesses my great-grandfather built from scratch to fold and he must have done everything to try to keep it viable: consolidated, brought the family in to work for nothing, made unwanted redundancies. As his flagship business, the French Gate address carried the dual weight of expectation and pride. It's written on that face in the photograph posed outside it during better days. Could Bill have pivoted? Could he have adapted things further to make it work? He would a few years later when in London, pushing a barrow of fresh fish around the streets. Perhaps it was too late to start doing that here. Too many overheads; too many mouths to feed. The tent collapsing in on him. After speaking to the couple on the bench, I wonder too if there wasn't shame involved. The loss of pride that becomes so terminal to the soul.

Atomiser rain. Dark, ridged thunder clouds are sheets of corrugated steel. I wait for the lights to change by the ring road that slices French Gate beyond the White Swan. Cars slick on the patchy tarmac.

The man on the bench pointed the location: a triangle of rough grass formed by a branch of the ring road splitting to link up with the route of the Great North Road, onwards, over the river, across the hump of North Bridge. 'Number 16 would have been where that grass triangle is.' These were his coordinates. Reaching them, I kneel, unfold the crumpled photograph and I leave it, under a stone.

*

North Bridge. And over it, the North Bridge Road. Another location underlined in the back of my notebook. Another point of contact on the line of the Great North Road. Another premises with that number *16* – digits that numerologists would have us believe symbolise 'the looking for, and the finding of, answers'. For more than a decade Bill owned 16 North Bridge Road: a fish and chip restaurant with staff quarters and rooms for the family to live in above. An address mentioned a few times in local press: the registered abode listed for numerous motoring offences. Site of a closing-time fight between Bill and two Arksey miners who refused to pay for their dinners. Men who, in the melee, broke the set of false teeth my great-grandfather was gifted by Doncaster Rovers. A place mentioned too in those regional newspaper reports of the tragic gas poisoning – of that unfortunate girl, Doris Coles, who fell asleep and never woke up.

I'm pressing on, northward, but the film is running backwards. From the French Gate of the 1930s to this: the first shop the family took after Bill quit the mines. The three-quarter-mile-long North Bridge, constructed to carry the Great North Road over river and the East Coast railway, was completed in 1910, replacing a smaller bridge and level crossing at Marsh Gate with a brick-arched and steel super-structure that transported travellers up and over, delivering them in and out of Doncaster town centre. Already mining up the road at Bentley Colliery by this point, Bill must have witnessed the demolition and rebuilding, and the new bridge's grand unveiling. He must have recognised the promise; the latent potential in passers-by pausing to eat before crossing.

As I take the rise, the drizzle fades. The ripple-clouds become a stif-ling, blanket grey. Bypassed now by another bridge, North Bridge is devoid of traffic: a shining curve like a river bending up into this leaf-smoke, late-afternoon sky. Where exactly number 16 stood is

impossible to know with certainty. North Bridge Road has also been altered, knocked back, cleared. The map has it on the north-east side of the bridge in what is now a shadow gap between a Boots store and the only house remaining on the road: a block-windowed, boarded-up villa. This isn't *their* place, but it is contemporary, and right next door. As close as I can get. Somewhere they passed daily and popped in for tea. Somewhere the ghosts might start to push through.

*

For the last few weeks, I've been looking for information on Doris Coles. Fifteen years wasn't long to get a name in the records in 1923. A line in the list of deaths in the district; a census (1911) showing her as one of seven children of George and Martha. No more to be gleaned about who she was, the shape of her short life; how she ended up working for Bill and rooming over the restaurant with the other waitresses, Agnes and Emily. But in the course of my searching, her name had triggered something else. Another newly digitised newspaper report of the inquest. This one, from the *Sheffield Daily Independent*, ran under the headline GAS TAP TRAGEDY. It was a longer article on the coroner's inquiry. In it, the testimony of Emily Loughton, a 'servant waitress', detailing how the three girls slept in the same room, how they had retired to bed around midnight on the night in question and, at around 12.45 a.m., Bill had knocked on the door saying: 'Now, Emily, what about that light?' Doris was already asleep, so, reaching over Agnes, Emily turned off the gas lamp, leaving the window open a few inches. In this fuller account, there were previously undisclosed details: how Agnes had woken in the night at the sound of Doris shouting out; how she tried to wake Emily but, on finding nothing wrong and smelling no gas, fell back asleep. Confused contradictions too: Agnes saying she thought the cause was probably the cuff of her nightdress catching the tap when she turned it off – the material tugging it open as she pulled away. Yet in her statement, Emily had remembered it was *she* who had reached over Agnes to turn off the gas lamp. But both had known nothing more until regaining consciousness the following afternoon. What happened, and how, will never be certain, but under a subheader 'The Discovery', there was the evidence of my great-grandfather. His words on the page. Snippets of his quoted voice. How he'd 'called the girls up at the usual time' but receiving no reply entered the room to be hit by the smell of gas. Finding the girls passed out, breathing heavily, he'd 'shouted for his wife', May, and together how they had attempted 'artificial respiration' while a doctor was urgently sent for, who arrived at 7.15 a.m. The information that a police sergeant also attended and inspected the gas tap. His report to the court that all was in 'adequate' condition.

I already knew the outcome: Agnes and Emily regained consciousness; Doris succumbed to an 'acute ingestion of gas'. I knew the verdict: the coroner's finding of accidental death. What I hadn't expected were the other details that the article revealed. That Bill and May and their children also lived above the restaurant in the rooms adjacent to the girls. That they must have sent one of their kids (presumably Ellen, the eldest at thirteen) to run for the doctor. That Bill and May had hauled the three girls out of that bedroom and given them mouth-to-mouth, desperately trying to get clean air into their poisoned lungs. What I hadn't experienced in the first account was the sense of shock and panic descending after Bill knocked on their door. The anguish and horror as he, May and their children, including my eight-year-old grandfather, did everything they could to keep Agnes, Emily and Doris alive. Suddenly, I'd been in there with them.

*

Back again. The family footage rewinding faster as I move up the Great North Road. The hand in the small of the back ushering me on, under a bridge, along the road to Bentley. C. G. Harper, writing at the turn of the twentieth century, is ahead of me:

> [P]ast Marshgate and over the dirty Don . . . a parting of the ways . . . [B]oth claim to be the true Great North Road and both were largely travelled. [W]e will go via York, the mail-route in later coaching days, and as flat and uninteresting a road as it is possible to imagine. Beginning with the suburban village of Bentley, with its ugly new cottages . . .

it continues with ruts and loose stones as its chief features, passing through lonely woods and pools and lakes, with a stray grouse or so, and astonished hares and rabbits as the sole witnesses of the explorer's progress in these deserted ways ...

Unknown to Harper, when he made his journey through what was still a rural village to the north of Doncaster, was that the investigations to locate the area's coal had begun. The Barnsley Seam would be struck at a depth of 624 yards in fields just to the north of Bentley, close to the 'deserted way' of the old Great North Road (now A19) to York. Negotiations would soon be underway between the landowners and the mining company: Barber Walker & Co. Two shafts were sunk at Bentley in 1906. By 1910, the colliery was employing 1,000 men twenty-four hours a day, 700 of them underground, ripping an average of 2,000 tonnes of coal in three shifts. Its miners were drawn from communities in Derbyshire, Yorkshire, Nottinghamshire. Given the existing pit interests of Barber Walker & Co. in these regions, they likely mustered this considerable workforce quickly by reassigning existing workers to the new mine, or offering opportunities for those seeking a change.

If the family folklore is right, my great-grandfather heeded the call, coming to Bentley from Nottinghamshire with his younger brother, James, and possibly an uncle, in time to help sink the shafts. That would put him at sixteen on arrival. Certainly the 1911 census has John William and James (the uncle, if he was ever there, already bowing out of the story) at Bentley Colliery, with both listed as 'Coal Miner Corporal'. This was somebody in charge of a 'district' or section of the mine, its roadways and ventilation systems – a seniority that suggests a certain length of service and earned trust, even at their relatively young ages of twenty-two and eighteen. Probable, then, that they played a part in the creation of Bentley Colliery. Early promotion the reward for risks taken.

What my great-grandfather would have witnessed was a fast-altering landscape. A vertiginous scene-cut from Harper's 'lonely woods' to a looming industrial behemoth capable of churning out conveyor belts of black gold in thick, slushy rivers. Building sprawl, a branch line, stockyards, gantries; wagons and slag heaps. Above it,

BENTLEY COLLIERY. 8-100.

the rising head frame and winding gear. All day and all night, that smoke-belching chimneystack.

Stretching over seventy-five acres from the pit gates south, the purpose-built company housing was a necessity. The domestic setting for the new migrant workers and their families. Bentley New Village had it all – school, cricket ground, football pitch, allotments. A grid of mining houses and alleys forming an instant community around the colliery.

Up Bentley Road in the quick-falling evening, I reach The Avenue – the street that was the main drag through the heart of the company village, delivering its workers straight to the pit gates. The 1911 census that records John William and James living here also confirms the number: 71. As I turn the corner into the road, the curved run of shops is mostly steel-shuttered, closed, or with glazing whitewashed from the inside. Second-storey facades shed ancient paint; a window is covered with slats from a pallet nailed over its frame. Interspersed between: two surviving takeaways; a baker's, a tanning salon, a launderette. The air smells of detergent and skunk. I think of Ellen's written recollections of The Avenue as a child – of meeting her dad off the tram, of him carrying her home on his shoulders. Reading that memory, I'd pictured sunlight, bustle, noise. Now, amid the descending dark, nothing moves. The street is funereally quiet. Its once-new, uniform houses, four in a block with featured gable ends, are a mix of pebbledash, render, painted-over red-brick. Two lads, wrecked eyes, ashen, sunken-cheeked, cans of something in hand, emerge dazed from a door and hurry into a car, tearing off for town. On a corner, about halfway up, I find 71. It has been split into two houses. Nobody answers the ring of the bells, my knocks. A dog begins snarling and barking across the street, then hurling itself at the door. I step back and look up at what must have been the main bedroom window. These haunted rooms where a part of us lived; where my grandfather was born. The presence. All the to-ing and fro-ing. A hundred years ago. An impossibly long time and yet nothing at all. There is a bowl of sun-bleached silk flowers on the bedroom sill. A net curtain, caught up in itself, hangs half-open, as though held by an invisible hand. As if someone, unseen, is peering out.

*

'At one time, there were green fields everywhere. On a little walk through a nearby field we were shown how to hold a piece of sugar in the palm of our hands, to give to a mare, who had a beautiful foal with her.' Ellen's earliest childhood remembrances of Sunday walks with my great-grandparents capture contrasts in the transitional territory around the colliery and its new village. Echoes of D. H. Lawrence's memories of his own Eastwood: 'a queer jumble of the old England and the new', where 'life was a curious cross between industrialism and the old agricultural England of Shakespeare and Milton and Fielding and George Eliot.' In these places, men ventured down into the earth. They emerged again from the darkness, blinking into light. Senses overawed. Sounds magnified. Colours saturated. When not in the pit, they roved fields and edge-lands, fished rivers, kept allotments, painstakingly tended flower beds. In his 1930 essay 'Nottingham and the Mining Countryside', Lawrence describes a collier's appreciation of beauty and an intuitive consciousness of the world around him: '[He was] deeply alive, instinctively . . . He loved the countryside, just the indiscriminating feel of it . . . Life for him did not consist in facts, but in a flow.' In the same essay, Lawrence romanticises a profoundly sensual, semi-sexual, relationship between the miners working underground: 'as a sort of intimate community, they knew each other practically naked, and with curious close intimacy, and the darkness and the underground remoteness of the pit "stall", and the continual presence of danger, made the physical, instinctive, and intuitional contact between men very highly developed, a contact almost as close as touch, very real and very powerful.' Back on the surface, this strangely tender yet tough masculinity underpinned much of life in mining communities. It was there in the sport; the hard drinking. Lawrence observes that the colliers 'brought with them above ground the curious dark intimacy of the mine, the naked sort of contact ... if I think of my childhood, it is always as if there was a lustrous sort of inner darkness, like the gloss of coal, in which we moved and had our real being.'

It's often suggested that this intimacy, this darkness, this connective tissue of understanding, meant places like Bentley could be largely self-regulating, self-policing. There existed a social trust. People looking out for one another. You knew everybody; everybody knew you. Those that broke the trust might find the community did not recognise them any more. They might find themselves ostracised. Whether this is true or rearview-mirror nostalgia, the hard line on loyalty when underground was unquestionable. Men risked their own lives to save their co-workers. Bill Cowen was dragged out from two roof falls on the same day. The hewers who saved him would have had to hack away tiny crawl spaces at enormous danger to themselves, through what they knew to be lethally unstable rock in the pitch-black and depleting air, just to reach Bill. Until we begin to understand these kinds of bonds, it is hard for us, in our times, to conceive of the way mining villages like Bentley might have operated. Hard too for us to understand and relate to the impact and lasting trauma an event such as that which happened here on 20th November 1931 could have on such a community.

Witness statements from inside the mine describe first a strong disturbance in the air; a flash, a heavy thump. One mentions a skein of blue flame whipping along the tunnel wall a moment before the shock was felt. 'Firedamp' was the term for the pockets of highly flammable methane released in the ripping of coal and Bentley was notorious for it. Even with its relatively advanced ventilation systems, its gates and seals and the religiously observed checks of gas levels by deputies, miners working at Bentley were known to be uneasy about its prevalence. Large volumes of air would mix in the 'roads' and make detection difficult. On that Friday, at 5.45 p.m., a sudden, fierce rush of wind and dust immediately told those near the main underground roadway that something was terribly wrong deep in the north-east section of the mine, where eighty-five men and boys were working. Soon after, a miner, Daniel Maloney, wandered out of a cloud of particulate dark with all his clothes and much of his skin burned off. Another, Arthur Kirkland, emerged in the same state, a hand missing. Despite this, he'd still managed to lift a tub off a boy, a pony driver who was trapped beneath, and drag him 300 yards to safety. As desperate calls went out for volunteers and breathing equipment, rescuers were already rushing towards the face with stretchers. One miner who'd just reached 'top' after finishing a long shift immediately descended to look for his son. What the men encountered was a scene of devastation. The explosion had flung broken bodies through the air and collapsed the ceilings of the roadways, filling them with debris. Lungs were robbed of oxygen as fires raged. Smoke filled the chambers. The dead and wounded were found stripped, scorched, blinded; the injuries so grievous to some that identification proved impossible. For seven hours, volunteers fought fire, heat, gas and rock fall and further explosions to rescue anybody living and recover the dead. When it was discovered that five men had been killed in a further stall, incredible efforts were made to reach the bodies, before they were eventually left entombed where they died.

Forty-five of Bentley's men and boys didn't come home that night, including Maloney and Kirkland, who, despite walking out of that hell, died later in hospital of wounds. At the following inquest, repeated evidence cited the extraordinary bravery and gallantry of those trying to save their comrades. The coroner commented: 'They risked everything. It was not a question of getting volunteers, but preventing them from taking unnecessary risks to rescue the men.' In a blurry photograph, one of the crew who'd rushed down to help is caught walking back out through the shocked crowd gathered at the pit head, face blackened, wearing a look of grim fatigue. This is Ellen's father-in-law, George Turner. A notice of the missing and dead was pinned to the gate. A message of condolence for the community arrived from the king. Medals were handed out for bravery. The funeral for thirty-two of the victims was attended by 30,000. Widows, one of whom was left to raise eight children alone, walked past rows of mourners ten deep along roads around Bentley New Village. The coffins were laid on three lorries draped with purple. Ahead, three more lorries overflowed with wreaths. The procession passed slowly down The Avenue, past 71, to reach Arksey Cemetery where a grave had been dug to bury the dead together. It was edged with evergreens. The coffins were laid in neat rows; the hole was back-filled and covered with flowers.

Sixty-two years later Bentley Colliery would be buried itself. A political move. A leaked confidential report revealed the colliery was running at its most productive, providing coal far more cheaply than Britain's South African imports. Even so, British Coal selected it for closure. Reserves abandoned underground; 450 livelihoods lost. The cog around which this community had turned was removed, leaving a

hole in lives as well as land. Then, in the late 1990s, after the last pit-head building had been torn down, a slow regreening. A return to that landscape glimpsed from the road by C. G. Harper. Grass breaking through the cracks. Trees springing up over the spoil heaps to form the wooded hill. Sinkholes coerced into ponds and thriving wetlands. Winding gears repurposed into a memorial sculpture. And everywhere, flowers.

*

I turn away from number 71, away from the faded silk blooms on the sill, the half-open net curtains, the darkness of the room behind. We'll never know for sure why the Cowens left Doncaster and no ancestor's face is going to emerge at the window to tell me. Track the footage back, though, and we might start to hazard a guess. Not a single incident, I suspect, but an accumulation: the death of Doris Coles; suspect arrangements with the authorities; unaccountable cash made and spent; deals, debts, the ruin of the Great Depression and, no doubt, the disaster at Bentley pit. For although he had been out of the mine for years when it happened, Bill would have known those who died. He would have worked alongside them at the faces and shared in that 'curious dark intimacy'; he would have served them in the shops. I wonder whether, when he walked down The Avenue, the opposite direction to where I'm walking tonight, his head bowed, part of that wave of mourning behind the coffins, if he thought of his sixteen-year-old self, arriving here to dig the seam. Of Thomas Burbanks, his partner killed the day he stayed home to help with the birth of my grandfather. Of his own near-death burials. Were it possible to look into my great-grandfather's eyes on that day in November 1931, with the economy in freefall, 3 million unemployed and the northern mining towns hit the hardest, I suspect the worry would be clear. A few more years of holding on but, with them, the ignominy of watching all he'd built collapse. The shameful business of handing in the shop keys, pawning possessions, the bailiffs at the door. Eventually, a running out of road and of options. One night a decision made.

It is telling that the family diaries uncovered in attics, the dinner-party recollections of my childhood, the inherited anecdotes – all go missing for these final years here. The desperation and despair needed to be erased. A gap in the cache of photographs. The Doncaster story forever paused at its high point: the boy done good; the holidays, expensive cars, respect and success. The grinning rows of family and workers lined up along the Great North Road in their finery, about to head off somewhere exciting. Climate, food, land, conflict, money – these are often given as the reasons for leaving our homes, but maybe memory can sometimes exert as strong a push, or a pull.

North, into fast-descending night – into air darkening so quickly it is as if lamps are being blown out. I walk up The Avenue towards the vanished mine. These things we perceive as permanent. These places we build worlds around – the collieries, the shops, the pubs, streets, houses – spaces filled with life and noise and conversation; of sorrow and laughter, of love and shock and shame. Of existences, known and unknown. Places that, for one reason or another, are left one day, abandoned, and slowly reduced to ruin. That in a century are torn down, buried. If we can be sure of anything, it's that it will be the same for those megalithic malls and Amazon warehouses of our time too. At the top of the road, where the pit gates stood, I cross into what is now Bentley Community Woodland – the once-scarred land returned to its lonely woods, pools and lakes. Even as we walk on, time spirals and cycles. It always brings us back to the beginning.

II

By the time I make it back to the car, it is late. Radio on, driving home, the news is even bleaker than this morning. Another sharp escalation in Covid cases. A grim quickening in the pace of this fast-shifting story. A new event horizon crossed while I wasn't paying attention. On-air are two guests discussing new figures that predict the impact of the virus on the UK population unless a full lockdown is instigated. What I hear is this: 'The modelling suggests 510,000 fatalities, maybe rising to as many as 800,000, depending on the severity of the virus, by the end of the summer.' Then a long space in which the interviewer evidently struggles to speak. Those words, the pause, the audible shock in the breath – things I doubt I'll ever forget. With a sickening churn, I think of the children, of Rosie. It's too late now to call, but I try her anyway. The phone rings, once, then clicks into voicemail. She must already be asleep. I picture her with Tom and Bea, arms around each other, lying in our bed together. The interviewer presses on: 'Who will make up this half million? The vulnerable? The old? The young?'

Before I reach over and turn off the programme, one commentator tries to contextualise the societal change that is now certain: 'There should be no question in anyone's mind as to what we're facing. This will be as significant as the world wars or the Great Depression.'

*

Somewhere north of Bentley, I switch roads from the A19 towards the A1 (M), cutting across the dark fields. Depthless dark beyond the headlights; a darkness of timeless space. Indiscernible shapes across night-blurred land, before the sky-glow of the great highway again – that ultimate of Main Roads, Travelling Roads and Returns. Indicating on to it, I think of the night, many miles south, when my great-grandfather first walked into my dream. What stories do we tell ourselves in these dislocated times? What threads of history, of our own histories, do we weave together to make sense of the long line from there to here? Well, we can be sure of one thing: they are only ever partial. Sometimes, though, the dead return to fill in the gaps. They reappear in the world of the living to point out a road connecting us back. They permeate our sleeping minds, compelling us to retrace steps along these recurring highways. They ensure their presence in the fleeting present. Perhaps this isn't for their redemption, resolution or release at all, but for ours. We stumble along the road to reach them because we seek guidance through our own difficult impulses, our own mutable times, through a chaotic world. They are the voice encountered in a storm of radio static. Tune it, listen closely, and an entire story may unfold. It may be a story of resilience and resolve, of adversities overcome. Of the fight to live well and the striving to provide for those we love. Of losses and disasters endured together, and the strength that must be found to start again. Maybe all of this can be mined as we go on. The dead are no more knowable, but their memories give us something to hold on to in the hard days ahead. When we too hear the thump down the tunnel and become engulfed by darkness, looking for a way back to the light. When it seems there'll be, once more, too many bodies consigned to the earth.

*

Beyond the exit I could have taken, the motorway is empty. At this hour, driving alone is freefalling. A drift. The road carries you to where you need to be. Blue signs flash by in the beams: 'A1(M) The NORTH / Scotch Corner 22 / Darlington 30'. Then, further on, turnings for Leeming Bar and Catterick. Passing under a pristine overbridge, close to Tunstall Beck, I know exactly where I am. I anticipate the slip road and take it, up a low-rising ground to a roundabout where a lane leads to a chained gateway providing a view back down on to the highway. I sit with the engine and the lights off and the windows down, listening to the wind blowing over the smooth six lanes, over the high grassy banks of the soft estate, through the shivering hawthorn growing along its tops. Gone now the shipping containers, the pile-drivers; the work crews in high-vis gear. Gone the archaeologists, the bones and the broken pieces; the fencing to hide our eyes from those opened horizons. Nothing marks the place where the body lay, where all those bodies lay for nearly 2,000 years. Only the road is old enough to remember everything. In the wake-wash of lights that accompanies a van barrelling down the central lane, the darkness comes alive. Shadow-figures appear to creep from cover. Spectres hover along the hard shoulder.

Ravages

(Catterick–Durham)

*His camps were scattered over a surface of one hundred miles;
numbers of the insurgents fell beneath his vengeful sword, he
levelled their places of shelter to the ground, wasted their
lands, and burnt their dwellings with all they contained. Never
did William commit so much cruelty; to his lasting disgrace, he
yielded to his worst impulse, and set no bounds to his fury,
condemning the innocent and the guilty to a common fate. In
the fullness of his wrath he ordered the corn and cattle, with
the implements of husbandry and every sort of provisions,
to be collected in heaps and set on fire till the whole was
consumed ... there followed ... so great a scarcity in England
in the ensuing years, and severe famine involved the innocent
and unarmed population in so much misery, that, in a Christian nation, more than a hundred thousand souls, of both
sexes and all ages, perished ... On many occasions ... I have
been free to extol William according to his merits, but I dare
not commend him for an act which levelled both the bad and
the good together in one common ruin ... [S]uch barbarous
homicide could not pass unpunished.*

Orderic Vitalis, *Historia Ecclesiastica*, circa 1110–1115

*So great a famine prevailed that men, compelled by hunger,
devoured human flesh, that of horses, dogs, and cats, and
whatever custom abhors; others sold themselves to perpetual
slavery, so that they might in any way preserve their wretched
existence ... It was horrific to behold human corpses decaying
in the houses, the streets, the roads ... for no one was left to
bury them in the earth ... There was no village inhabited
between York and Durham; they became lurking places to
wild beasts and robbers, and were a great dread to travellers.*

Symeon of Durham, *De Exordio Ecclesiae Dunelmensis*,
circa 1100–1125

In Overtun. In Catal. In Hanbreton. In Tadestorp. In Useburne. In Brantune. In Bure. In Chircebi. In Calduelle. In Cernhow. In Cinderbi. In Holtbi. In Langtun. In Catrick.

Winter, smoke-mingled mist. Stumpy, crucified trees. Black limbs charred by raging fire, snuffed out by hard rain. The acrid fog of smoulder after flame swirls over a swamp of muddy ash. A man and a woman stare into the grey, waiting for any disturbance. The faintest noise. Movement. Both are masked, breathing through a bound rag covering mouth and nose. They stare and they listen and they count to a thousand in their heads. Then the man rises awkwardly on to a knee, scans again, and hauls himself up using his spear to lean on. When he limps into the mist, she follows.

Halfway through the grove of dead trees, she remembers when this was an apple orchard. She sees it as it was in spring, five years back. Cast about are hoes, forks, billhooks. Bent or with hafts split. Sacks of flour, spiked and strewn, rot in icy puddles; under a tree the body of a tied goat has been scavenged. Its head remains, eyes pecked out, and a ribcage. Even from a distance, it's clear there is nothing left of the homesteads but charcoaled timbers and blackened bodies. Blistered skin stretched over skulls.

With his cloak over his face, he waves her back. Under the rubble, where the rain and frost hasn't reached, embers still glow. The smell of scorched flesh had been heavy in the air a mile away; here it is diabolical. He coughs, retches, lifts the mask and spits. Ushering her to move upwind, they walk the length of the village in silence, him limping ahead, her cutting between plots and over fences looking for anything of use. They skulk all the way to the old road, where he crouches and listens, then they turn back again. Picking through the paddocks and the fields they find only frozen corpses. All of them are men. Some had tried to run for the woods. Some had turned to fight. He reads all of this in the patterns in the mud. The horses. The women and children being rounded up and barricaded in the longhouse with the animals and all their winter stores. The stacking of firewood around the doorway. The oil in the thatch. The burning.

There is no need to ask her if this was the place, for he witnesses her kneeling by one of the fair-haired men in the fields. The way she studies his face as she unhooks the fire-steel from his belt, and unties the buckskin pouch of tinder around his neck.

He limps to her and says: 'The snow will come soon. With the darkness.'

She looks skywards and nods.

'We cannot stay in this place.'

But she knows this already.

At the edge of the orchard, she retrieves the shield and their bundles from where they concealed them under dead leaves and bramble. Their packs contain furs, gloves, a stew pot, water gourd. A few trinkets. All that could be grabbed when they first fled from Eoforwic. She drinks from the gourd, rinsing the ash and grit from her mouth, then vomits. Squatting and hidden, she muffles her face with her cloak and rocks, before catching her breath and wiping her tears with a sleeve. She hauls their packs through the orchard mud, the shield across her back, and sees again the spoiled grain sacks. She cuts each open with her seax. The flour is rancid and icy in her hand.

They stalk eastwards from the village, over frost-hard barren fields, moving in the opposite direction to the road where a long strip of Roman ruins had undulated the woods. Where they'd heard faint shouts and screams to the west. Through the mist they see a skeletal circle of trees only partially burned. After listening and watching and counting to a thousand, they move into them and rest beside a fallen oak with a hollow excavated by its ripped-out roots. As darkness falls, they stack wood over the hole and cover it thickly with cut pine boughs. Snapping twigs from the dead oak, she stumbles upon a seam of ear fungus growing along an elder. These they soak in the last of their gourd-water with pine needles, before boiling it in the embers of a small, hot, spitting fire. They drink the broth in turns, then smother over the charcoals. Hunkering down in the hollow, pulling pine boughs over themselves, they shiver in their furs and cloaks.

He whispers: 'What was it? The name of her village?'

Hartwel, she thinks, but she whispers back: 'I reccan-ne. It is gone.'

Around them, the deadening wood. The quiet that comes with the fall of snow.

This is the time of ghosts.

*

In Hartwel. In Cudun. In Bercbi. In Smeatun. In Hornbi. In Natun. In Wercerel. In Griserbi. In Egbyrtun. In Hain. In Torp. In Morcha. In Ercerbi. In Bartun. In Neuton.

They continue east through the snow for two days and nights, follow-ing the river, believing it may keep them away from the scouts and raiding parties along the road. Ahead, the distant escarpment of moor. Bright sword-grey light over white. Slow progress along the river's banks, avoiding trackways between settlements and their pathways weaving down to the water where the boats are holed and burned at the jetties. They wade thigh-deep through fields, through drifts, in blizzards of silent flakes, staying wide of the kindled villages. Clothes sodden, feet and fingers numb, stomachs cramping with the hollow-ing hunger, they watch for smoke and kites on the horizon. They search for food. Twice they see great fires. They move in the same cautious way they have since leaving Eoforwic. At nightfall they melt snow for water, fill the gourd and huddle in the woods. When needing to rest out in the open, they dig into drifts and lay furs on snow. Fires lit in pits are extinguished before their heat can do much more than warm the wet layers they are wearing. They lie in the darkness, pain gnawing at their guts; eyes ringed with death. More than once she hears her sister singing to her.

He dreams and, in his dreams, he sweats. That day. Hot under armour. Rising in the saddle as the scream goes up and his brothers crest the road's rise at Elmeslac. Him burning with bloodlust and the yells of the Danes worried and clamouring at the sight of Harold's banners and the huscarls' mail flashing silver in the sun like a striking fish. He dreams of thrusting a spear into the shield wall, that seething mass trapped on the wrong side of the river. Following his brothers, jabbing into faces, necks and chests as the Danes swarm, half-naked and red with sun, baying and swinging their axes and bills. In his dreams he smells the piss and the shit and the fear and tastes the stink of shock and hears the sound of skulls split under the sword. He sees the headless and armless, the throat-slit. He chases them as they panic and sprint for the bridge and fall. In his dreams his horse is under him, twisting with a gaping hole in its throat, and he is dragging his useless leg free, trying to stand, but the stub of a broken spear sticks out of his blue cloth trousers. Blood bubbles up, black and thick and hot from the wound.

On the third day they scale the moor up a flank of thick pine trees. The snow has become hard rain. The whole earth slippery, cold. Rain ticks and drips through the stunted branches as they scramble up the needly hillocks and rocky outcrops. At the cataract of a wide beck, where it tumbles twenty feet into a bowl of trees beside a small beach, he fills the gourd as she strips off her overdress to wash her neck and face. Then she gives a shout and he looks up to see her scrambling on her hands and knees beside the waterfall. In a wedge of rock halfway down, a young deer has slipped and fallen and caught fast, its neck broken. The torrent rushing over it, that has kept it from the wolves, washes its lolling head from side to side so it appears to watch her placidly, curiously, as she approaches. Soaking and gasping in the freezing water, they drag it free. Only its flanks and belly are green and spoiled. The rest they skin and butcher quickly, washing the head and guts and skin and hooves downstream. They suck at bloody, fatty fingers as they cook loin and legs over embers beside the water and devour as much as their bellies can hold. Both sleep where they lie on the little beach of stones, under the pines, then wake and eat their fill again. They keep the fire stacked high and dry their cloaks, underclothes and furs. 'T'who shude we-pray na?' she asks him.

The man shrugs. 'The deer?'

She takes the bones she has bound into a cross and throws it into the cataract.

An hour before dark, the rain ceases. The temperature drops. As the woman sleeps by the fire, he limps into the trees and starts to haul bigger branches towards the camp. Then he is aware, as if stung, that he is being watched. He feels no weapon on his belt and so pretends to be oblivious, keeping the human shape up-slope in the edge of his vision. Dragging the firewood towards the fire, he quietly picks up the spear from their things, then spins and crouches with his arm raised to throw and yelling for the figure to show himself. Terrified, a boy in a hood caught midway across in the open ground behind screams, stumbles and falls back.

It is a boy, but a boy on the edge of manhood. A Dane lad, off the moors. His clothes are ragged. More mud than weave. Eyes wide and wild as a snare-gibbeted hare. His left foot has no boot and it is white as bone. The woman wakes and scrabbles for the sword as the man stands over the lad, spear on his chest, shouting: 'Are you alone?'

'Ay,' the boy replies. 'Plaes . . . Am-began . . . plaes.'

'Where are your people?'

The boy looks to the woman as she draws the blade from its sheath.

'Plaes . . . ne. *Ne.*'

'Where are your people?'

'Ded.'

The man nods at the woman. She creeps into the trees to check his tracks.

'Where are you from?' the man asks.

'Plaes . . . Am staevrin . . .'

'Where are you from?'

'Chizesburh.'

'Is that over that way?' The man points east. 'Over the moors?'

The boy nods.

'They are that way too?'

'Ay . . . I wer up-fell wen tha-cam. Wen I cam-bac it wernt . . . it wer . . .'

He stares at the man, as if he might explain.

'Did you see them? The Bastard's men?'

He nods again.

'Where were they headed?'

'Al-ower. Easte. Southe. On hosses. Ridin t'ards see.'

The man curses.

'Ay. I sin tha-fires alower moor. I sin camps an tha-fire ower harburs . . .'

'The harbours?'

The woman walks back with the sword sheathed and shakes her head.

'Ealdgyth,' The man says. 'This lad has seen . . .'

'I hearede his wordes. Let-him stande.'

Before it is dark, the man heaves himself up the slope, trying to keep pace with the lad, tracing his tracks to where the ground levels and opens over tussocks of snow-speckled heather. The wind scours their faces. From afar they can hear dogs and smell burning. They count five, perhaps six, great plumes of drifting smoke. At the camp the woman gives the boy some ribs and charred fat and they sit in the firelight staring at the flames, chewing on bones. When the boy sobs and moans in his sleep, the woman goes to him, laying her furs over his thin body. She cradles him like a child, feeling the sharpness of his ribs under her fingers. Shushing him, she sings softly into his hood. At dawn, she wakes to find that he has gone. And gone with him, the rest of their meat.

They retrace their steps west, back towards the road, hunger and speed forcing them to take risks. They forgo the safety of river and wood for trackways. The rain comes and goes. The cold doesn't change. Banks of freezing mist. At village edges, cloaks over faces, they stare and wait and count to a thousand, then loot the homesteads without care, kicking through the cinders, turning over middens of burned grain and the tarred bones. Bodies are nothing but hollow shells of ash. They disturb crows and kites too fat to fly, grinning dogs, rivers of rats. They find a clay pot of dried beans under a smashed door and eat them all. They move urgently and quickly. He wakes often in the night from the same hot dream with the same hot wound searing fresh in his thigh.

In the ploughshares around the place that used to be Ercerbi, they find the first traces of survivors. Scratch camps. The bones of dogs and horses with teeth marks all over them, tossed into cooking pits. That evening, when they reach the road, close to the place that was Bartun, they pass naked corpses hanging from beech branches, creaking in the breeze. *Silvatici*. All have their genitals cut away. Bellies split open. One has had the ornaments of a thegn wrapped around his neck and hammered into his flesh. The woods are silent, terrible. She tells him that they cannot stay here. It is dangerous. There are many tormented spirits. He knows this. So, they wait and listen and quietly cross the icy surface of the road, like a wide, frozen river, before following its course north, staying close, picking their way through the under-growth in the dark.

Soon he can drag his leg no further. When he slips on a root and stumbles, he stays there, face down, heaving for air. She feels his head. Feverish, sweaty. She gives him water and then forces him to climb a small rise in the wood where she unloops his shield from his shoulders and helps him on to it then layers his cloak and fur on top. He reaches for her hand, holds it firm. 'No fire, Ealdgyth. No fire.' But she ignores him and searches around the rise, feeling in the dark, peeling bark from the ghostly trunks of birches, snapping their standing dead-wood. Her foot slides in the fresh scat of boar and she returns with the spear, sitting, waiting, but nothing moves. When she stands again and glances east from the rise, over the road and the trees, the moon is up and a million stars glitter in the jet-black night. Below, all along the horizon, she sees the many night fires of William's men, scattered across the dark, skull-curve of the earth.

*

In Manfeld. In Stapletun. In Berford. In Scarcreghul. In Stenuegher. In Stenuegbe. In Ecelbe. In Mortham. In Hail. In Cowtun. In Laytun. In Wyeclif. In Dun.

In the morning she hauls him as far as she can, delirious and hacking, into a wooded valley west of the road where the brush is thickest. Near a frozen beck, amid bramble and thorn, she buries him under branches, whispers to him to cough into his cloak and returns for the shield and their packs. Halfway back she hears shouts and cries and stops and steadies her heartbeat to determine direction. White mist. Glittering oaks and birches and beeches. She moves when it is quiet. At the little rise where they slept the night before, she looks at

327

the road. More shouts, screams. They sound as if they are to the north and east. After they fall silent again, she collects their things and covers up their dead fire. She straps the heavy shield across her back and stands, then immediately crouches again. The sound is slow, plodding, but it is unmistakable: hooves on stone.

The cart is weaving drunkenly down the middle of the road. A lone ox, slipping on the cobbles of ice, heaving at the harness, is tormented, unable to lie down. It is done. She watches the beast collapse in its bonds, its head and neck still tied to the bar. She waits and counts, and keeps herself hidden. The ox rises, slips and slumps again. She waits even as snow begins to drift like goose down, until the shapes among the trees edging the road resolve into wolves. Then, picking up the spear and gripping the handle of her seax under her cloak, she slips down and walks purposefully towards them, her eyes fixed on theirs, holding out the spear. She is nearly upon them when they turn and trot into the trees. In the back of the cart is a dying man half-covered with bloody straw. His mail and tunic are black with blood and he holds both hands over his viscera. Death has its claws in him. His skin is milk, mouth lost in a bloody beard, but he blinks and gazes at her. He is of William's men. In a single movement, she walks to the front of the cart and punctures the ox's throat. Behind the seax comes a long spurt of hot blood. She cuts away its harness and, working quickly in the thickening snow, she kneels and slices and hacks at its flesh, her hands slippery with the running blood, removing a hindquarter and chunk of rump and dragging it back over the road to the trees. She returns and cuts off some of the flank and then hauls all the meat to the little valley where she left the man, covering it with moss and snowfall. She runs back again for their packs and weapons and shield. From the rise, she sees the wolves now tearing strips from the entrails of the ox, yapping and chewing and shaking the drift off their coats. One raises its paws on to the back of the cart. She watches it leap up, look about and fuss at something. A boot or a leg. Then it bows its head to bite. Already kites throng the branches of the surrounding trees. They scream to each other.

It was a risk and she knows it, so she is careful to mask her own tracks, even as the blizzard blankets the ground behind her. By dusk, as the flakes slow and stop, she has made a deadwood shelter by the beck,

the fresh fall acting as a layer of insulation on top. She tightens her
cloak and tucks the furs about him, lifting his head to sip the warm
liquor she has made from the stewed ox meat. She thinks of the evening
she found him like this four years before in the woods further south
along this same road, near Eoforwic. He had been trying to ride south
with his brothers to meet the Bastard, but his leg-wound had proven
too raw for the saddle. He'd bled badly. The huscarls had propped him
up with weapons, food and fire and sworn to return for him. She had
found him two days later, half-dead, as she had hunted for hare. He had
lain in their stall for two weeks and she had nursed him with yarrow,
her father helping himself to the man's coin each night for payment. His
leg had healed slowly until he could stagger with a crutch, but by then
everything had changed. Word had reached them from the south of
Battle. Her father was sickening-to-die from a stray dog's bite. Her
brother's body was strung up for theft and left by the old Roman wall.
Her sister had already gone north with her fair-haired farmer to Hartwel. Before long there was only the huscarl and her.

She makes a smoulder-fire from logs to last the whole night because
they are hidden in their dell and the smoke only crawls over the
ground. While he sleeps, she lies beside him or keeps vigil at the edge
of their camp and looks out for fires. For two days, she does this until
the hind meat begins to dwindle and the snow melts under rain. When
he opens his eyes and asks for ale, she laughs and then, laughing,
weeps.

'We kepe-nartha, tha-reccan?' she asks, that evening.

He nods, chewing on the flame-blackened meat.

'I hearede . . .' She pauses. 'How-el from tha-way. An-easte. Wen
tha-slept.'

He sucks his fingers, wipes his beard. 'But it is all there is. North,
south. You heard the Dane lad. They are at the harbours, eastward,
and we know what they have done to the west. No soul can live
through the winter if they stay here. Even if they do, there is only
death waiting for them in the hunger-spring. All will starve.'

'Go-weara then?'

'To Dunholme. Further, even.'

She cuts the ox-flank into smaller slivers and cures them over
the fire.

On the third morning, he is strong enough to rise and hobble and they pack up and push through the undergrowth on a wide curve that brings them out near the road two miles from where the ox had been killed. The low sun tracks their progress through the trunks. Each time they rest, they let its weak warmth fall full across their faces.

They move slowly for a day, eating their jerky sparely, keeping the road on their right. They pass burn pits and scavenger fires. She carries a heavy stick the length of her forearm to throw at game in the hope of stunning something for long enough to catch it. She clips a wood pigeon in a clearing fringed with elder, drops her pack and runs, but cannot reach it before the bird spins and flaps in a frantic circle into the crown of a holly. It sits clucking out its distress, unable to fold its broken wing back into its body. On the other side of the clearing, they find ploughshares where human corpses have been exposed by melted snow. They pick their way over winter beet that has been hacked to pieces and lies jellied. They know without speaking to one another what has happened – that these farmers were forced to destroy their own crops and smash their own tools to pieces, before each was made to kneel in the field and then beheaded.

An hour before nightfall they make camp among boulders overgrown with mosses in an expanse of pine with wide areas of clearing where the light forms pools. Etched across the rocks are carvings. Interwoven rings. Concentric circles. These coat the entirety of the largest stone in patterns. The place has its own strange, blue light. The soft ground is criss-crossed with animal prints. Deer, boar. She has borne the weight of the shield and the packs all day and now she breaks firewood as he limps off to hunt in the dusk, following fresh tracks. A mile deeper into the wood, he glimpses a glow before he smells fire, for the wind is blowing from the east. There is no moon and the pines are dark so he creeps as far as he dares, until he can see the shadows gathered around the flames. He counts four ragged outlines. Another. Five. And then he smells whatever it is they are searing in the flames and it makes him gag. He hurries back empty-handed and tells her that they must forgo the fire. She shows him a dark hollow she has found in a space under the boulders, then climbs into it. They layer its damp floor with cut boughs, before he passes down their things. Only the shield is left and he covers it with sticks and pine mulch. They eat the last of the ox-flank raw in the dark and then lie entombed in their bowl of earth and stone, clinging to one another.

When she wakes, it is late. She hears her sister singing. Murmurs. Voices. She sits up, and listens again. It is men chanting. A high, tremulous voice; many answering back. She rests her hand over the man's mouth. He wakes and immediately understands. Peering out, they see, through the trees, forty or more bareheaded figures in a wide glade in the pines. The crowd kneels before a short bald man in robes who holds aloft a wooden cross. Shafts of gold strafe the gathering. Clouds of breath drift from the men. The accents are strange, but they recognise the words being shouted through the wood: *Deus tu conversus vivificábis nos. Et plebs tua lætábitur in te.*

Encircling this mass, as if watching, five bodies are noosed from the branches. She motions to him: *Do we run?* He shakes his head, points down: *We hold here.*

*

In Burg. In Flaneburg. In Calretun. In Biletun. In Burtun. In Suarbi. In Gantun. In Galmetun. In Wilerbi. In Bretlinctun. In Waletun. In Hovertun. In Pocleitun. In Gryfe.

They wait in silence in their burrow for William's men to finish prayers and disperse. Three of them come to piss close to the rocks and in their small cave beneath, the huscarl shifts his weight, manoeuvring the spear to strike, but the men do not see beyond the frosted clump of reeds she pulled into place the night before. Even after they have left and the sound of them mounting horses has faded, they wait, counting to a thousand before they emerge. She crawls out, keeping low, moving towards the glade where she discovers a half-empty ale pot which she carries back. They drink its contents, then she returns it. She knows the huscarl is angry with himself, for he walks with a rage, faster than he did before, dragging his leg when it cramps and refusing to rest for very long. He won't share in their meat either. 'One more day,' he says. 'I will eat some then.'

The quandary is this: the road is the quickest way northward. They know the Romans cut the truest paths through this territory. Yet there are far more chances of encounter on it. That night he asks her what risks she will take. She tells him that she will take whatever risks they must for them to live. He nods and stamps out the fire.

The following day they become lost in a dense wood and when they double back to the road, they find themselves instead in a plateau of open ground. Heath and rowans. Doubling back again, they cross a moor threaded with peat streams and find they are in a different forest. They smell fire but see no smoke. They move swiftly, hungrily, watching constantly. They wait. Count. They loop two burned villages and avoid the blackened dead and the air of disease and discover old men, old women and young children huddled together in groups in the woods, dead from hunger or cold. They find the corpse of a man with his limbs hacked off. Another lies on his face. The flesh of his buttocks has been cut away. More than once they glimpse human bones in the ashes of fires. The rain, when it comes, is heavy. Snow threatens, but doesn't fall.

There is only silence. Silence laying across the fields and woods and hills.

Heading east again for a day and a night through thick brush, they come out near Alciland and drink from the spate river to sate the aching and the longing in their stomachs. Then they cross it on a wooden bridge. When they find the road again, they hear shouts and drop their packs and run to hide. From a treeline, they watch three men, a woman and child hobbling southward. All are sickly thin, wrapped in rags. One of the men spies the possessions on the ground and with a yelp begins tearing through them looking for something to eat. In desperation, he chews on the leather strapping binding the pack. The huscarl swaps his spear into his strong hand and steps out, disguising his limp as best he can. The woman follows with her seax drawn. The woman with the child sees them and shrieks and points and the man ceases his looting and looks up. He has no weapon and no strength to run. He cowers on his knees and moans and cries with his arms outstretched as they approach, his face pressed to the ground. The huscarl picks up their packs and begins to step backward but the woman stops. She cuts off some of the excess strap leather and throws it to the man who stares at it in the mud. A few paces on, they hear the woman with the child calling to them. 'Be-wear. Be-wear na. They ar a-narth a-her. A1 wi-hosses and men. Al-alang the stan. Be-wear na.'

Heeding her words, they walk further through thick, ghostly birches, taking a trajectory away from the sinking pale sun. Both know they are starving and they must hunt and so they follow deer tracks, springing woodcock, triggering a doe into flight before they are forced to abandon their efforts at dusk. They sleep badly with the cramp of hunger and the howl and yitter of wolves in the night. The next afternoon, lost again, turning in circles, they eventually pick up a trackway and, in the morning, they find that it heads in the direction of the rising sun. It is pitted, pooled, imprinted, but it is quiet. They follow it, the man forcing them forward always, dragging himself towards the sun, breathing hard with exertion. When they set off again after drinking through the ice from a spring-pool, he marches ahead, spear as a walking stick. Approaching a bend, he hears the woman cry. 'Men,' she screams. 'In tha trees . . .'

An order is shouted from both sides before he is able to react. *Hald-ye. Hald.* His movement is instinctive. A dropped knee; the swinging of the shield to the front. The tearing from its ties. The spear is up. *Haald-ye* comes the shout again. There are six men – four to one side, two to the other. Their clothes, leather and wool, are mud-dull and heavy with rain. They are hooded. They look like trees come alive. Three carry swords. One has an axe and a shield. He is the one that walks forward. 'Wat ar-ye? Not the Bastud's man ar-ye? Wat ar-ye? *She* be-a Dane. But ye-man. *Speke* man.'

The huscarl keeps his spear raised. 'You Silvatici?'

'Ay. An ye ar-notte? Wat ar-ye?'

'I was oathed to Godwinsone.'

'Ye-ar a fyrde-man?'

'No.'

'Wel. Godwinsun be long-ded ma-wesexbrutha.'

One of the men walks closer, pointing with his blade. 'Ne. He is ne-fyrdeman, brutha. Nay wesexmane. H'is *hooscar-le*. See tha sworde. Tha-crafte. Si tha shealde.'

'A'ye hooscar-le?'

'Ay.'

'Who ye fer-na? The Aethling-a?'

'I am for me. For her.'

The man with the axe looks at the woman. He lowers his shield.

'Cum brutha, an-sista. Ne quarrele-her wit-tha. An-I reccan ye staevrin . . .'

The huscarl doesn't move. 'We need to go on.'

'*Go-on*? Weara brutha? Ye reccan t'aske th'Bastud to shaer-his mete?'

The others laugh.

'No. We need to go onward. North.'

The man with the axe pulls back his hood and smiles. His lank hair is twisted and tied up into a horse's tail. He is missing an ear. '*Ye* want-te go-on hooscar-le. *She* be Dane-blud and staevrin. Cum womane this Wessexmane is stuborne. Speke t'im.'

But she does not speak. She keeps her eyes fixed on the men, alert.

'Ay, wel fuc-ye then.'

The men turn and begin to melt back into the trees. It's then that the woman spies the child. A girl with auburn hair has been concealed in the dead bracken, watching. Now she stands and reaches out her arms as the man with a missing ear passes her. He scoops her up and hoists her over his shoulder. Seeing this, the woman steps from behind the huscarl. 'Heldye brutha. Plaes,' she yells. 'Cum-brerna. Cum-brerna na . . .'

The men stop and turn, and wait.

'What did you say to them?' says the huscarl.

'That we-wil go with them. Thes ar goode-men . . .'

'They are Silvatici. They are hunted men. We must go . . .'

'And staevr? Cum-na, love. They hav fude. See tha t'yurla is-wel. *See* her.'

They number thirty-three in camp in a clearing two miles deeper into the forest. Six further men act as sentries at the wood edges, and there are twenty-two horses taken a year earlier from Robert de Comines. All are fighting men, save for the young girl who sits alone under a skin tent with a hound. There is the meat of a boar roasted the night before and clean water. The huscarl and the woman take their fill of them.

After they have eaten, the man with a missing ear sits with the huscarl and they talk of the burning of Eoforwic, of Copsig and Gospatric, and the treachery of the Danes in the Humber. The man asks again where it is they seek to go and when the huscarl tells him, he explains that Dunholme was burned too, but that he has heard the monks have returned from Lindisfarne with the body of their saint. The protector. The one who made the fog at Nartallertun that turned back the Bastard's men. *Cuddy.* And that men have come from the north now and it is safe. The huscarl and the woman make a bed away from the others. When the fire is out, they curl up in furs. In the night, swaying with ale, the man with one ear staggers back to where they sleep and watches them.

He returns at first light, waiting for them to wake. When they do, he hands them hard bread and some boar meat wrapped in skin. He tells them they are leaving to hunt after William's raiding parties. They ride south on the road to slaughter all they meet without mercy. He says: 'I sin yer leg is weke hooscar-le. It trobles-ye yet? Can-ye stil-fite?'

The huscarl looks him in the eye. 'Better than most, still.'

The other smiles. 'Brutha, I hoep-so.'

'If you mean for me to ride with you, I cannot. My oath is hers.'

The man with one ear crouches down and picks up a stick. 'Nay. I-wud ne aske ne-man to breke oath. I aske ye-to mek-anutha.'

He draws the stick through the frost. 'Tayk ma t'yurla to Dunholme.'

The huscarl looks at the woman, then back. 'What?'

'We-begn but-a haf-daye a-Keringdun on a-stan. Ye tayk-the stan a-nartha . . .'

'No. We cannot take the girl . . .'

'Dunholme but a-daye, a-daye and haf, furtha . . .'

'No, *ne.* Tell him, Ealdgyth. In his tongue.'

But the woman doesn't speak. She lets the man continue.

'Ye ne-tayk-ye th'stan-her-a. Reccan-ye?' He dots the line drawn and jabs at it. 'An ye mak-er Dunholme up-riva Weyar. Reccan? Up-riva Weyar tru-woode.'

The huscarl hauls himself up using his spear and puts his hand on the man's shoulder. 'Hear me, friend. We cannot take your girl . . .'

The man shouts: '*Ne.* Heare-me. Reccan-ye al a-saye?'

He rings the rough map drawn in the frost, stands and throws the

stick into the undergrowth. Others in camp, midway through sad-
dling, look over. The man missing an ear bows his head, spits, then
turns around and faces up to the huscarl again. He speaks quietly. 'Ye
of-al reccan-wat cums. We wil-ne be-bac. We *will not be back.*'

They stare at each other in silence. The huscarl had known his
meaning even before he said it slowly, clumsily, in his tongue. The
man with a missing ear looks to the woman. 'Sista, plaes. Tayk t'yurla
a-Dunholme. Kepe-a sayefe-a. She be-yers na.'

And after a moment, the woman nods.

*

*In Huton. In Rudbe. In Scutescelf. In Smedun. In Deytun. In Hun-
dredstun. In Tuntorp. In Scardiztorp. In Aclem. In Cerchbidayl. In
Paynstorp. In Sudcniton. In Xistendale.*

When the girl tires, the woman carries her, binding her across her
back with a pack strap. The child cries, sniffing, burying her head into
the cloak and then, eventually, she sleeps, her tangled copper hair
tumbling down the woman's neck. A hidden sun turns the sky pale
grey. The ground is sodden, but it does not rain. As the Silvatici had
promised, they sight the ruins of Keringdun in just over half a day
moving through thick cover fringing an old stone road. They see no
one and, aside from robins and rooks, they hear only the distant giddy
yips of a pack of hunting hounds turned loose, gone wild. As they
trudge through the muddy pools and climb over black roots, the
woman whisper-sings to the girl. Songs she can recall. Songs she and
her sister learned from the women who sang in the ale halls when she
was young and carried the beer and swept the straw. Song-poems of
the sea and the sword. Of battles and bravery. Funny songs that would
send all who heard them into fits of roaring belly laughter. The songs
that made men cry. They rest on a rise of ground with visibility over
the frozen sprays of the bare tree canopies and when the sun emerges
briefly, they see the glint of the river in the plain below. The woman
cleans the girl's face and hands with a wet corner of her cloak and
gives her some of the bread, which she eats slowly, keeping her grey-
blue eyes fixed on the woman's face. The woman beams at her and

tells her that she has the most beautiful eyes she has ever seen. One day, she says, she will barter her some beads just as beautiful and she'll thread them on leather for her to keep and wear.

They leave the road and make for the river as the Silvatici had instructed. It is wide and wild and it flows around small islands of thick willow and the tributary banks to form a delta. Great stretches of its edges are frozen; the ice stone-set around reeds. They follow it downstream and smell old fires and soon come across a torched hut with collapsed mud walls with a cindered jetty and two boats destroyed. The old ferryman has been stripped, bound against a tree and used as a target. The entirety of his thin body bristles with arrow shafts. Further on, a shingle island formed out in the flow is covered with wading birds and geese. As the huscarl and the girl drink from the gourd on the riverbank, watching, the woman crosses over the connecting ice, carefully picking her way to creep up to the island's overgrowth with the spear. She waits then lifts her head and prepares to throw when all the birds are suddenly up and away in a flap of wings and shrieking honks, skittering into air. When she turns to look back at the bank, she sees the horseman breaking the treeline above where the huscarl and the girl sit on their packs. She sees the huscarl dragging himself up and driving the girl on to the ice, commanding her to run, *run*. The woman drops the spear and dashes to meet the girl as a second and third horseman emerge from the wood. Then two men behind them running flat-out on foot. The huscarl glances up at the woman for a second and then he lifts his shield and unsheathes the sword and turns to the first rider as he descends upon him. Half-way across the ice, the woman pulls the girl into her arms and then scrambles back towards the island, the ice cracking and splintering underneath her pounding feet. On the other side of the low shingle, the water flows swiftly, deeply. Holding the girl to her chest, she looks back as the huscarl meets the lead horseman with his shield raised, shifting to the right when the sword blow comes so it is only glancing. She sees the rider rise in his stirrups and hack down with his blade again into the shield-wood and then turn the horse to try to circle behind him, but the huscarl has already torn his sword across the back of the horse's foreleg releasing a thick spray of blood and the animal lurches on to its knees, tumbling its rider over its head. In a single movement, she sees the huscarl fall on the winded man, slamming his heavy shield down into his throat and stabbing the sword into his chest, ripping it clear and spinning around to meet the others. She can hear his roaring and swearing at them. One of the horsemen breaks left and gallops towards the thicker river ice, his eyes fixed on the woman and girl. These are William's men. This rider wears the helmet and the shield of the king's troop and bouncing against his saddle are human heads tied by their hair.

When the second horseman hits the huscarl, he spins and stumbles, but climbs up again under his shield. The rider shifts his weight in the saddle and sweeps the blade underneath, slicing the huscarl's forearm to the bone. He staggers, drops the oaken shield and then lifts his sword with both hands. The rider kicks at the horse's flanks and swings down once more and blades smash together, but the huscarl uses his skill to shift the rider's momentum, twisting his own sword under the rider's in a circle, dragging it over the horseman's thigh as he passes. The cut is lethally deep, severing all to white-wet bone. The rider instinctively pulls the nose of his horse away and gallops upstream holding his leg but he barely makes fifty yards before he slumps sideways and falls into the bullrushes. The huscarl's entire sleeve is now black with blood and he coughs blood from his mouth. The third rider has breached the reeds and is guiding his horse on to the thickest ice. The huscarl yells for the woman to *run* but there is nowhere left to go. The two men on foot are almost upon him now. She sees one raise a spear, then suddenly its point is protruding through the huscarl's shoulder. He sags to his knees, then pushes himself up on his sword and raises the blade again. This is the last time she ever sees him. Him turning to strike; his face a blooded mask.

The river ice cracks under the rider making for the woman and the girl. His horse begins to swim, straining its neck, pulling for the island. The woman holds the girl's face in her hands. 'Swimne-ya? Swimne-ya?' But the girl is in shock. Lifting her, the woman tells her to hold her neck, *hald-fast*, and then running down the shingle to where the river flows fastest, she shuts her eyes and jumps into its current.

*

In Denerbi. In Hoptun. In Waltun. In Mulehale. In Mulhede. In Toc-withe. In Bordleby. In Aschebi. In Yarme. In Beristade. In Chenareburg. In Ripeleid . . . <u>Wasta.</u>

Pain. The black shock of freezing water. Then bobbling and flailing for air. Under again. The roar of river. Silence underwater. The weight of the girl. The two of them surfacing briefly in spluttering gasps until, on a bend downstream, she strikes hard against a slumped alder and feels its twigs whip over her skull. She grabs up and holds and pulls the girl with her. Then the drag against current, the numbness as she hauls them out on to the frozen mud and into the willows of the bank.

When her breath comes back in a great inhale and she feels the stabbing cold all over her body, she checks the girl who is shivering, her eyes wide with shock. She hugs her and rubs her for warmth and the girl looks up at her with those blue eyes, her soaking hair plastered across her freckled face. She rocks her on her lap and then she carries her deeper into the woods. Trees grow thickly on ground that rises to the north. Sycamores, oaks. They push into them, up the banks and through the low-lying thorns and brush. When the girl's shivering becomes uncontrollable, the woman feels for the tinder pouch and the flint and steel she took from her sister's husband in Hartwel and that she keeps tied about her neck. She strikes sparks into the wet papery birch bark and, after a while, a thin edge takes and curls and a fine line of smoke rises. This she feeds gently with deadwood until it sizzles and squeaks into flame. She strips, makes the girl undress and hangs their clothes around the fire until they steam. They sit together for warmth and keep the fire fed, then dress again and sit awhile more until the heat can be felt through the wool of their tunics and their skin tingles and the girl stops shivering and sits dull-eyed staring into flames. The woman rocks her on her lap, kisses her head.

The girl says she wants bread and warm milk and the woman tells her she is sorry she lost their things. When the girl asks if the man will bring them food, she tells her that he can't now. That he walks with them, but they cannot see him any more. She tells the girl she knows how hungry and cold she is, but that they have to keep moving.

Evening is falling as they blunder up through black trunks, pausing to listen and to look. They rest for a few hours in the thickness of a holly grove by a small fire set in a dip. She knows it is too cold to survive the night without shelter and in the near-dark she covers a tunnel of stacked branches with leaf litter until it is as deep as her elbow and it is as if the earth-floor of the woods has been lifted and they have crawled inside. She holds the girl against her as she trembles until she feels her breathing slip into sleep.

It is colder in the morning. They wait for the weak sun to gild the trunks and then leave. There are fresh wolf tracks in the frosted forest floor. They walk all day to keep warm and the woman carries the girl as far as she can and then holds her hand. Before dusk they find a frozen beck and follow it uphill until another wood. They breach the treeline into pasture dotted with blurs of hawthorn and where cows have been slaughtered and left ungutted. They pass with noses and mouths covered. Beyond, a small track leads them down again into bare trunks. As they descend, she glimpses through the wooded heights, above a looping hairpin bend in the river below, a high tongue of land opposite. Ringing the entirety of the cliff edge is a wooden palisade.

They stumble down to the river, close to a crossing where the water is narrowest and shallowest, then wait near the pontoon of bound logs that bridges the flow. After counting to a thousand, the woman carries the girl on her back over the Wear in the blackness, planting her feet on icy timbers. On the other side, at the foot of the cliff, she looks for and then follows a path into the trees around the peninsula's western edge, until they find the steep, worn track that cuts up towards the palisade, towards a broad gateway that is lit by flame-glow. She becomes aware that they are being watched.

The girl whispers that she knows this place. That she has been here before.

There are twelve men with torches waiting for them at the top of the path. Four more emerge from behind, carrying spear and shield. These shout to the men at the gate that the woman and child are alone. Then they disappear into the trees. The men ask of the woman if either of them is sick. She tells them no, they are not. They ask if they have seen any raiding parties and where they were. The woman nods and says across the river, a day's walk back. They ask her where they have come from and she tells them from Eoforwic. *Eoforwic*, one of the men exclaims, shaking his head. He says that they cannot take all of them. *How can we take them all?* The woman asks them where they are and they tell her Dunholme. Then the men send one of their number for the brothers.

Three men in coarse white robes arrive at the gates and the eldest of them asks the same questions again. The woman sags with hunger. She begs for the girl to have something to eat and be warmed by a fire and the brother answers yes, for they are under Cuthbert's protection now and they needn't fear any longer. Once they have their strength, they will be expected to stay and to work, to rebuild what has been burned in the city, to weave and brew and, in time, to grow and tend animals and the sick and ravaged land, for there are many mouths to feed here and many more will come before the spring. But they can eat their fill and be warm and sleep within the palisade and they will be safe here. And do they agree to all of this? In God's name?

They are led through the gates and through streets between the silhouettes of houses and stores, some damaged, some razed completely, some being repaired. In the alleys, armed men sit wrapped in cloaks in small groups around fires and throw bone dice. In a dim clearing where the longhouses have been torched to rubble, rows of rough tents have been slung between the ruins with animal skins and reeds as covering. Arranged outside them, by large cooking fires, women and children call out as they pass and ask where they are from and if they've seen certain children or men wandering on their way and if they can recall their names at all or what they looked like. Some bless them as they pass and offer them to sup from their own meagre provisions. Beyond the camp, they walk between corrals and enclosures of oxen and sheep. They hear them bleat and smell them and feel the heat of them in the bitter air.

The men in robes lead them to a wide plateau of earth and mud where a huge stone-walled church stands, the likes of which the woman hasn't seen since Eoforwic. The windows in its tower are illuminated weakly from within. Around its wooden doors, monks in dark cassocks gather and talk. More brothers appear walking in procession from a half-repaired longhouse, clapping hands and stamping for warmth.

'You'll want to give thanks to Cuthbert for your deliverance before you eat,' the elder monk says. The woman breathes deeply and finds the strength to nod.

They are led past the monks into the church, much of which has been ransacked, but its roof is untouched and the stacks of splintered wood and pot have been swept to the sides to leave a bare, inlaid stone floor. In the middle, upon a wooden tier is an embroidered cloth stitched with gold thread that shines in the guttering haloes of candles. Laid upon it is a warped wooden coffin carved and painted with figures, symbols, letters.

'We have brought him home,' the man says. 'You may pray to him.' And she does.

Outside, abutting the church, a lean-to. Coals glow in a pit under a beamed roof thatched with reed. Another man in robes who has the pimply face of a boy is instructed to hand the girl and the woman bowls of barley broth with some cold mutton. He fetches this, but warns them not to eat too quickly, saying he has seen many like her die on that very spot from giving in to greed when their bodies are still ravaged with hunger. The woman, standing, scarred and starving, stares at him and he reads her mind. He walks to a shelf and finds her a pot to dip in a cask of ale and gives the girl a soft apple and a thick cloak too big for her. He fishes out a couple of wool blankets from a chest, then he shows them to a row of stalls in the dark at the back of the lean-to, close to the fire where they might take some straw and make up a bed for tonight. They lie there under the blankets, their arms wrapped around each other, foreheads touching and they listen.

They listen as he mutters and feeds the charcoals with new logs.

They listen to the fire surging, then stilling with the wind. They listen to the far-off conversations of the refugees, the night-cries of mourning and night-terrors of children and the bleatings of sheep and the distant frequency of the river. Then suddenly, more loudly than everything, they hear the stone-echo harmonies of the brothers as they begin to sing in the stone church. And it sounds like a kind of weeping.

When the woman wipes the tears from her face, the girl stirs and grips her arm and blinks up at her. She asks if she is leaving and the woman whispers, no, she is not.

She looks into the girl's grey-blue eyes, kisses her head and strokes hair from her face. She tells her that she is with her now. And that is all. And that is everything.

This is the time of hope.

Resurfacing
(Durham–Caithness)

I

The singing begins as I write in my notebook. The voices of the choir filling the cathedral. April, just. Light over Palace Green. The sound of the city traffic, birdsong. A falsetto of Latin verse. That soaring response. Minor into major, into minor.

Durham. Cuddy's shrine. CVTHBERTVS. PROTECTION. The journey of the monks. 100 years of fleeing. Pilgrimage. The coffin wanderings – up and down Dere Street / The north road. Cathedral rebuilt by the Normans after conquest / harrying as a statement. Stunning, overpowering. A FORTRESS. Unchallengeable. Oppressive. Lion head door knocker (north porch) promised sanctuary to all who touched it. A fitting place to come now, post-Covid. With this light through the stained-glass. Lit 3 candles, Rosie, Tom, Bea. A prayer whispered above his body. Protection on the road ahead.

Minor into major into minor. Old notes over new notes. Words written before the world changed completely, before it fractured, fragmented. I flick back through years, pages, lines scribbled in London, Ickwell Green, Grantham, Doncaster, Catterick. I find roads walked, rewalked. Memory overlaid. Descriptions of people, place, histories. The call in Latin. Harmonies layering harmonies. Stone-echo vanishing into silence. The singing quiets. I check the time and head to the station to meet Mum off a train. We drive north.

A167 to Chester-le-Street. Roman town. Cuddy's road. The old Roman road. The Street. Strata. Pick up the A1(M). Follow line to Newcastle.

Recall my 1st sight of the deep valley of the Tyne. Visiting a mate at university '96? / Drinking on The Metro. The mix of bridges spanning that rift of river; 1st view of the city. Glints of roofs and houses and offices. The fine cut of Grey Street. The cut of the wind. Coming out of a pub and finding the sudden brackish smell of sea in a street. The plunging down dark streets to water. This time we keep west, on the A1 bypass / loop around / under ANGEL OF THE NORTH. The moor behind. Then <u>Morpeth</u>. Moor-path. The coaching inns. Handsome high street. Lunch in The Plough. Friendly / fraught. 'Eat Out to Help Out' stickers. QR code menu. Empty sanitiser stations. Mask signs. Wrong orders come. 'Please bear with us. These are difficult times. We're all <u>trying</u> to get back to normal . . .' And we do.

We are beyond the wall now. *Trans Vallum.* Deep into the border country, following green A1 signs for Coldstream, Alnwick. Northumberland. Great skies and corrugated fields. Birch. Willow. Sycamore. Low barns. The tarmac flowing beneath us like a grey river. Notes made at service stations when we stop for petrol, coffee, loo breaks. Through the windscreen, Mum photographs the passing landscape we both know well.

<u>Alnwick</u>. The Castle. The Percys. Thomas? PILGRIMAGE OF GRACE. The march down the road. Catholic rebellion against Henry 8. Economic? Political? Failure. Mum asks – do you remember coming here when you and your brother were little? I try / picture a cottage instead. Somewhere close but near an old railway. Red gate. Rain. Three-bar fire. Making Airfix Spitfire kits on the floor. A cold bedroom. But the castle? My memories of it are with my own children – with my brother's children. Tours of its grand interior / Tom on my shoulders. The dress-up. The broomstick flying lessons. Day trips from the Northumberland coast – shared holiday homes in Beadnell and Craster before the pandemic. The kids still young enough to believe in magic. Walking to the beach after dinner with a toddling Bea to collect hag stones. Sitting on rocks / tide licking our feet. A challenge: dropping stones into the steel-blue waters. Letting her win. Her telling me that I just need to learn to let go. <u>Watch</u> Daddy. <u>See</u>?

The A1 / Great North Road all the way. Long ribbon-road. Two-lane through arable heaven. The land dipping east down to white-cap, wave-break rolls over shore-rock. Sands, mudflats, the great North Sea. 'Holy Island', a finger sign points. Lindisfarne. The Farnes. Tidal island and seabird outcrop where Cuddy saw out his last twenty years. Where his body was found intact ten years after death. Where he was declared a saint. Teasing coast. Suddenly there, then far. Flashes: black rock, sea. Cirrus over blue.

> _Berwick._ _Park up by the wide Tweed, under walls. Sun on the smooth,_
> _swift water. Wide prospect of old stone road bridge. 15 arches / span-_
> _ning river. James 1 (James 6 / Scotland). Early promise of UNITY after_
> _bringing the kingdoms together (1603). Centuries wrecked and sacked_
> _by the English and the Scots. The bridge a staple; a stitch; a suture._
> _Narrow alleys up from river. We walk steep, shops-shut streets. A little_
> _bar – open but full. LOWRY paintings on alleyway boards. Stick fig-_
> _ures in the vistas. Tea at YHA cafe. 'We can fit you in!' Stereo playing_
> _Sting's The Great North Road._

Across the border. Municipal saltire sign: _Welcome to Scotland. Fàilte_ _gu Alba._ A1 four-lane gunning north. Wind skittering over grey sea. Farms on rising ground to the west. Gorse. Cattle. The stark white block of Torness nuclear power station. A curving inland, past Dunbar, place of Cuddy's birth, around the buttress of the Lammermuirs. Coast and high moor. Falling miles to Edinburgh mark us as making good time. The only hold-up is short: ten minutes at temporary lights in the long approach to the city centre. Trucks. Cones. A sign (white on red) spells it out: WE ARE RESURFACING.

II

The body has lain in the dark for a dizzying span of time. Since being placed in a stone-lined kist, constructed in a hollow carved into the Caithness bedrock near the northernmost tip of mainland Scotland, the earth has made its journey around the sun more than 4,200 times. Around those concealed bones, through the light and dark of a million and a half days and nights, the world has spun through inconceivable changes.

It is February 1987. Father and son William and Graham Ganson are beside the road in an area that is now known as Craig-na-Feich, in Achavanich. They are quarrying stone with a digger, hacking into a little ridge of rising ground for material to be used for the upkeep of a road. As they gear up the engine again and drag its toothed bucket across and down into the earth, the bank they've been gouging out gives way. Revealed: a huge slab of heavy stone and – where it has slipped position – the darkness of a space within. There is a raised hand, an urgent shout. The digger's engine is cut. From the void beneath the rubble-filled digger bucket there is a human skull staring back at them.

A jolt, you'd imagine, at that realisation. *Soil and stone into spoil and bone.*

The police are called. The officer understands the age in the skull immediately and summons a local archaeologist, Bob Gourlay, who excavates and records the kist and its contents. The remains of what appears to be a young woman. A cattle scapula. Pieces of worked flint. An ornately decorated earthenware vessel, a 'beaker'. Everything is recorded carefully, from the position and orientation of the body to the construction of the kist and the placing of the grave goods.

Measurements are made. Photographs taken. The finds sent to experts elsewhere – the beaker for analysis to Edinburgh to determine what its contents were, whereupon it develops a crack and breaks apart. On receiving it back, Gourlay repairs it, then types a pamphlet detailing his results. Body, beaker, scapula, flints are dispersed and reburied in the vaults of museums. The earth will make its journey thirty more times around the sun before they surface again.

*

It is early evening and I am walking from the hotel to look for the end of the road. After the long drive north, it feels good to be out. A descending sun is spilling amber over Edinburgh, sending the skyline shadows of the Old Town with its elegant spires, towers and sheer, austere facades, stretching out towards Leith and the unseeable North Sea.

All our roads end. Don't we know that? Haven't we felt it lately, keenly, in our bones, in our homes? Those months of daily, teatime briefings on infection rates, growing numbers in intensive care, of new, incomprehensible thousands of dead. Far too many people have reached the end of the road too soon, carried there by the harrying plague of our age. Far too many have had their lives torn apart completely. The rest of us, the lucky ones, emerge from two years of suspension, but not one of us is unaltered. A month on from the final lifting of coronavirus restrictions and it still feels more novelty than normality to be free to be anywhere again. To take the air of a place that is not your own. To breathe without a mask. To walk among strangers once more.

A couple holding hands outside a closing kirk. A piper packing up on the street corner. I hear American voices: 'Did you do Greyfriars yet? You *have* to . . .' Chinese students mill around one of the many gift shops ('Thistle do Nicely') with bags full of tartan souvenirs. There is life between the falling stripes of shadow and light. There is chatter, music on the breeze, but everything quieter, more muted, than I ever remember this city being. Except, that is, for all the roadworks. Here too, on the Royal Mile, the *Via Regis*, a nineteenth-century regal rebrand of the stretch of road between Holyrood and Edinburgh

Castle, the cobbles have been lifted. Orange barriers pinned with diversion signs surround the parked-up diggers and pallets piled with bags of cement. Explanatory boards read, pointedly: WE ARE IMPROVING YOUR ROADS.

All our roads end. The question is always where, and when? Unsurprisingly perhaps, that great shape-shifter of a highway, the north road, has no more a fixable finish line than it does a definitive origin, or a singular course between. It depends on which point you turn the clock back to. For many centuries, though, most would agree that the road up from London to Scotland finished in a suitably crescendo-like conclusion. A slow rise followed by a dramatic drop. Approaching Edinburgh from Musselburgh, the route looped around the Salisbury Crags and Arthur's Seat before a steady climb up what would become the Royal Mile, along a glacial ridge formed behind a huge core of extinct volcano familiar to all now as Castle Rock. Perched on top of this natural fortress, Edinburgh Castle. Before that, a hill fort, Din Eidyn. Had you followed the line up through Britain, it would have terminated at these gates. Beyond, only a sharp fall into a void. Behind, the road from whence you came.

The sea can be seen from this spot. Over the railings of the esplanade, the wide gathering place in front of the castle's gatehouse, over budding trees and banks of daffodils, over the pomp and splendour of Edinburgh's Georgian New Town, a seam of grey-blue water. Darkening fell above. Up here, the wind snaps the flags. Seagulls reel. The castle has shut for the night, so I turn and head back down the road already travelled, down the slope of the Royal Mile's handsome, steepled gully, down Castlehill and Lawnmarket, down High Street and Canongate, to find another ending.

When the first highway maps began to be committed to paper, the terminus of the Great North Road was marked as halfway up the Royal Mile, at 'Netherbow Port'. 'Port' as in gate, as this was the most important of the six ancient gateways to the medieval city and the meeting point of the two burghs of Edinburgh and Canongate. The imposing fortified and towered arch dividing them was the Scottish equivalent of Hicks's Hall at Smithfield: point of origin or departure, depending on which way you were travelling. By the time the gateway was demolished in the 1700s, the road passing through was a stinking thoroughfare slipping between heaped tenements. Forced upward by the city's encircling defensive walls, the buildings of the Old Town had risen ever higher as the wealthier sought cleaner air, above the poverty and the pestilence of the warren-like wynds and closes below. Above the squalor, smoke and filth of the poor families crammed into single rooms. Above the noise and the choke-smoke of trades being practised beneath; the open fires and open-sewer stench of pools and rivers of effluent. Above the streams of blood and guts sluicing down the road. In this likeness, at least, Netherbow might have been twinned with Smithfield.

A new slab of stone carved with the old name is set into the wall. At the top of an ancient flight of steps, looking east towards Aberlady Bay, an information board: *Beyond Here is The World's End*. For a large proportion of the 50,000 residents kettled into the Old Town in the early eighteenth century, this would have been true. The Netherbow gate was a tollhouse that canalised the road and charged its travellers. Fees levied, whether going in or out. Poorer inhabitants could never afford to leave the confines of the city. This was the end of their world. The village of Holyrood, half a mile downhill, as distant and unreachable as London, or Australia.

All roads end. And here is the trace of a gate once demarking not just the Great North Road's conclusion but the world's end. I think of how neat that would have been. Back at the start of all this, I had a mind to walk the last fifty miles or so from Berwick to this point. Two days of ecstatic, footsore slog flipping that world's-end contention the other way – finishing by looking north into a setting sun. Details in my notebook record the idea, but plans change, out of desire, out of necessity. We've learned this too these recent years. Endings aren't always when or where we imagine.

My phone buzzes in my pocket. Mum is messaging from the hotel, checking what time we arranged to meet for dinner. I reply that I'll see her in the restaurant in twenty-five minutes, reminding her that we'll need to be asleep early tonight and away in good time in the morning. For tomorrow brings another, longer journey north.

*

The old highway had leaned into my life again at the moment when reaching its end seemed impossible. At the height of the pandemic, when all rhythms and patterns of existence had shifted, the Great North Road took it upon itself to arrange the pieces, to bring together coincidences that offered a new course. It was during that first year of lockdown when there was little more to living than struggling through days of stalled time. Those unreal, unravelling weeks and months of lives and livelihoods coming undone. The world shocked and scared. For Rosie and me, constrained and strained with worry, work and the demands and disruptions of home-schooling the kids, it felt like a rerun of those early days of having a new baby in the house. Minutes catching on moments and stretching into hours; days vanishing in a matter of seconds. The four walls closing in. The universe shrinking to the immediate and the essential again. Everything on hold. All plans shelved. All horizons narrowed. Every road abandoned.

It brought a familiar sense too of the future slamming hard into the now. The miles ahead vanishing. Likewise, a feeling of the past proximate in the present again. In the furnace-heat of that first summer of seclusion, as nature erupted wildly in our absence, I read a feature in a magazine about an uptick in recovered memories being experienced across global populations enduring lockdowns. The sealed-in mind, as the story explained, has a tendency to seek escape wherever it can, habitually turning inward where outward flight is impossible, resulting in the unlocking and resurfacing of previously forgotten things. It rang true. Outside our bolted doors and windows: the eerily empty, sun-streaked ghost towns and cities, regreening after our withdrawal. Inside: unsettled, room-bound brains left to mine their deepest recesses and darkest corners. Home grounds becoming haunted spaces caught between times. Phantoms, known and unknown, appearing in our living rooms and stalking the long highways of memory. All those old shadow selves, those discontinued selves; all the vanished people, places and possibilities that once had to be sought out at the edges to be reckoned with were now overrunning our newly fixed positions, catching us as we slept.

My dreams were vivid, various, but with one place and time recurring in particular: living on the edge of the moor with Mum. I told myself it was a subconscious yearning for space. A response to being incarcerated for too long with only a tiny yard, overstuffed with pots, washing line and bikes, in which the children could play. Each day I wished the kids could jump the fence and run. The open moor was the place I'd done that at their age – surely my dreams were a lamenting that I couldn't give them the same? Except there was more to it. Scenes too specific; events clear, as if they had happened yesterday. One that recycled repeatedly involved sitting and waiting in our house under the looming shoulder of moor – for *what*? I don't know. The memory refused to resolve. Somebody to return? Someone to collect me? But I'd be sitting alone in the kitchen, watching a rectangle of light stretching from one side of the room to the other, a clock ticking. Scentless bunches of lavender hanging off the beams gathering dust. Motes drifting in the air. The building settling with its own stillness. The growing silence of the empty rooms around me. The dead hours of watching and waiting and listening as day darkens into evening, long after it was clear that no one was coming.

After a while it occurred to me that the resurfacing of these memories, this mix of recollection and projection, might be stemming from concern. My mum still lives on her own in the village below that moor, and I worried about her enduring the weeks and months of detention by herself. I imagined her alone and missing us: her family, her grandchildren. My mind was defaulting back to the isolation and loneliness we had endured together before, reminding me that harder even than juggling all that Rosie and I had to each day was living again in that stillness and silence, watching the light moving, the hands of the clock crossing, uncrossing. Waiting with the knowledge that no one was coming. So, I called Mum more than usual. We arranged games with the kids on Zoom, sent texts daily that were records of the seasons changing. I made her a promise: *when all this is over, we will go somewhere together.*

At the same time, a sense of something unfinished was acting on me like a cough you can't shake. The A1/Great North Road was strictly out of bounds unless you were a stretched-to-the-limit first responder, delivery driver or part of the rule-inverting cabal of ministers and advisers (mis)guiding the country through the unfolding disaster. In the limited windows I had to myself, I was reduced to travelling the road north through Newcastle and Northumberland and up to its conclusion in Edinburgh, via the same stack of out-of-print highway books, novels, newsletters and pamphlets that had first set me on the north road five years earlier. Old lines of flight for this new world in flux. To trace again the constancy of this ever-changing highway felt reassuring. As Frank Morley found, picking about the ruins of London after the Blitz, the north road is an attestation. Even amid devastation and these hard transitions into different historical eras, it goes on. When, or if, I might reach the road's end, though, was anyone's guess.

It was Norman Webster's book *The Great North Road* (1974) that kept me company most. Its straightforwardness and conviction compelling. The way the author removes himself completely in his meticulous route details. The rolling tense of the text ('Thirlestane castle is passed, but the road turns right a mile before the town ...') creating a sensation of momentum – of a road trip in real-time. The only place his surety slips is across the book's final pages. Webster unexpectedly sidesteps any full stop: 'If Edinburgh brings finality to the Great North Road,' he writes, 'the Thurso Mail from London was only half-way on its journey ... through Edinburgh to Perth ... and over the muir of Caithness to Thurso, 783 miles from London, a reminder that the northern highway does not end in Midlothian but goes on ... the signs continuing to read "To the North".'

There is an unexpected fraying in form and course. Webster's tone philosophical. The terminus abstracted. He writes: 'In perspective the Great North Road is seen as an introduction to northern Britain, the goal lying indeterminately ahead like some Ultima Thule ... seemingly as elusory as Pope's in his *Essay on Criticism*: *Ask where lies the North? at York, 'tis on the Tweed; In Scotland, at the Orcades.*' Roads run on, the thing you seek vanishes over the horizon, endings are relative. Such are the inferences. With what we were living through, this resonated.

At the end of that first year, a 'Kent variant' of Covid began spreading up from the south-east where it was first detected, through London, into the heart of the country. The data revealed it to be following, at something like walking pace, the A1/Great North Road. It was even rechristened *Alpha*. More virulent, more transmissible, more lethal, it snapped focus back to personal susceptibility. Infection was deemed unavoidable. Serious illness or death a dice roll depending on vaccination status, age, affluence, location, genetic predisposition and, most prominently, underlying health conditions, whether known or unknown. DNA agencies had begun doing big business accordingly, uncovering what was hidden in the blood against checklists of potential buried, inherited nasties. A swab might spotlight undetected risks to children and parents, the blurbs promising '150+ comprehensive health reports'. Phrases like 'blood bio markers', 'genetic variant analysis', 'carrier status insight' and 'disease predisposition testing' were persuasive. The discounts generous. The messaging was perfectly positioned to imply that this was a fascinating way to travel virtually through space and time – to connect with communities of people and relatives you didn't know existed. A promise of new answers to questions being asked, once again, by a nation lost and traumatised: *Who are we? Where have we come from? Where are we going?*

When they landed a few days before Christmas, I scrolled the DNA results on my phone in a supermarket. Something of an early present. Nothing sinister in my line that could have been passed on to Tom and Bea. Nothing that might put them at any higher risk. Relieved, I clicked open the other reports. An ancestry map seemed to back up the Cowen family histories I'd been uncovering. Blooms of blue; DNA markers from the last 250 years showing concentrated patterns of presence in the west of Ireland (Mayo), central and northern England, Yorkshire, London. Then, at the bottom, in its own box, a headline: *You share an ancient maternal-line ancestor with a prehistoric woman from northern Scotland.* The text explained that four millennia ago, a young woman had been laid to rest in a small tomb in Achavanich, Caithness, close to the North Sea at the edge of Scotland. Buried with her, a beaker, pieces of flint, a cattle scapula. Thirty years after she was chanced upon by two men digging rock for a road, there'd been a project to learn more about her, including DNA testing. This identified her maternal haplogroup – the line of DNA passed from mother to daughter through the generations – and the report confirmed this to be the same as mine. H5b. At the bottom, a CGI portrait looked, at first, like a photo. A living face staring back at me.

At home I read deeper into the story and the project that sought to better understand this woman and her world. I compiled features

from papers and websites and copied a map showing an approxima-
tion of the kist's position beside the road in Caithness. I emailed them
to Mum together with the ancestry report, hoping it might prove
something of a distraction. Something to think about. Something of
interest to share with friends. But it was, I stressed, as distant an
ancestral link as we might find.

Having done some digging, it appeared that belonging to this
maternal haplogroup was not exactly rare. H is one tributary in the
great human river that has, at its source, a single woman who lived
somewhere in east Africa sometime between 120,000 and 150,000
years ago. Yet on a Zoom call later, giddy with the news of discovery,
Mum had asked if we could, one day, go and visit the burial site. If we
could stand where 'her family' had. *Maybe this is the journey that we
should make when all this is over?* It would be the furthest north in
Britain she'd ever gone and she wanted to see the mountains, the sea,
the birds. We were heading into another Christmas apart. There were
growing rumours of a new lockdown beginning in January. 'It's a long
way and I can't do these trips alone any more.' She'd said: '*Please.
Could we go together?*'

That night, I picked up my tattered, taped-together copy of Norman
Webster's *The Great North Road* from the bedside table and leafed
through it. I wanted to locate again the mention of Caithness I knew
to be in there. I found it not only in that last paragraph on the Thurso
Mail, but in the very last sentences of the book. Reading them once
more left the impression of a command as much as a conclusion: 'The
story of that further journey which, beginning at Edinburgh and
ending in the extremes of Caithness, passing through country wild
and varied, is yet to be written.'

*

We check out of the hotel early, then drive north from Edinburgh over
the Firth of Forth before the rush-hour traffic can snag our progress.
Achavanich is a blue dot on the satnav. The road to reach it lies like a
length of hurled rope. Were it possible to climb on to the hotel's roof
and fly in a straight line, we'd land at the site of the kist in about 170
miles. But our earthbound route meanders nearly a hundred more,

beholden to Scotland's extraordinary topography – weaving past towns and cities, around glens and lochs, bridging rivers at their narrowest points. It loops the bulk and the loom of the Cairngorms, those high plateau heart-hills of the eastern Highlands, then strikes out even further still, up beyond Inverness, stitching around the coastline like a hem.

What the distance gives us is time to listen. I've stacked up podcasts on the history of the Chalcolithic and early Bronze Age, including a few dedicated to the Achavanich burial itself, featuring interviews with the driving force behind the rediscovery and research on the project, Maya Hoole. Before I left home, I had emailed Maya to outline our journey on the off-chance she might be able to share the exact location of the kist. At the same time, there'd been the opportunity to ask about her name: *Hoole*. The only other person I've ever met with that surname being Rosie. Maya had messaged back with a dropped pin in a Google map and to confirm that she had never encountered another Hoole that wasn't a relative either. Did we know from where Rosie's family hailed originally? Calls had been made to her parents. Locations checked. No DNA testing was required to determine they were likely distant cousins.

Maya had been working as an early career archaeologist looking for images to post on social media when she first stumbled across a photograph of a beautifully decorated Bronze Age beaker and the details of the rescue excavation in Caithness in 1987 that had unearthed it. When she'd tried to find where the beaker might be, she'd hit a brick wall. The old Caithness Museum where all the recovered objects had originally been sent had since closed, reopening as a Viking Centre, before closing down again. Scotland, as with all parts of Britain, finds itself overwhelmed by its own rich histories. What to do with everything once the funding dries up is a perennial question. Behind the museum displays are countless thousands of boxes of finds and excavation materials filling shelf after shelf of storage. Objects get separated from written records and disappear again. Curious about the beaker, Maya spent months digging for answers when, in 2014, a web search one morning returned a list of artefacts available for public sponsorship from a museum in Thurso. There, in all its motif-patterned beauty, was the same beaker she'd seen in the photo. She made contact. Yes, the museum had it. Was she interested too in the bones of the young woman it had been placed beside? It marked the beginning of a project that grew into something more significant than Maya could have imagined, transforming that Bronze Age burial site at the edge of Scotland into one of the most researched and illuminating of its kind.

*

Skirting Perth on the motorway, we pick up the A9, the road that will take us all the way to the kist. The four-lane is smooth, easy driving. Overbridges. Laybys. Deep verges of leafing birch, gorse, spruce; far hills brooding over tilting plains of field. Rain spatters steadily then stops. From Dunkeld to Pitlochry, our road weaves beside the River Tay; a twisting, shimmering surge meandering through wet green pasture. The pattern becomes the same as yesterday. Mum snapping away on her phone at passing views. Rest stops in search of coffee and conveniences. In the Motor Grill restaurant at Ballinluig Services there's no chance of placing an order for two hours.

I've stacked up podcasts, but I've made playlists too. Sets of songs and old albums we used to have on record and tape in the front room. Songs I remember Mum playing in the car when I was a kid in the summer holidays – when I'd watch her from the back seat singing, stumbling through words to get to the chorus, drumming the wheel, happy. Us giggling at her trying to hit the right notes. 'Strawberry Fields Forever'. 'The River'. 'Goin' Back' by the Byrds. Mersey Beat bands; late-1960s folk-rock. Country. The sky clears and the road carries us around tinfoil lochs and through passes into the hanging silence of the mountains and glens edging the Cairngorms. I let the songs play in succession and watch her remembering them again, each opening a little cave of time in the confines of our car.

At Aviemore we pull in and find a little walkers' café with cheery waiters and damp cagoules drying on radiators. Mum chooses the table in the upstairs room and begins conversations with the other customers. She lets our tea stew in those red-hot, stainless-steel teapots and deliberates over the cake display. She shows me the phone pictures she's already taken. I'm sharply aware that I know what she will do before she does it. What she'll say. I could tell you that this is because we've spent two days in the car, or forty-five years as mother and son before that, but there is something else. After the break-up of my parents' marriage, situations like these in cafés, shops, supermarkets, or when we'd bump into people Mum and Dad knew, would see us slip into roles. A pretence of normality. Things were falling apart at home, we were in all sorts of pain, but in public we'd pretend that everything was fine and dandy, carefully and consciously holding it all together for others. I struggled with enacting these parts as if nothing was wrong when we both knew that it was. Yet I went along with it. I learned my role. I memorised our parts because I wanted things to be OK and to protect Mum. What it did, though, was further deny the acknowledgement of what was actually happening. It made me feel even more alone. Perhaps that should be OK thirty years on, except that we still struggle to acknowledge those times now. They are a blind spot that has been there ever since. We are better than we were. I try to be open, sensitive, but when I bring those years up, the conversation always remains general or gets moved on. I wonder now whether she also feels the physical tension of those days flashing up out of nowhere like I do, or what version of events she even recalls. Or whether, in seeking to move on, she has forgotten and I'm alone in dredging all this up. I want to ask these things, but I can't because she is happy. More than anything else, I learned in those difficult years that was the thing I desperately wanted her to be again.

I pour the tea, halve my cake and push it over. She smiles, does the same.

Back in the car, the satnav blinks on. The route still shows 120 miles to Achavanich. We won't be there before mid-afternoon. Mum's phone is out before we pull away. She's snapping a peregrine careening off the mountain behind the car park.

I ask her to choose whatever song she wants to hear next from the playlists. 'Mmm.' She chews her cheek. 'Can't we learn a bit more about my ancestor instead?'

*

Ava. It was the name Maya and the archaeologists and experts originally gave the project. Ava, from the middle letters of Achavanich.

However, it soon became interchangeable with the found body itself. Ava likely had a name in her own time, and while it is impossible to know what it was, we should remember that she once did. That it was known and spoken by a mother and father, perhaps a son or daughter.

Ava's burial in the stone-lined kist was not usual. Whoever dug out a tonne of Caithness flagstone to create the pit to put her in did so by hand. This was a considerable undertaking. Using antler tools, it would have taken a single person days or could have involved multiple diggers working together from her community. Either way, it was a serious commitment for an early Bronze Age farming population and in contrast to the sand and gravel that other Beaker-era kists found in the north-east of Britain were dug into. So, was she in some way particularly revered, or feared? That's what the archaeologists ponder. Opinion tends to lean towards the former. Whoever laid her 5' 5" body down did so with real care and in ways that must have been significant to them. She was dressed and buried soon after her death. Time was taken to carefully contract her legs, possibly binding them up post-mortem, so that the knees were nearly touching her shoulders. Her body was positioned on its right, as is common for female beaker burials, her right arm across her chest, her head turned to the side. There is a shying away from using the word 'foetal' in any description because it introduces assumptions, projections, biases – but it is hard not to think of it when you hear the experts being interviewed. While it may well have been a sudden disease or long illness that did for Ava, death as a result of complications during childbirth is clearly in the back of everybody's mind. Especially when there has been no other obvious trauma discovered to the surviving bones. Especially when you consider that she died between the ages of eighteen and twenty-five.

Pollen analysis reveals that flowers may have been placed in the kist. Coincidental maybe, but some have medicinal connotations: meadowsweet for pain; sphagnum moss and St John's wort for the staunching of blood. Also found was the presence of cotton grass, fern, bracken, heather, the pollen of birch, alder, hazel and pine. Laid on top of her was an offering and – if it's not too much of a reach either – food for the journey into the afterlife. The shoulder of a sub-adult cow. From her stable isotopes we know Ava ate a diet rich in meat despite living close to the sea. Her short life, by our terms, knew sickness and malnutrition; it knew hard work. To one side of her head was placed a flint scraper. To the other, carefully, was put the beaker.

*

Mum asks whether I could identify meadowsweet, sphagnum moss, St John's wort. I tell her that of course I can, because she taught me what they look like. I tell her too that I've been trying to get the kids to memorise wild flowers with varying degrees of success. She laughs, tells me I have to be patient. I remember suddenly, strongly, an afternoon, end of summer, when she'd showed me how to cut lavender from a bed, how to bunch it, bind its stems together and hang it from the kitchen beams to dry.

Northward towards Inverness and the Great Glen. Nordic skies of cold blue scratched by straight lines of plane vapour. Pines knocked down like skittles. Logging wagons. On the metal grey back of a sign on the other side of the road, someone has sprayed FLAT EARTH, then FE, FE, FE on every sign that follows for maybe four miles. It is anything but, though. Glens, mountains, flood plains with swerving, glinting rivers. The road curves and lifts and then we are on the raised edge of a huge expanse of muted yellow and brown. We are looking down and back across a plain. In the distance, the subtle shades of green and russet of enormous, pleated mountains, their tops white with snow. What comes to mind is a sweeping Peckinpah panorama from a Western. As I'm thinking it, a train slips through the middle of shot, catching the sun.

Mum has her window down to get a clearer photo. I slow the car.

There is time to listen, time to look. Time to talk also. We try to recall when it was that we last spent this long together, just us, reminiscing about trips to Scotland we made when I was young. Holidays in Gairloch, Wester Ross. Oban. Iona. Long drives like these through the Highlands. I think of my brother and me in the back seat, blurs of epic scenery. Dad driving. A time near a loch when he nearly fell asleep at the wheel and came to a stop in the rough, reedy ground, shaken but unhurt. There were two weeks on the Isle of Colonsay one year. A flat in an old house filled with light. Giant rhododendrons in the garden. I must have been thirteen or fourteen then, and it was the last summer we had together as a family before things began to change. We walked across the sands at low tide to Oronsay. Watched seals. Walked the island in loops. Everyone read a lot. I remember it being quiet. Long silences in the afternoons. Maybe a fraying was already happening. Mum chuckles. 'The golf course! Do you remember that?' Then I do. I remember Mum, Dad, me and my brother on a ramshackle fairway behind the house. None of us knowing how to play. Falling about laughing as every one of our sliced shots was carried by a hurricane sea-wind down one of the rabbit holes peppering the greens, until the whole game had to be abandoned. I'm smiling thinking about it. Funny what stays with us, what slips.

Doors are opening. As we drive on, I feel it is OK to push them a little. I talk about the house on the moor and innocuous things I remember from the years when things were really hard. Other funny moments, because they also happened, even amid everything. And humour, well, it's a road in, isn't it? I mention the night I was asleep after coming in from a club at 3 a.m. and Mum woke me an hour later to deliver a breeched lamb that couldn't get born. How she'd held the torch as, fortified with Dutch courage, I'd got my hands dirty. How after I'd turned that slippery mass and tugged it out, I lay there in the straw of the shippen, lamb on top of me, my face splattered with birth-mucus. How I'd stood, walked outside, then thrown up. I mention the UFO watchers who'd arrive sporadically at our door and ask if we'd seen the bright lights on the moor tops the night before. Or if we had ever encountered an alien *personally*. I ask Mum questions that I know the answer to because it opens old ground – like the name of the poem she wrote and had published in a magazine when we had to sell the house. That was called 'Leaving the Moor'. I tell her it was a brilliant piece of writing filled with emotion, beauty, poignancy. She is thrilled that I remember it. She says she still has it somewhere. 'You can have a copy if you want?'

*

The experts explain that the preferred parlance of archaeologists today is *beaker-associated* people. I get the point. Why would we reduce a complex people and a transformative period of history involving trade links across Britain capable of moving a button of Whitby jet or Cornish tin to Scotland at speeds that would give modern courier companies a run for their money; that saw incredible innovation, culture, craft and ritual, to a pot buried with (some of) the dead? It's hard, though, not to smile at what sounds like sensitivity, as if they made contact to request a more respectful descriptor.

While Mum scrolls through my mobile, loading up another podcast, I ask how she will feel being surely classified in time as a *phone-associated* person. She laughs, slaps my shoulder. God knows, though, I've read of people requesting a burial with their handset. For a phone to be placed carefully by their head. A chance to audit those millions of photographs. Something to do on the long journey into the afterlife.

We learn that one of the most revealing parts of Ava's story is her own ancestry; the deeper revelations of her DNA. The team discovered that she has no real match to the pre-existing Neolithic peoples who resided in and around Caithness at the time, meaning Ava and her family were recent incomers to the area. She was born and raised where she was found, but her parents or grandparents originated somewhere close to the modern-day Netherlands and travelled to Scotland via trackway and sea, probably along well-used trade routes. This places them into a much larger story of the migration and settling of beaker-using people into Britain beginning about 4,400 years ago.

The prevailing thought in the first half of the twentieth century was that these beaker-users brought war to these shores. They were a foreign invasion force coming here with their tools, tanged and barbed arrowheads and their mastery of completely new technologies – such as refining metal. The DNA evidence reveals that, indeed, their arrival brought about a 90 per cent replacement of the pre-existing Neolithic population of Britain in the DNA record within a couple of hundred years. However, the dominant theory today is that this mass cultural and genetic takeover was a more complicated picture; one that involved immigration, adoption and adaptation, rather than all-out war.

What the Ava project has done is put a human face on these times. A face we might see ourselves in and relate to, whether part of the same haplogroup or not. Before her DNA tests were returned, a forensic artist named Hew Morrison had rendered over a scan of her skull and teeth layers of skin, sinew, muscle and fat. Human eyes were able to look into her open, handsome features with all their idiosyncrasies again. Initially, the brief was to give her blue eyes, light skin, reddish-brown hair. Fair guesses, except that the DNA painted a different picture. She had, in fact, dark hair, olive-toned skin and brown eyes. The image needed revising.

What was inside the treasured and carefully placed beaker beside that face remains a mystery. Nothing could be found that could be analysed. Fermented milk is one guess. An ale flavoured with honey or flowers another, based on similar burials in the region. All the team agree, though, that it would have been something potent and nourishing to wash down that slab of beef. Into her patterned beaker would have been poured a good drink to get Ava wherever she needed to go. A last one for the road.

*

Cans of pop. Cheese toasties. Once over the firths and into Caithness, the café is the last place open for food if we don't want a detour off the A-road. Terracotta tiled floor, panelling. Faded prints of Venice. The woman serving us is friendly, inquisitive. 'What brings you up this far?' Mum relates the story. 'You're Scottish then! Good!' The woman beams back. She admits she's never heard of Ava, but suggests we visit Badbea, a clearance village just up the road from Helmsdale, en route to Achavanich.

The sea to our right, eastward. Uninterrupted horizons. The A9 has become a coast road. Kitted-out VW sleeper vans with European plates. Escapees in beanies tiptoeing back from a swim or huddled over a cooking stove. A Transit van is jacked in a layby with a wheel missing. Another has 'Wild & Free' in a huge decal across a window. Inland, a buzzard drifts in lazy circles. I think of what Norman Webster wrote in *The Great North Road* about Caithness as 'wild' country. True enough, but we'd all do well to remember it was a populated, peopled place in times more recent than Ava's. Badbea and its ruins, ten minutes' walk from the road, drives the point home with arresting contradictions. Sublimity and desolation in a single space. Forsaken homes by the sea. Another end-of-the-road/end-of-the-world setting.

The tiny homesteads, once shared by residents and animals alike, were built by those ejected from their former lands in the hills, glens and straths by lords who reckoned sheep as a better commercial prospect than meagre rents and returns from tenant families. Across the Highlands, punitive proprietors emptied land in the spirit of 'improvement'. Evicted populations, forced into sea-edge survivalism, turned in desperation to spinning wheels, herring boats, kelp foraging, poor plots, illicit distilling. The Duke of Sutherland, from the neighbouring county, is the most cursed of names in the histories of the clearances, but in Caithness, Sir John Sinclair (1754–1835), the highly educated MP, statesman, agricultural reformer, slave owner and scion of the Scottish Enlightenment, played his part. At least 300 people pushed to the edge. Sinclair, it seems, had more of an interest in archaeology and the preservation of the relics of the past than his living tenants. His documents on Scottish Neolithic and Bronze Age sites were some of the first records made of any of them. He would have been delighted, no doubt, to have discovered Ava's remains on his enormous estate.

At Badbea, eighty of the displaced and driven-out from Caithness and Sutherland constructed dwellings from whatever might be thrown together. There was nowhere else to go. This lethal lip of land overlooking the Berriedale Cliffs, where children and animals were tethered to rocks in bad weather to save them from going over, was deemed far too perilous for Sinclair's precious Cheviots. Still, folk lived out gruelling lives here, brought up children, worked boats, survived the batterings of winter storms. Badbea was finally abandoned in 1911 for what its emigrants hoped would be a better end of the road in New Zealand and North America; their bones buried in the soils of distant lands, away from their ancestors. Sinclair elected the ruins of Holyrood Abbey for his own. A stone sarcophagus. A kist, by another name.

*

The road runs inland, turning from coast-tracing to cut up to Thurso. A narrow two-lane through mottled expanses of blanket bog, reed and pools, part of the important peatland region stretching across Sutherland and Caithness that is being rebranded 'Flow Country'. Wind-worn crofts with mazy fences, stacks of machine parts, tyres.

Just short of where Maya had dropped the pin on the map, close to a little loch, we pull up on to the roadside gravel and cover the last of the distance on foot, walking along the empty road. Breakers of dark-bellied cloud and a shining sun. There is a ridge of rising ground. Protruding strata of flagstone. A terrain of reed, woody heather and moss in tussocks of ochre-green, brown. You can still see where the Ganson men brought in the digger. The hollow in the bank. Mum walks up and into it ahead of me.

At the place the kist was found I stand with the sun at my back and my shadow falling over the ground. For a million and a half days and nights Ava lay here, tucked into her underworld, but there is no body now. No grave goods. The tomb empty. Only broken shards of the lichen-covered flagstone where the hollow was made and, by chance, where her head would have been, a bird's skull hidden in the heather, bleached by sun and rain. It has a long, thin, pointed beak. 'It looks like a snipe to me,' says Mum.

For nearly an hour we walk around the site, together and alone. I try to picture the landscape Ava's brown eyes saw. Marshy belts of pine and alder, birch and hazel. Deer. Wolves. Cattle and pigs foraging the deep, wet grass beside pools and streams. Dwellings that smelled of dung and smoke. And those things that don't change: sun, clouds, blue skies. The snow-capped mountains to one side; the open sea to the other.

Because there is nothing here to tell us what to think or feel, no signage, no messaging, we are free to follow our thoughts. With my back to the kist's rock, I watch Mum make her way to the road to take another photo. I quickly snap one of her. Silhouetted, appearing small and alone against the huge backdrop, it is as if she might, in just a few steps, disappear into it. I remember something she said in the car about it being a shame that her family line of mitochondrial DNA, passed from mother to daughter for so many thousands of years, is coming to an end with her. And I realise something that has been staring me in the face all along. Mum knows exactly how related she is to Ava – to her 'ancestor'. Her knowledge of biology is far greater than

mine. I've missed the point completely. This journey was about us spending time together. That's what she always wants and what she's always wanted. If I think about it, I can't remember a single occasion where if me or my brother was passing, she didn't drop everything to accommodate us. Or a time when I've asked her to come and stay that she hasn't done everything possible to make sure it happens.

We make journeys through life. This *is* life. We all exist in the Flow Country, whether we are ready to accept that fact or not. The world spins through inconceivable changes and, in our brief time upon it, we do too. Come the end of the road, maybe all we can hope for is the love and care of a family or community to see us on our way. Someone to dress us in best. Someone to fill a cup with good drink.

I walk over to stand with Mum. She loops her arm into mine and asks whether we shouldn't be getting off. There is a long drive yet, south, to our hotel for the night on the banks of Loch Ness. I ask whether she's *absolutely* sure she's got every photograph possible, and she slaps my arm again. She thanks me for doing all this. The booking, the driving. The sorting. Not just the trip either. She pauses. 'I know how hard things were back then. I know how difficult it was for you. I do know . . .'

She squeezes my arm. And it's enough. I squeeze hers back.

I retrieve the snipe skull and a few shards of the broken flagstone. I take a last long look over the kist. The light dulls and flattens. When I turn, my shadow is gone.

III

The car-hire return is subterranean, close to Waverley station. A drive-in and leave-it, keys-through-a-letterbox operation. I buff out a few scuffs in the dark. A notice: MAKE SURE YOU TAKE *EVERY-THING* WITH YOU. Inside the glovebox, my notebook. I resurface on to New Street and follow it under the A1 to the Jacob's Ladder pathway.

> *Edinburgh. 140 steps – top of CALTON HILL. Designs (19th C) on being the Acropolis to this 'Athens of the North'. Monuments & Memorials, Corinthian columns. The Nat. Monument the new Parthenon. Never finished. Tower for Nelson. A Greek-style circular temple for Dugald Stewart (philos / 'key player' of Scot. Enlight.) by Playfair.*

I've known this hill for something like twenty-seven years, since I tried (and failed) to come to Edinburgh University to study art. Where I was told in a corridor by one of my interviewers that they doubted my heart was really into what I was choosing. That I should think long and hard about what it is I want to do with my life. I was eighteen. It was on Calton Hill I met a friend already studying here and who was putting me up. We drank. We talked about our hometown. I remember us laughing in the sun and air.

> *THIS VIEW. Another vantage point. Fading COVID warnings on railings about keeping space; keeping distance. From here – the full sweep of the city. 'Greatest view in Scotland' (RL Stevenson). Pentland Hills. Salisbury Crags. Castle Rock. The clustered collage of domes, steeples, towers, spires making up the Old Town and New. Here,*

Alexander Smith: 'The New is there looking at the Old … two times
are brought face to face.' From here, the finish line. The official end of
the A1 / Great North Road.

In 1815, Netherbow was abandoned in favour of a new terminus –
the new General Post Office in Edinburgh's New Town. In time, this
grand entry–exit via Waterloo Place would be considered the noblest
approach of any European city. Here, the London Mails swept in
along Georgian avenues lined with elegant architecture, beneath the
brows of Calton Hill and Arthur's Seat. It is here, in Norman Webster's opinion, that the accident of that word 'Great' in the north
road's name finally becomes justified.

*

In the hotel room, after dinner, I unwrap the snipe skull and the stone
fragments from my rolled-up jumper and I place them on the table, on
top of Webster's book. I climb into bed and search for 'Ava' on my
phone. The first result is a spammy baby-naming website. *Ava – from*
Avis, it tells me. *The Latin for bird, or birdlike.* I smile, clear the
search box, and then type in 'snipe'. *Water bird/wader. (Resident. NE*
Scotland). Wetlands and marshlands. I scroll down, read, then get up
to find my notebook again.

> *SNIPE. A creature of transitory / liminal spaces. Camouflaged. Hard*
> *to hunt. (From snipe we get 'sniper' …) A bird for: 'those who are*
> *searching for answers'. In Eastern mythology it represented freedom,*
> *liberation. In Greek symbolism: the spiritual journey. In early cultures,*
> *snipe synonymous w/ guidance on the difficult path to enlightenment.*
> *The bird of luck and PROTECTION on the road through life.*

The Henge

(A1(M), Junction 49)

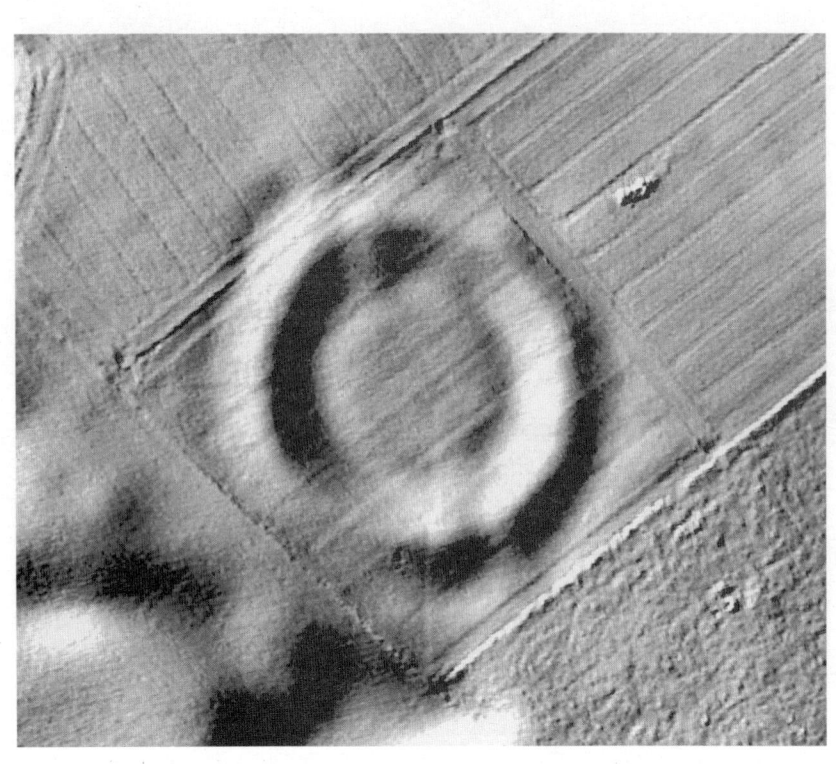

There are four of us this late afternoon, walking along the edge of the field behind the new house, following a path through a gap in the hedge and up a hump of hill on to the ridge. The hinge of the year. Days still thick with last-gasp summer warmth, but a cold clarity to the light. Northern England on the cusp of October. Greenery beginning to go over. Rooks chattering in the crowns of oaks. The exhausted land settled, and settling.

Our son bounds ahead of us. My daughter is holding Rosie's hand and singing. The track is leading us between wheat stubble and a holly hedge. Across a thin road, a farmhouse with a cluster of empty barns and crumbling pig sheds glowers back down the path. Screened by curtains of leylandii and ragged skirts of dock and nettle, it exudes abandonment. Behind, the slope meets a sky of cloud and pale blue in a curving horizon.

At the road, the children petition to turn back, hauling on our hands. They are too excited about their new home and the other kids in the village to play with to go any further. Rosie, still trying to get some heat back into her limbs after a long swim in the river, volunteers to take them, admitting she'd prefer a cup of tea to a bit of trespass.

We wave to each other. I watch them return, until a fold in the field hides them from view, then make my way through the quiet farmyard and up the narrow track beyond to crest a little hill. From here, on a clear day, I've found you can see miles in every direction. You can see the ground gradually falling away to the west, down to the tree-thickened curve of the River Ure. You can see, east, the suggestion of a trackway taking you all the way to Dere Street, the old Roman road, the A1(M).

Tracing this path requires a sliding under barbed wire. The stalking along the grassy, hummocky borders of huge, sloping fields ploughed into smooth, sun-shadow squares of deep red-brown earth. The crouching and hiding from the windows of a grand farmhouse and its outlying, red-brick workers' cottages. The scaling of a felled trunk and electric fences. I send up lapwings and spring two roe deer that bounce over the earth into a brushy treeline. I am traversing a bank to keep myself concealed when a hare suddenly stands, stares and then runs at me, brushing past my leg, heavily, like a Labrador. The further I walk along the line, the more convinced I am that this must have once been a road. Stone underlays my steps in a seam. The route sticks to the high ground and, on the map, I see the logic: an easy right angle off one of the most important roads in Roman Britain. A line threading across an expanse of moor, down to what is a natural crossing point on the Ure. At its other end, where it joins the highway, there are more features. Things visible to the naked eye on satellite images. The bumps of barrows or burial mounds, dotted across an elevated plateau above the A1(M). Close by, just to the north of a square of plantation wood given over to pheasant shooting, there is a field entirely filled with the ghost-print circle of a henge.

*

Moving had been on the cards for a while. Weary of the din and disarray of the growing children, our old house had let it be known in subtle ways that it was time for us to go. Rooms began to look like they needed decorating. Unsolicited approaches from estate agents started arriving through the letterbox. The kids declared daily that they no longer wanted to bunk up together. Those moor dreams during the pandemic already had me yearning for somewhere with a little more than a four-by-four-metre backyard – lockdown after lockdown seeding the idea that we might swap a decade of stacked living in a terrace on the edge of town for anywhere with some outdoor space.

A search area was drawn, then redrawn, shifting further north and eastwards until it appeared to be falling suspiciously close to the old highway. Rosie enjoyed pointing out that I was gravitating to the north road, suggesting it was the plan all along. But when we landed on a place that seemed to have all we needed, she agreed.

The process of extracting ourselves from long-lived-in rooms proved harder than we thought. Stripped of furniture and pictures, with shelves cleared and boxed up, those same spaces that only a few months earlier we'd been sick of the sight of, that had felt so stifling and haunted, now recalled the excitement of first moving in. It was difficult not to think of all the house had witnessed since: the stairs where Tom learned to haul himself upright and would turn to give us his proud, little gurgle-laugh. The one stretch of worn carpet where Bea mastered rolling over and crawling. The kids spilling veg from the allotment through the narrow hall, teeth marks in most of it. The bedroom where, for so many nights, I held a restless, wide-awake Bea for warmth as we watched the dark dissolve into day. The window where we would hear swifts and glimpse their hurled-anchor fly-pasts; where Rosie first told me she was pregnant as the first snow of that winter fell. All the parties, playing, people. All the magical years. I'd wondered: *Where does it go? All of this precious existence? All of this sacred time?*

Dismantling the bunk beds in the kids' room, my hand bumped up against Tom's old play mat, rolled up and squashed beneath. It was the one he used to push second-hand toy cars around, navigating its cartoon landscape of lush green fields, woods and wide, empty roads. I remembered how it had been on the floor the day my dad came over and mentioned the north road; when he'd told me about the dig happening along the A1. I unrolled it again and shouted downstairs for Tom. Nine now, his world has moved on from toy cars with missing wheels, but he smiled to see it. I watched him, on his knees, brushing away the dust, his eyes remembering every detail.

'What should we do with it, Dad?'

'We should give it a hoover and take it to the charity shop.'

He'd looked at it for a while longer. 'I'll miss it so much, though . . .'

'I know.' I declined to point out it had been under his bed for years.

'But yeah, OK,' he sighed, eventually. 'You can clean it.'

*

I'm reminded of the play mat again as I approach the plantation pines and stop to check Google Maps, scrolling its satellite imagery for a precise location for the henge. All lush fields, woods, wide-empty roads. There is a cottage ahead of me – a keeper's digs for the pheasantry, hidden at the edge of the wood. I crouch beside an elder to remain concealed. The high-altitude images on my phone screen reveal retrospect more clearly than here on the ground. I find the blue line of the A1(M), drag the map north and then west a few fields. The henge is blurry, but there. Closer than I'd thought. A great ring, water-marking the earth along the boundary of a square of trees.

Given its visibility and size, it had been a surprise to discover that this ancient monument was – like the kist at Achavanich until its rediscovery – comparatively unknown and uninvestigated. The Hutton Moor Henge, as it is officially classified, appeared in the Historic England scheduled monument listing of 1927. The earliest description I could turn up was from a local antiquarian named John Richard Walbran. In 1851, he wrote that the evidence this area was once venerated and a centre of governance for 'the Brigantes Celts' was, in part, because of:

> ... *a remarkable earth-work on the high land ... commanding extensive prospects up and down the Vale of Ure, as well as of the distant ranges of hills which form the side screens of the great Yorkshire plain. Like Abury* [Avebury] *and Stonehenge, which it rivals in antiquity, its outline is that of a circle, of which the diameter is not less than 680 feet ... enclosed by a lofty mound and corresponding trench ...*

Walbran also records two 25-foot openings aligned roughly north-north-west and south-south-east opposite one another in the circle of ditch and high-banked mound. Entrance and exit, he suggests; the henge once being intersected by a long avenue. His conclusion on the usage of the place is '. . . as a temple for the performance of Druidical rites . . .' confirmed by the nearness of eight, large 'Celtic' barrows. He mentions that he has already excavated two of these previously, finding '. . . nothing but a few calcined human bones, the ashes of the oaken funeral pile, and some fragments of flint arrow-heads, such as are still used by North-American Indians.'

Walbran made the connection to various other 'temples' in the vicinity. Namely, the three Thornborough henges arranged in a slightly off-straight line at West Tanfield, and another 'earth-work' south of Hutton Moor Henge: 'in a large field called *Cana*'.

These henges and the later barrows around them were constructed between the Neolithic and the Bronze Age, some 6,000 to 3,500 years ago. Staggeringly, they were potentially in use, built and rebuilt, for thousands of years. For what exactly? We know little more now than Walbran did. 'Ritual', 'rite' and 'ceremony' are loaded words, but we are forced to come back to them time and time again. What was perhaps less discernible in the nineteenth century is the way these monuments appear to correspond. Until the age of flight, aerial photography and precision cartography, it was harder to glean how this run of Neolithic and Bronze Age features, stretching from the Devil's Arrows standing stones at Boroughbridge all the way to the henge and cairn at Catterick, forms a corridor aligned with the Rivers Ure and Swale. The way they overlook what had been a routeway through the Vale of Mowbray since the Mesolithic. The line the Romans would straighten, widen, harden with stone. The line that is the A1(M).

*

Through the plantation wood, I keep my head down. I am out of sight of the glare of the keeper's cottage, but the shadowy density and noiselessness of the trees is unnerving. The scrub grown over mounded earth resembles barrows. To look into the dark is to half-see shadows flicking between trunks. The field, when I reach it, is a relief: a discernible circle of henge undulating rough pasture lying open to the sky. With the drawn curtain of trees behind, I walk into the henge's centre and sit down.

The consensus is that these henges would have been something to behold, drawing pilgrims to them in large numbers, up processional causeways, across perimeter ditches, into a colossal, wide, four-metre-high ring of banked earth that gleamed and glittered white. Gypsum, the calcium sulphate mineral found in this area, was hacked out with antler tools and layered thickly on the sides, meaning the henges caught light: the rising and setting sun, the glow of moon. This human-bone whiteness has led some to wonder if the henges might have been associated with the dead. Gypsum areas are notorious for sudden, sporadic sinkholes and hollows opening like doors to an underworld. Was this part of the ritual function of these henges? To emulate portals? To corral the departed in congregation with those present? Others speculate that the gypsum brightness reflected the constellations. They note that – save for the entrances – the high banks blocked everything in the landscape, leaving only sky if you were one of the 2,000 people that could gather within. Perhaps *this* was their point? The two entrances, all of which follow variations on the same north-north-west/south-south-east axis, aligned with a rising Sirius, the dog star, the brightest in the constellation Canis Major. They would have framed the solstices – the sunsets of midsummer and the sunrises of midwinter – with all the significance this surely held.

For the Neolithic farmers that built and maintained these monuments with enormous, organised labour forces, a thousand years before the building of the pyramids, the seasons, the stars, the vanishing and reappearing sun over the horizon, the crossing from the spell of death to the promise of life – all were instrumental to existence. So too the rock, the earth, the being and the breath of each other and of those there before, but gone. Perhaps the henges embodied all these things at once.

In his paper on the Thornborough site, archaeologist Jan Harding suggests that in some way they were: 'bridging the divide between the living and their ancestors, especially if the stars above, the gypsum below, and human bone were perceived as of the same substance . . .' Which, as we have come to learn, they are. Harding stresses too the role of the journey in this corridor of Neolithic monuments, believing that symbolism was written out all along this connecting routeway with the notion of movement through this landscape integral to its formation. He quotes the archaeologist Blaise Vyner's description of a clear 'Great North Route' suggested by these aligned henges, because of the way those double entrances also seem to perfectly reflect the course of the ancient trackway they ran alongside. The road that predated their building.

And the road that remains. That always remains – 400 metres to the east of where I'm sitting and, particularly now, the sound of it. The long, slow inhale and exhale of breathing again. It is not lost on me that for millennia people journeyed great distances to reach here. If I close my eyes, I can hear them still. The whispers and howls in the passing wheels and engines. Voices rising, then falling away.

It is not lost on me either that the first time I heard the road come alive like this was just a few miles to the north of where I am, close to Catterick. There, where all of this began. And here I am back, almost, at that start once more. This circle around me.

*

After a while, I stand up and walk to the edge of the henge. I look down towards the north road. Its ceaseless flux and flow. I think of the day I unearthed the body by the side of the highway and of an empty kist at Caithness. I think of all the miles in between. I think of London, of maps and the heat of its maze-streets, the crush of history, the glint of sun on glass superstructures, the flood of forgotten memory. I think of walking with A beyond the gravitational pull of its centre, into the hinterlands. Of a million interstitial places: warehouses, industrial parks, retail parks, car parks; of great estates and tents pitched in layby-woods and under flyovers. I think of thin places: battles, graves, memorials; of shocking coincidences and correlations. I think of civil wars, rituals, suffering and celebration. Of old gods and children singing through the trees. I think of a Britain beautiful, dark, ugly and shining. Strange from its earth to its heavens.

I look north and I look south and feel everything pouring in. Roadside suburbs on summer evenings; tarmac wet with rain and blanketed in snow. Words nailed to a tree – *You, who walk to think / May seek your path in life* – and carved in stone dedicated to the god of highways. I think of a murdered man's name etched into a beech, of hidden injustices. A ship carrying pilgrims over an ocean and rockets aimed at distant planets. I think of the signs, the language of the road. Their shift from instruction to meaning. The wreaths of flowers, reams of litter. Flags, crosses, ruins. Fields, coasts, rivers under endless blue. Tunnels of trees; April sun in an ancient city; mountains, skies and pines. I think of post-industrial backwaters, boarded streets; nose-to-bumper lorries bombing down grey arterial highways. I think of lost voices calling out to me, looking for a home.

I remember the mine under the hill; roads forming the shape of a human body. I think of a man choking in the darkness and the dust, the faces of his family flashing through his terrified mind. I think of my children and of all the miles in between.

*

A week ago, Dad had dropped by the new house. The bell wasn't working and coming downstairs I'd found him waiting on the other side of the door. He had brought with him a DVD and, after coffee and cuddling the kids, he asked if I had a way of playing it.

Jump and flicker. Black and white flashes resolving into the colour figure of a man in a dark suit leaving a car. A glance at the camera, a grin. A cigarette in his hand. I recognised my great-uncle Walter immediately. A cut. Two more people. A couple heading into a cottage. My grandfather, Bartley, walking with stick; my nana Joan. Hailed by whoever was holding the camera, they stopped, looked over. Walter and Bartley, the brothers, sharing a joke in the doorway. The little cottage, the shuttered windows, the hydrangeas, the fox terrier fussing about everyone's feet. Squire's Mount, Hampstead. Cut again. Ellen, strong, striking, dressed impeccably with her sister, Peggy, and the children in tow; a shot of the kids alone, squinting down the lens. My dad as a boy, the same age Tom is now, walking with his sister.

Cut. A different reel. A huge, handsome man leaning down to talk to an old woman in a wheelchair, wrapped in a headscarf and blanket. A kiss on either cheek. 'That's Ifor Jenkins,' Dad said. 'Richard Burton's brother.' When I asked who the woman was, he'd said: 'That's your great-grandmother. That's May.'

Cut. Then he was there. The man I knew would appear. Filling a window frame, then walking through the front door. Hat, bow tie, suit. Pipe clamped between his teeth. Older, broader, but still as sharp as you like. Still centre of things. John William Cowen. Gone the flint stare now. In its place an expression of contentment.

'How come I've never seen this before?' I asked Dad.

'I had no idea it existed until yesterday. My cousin John sent it to me.'

For how long – twenty minutes? – I watched them all, living and breathing in the room with me. I saw them gather for Bill and May's

golden wedding anniversary in 1959. Christmas 1963. The cast steadily growing. The war generation communing conspiratorially in the
corners with their drink and cigarettes; the younger lot, Dad included,
dancing awkwardly in a small flat in Swiss Cottage. The kids twisting,
holding up a copy of 'Please Please Me' by the Beatles. Two of the boys
playing tennis rackets and shaking their heads in time. More footage
cycled through. An odd effect, but I could see Bill and May ageing at
the parties, the birthdays; whenever any of the family seemed to be
leaving or returning from abroad. I could see the same streets I walked
up and down when I lived in London. Then in one sequence the camera
lingered on my great-grandfather and he appeared to say something.
Briefly, but definitely, he broke the line of the gaze of everyone else
grouping for the shot. He looked down the lens of the camera in a way
that felt as though he was staring directly at me. Meeting my eyes, he
nodded, and then he smiled. It was as if he was making a point. As if
he knew that, in time, somebody watching this film back in a room
somewhere would see him do this. Like he knew what would follow.

Another cut. This time to a church in a blur of colour. 1968. A
close-up of a stained-glass window. Light streaming. A summer's day.
The people lining up outside looked elderly but they might have only
been in their late forties. The wilting war generation, turned out in
best suits and hats. It had taken me a moment to realise what I was

seeing. I knew that church from when I was growing up. Holy Trinity in Skipton. Suddenly I recognised the young couple holding hands and emerging out of its doors.

Cut. Overexposure cooling into focus. Mum and Dad on their wedding day.

I sat next to Dad and we watched these final silent CineFilms in silence. Flickering reels of the church, close-ups of the exterior with family congregating; confetti being hurled into the air, catching in hair, on shoulders. Relatives, arms around each other, mugging for the camera. Shots of shoes, rings, bouquets. My parents as young as anything, handsome, brimming with life. And here's the thing: I watched and I didn't feel any of the grief or the pain or the hurt that I might have done once at being surprised by these scenes. My mind didn't snap back to the end of it all. I didn't have to make up an excuse and leave the room because there was a pressure in my chest and a swelling of emotions that I was helpless to contain and unable to explain. I watched Mum and Dad and I smiled and laughed with them. I felt the joy of two people I love, half the age that I am now, setting out on a journey together.

Cut. A last reel of footage: shots of two cars driving down a wide, empty road. The kind of shots you see in road movies. One car overtaking the other, before the camera turns to catch the other coming up

fast on the outside. Who was filming or why, I couldn't tell you. But there was a wide shot of a two-lane that seemed immediately familiar, filmed through a windscreen. A ribbon of highway through curtains of sun-dappled trees. Then open road again. A final shot before the tape evidently ran out: a skewing sideways of the camera to catch a passing road sign, to record where they were. It was this frozen end frame that was left on-screen until I turned it off. A sign. White and yellow on green. The blurry words 'London 23 / Hatfield 2.' And above them: 'A1'.

*

I think of all the miles between and I wonder what we are supposed to make of these overlapping strata, these spirals. These ghosts, doubles and echoes. These recurring coincidences and connections. Something? Nothing? I tell myself that they are surely chance. The chaos of unstable history serves up random patterns and we, the pattern-making species, unsurprisingly find them everywhere. To draw meaning and purpose from the mess and muddle is a part of what makes us human. But out here, by this rift of a road, I can't help wondering again about the possibility of life as somehow being deeper, weirder, more mysterious than we know. Perhaps our routeways through this world are also marked with, if not monuments, then moments of symbolism. Things that might be perceived and understood when we travel far enough to come full circle.

*

We all walk a long road. Might we all agree on that? A great north route; a great north road. It was true back in the dizzying reaches of time; it is true today. Life remains a line through unknown territories, fields and woods. It is a series of choices and chances, of turnings taken and not. There is joy and there is pain but, as we travel, we learn we cannot live fully, openly, lovingly as we should without experiencing both. Five thousand years on we're still trying to make sense of these actualities – of where and when we find ourselves, of the immensity of existence and of the beauty and brutal briefness of our placing here on this planet, amid these wheeling constellations.

We pace out our days under the same arcs of a blazing, life-bringing sun and a bone-white moon and, just like those drawn to these henges in the depths of midwinter, in song, in celebration, in quiet, awestruck reverence, along the way the dead and departed return to us. We bridge the divide and commune with these ghosts in order to lay them to rest.

For a long time and for reasons I understand now, I believed the only road was escape. That moving down the highway meant forging ahead at any cost and letting go of everything behind. That living was an act of leaving and forgetting – the cutting-free of the baggage of the past and a constant striving to live on the cusp of imminence, on the tip of a breaking wave. But I have also known what it is to be caught in the current of memory. To wish we could reverse time. To drive onward but with eyes fixed on the rearview mirror. To hold on too tightly to those things that were here, but are gone.

If following this highway these years has shown me anything it is that the same might be said of this country, of this world. To ignore, to forget and to disassociate ourselves from the tide of history that has washed us here is easy. Likewise, in moments of great upheaval, we have seen how tempting it can be to try to live in the past. But the challenge, and the necessary change if we are to have any chance of making it, is to learn to reckon with both of these things. To hold them both together as we proceed. We must live fully in the realities of a complicated present and face an uncertain future together, without being beholden to what has been passed down. Yet it is impossible to do so without being clear-eyed about that history and the enduring influences that continue to work so powerfully on, and through, us today. If we are to answer the questions of who we are, how we got here and where we are going, we must be honest, aware, compassionate. We must look back – not to dwell there, to recreate or edit what happened; rather, so we can face the truths of it and use these truths to engineer and realise a different future. One in which all our fates and the fate of this planet are changed for the better. This is the crossroads we stand at every morning. To know the road that brought us here; to confront it, come to terms with it. To live with it, but not in it. To let it inform the roads we need to take and give us the strength to take them.

We know what these roads are and we know the obstructions that prevent us altering course. Our denial of the truth. Our disenchantment. Our apathy. Political inaction in the face of irrefutable evidence. The myths, failures and foolishness of leaders. The grip of self-interested power, of plutocracies. Systems in which the wealth of billionaires is taxed at a lower rate than the income of the lowest paid. Growing inequality that sees communities hollowed out and cities divided between those with staggering riches and those struggling to survive. The drift into populism, authoritarianism. Deregulated markets and a culture insistent that value and meaning can only be attained through possessing, self-obsession, indulgence and individualism.

I know it's late, but we cannot give up. For so long as the road continues, the future is still ours to shape. Even in the turmoil there are signs of fellowship, of congregation. Good things being done. As in these sacred places so long ago, there are voices rising in the darkness that sing of hope and transformation. They sing that even in the dying light, we will not abandon each other. We will stand together, shoulder to shoulder, and rail against this spell of death. That winter will pass into a season of life.

*

Time, as ever, is pressing. Headlights on the north road are like sparks along a fuse. The highway is a shining line leading everywhere, but I know where I want to be. I turn and walk back along the woods and the field edges, past the burial mounds and down from the ridge. The sky behind the hill dims. Ahead, lights are flickering on in the houses. A darkening band of blue has a glow growing at its western edge. Smoke-curls of dusk drift up from far-off, quietening woods. The land disappears into distance, into a screen of stars beginning to emerge beyond. As I draw closer, I see children playing in our garden. When Tom and Bea catch sight of me, they rush up the path, all red-faced and out of breath, calling to me: *Dad! Dad!* They wrap themselves around my waist. I kneel and kiss them, then lift them up, an arm under each, and carry them home. A beat in my chest as I think of a turning that I know is coming. The day when their arms no longer wrap around me instinctively. When Rosie and I must kiss them and set them on their own roads. What can we do but hope we did all right; that the mistakes they make are not history's, nor ours, but their own? What can we do but let them know we love them as much as a heart can love? That we go with them wherever they go? That time is all we ever have, and all that matters? Time, and what we do with it.

I put them down and they run to their friends. A flare of last light in the west is falling over everything, catching their hair. They carry its flame, its fire, down the path.

Acknowledgements

This book has been written in various places and at various times over a decade. Across these years, along the way, so many people have listened, supported, shared their stories or travelled the road with me. There are too many to list here, but my thanks to all of you. Robert Macfarlane was there at the beginning, there at the end, and there have been some unforgettable days of tracing the highway between. To him I owe a great debt. Special thanks are due also to Steve Sherlock for opening horizons; to A for bearing witness; to Nick, Claire, Sue and James Monkhouse; my brother Matthew Cowen (for the history and the late-night whisky) and his family; John Turner, Jason Conrad, Stuart Cowen, Sophie Cowen, Karen Cowen and the all the wider Cowen clan, and for all the untold stories and hard miles of critiquing and creating, to Theo Cooper and Danielle Treanor. In Edinburgh, I'm grateful to James Nelmes. Also, for his Old Reekie memories, Euan Ferguson. For her tireless and inspiring work on Ava and Achavanich, Maya Hoole. To Greg Heath for the vision and the care. From the band days: Spike Graham, my soul-brother, plus all The Kites, and Charlie Westropp and the Dissidents: forever *Saturday Night and Sunday Morning*. For the words, the art and the thinking in Leeds: Mike Parkinson, Christopher Walbank, Ken Briggs, Derek Fry, Simon O'Sullivan, Marcel Swiboda, Martin McQuillan, Griselda Pollock, Fred Orton.

It was the brilliant Sarah Rigby who first saw *The North Road* and believed in it enough to keep it in her heart, even as the world changed. Likewise, Jocasta Hamilton. I'd like to profoundly thank my wonderful editor at Random House Penguin, Zennor Compton, and her fantastic colleagues, Helen Conford, Joanna Taylor, Jessica Fletcher, as well as Sarah-Jane Forder for her sterling copy-editing. Pete Pawsey for turning photographs into art. Thanks, too, to Ceara Elliot for her cover, and Laura Brooke and Ania Gordon for the publicity and marketing. Lastly, but never leastly, to my brilliant agent, fierce shield and friend, Jessica Woollard, for always commanding me to take risks and to never apologise for being myself. Also, to Esme Bright and everyone on the team at David Higham Associates.

I'm grateful to many and various other writers, creators, artists and photographers who have provided inspiration (whether aware of it or not) and supported this book in various ways, especially Adam Thorpe, Benjamin Myers, Horatio Clare, Nick Hayes, Tim Dee, Philip Hoare, Melissa Harrison, Amy-Jane Beer, Katharine Aalto, Nicholas Hogg, Joanne Harris, Iain Sinclair, Alice Munro, Kerri ní Dochartaigh, Amy Liptrot, Stephen Moss, Nick Drake, Max Adams, Niall Ferguson, Simon Schama, Dan Richards, Tom Bullough, John Mitchinson, Jackie Morris, James Rebanks and Helen Rebanks, Nicola Chester, Will Atkins, Helen Jukes, Josh Shinner, Willem Dafoe, Alison Vainlo, Alan Bennett, Michael Palin, Tony Harrison, Liz Berry, Helen Mort, Alice Oswald, Ted Hughes, Annie Dillard, Sam Shepard, Gary Snyder, Jim Harrison, Sharon Blackie, Geoff Dyer, Jay Griffiths, Bryan Washington, Adelle Stripe, Linda Cracknell, Mary Colwell, Sara Maitland, Johnny Flynn, Paul Graham, Jon Nicholson, Steve MacLeod, Naomi Klein, Tim Binding, Robin Robertson, Karl Ove Knausgård, Joseph Hutchinson, Gerald Stern, Seamus Heaney, Michael Dennis Browne, Deborah Digges, Dave Eggers, Wyl Menmuir, Raynor Winn and Michael Smith.

I reserve my deepest gratitude and love to Dad and Mum; like me, this book would not be without you both. Your support, understanding and encouragement have been the difference. And to my constant northern stars: Rosie, Tom and Bea. It has been a long and, at times, hard road, but you have only ever shown the greatest love and patience. What I've learned is this: when I set the coordinates by you, I am always home.

Credits

PHOTOGRAPHY CREDITS

p. 249: photograph © Paul Graham

The author and publisher gratefully acknowledge the permission granted to reproduce the copyright material in this book. Every effort has been made to trace copyright holders and to obtain permission. The publisher apologises for any errors or omissions and, if notified of any corrections, will make suitable acknowledgement in future reprints or editions of this book.

TEXT ACKNOWLEDGEMENTS

Epilogue: Quote from *Ulysses* by James Joyce

p. 34: Quote from 'The Road Not Taken' from *The Collected Poems* by Robert Frost

p. 69: Quotes from *The Waste Land* by T.S. Eliot

p. 165: Quote from 'The Road' from *Water Inside The Water* by Susan Mitchell

pp. 148–9: Reference taken from Ted Hughes' letter from *Letters of Ted Hughes* by Ted Hughes and (editor) Christopher Reid

p. 150: Quotes from *The Green Man* by Kingsley Amis

pp. 194–5: References taken from the 'The Environmental Revolution', part of a collection of essays from *Winter Pollen* by Ted Hughes

pp. 200–201: Quotes from the poem 'Little Gidding' by T.S. Eliot

p. 207: Excerpt from *Edge of the Orison* by Iain Sinclair

pp. 255 and 259: Reference to lyrics from 'Suzanne' by Leonard Cohen

p. 257: Reference to lyrics from 'Drive All Night' by Bruce Springsteen

p. 258: Reference to lyrics from 'Sisters of Mercy' by Leonard Cohen

p. 259: Reference to lyrics from 'Born Slippy' by Underworld

pp. 261–2: Reference to lyrics from 'Stolen Car' by Bruce Springsteen

p. 291: Quote from *The Long Take* by Robin Robertson

p. 291: Quote from 'The Uses of Sorrow' from *Thirst* by Mary Oliver

pp. 356 and 358: Quotes from *The Great North Road* by Norman William Webster

Sources

Ambers, Janet, Matthews, Keith and Bowman, Sheridan, 'British Museum Natural Radiocarbon Measurements XXII', *Radiocarbon*, 33:1, 1991, 51–68.

American Progress, painting, painted by John Gast (1872).

Amis, Kingsley, *The Green Man* (Cape, 1969).

Bartlett, Robert, ed. J. M. Roberts, *England Under the Norman and Angevin Kings, 1075–1225* (Oxford University Press, 2000).

Bellow, Saul, *Humboldt's Gift* (Penguin, 1996).

Bradford, William, *Of Plymouth Plantation* (CreateSpace Independent Publishing, 2016).

Bunyan, John, *The Pilgrim's Progress* (Penguin, 2003).

Burne, Alfred, *The Battlefields of England* (Methuen and Company, 1950).

Cambridge Digital Library, 'Britannia (Atlas.4.67.6)', cudl.lib.cam.ac.uk (accessed 19/11/2024).

The Church Historians of England, trans. Joseph Stevenson, *The Historical Works of Simeon of Durham, Vol. III, Part II* (Seeleys, 1855).

Cohen, Leonard, *Sisters of Mercy* (Hipgnosis, 1967).

Cohen, Leonard, *Suzanne* (Hipgnosis, 1967).

Dalton, Paul, *Conquest, Anarchy and Lordship: Yorkshire, 1066–1154* (Cambridge University Press, 2002).

Davies, Hugh, *Roads in Roman Britain* (The History Press, 2008).

De Quincey, Thomas, 'The English Mail-Coach, or the Glory of Motion', in *Miscellaneous Essays* (Tickner, Reed & Fields, 1851).

Dickens, Charles, *Great Expectations* (Penguin, 1996).

'Digging Up Town's Forgotten Past', *Comet* (19 January 2006).

Domesday Book (Folio Society, 2003).

Egan, Pierce, *Boxiana; or, Sketches of Modern Pugilism* (W. M. Clark, 1830).

Egan, Pierce, *Sporting Anecdotes, Original and Selected* (Sherwood, Jones & Company, 1825).

Eliot, T. S., *Four Quartets* (Faber & Faber, 1944).

Eliot, T. S. ed. Frank Kermode, *The Waste Land and Other Poems* (Penguin, 2003).

Faulkner, William, *Requiem for a Nun* (Vintage, 1996).

Fidge, George, *The English Gusman* (1652).

Fitzstephen, William, *A Description of London from the Twelfth Century* (Cambridge University Press, 2024).

Four Quartets, BBC radio programme (22 December 2016).

Frost, Robert, *The Collected Poems* (Vintage, 2013).

Goodman, Anthony, *The Wars of the Roses: Military Activity and English Society, 1452–97* (Taylor & Francis, 1981).

Gourde, Leo T., *An Annotated Translation of the Life of St. Thomas Becket by William Fitzstephen* (Loyola University, 1943).

Gourlay, Robert B., 'A Bronze Age Beaker from Achavanich, Caithness', Highland Regional Council, 7 September 1988.

Graham, Paul, *A1: The Great North Road* (MACK, 1983).

Harding, Jan, *Cult religion and Pilgrimage: Archaeological Investigations at the Neolithic and Bronze Age Monument Complex of Thornborough, North Yorkshire* (Council for British Archaeology, 2013).

Harper, C. G. *The Great North Road* (Cecil Palmer, 1901).

Henry of Huntington, ed. Thomas Arnold, *Historia Anglorum: The History of the English from AC 55 to AD 1154* (Cambridge University Press, 2012).

Hind, James, *The Declaration of Captain James Hind* (1651).

Hoole, Maya et al., '"Ava": A Beaker-Associated Woman from a Cist at Achavanich, Highland, and the Story of Her (Re-)Discovery and Subsequent Study', *Proceedings of the Society of Antiquaries of Scotland*, 147 (2018), 73–118.

Hughes, Ted, ed. Christopher Reid, *Letters of Ted Hughes* (Faber, 2009).

Hughes, Ted, *Winter Pollen* (Faber & Faber, 1995).

Jackson, Kenneth H., *The Gododdin: The Oldest Scottish Poem* (Edinburgh University Press, 1969).

Joyce, James, *Ulysses* (Shakespeare and Company, 1922).

Lamb, Caroline, *Ada Reiss* (Murray, 1823).

Lamb, Caroline, *Glenarvon* (Valancourt Classics, 2007).

Lavelle, Ryan, *Alfred's Wars: Sources and Interpretations of Anglo-Saxon Warfare in the Viking Age* (Boydell & Brewer, 2012).

Lawrence, D. H., 'Nottinghamshire and the Mining Countryside', *New Adelphi* (1929).

Margary, Ivan D., *Roman Roads in Britain* (John Baker, 1967).

Miles, Henry Downes, *Pugilistica: The History of British Boxing Containing Lives of the Most Celebrated Pugilists* (J. Grant, 1906).

Mitchell, Susan, 'The Road', in *The Water Inside the Water* (Perennial, 1994).

Morley, Frank, *The Great North Road: A Journey in History* (Hutchinson, 1961).

North Country Mails at the Peacock, Islington, painting, painted by James Pollard (1823).

Nottinghamshire Archives, *A Critical Review of the State Trials, Nottingham Assizes: The Trial of Captain Mitford Henry, Esq; on the Statute of Stabbing Before Mr. Justice Powel, at the Summer-Assizes, for the County of Nottingham, in the Year 1721. 8 Geo. I* (1721).

Oliver, Mary, 'The Uses of Sorrow', in *Thirst* (Beacon Press, 2006).

Orderic, Vitalis, *Historia Ecclesiastica* [will need edition for this – CH].

Paine, Thomas, *The Rights of Man* (Penguin, 1984).

Robertson, Robin, *The Long Take* (Picador, 2018).

Roebuck, Peter, *Cattle Droving Through Cumbria* (Bookcase, 2016).

The Royal Mails Starting from the General Post Office London, painting, painted by James Pollard (1830).

Schama, Simon, *A History of Britain: The British Wars 1603–1776* (Ebury, 2001).

Sillitoe, Alan *Saturday Night and Sunday Morning* (W. H. Allen, 1958).

Sinclair, Iain, *Edge of the Orison* (Penguin, 2006).

Smith, Rick, Hyde, Karl and Emerson, Darren, *Born Slippy .NUXX* (Universal Music Group, 1996).

Springsteen, Bruce, *Drive All Night* (Sony Music Group, 1979).

Stubbes, Philip, ed. Frederick J. Furnivall, *Anatomy of the Abuses in England in Shakspere's Youth, A.D. 1583* (N. Trubner & Co., 1877–79).

Symeon of Durham, *De Exordio Ecclesiae Dunelmensis* [as with this – CH].

Thomas, Edward, *Collected Poems* (Seltzer, 1921).

Traill, H. D., *Social England: From the Earliest Times to the Accession of Edward the First* (Cassell, 1894).

Vainlo, Alison, 'Bentley Village, A History', bentvillhistory.blogspot.com (accessed 19 November 2024).

Walbran, John Richard, *A Guide to Ripon, Harrogate: Fountains Abbey, Bolton Priory, and Several Places of Interest in Their Vicinity* (W. Harrison, fifth edition, 1851).

Williams, Ifor, *Canu Aneirin: Gyda Rhagymadrodd a Nodiadau* (Gwasg Prifysgol Cymru, 1938).

Winslow, Edward, *Good Newes from New-England* (Project Gutenburg, 2021).

Wood, Michael, 'Brunanburh: Where Did the Battle That Saved England Take Place?', *BBC History Magazine* (18 October 2019).

Wormser, Baron, 'More Money Than God: William Bradford's Of Plymouth Plantation 1620–1647, *Solstice*, Winter 2021.

Woulfe, Patrick, *Irish Names and Surnames* (M. H. Gill & Son, 1923).

Wyntner, Andrew, *The Quarterly Review* (John Murray, 1854).

Selected Bibliography and Further Reading

Ackroyd, Peter, *Civil War: The History of England Volume III* (Pan Macmillan, 2015).

Ackroyd, Peter, *Foundation: The History of England Volume I* (Pan Macmillan, 2012).

Ackroyd, Peter, *Hawksmoor* (Penguin, 1985).

Ackroyd, Peter, *London* (Vintage, 2001).

Ackroyd, Peter, *Tudors: The History of England Volume II* (Pan Macmillan, 2013).

Adams, Max, *In the Land of Giants* (Head of Zeus, 2015).

Bagshawe, Richard W., *Roman Roads* (Shire Archaeology, 2000).

Bede, *The Ecclesiastical History of the English People* (Oxford University Press, 2008).

Bell, Graham, *Yorkshire Battlefields: A Guide to the Great Conflicts on Yorkshire Soil, 937–1461* (Wharncliffe Books, 2001).

Bergson, Henri, *Time and Free Will: An Essay on the Immediate Data of Consciousness* (Dover Press, 2001).

Birtley, Andrew, *The Vindolanda Guide* (The Vindolanda Trust, 2015).

Birtley, Robin, *Roman Records from Vindolanda on Hadrian's Wall* (Roman Army Museum Publications, 1990).

Blair, Peter Hunter, *Northumbria in the Days of Bede* (Book Club Associates, 1976).

The British History Podcast, 'The Achavanich Beaker Burial Project: Ancient DNA with Maya Hoole' (May 2017).

The British History Podcast, 'The Achavanich Beaker Burial Project: Discovering Ava with Maya Hoole' (December 2018).

The British History Podcast, 'The Achavanich Beaker Burial Project: The Beaker People with Dr. Alison Sheridan' (May 2017).

Boswell, William C., *Along the Great Northern Road* (Jarrolds, 1939).

Bradley, T., *The Old Coaching Days in Yorkshire* (Yorkshire Conservative Newspaper Co., 1889).

Briggs, Asa, *Victorian Cities* (Penguin, 1963).

'British History Online', british-history.ac.uk (accessed 19 November 2024).

Bunyan, John, *The Pilgrim's Progress* (Penguin English Library, 1965).

Cookson, Gillian and Sanderson, Ian, eds., *Yorkshire Archaeological Journal, Volume 85* (Maney Publishing, 2013).

Cowan, E. T. and Henderson, L., eds, *A History of Everyday Life in Medieval Scotland 1000–1600* (Edinburgh University Press, 2011).

Crace, Jim, *Harvest* (Picador, 2013).

Crane, Nicholas, *The Making of the British Landscape* (W&N, 2016).

Davies, Hugh, *Roman Roads in Britain* (Shire Archaeology, 2008).

Dee, Tim, *Four Fields* (Jonathan Cape, 2013).

de la Bédoyère, Guy, *Roman Britain: A New History* (Thames & Hudson, 2006).

Deleuze, Gilles and Guattari, Félix, *A Thousand Plateaus: Capitalism and Schizophrenia* (University of Minnesota Press, 1987).

Derrida, Jacques, *Specters of Marx* (Routledge, 1994).

Devine, T. M., *The Scottish Clearances: A History of the Dispossessed, 1600–1900* (Penguin, 2019).

Dillard, Annie, *The Abundance* (Canongate Canons, 2017).

'Durham Mining Museum', https://www.dmm.org.uk/ (accessed 19 November 2024).

Eliot, T. S., *Collected Poems 1909–1962* (Faber & Faber, 1963).

Fell, D. W. and Johnson, P., *The Evolution of Dere Street from Routeway to Motorway: Evidence from the A1 Dishforth to Barton Motorway Scheme* (Northern Archaeological Associates).

Ferguson, Niall, *Empire* (Penguin, 2009).

Fermor, Patrick Leigh, *A Time of Gifts* (John Murray, 1977).

Firth, J. B., *Highways & Byways in Nottinghamshire* (Macmillan & Co., 1924).

Foster, Hal, *The Anti-Aesthetic* (Bay Press, 1983).

Fraser, Lady Antonia, *Cromwell: Our Chief of Men* (Orion, 2002).

Frost, Percival, *Newton's Principa, Sections 1–3* (Macmillan & Co., 1863).

Fry, Michael, *Edinburgh: A History of the City* (Pan Macmillan, 2010).

George, Josie, *A Still Life* (Bloomsbury, 2021).

George Kay, F., *Royal Mail* (Rockcliff, 1951).

Gleick, James, *Isaac Newton* (Fourth Estate, 2003).

Graham, Frank, *Alnwick: A Short History and Guide* (Butler Publishing, 1994).

Graham, Paul, *A1: The Great Northern Road* (MACK: 1983).

Graham, Paul, *Troubled Land* (Grey, 1987).

Grainge, William, *Harrogate and the Forest of Knaresborough* (M. T. D. Rigg Publications, 1988).

Goddard, Frank, *The Great North Road* (Frances Lincoln, 2004).

Hall, Ian, *The Great North Road (Highway and Byways of Northumberland)* (Wanney Books, 2017).

Hanson, W. S., *Agricola and the Conquest of the North* (Batsford, 1987).

Hardyment, Christina, *Writing Britain: Wastelands to Wonderlands* (British Library, 2012).

Harper, C. G., *The Great North Road* (Cecil Palmer, 1901).

Harrison, Melissa, *At Hawthorn Time* (Bloomsbury Circus, 2015).

Harrison, Tony, *Selected Poems* (Penguin, 2013).

'Herts Memories', https://www.hertsmemories.org.uk/ (accessed 19 November 2024).

Hindle, Paul, *Medieval Roads and Tracks* (Shire Archaeology, 2016).

Hoole, Maya, 'The Achavanich Beaker Burial', https://achavanichbeakerburial.wordpress.com (accessed 19 November 2024).

Houseman, A. E., *A Shropshire Lad* (Dover Publications, 1990).

Hughes, Ted, *Collected Poems* (Faber & Faber, 1995).

Hughes, Ted, *Crow* (Faber & Faber, 1995).

Hughes, Ted, *Winter Pollen* (Faber & Faber, 1995).

Hughes, Ted, *Wolfwatching* (Faber & Faber, 1995).

Hutton, Ronald, *The Making of Oliver Cromwell* (Yale University Press, 2021).

Hyer, Maren Clegg and Owen-Crocker, Gale R., *The Material Culture of the Built Environment in the Anglo-Saxon World* (Liverpool University Press, 2015).

Inglis, Harry, *The Great North Road Map – Part 1* (Gail & Inglis, 1898).

Jack, Ian, ed., *Necessary Journeys* (Granta, 2001).

Jamie, Kathleen, *Sightlines* (Sort of Books, 2012).

Jefferies, Richard, *Nature Near London* (Chatto & Windus, 1887).

Jones, Barri and Mattingley, David, *An Atlas of Roman Britian* (Blackwell, 1990).

Jones, Charles, *The Forgotten Battle of 1066: Fulford* (The History Press, 2007).

Kennedy, Barbara M., *Deleuze and Cinema* (Edinburgh University Press, 2000).

Kerouac, Jack, *The Dharma Bums* (Penguin, 2000).

Kerouac, Jack, *On the Road* (Penguin, 1991).

Lopez, Barry, *Horizon* (Penguin, 2019).

Loyn, H. R., *Anglo-Saxon England and the Norman Conquest* (Longman, 1962).

Macfarlane, Robert, *The Old Ways* (Penguin, 2013).

Macfarlane, Robert, *Underland* (Hamish Hamilton, 2020).

MacGregor, Neil, *A History of the World in 100 Objects* (Allen Lane, 2010).

McCarthy, Cormac, *The Road* (Picador, 2006).

McInerney, Jay, ed., *Cowboys, Indians and Commuters* (Viking, 1994).

Morley, Frank, *The Great North Road: A Journey in History* (Hutchinson, 1961).

Morris, Marc, *Anglo-Saxons* (Hutchinson, 2021).

Mort, Helen, *Black Car Running* (Vintage, 2019).

Mothersole, Jessie, *Agricola's Road into Scotland* (Bodley Head, 1927).

Mountfield, David, *Stage and Mail Coaches* (Shire Publications, 2003).

Munro, Alice, *Dear Life* (Vintage, 2013).

Munro, Alice, *The Moons of Jupiter* (Vintage, 2004).

Muir, Richard, *Shell Guide to Reading the Landscape* (Book Club Associates, 1981).

Myers, Benjamin, *Cuddy* (Bloomsbury, 2023).

Naipaul, V. S., *the Enigma of Arrival* (Picador, 1987).

National Highways, 'A1 Leeming to Barton', nationalhighways.co.uk (accessed 19 November 2024).

Newton, Isaac, Cohen, I. Bernard, Whitman, Anne and Budenz, Julia, *The Principa: The Authoritative Translation: Mathematical Principles of Natural Philosophy* (University of California Press, 2016).

Nicholson, Jon, *A1: Portrait of a Road* (Harper Collins Illustrated, 2000).

Olusoga, David, *Black and British: A Short Essential History* (Pan Macmillan, 2020).

Parker, Mike, *Mapping the roads: Building Modern Britain* (AA Publishing, 2013).

'Past in the Present', https://pastinthepresent.net/ (accessed 19 November 2024).

Pearson, Parker et al., 'The Beaker People: Isotopes, Mobility and Diet in Prehistoric Britain', Prehistoric Society Research Paper 7 (2019).

Perry, Richard, *A Naturalist on Lindisfarne* (Lindsay Drummond, 1946).

Pevsner, Nikolaus and Neame, David, *Yorkshire: York and the East Riding* (Penguin, 1972).

Pine, Emilie, *Notes to Self* (Penguin, 2019).

Platt, Edward, *Leadville* (Picador, 2000).

Prebble, John, *The Highland Clearances* (Penguin, 1973).

Protz, Roger, *Historic Coaching Inns of the Great North Road* (CAMBRA, 2017).

Purkiss, Diane, *The English Civil War: A People's History* (Harper Collins, 2007).

Rackham, Oliver, *The Illustrated History of the Countryside* (W&N, 2003).

Readers Digest Association, *No Through Road* (Drive Publications, 1975).

Read, Herbert, *Art & Society* (Faber & Faber, 1956).

Riding, Jacqueline, *Jacobites: A New History of the '45 Rebellion* (Bloomsbury, 2003).

Roberts, Alice, *Ancestors* (Simon & Schuster, 2021).

Ross, David, *Scotland: History of a Nation* (Lomond Books, 2013).

Rowland, T. H., *Dere Street* (Frank Graham, 1974).

'SABRE – The Society for All British and Irish Road Enthusiasts', sabre-roads.org.uk (accessed 19 November 2024).

Sanghera, Sathnam, *Empireland: How Imperialism Has Shaped Modern Britain* (Viking, 2021).

Schama, Simon, *A History of Britain: At the Edge of the World? 3000BC–AD1603* (Ebury, 2000).

Schama, Simon, *A History of Britain: The British Wars 1603–1776* (Ebury, 2001).

Schama, Simon, *A History of Britain: The Fate of Empire 1776–2000* (Ebury, 2002).

Schama, Simon, *Landscape & Memory* (Harper Perennial, 2004).

Scott, Walter, *The Heart of Midlothian* (Nimmo, Hay & Mitchell, 1885).

Sebald, W. G., *Austerlitz* (Hamish Hamilton, 2001).

Shaviro, Steven, *The Cinematic Body* (University of Minnesota Press, 1993).

Shepard, Sam, *Motel Chronicles & Hawk Moon* (Faber & Faber, 2018).

Sinclair, Iain, *Living with Buildings* (Profile, 2018).

Sinclair, Iain, *London Orbital* (Penguin, 2003).

Sinclair, Iain, *London Overground: A Day's Walk Around the Ginger Line* (Hamish Hamilton, 2015).

'South Witham Parish Council', https://south-witham.parish.lincolnshire.gov.uk/ (accessed 19 November 2024).

Thomas, Edward, *The South Country* (Little Toller, 2009).

Thorpe, Adam, *Ulverton* (Vintage Classics, 2012).

Tolstaya, Tatyana, *Aetherial Worlds* (Daunt Books, 2019).

Vainlo, Alison, 'Bentley Village, A History', bentvillhistory.blogspot.com (accessed 19 November 2024).

Virgil, trans. Peter Fallon, *Georgics* (Oxford World's Classics, 2004).

Vyner, Blaise, *The Archaeology of Roman Dere Street* (2012).

Webster, Norman, *The Great North Road* (Adams & Dart, 1974).

Wilson, P. R. et al., *Cataractonium: Roman Catterick and Its Hinterland, Parts I and II* (CBA, 2002).

Woolrych, Austin, *Battles of the English Civil War* (Pimlico, 1991).

Yourcenar, Marguerite, *Memoirs of Hadrian* (Penguin, 1951).

Žižek, Slavoj, *Too Late to Awaken* (Allen Lane, 2023).

Index

Italic page numbers indicate illustrations.